S0-CFH-712

Jerome Rothenberg's Experimental Poetry and Jewish Tradition

Jerome Rothenberg's Experimental Poetry and Jewish Tradition

Christine A. Meilicke

Bethlehem: Lehigh University Press

Associated University Presses
2010 Eastpark Boulevard
Cranbury, NJ 08512

The paper used in this publication meets the requirements of the American National Standard for Permanence of Paper for Printed Library Materials Z39.48-1984.

Library of Congress Cataloging-in-Publication Data

Meilicke, Christine A., 1968–
Jerome Rothenberg's experimental poetry and Jewish tradition / Christine A. Meilicke.
p. cm.
Includes bibliographical references and index.
ISBN 0-934223-76-9 (alk. paper)
1. Rothenberg, Jerome, 1931—Criticism and interpretation. 2. Jewish religious poetry, American—History and criticism. 3. Experimental poetry, American—History and criticism. 4. Jews—United States—Intellectual life. 5. Judaism and literature—United States. 6. Judaism in literature. 7. Jews in literature. I. Title.

PS3568.O86Z77 2005
811′.54—dc22 2004020425

PRINTED IN THE UNITED STATES OF AMERICA

For my parents
and Jitesh

Contents

Acknowledgments

A GREAT NUMBER OF PEOPLE HAVE SUPPORTED MY RESEARCH FOR this book. In particular, I would like to thank Jerome and Diane Rothenberg for their openness, kindness, and friendship and their willingness to share with me some aspects of their lives and work. They also introduced me to other poets and collaborators. Jerome Rothenberg answered my questions by e-mail and in conversations with great diligence and patience. He also gave me permission to quote from our communications and his manuscripts.

I am also very grateful for the correspondence with the poets David Meltzer, Karl Young, and Jack Hirschman, who provided me with interesting background information about the Jewish poetry scene in the 1970s. Eleanor Antin communicated with me regarding her own projects, which involve reappropriations of Jewish history. Bruria Finkel shared with me her fascination with Abraham Abulafia and sent me diverse material relating to that interest. Charlie Morrow gave me important insights into the performance movement and talked to me about his experiments with rituals and shamanism. Thank you for those inspiring communications!

Since this book contains many interdisciplinary references, I relied on the advice of a number of people: Professor Michael Davidson made some challenging critical suggestions; Professor Moshe Idel answered my questions on the meditation techniques of Abraham Abulafia; Professor David Roskies corresponded with me on aspects of the Klezmer movement; Rabbi Arthur Waskow talked to me about his involvement with theater and performance. I am very grateful for their critical and inspiring remarks. I would also like to thank Professor Alvin Rosenfeld who first recommended to me a book by Jerome Rothenberg.

Of course, much gratitude goes to the supervisors of my dissertation, Professor Alfred Hornung and Professor Dieter Lamping, who have been encouraging and supportive all along. Professor Reinhold Schiffer has also been very helpful in the initial stages of my research and encouraged me to pursue the subject. The DAAD (German Academic Exchange Program) provided me with a scholarship for twelve months (1999–2000). This enabled me to do research in the United States. Likewise, the English and Comparative Literature Department at Columbia University has been very generous in granting me the status of a visiting scholar and then further supporting my research with a stipend for the academic year 2001/2002. I am also indebted to the University of California, San Diego for giving me the status of a visiting scholar and letting me use the Archive for New Poetry at the Mandeville Special Collections Library. Many thanks to my copyeditor Karen Miller, who read the text with great care and thoughtfulness.

I also would like to thank my friends Dietmar Becker, Brad Sabin Hill, Andrew Levy, and Joel Lewis for many exciting conversations and their willingness to read and comment on some of my writing. And finally, much gratitude goes to my husband, Jitesh Surelia, whose presence was essential throughout this project.

A Note on Transliteration

FOR TRANSLITERATIONS FROM THE HEBREW AND THE YIDDISH, I AM following the conventions established by the *Encyclopaedia Judaica*.[1] However, divergent transliteration systems, which occur in quotations by other authors, are left unchanged.

Abbreviations

In citing works in the notes, some short titles have been used. Works frequently cited have been identified by the following abbreviations:

BJB Jerome Rothenberg, Harris Lenowitz, and Charles Doria, eds. *A Big Jewish Book: Poems and other Visions of the Jews from Tribal Times to the Present*. Garden City, N.Y.: Anchor Press, 1978.

DS Jerome Rothenberg. *That Dada Strain*. New York: New Directions, 1983.

G Jerome Rothenberg. *Gematria*. Los Angeles: Sun & Moon Press, 1994.

JR Jerome Rothenberg. "Jerome Rothenberg: A Dialogue on Oral Poetry with William Spanos." *Boundary 2* 3.3 (spring 1975): 509–48.

K Jerome Rothenberg. *Khurbn & Other Poems*. New York: New Directions, 1989.

NA Jerome Rothenberg. "Nokh Auschwitz." In *Jewish American Poetry: Poems, Commentary, And Reflections*." Ed. Jonathan N. Barron and Eric Murphy Selinger. Hanover, N.H.: Brandeis University Press, 2000. 137–45.

P Jerome Rothenberg. *Poland/1931*. New York: New Directions, 1974.

RI Gavin Selerie and Eric Mottram, eds. *The Riverside Interviews: 4: Jerome Rothenberg*. London: Binnacle Press, 1984.

S Jerome Rothenberg. *Seedings & Other Poems*. New York: New Directions, 1996.

TS Jerome Rothenberg, ed. with commentaries. *Technicians of the Sacred: A Range of Poetries from Africa, America, Asia, Europe & Oceania*. Rev. and expanded 2nd ed. Berkeley: University of California Press, 1985.

VB Jerome Rothenberg. *Vienna Blood & Other Poems*. New York: New Directions, 1980.

Jerome Rothenberg's Experimental Poetry and Jewish Tradition

Part I
Reappropriating Religion

Introduction: "All Poets Are Jews"

> If the poet's name is god how dark the day is
> how heavy the burden is he carries with him
> *All poets are jews*, said Tsvetayeva.
> *The god of the jews is jewish*, said a jew.[1]

THE ASSERTION THAT "ALL POETS ARE JEWS" IS ONE OF JEROME Rothenberg's favorite propositions. His universalist understanding of Jewishness is balanced by a more particularist stance, which acknowledges the specificity of Judaism, but takes it again as "a central & sufficient instance"[2] of the human. This tension between universalism and particularism underlies the rewriting of Jewish traditions by Jerome Rothenberg, a contemporary American-Jewish poet whose use of mystical and magical Jewish sources goes back to the 1970s and has continued since then. This book investigates the reappropriation and transformation of Jewish tradition in Rothenberg's poetry.

American Judaism today has many strands. It is so far from being a monolithic block that some scholars have even spoken of "religious warfare between Jews."[3] Hence there is no general agreement among American Jews on any aspect of Judaism or Jewishness. This plurality is germinal to Rothenberg's own understanding of Judaism. Asserting the role of the poet as the "marginal" defender of diversity—in Judaism as well as anywhere else within his reach—Rothenberg "speaks . . . with many voices,"[4] one of which is Jewish. Clearly, Rothenberg's Jewish voice emerges from the diaspora. It grows out of the awareness of being in exile. For the poet, exile implies loss in many different forms:

- a sense of exile both as cosmic principle (exile of God from God, etc.) & as the Jewish fate, experienced as the alienation of group & individual . . . ;

- from which there comes a distancing from nature & from God (infinite, ineffable) . . . ;
- or, projected into language, a sense (in Jabès's phrase) of being "exiled in the word."

(*BJB*, xxxv)

Such an overall sense of loss prompts the search for recovery, a kind of "rebellion against exile, alienation, division."[5] One way of overcoming alienation is to draw on tradition.

According to Charles Liebman, tradition is a "set of norms and values and beliefs which an individual or society attributes to its own past and which are of some relevance, positive or negative, for the present."[6] The term "tradition" is derived from *traditio* (Latin, "to transmit") and in Judaism refers to the "continuous transmission from generation to generation."[7] According to rabbinical Judaism there is an unbroken chain of oral and written Jewish tradition going back to the revelation of the Torah at Sinai. However, this belief was challenged by the enlightenment and the historical-critical study of texts. When the German-Jewish *Wissenschaft des Judentums* applied the historical-critical method to Jewish tradition "modernity ate away much of tradition. Its sharp teeth cut through the links in the chain."[8] Modernity thus provoked several splits within Judaism. In America there are now at least four major Jewish denominations: Orthodoxy, Conservative Judaism, Reform, and Reconstructionism. Each fosters a different attitude toward tradition and observance. Moreover, many American Jews are unaffiliated or secular. In the eyes of all those Jews who do not identify with Orthodox beliefs—and Rothenberg is one of them—the "chain of transmission" is broken. A collective tradition has been lost. Out of this acute awareness emerges the need to recover tradition.

Rothenberg's reappropriation of Jewish tradition contributes to the construction of a contemporary Jewish diaspora identity. American-Jewish poetry actively participates in recreating Jewish consciousness and conscience. Yet, he does not limit himself to Jewish texts and traditions. Rather, his writing is characterized by an extraordinary cultural and literary scope and inclusiveness. For example, the poet's oeuvre consists of more than sixty books, among which are several innovative anthologies of oral literature, Jewish poetry, and modern/postmodern poetry.[9] Rothenberg's own writing ranges from translation and poetics to poetry, and centers on three major issues: Jewishness and Judaism, Native American cultures and poetry, and dadaism. It is his conviction that the universal may be found in the particular and vice versa. By giving primacy to Rothenberg's Jewish poetry, this study focuses on the particular rather than the universal. However, the special instance of rewriting Jewish tradition might be paradigmatic of broader trends in American literature and culture.

Rothenberg's "Jewish poetry" will be situated in two major contexts—American Judaism and contemporary American poetry with American-Jewish poetry as its subcategory. Out of this contextualization two propositions emerge:

First, in reappropriating Jewish tradition Rothenberg attempts to create what Michael Meyer calls "a generational link with the Jewish past."[10] Such a connection with the past is essential to the construction of a Jewish identity. From the vantage point of contemporary discussions about the general constructedness of identity, Jewish self-definition is a continuous process and parallels other processes of self-definition and constructions of identities among other groups of people.[11] By demonstrating different ways of tapping into tradition, Rothenberg provides different options of fashioning a contemporary Jewish identity.

From a sociological point of view, the poet's interest in the tradition of his ancestors, which first figures in his book *Poland/1931*, is illustrative of third-generation immigrants to America.[12] This generation rediscovers the culture their parents repressed in the course of assimilation. In searching for their ancestral roots, the new generation rejects its parents' culture and turns back toward the grandparents.[13] The lost world of the *shtetl* and Ḥasidism, *wunderrabbis* and Yiddish language comes to be employed in the symbolization of Jewish identity. The klezmer revival in the United States originated in the 1970s at the same time as Rothenberg's first Jewish books. Both share the involvement with the Jewish past and the attempt to bring its desirable aspects into the present. Hence Rothenberg's poetic rewriting coincides with other contemporary approaches to tradition as exemplified by the Jewish counterculture and the subsequent formations for Jewish renewal. Therefore, I argue that Rothenberg's writing illustrates these approaches, despite his nonaffiliation with any of these groups. The same "malady"—an overwhelming sense of loss—calls for the same "remedy"—the reappropriation of Jewish tradition, taking into account present needs. That such recovery can never be complete goes without saying.

Second, his association with the avant-garde affects Rothenberg's reappropriation of Jewish tradition. (In this book the term "avant-garde" is used generically to designate various experimental strands of literature.)[14] The poet employs and modifies a great number of experimental literary strategies, which might also be called "appropriative strategies." He explores how these various devices can be used for the recovery of the repressed or lost. Rothenberg's sense of loss is so profound that it extends beyond the issues of Jewishness. He deplores the deprivation of a "primal poetry or art or theater or music,"[15] or, in other words, "a primal poetics." Out of this recognition grows Rothenberg's concept of "ethnopoetics." It advocates a type of poetry that is created on the basis of these suppressed and marginalized traditions, "a redefinition of poetry in terms of cultural specifics, with an emphasis on those alternative traditions to which the West gave names like 'pagan,' 'gentile,' 'tribal,' 'oral,' and 'ethnic.'"[16] In this ethnopoetic process of rewriting, Rothenberg draws on cultures and historical periods in which poetry is/was more central than in our Western world today, for instance in shamanistic cultures. Thus, he derives a poetics that aims at the re-empowerment of contemporary poetry and language.

In this context two fundamental concerns will be traced throughout this book: the destruction and renewal of language, and the search for totality, wholeness, and unity (holism). Both instances reveal that Rothenberg's poetry and poetics transcend the confines of academic formalism, the habits of the New American Poetry and the negations of avant-garde Language Poetry.

In the above proposition two aspects of Rothenberg's writing are singled out for the sake of clarity. Yet in effect this book investigates the *interaction* of these two outlined factors. It explores the interpenetration of American Judaism and American poetry. Both contribute to the creation of an American Jewish avant-garde poetry and a contemporary diaspora identity beyond traditional Judaism (Part I: Reappropriating Religion), and after the Holocaust (Part II: Reappropriating History).

Finally, it should be noted that Rothenberg's reappropriations reach beyond Jewish culture. He has published numerous expansive anthologies in which he rewrites other "traditions":

the tradition of a sacred poetry in *Technicians of the Sacred*, the tradition of Native American poetry in *Shaking the Pumpkin*, the tradition of American poetry in *America: A Prophecy*, of American avant-garde poetry in *Revolution of the Word*, and the tradition of international avant-garde poetry in the two volumes of *Poems for the Millennium*.[17] Of course, so much rewriting also had an impact on Rothenberg's approach to Jewish tradition. And conversely, the analysis of his appropriative strategies with regard to Judaism may also provide a model for further investigations of his other rewritings.

The Terminology of Reappropriation

Michael Meyer uses the term "reappropriation" to mark the "return to tradition" among Jews beginning at the turn of the twentieth century and continuing into the 1960s.[18] Alternatively, the sociologist Liebman defines "reappropriation" generically. He contends that the reappropriation of tradition is a "continual process wherein the tradition is reappropriated so that it may retain its relevance for the contemporary society."[19] Combining these two views, one could say that reappropriation has always existed, but what changes are the circumstances under which such appropriation takes place and its legitimization. Liebman himself suggests that the central difference between past and present (postmodern) reappropriations lies in the self-consciousness of the act. He poses an important question, which may also be applied to Rothenberg's act of rewriting Jewish tradition: "Does it [a certain society] really believe it is behaving in accordance with Tradition, or is it manipulating the Tradition [without acknowledging it to itself]?"[20]

For the study of literary reappropriation, it is conducive to draw on terms that also are used in the historical and sociological analysis of Judaism. The terminological overlap allows us to compare Rothenberg's reassemblage of Jewish tradition to similar activities in religious Jewish circles. Another useful term is "transformation." Marking the very general process of transforming a text, any derivational practice may be called "transformation." This book takes "transformation" to be synonymous with "rewriting."

While the broad term "rewriting" generally refers to the contemporary practice of reinterpretation, the word "reappropriation" delineates a more specific procedure. Different portions of this book explore Rothenberg's "appropriative" literary strategies with respect to Jewish tradition. The most prominent appropriative devices are collage, assemblage, palimpsest, parody, pastiche, and forgery, found poetry, theft, and translation.

Many of these strategies emerge from contemporary avant-garde experimentation, but Rothenberg puts his own twist on them. Appropriation is fundamental to his work. The fact that he is often criticized for appropriating materials of other cultures indicates how much his writing depends on appropriative devices. One may even claim that Rothenberg's oeuvre illustrates the concept and practice of appropriation and therefore also raises questions and controversies surrounding this complex issue.

Another set of suitable words refers to the displacement and dislocation of materials. Appropriation may be discussed in terms of decontextualization and displacement: something is taken from one place and brought to another. Translation, for example, implies the "carry-over" of texts from a different culture or a different historical period. In this very broad sense, appropriation and translation both involve displacement. Rothenberg observes that "all translation . . . represents a traumatic event: this shifting, this rupture of language: going from language to language."[21] In other words, translation entails loss. But Rothenberg, a prolific and skillful translator, also recognizes the creative potential of this situation: "But precisely this is what makes it ever really worth bothering: an area left open in which (sometimes) a new poem can be written. This involves some sense of re-creation."[22] The poet engages in the translation of such a wide variety of texts and rituals that Eric Mottram speaks of this far-reaching attitude in terms of a "politics of translation."[23] In fact, he claims that the poet's attitude toward translation is indicative of his general approach toward other cultures and—one may add—to the past.

All the terms mentioned so far are associated with the notion of change, which is fundamental to Rothenberg's "tradition (or poetry) of changes."[24] Rewriting is taken to be a continuous process. At the roots of this poetics of change lies the idea of

> metamorphosis & the poet's freedom to reconsider & review the common sources. . . . So, by contrast to the "literal" view that repeats the past by rote, the alternative tradition makes-it-new

at every step—& in this sense "tradition" & "experiment" or "change" come very naturally together. (*JR*, 525)

"Alternative tradition" refers to the notion of a suppressed subculture, of which Rothenberg finds traces everywhere. This "Great Subculture" (Gary Snyder) constitutes a countertradition that opposes anything established. The assumption of a repressed tradition also informs Rothenberg's rewriting of Jewish tradition; it will be studied in this book.

May it suffice here to present one example of Rothenberg's reinterpretation of Jewish tradition. The anthology *A Big Jewish Book* is preceded by the following epigraph:

> Rabbi Eliezer said
> "prayer 'fixed'?
> "his supplication bears no fruit
>
> . . . .
>
> the question next came up: what
> is FIXED?
> Rabba & Rabbi Yosef answered
> "whatever blocks the will
> "to MAKE IT NEW
>
> (Talmud)[25]

In this translation Rothenberg transforms a Talmudic text into a contemporary poem that expounds his poetics. The capitalized word "FIXED" and the phrase "MAKE IT NEW" allude to a Poundian principle. By foregrounding these words typographically, Rothenberg draws attention to the similar ways in which tradition is rewritten by rabbinical Judaism and modernist poetry. Both types of rewriting avoid fixity. However, in making this analogy Rothenberg deliberately ignores obvious differences between these two approaches to tradition. Surely, the poetic license of a contemporary poet differs from the conventions of normative Judaism determining who is allowed to reappropriate and reinterpret tradition. In a traditional Jewish context, only someone who was trained in the study of the Talmud has this privilege. But today, outside the Orthodox realm, "there is no consensus on who has the right to appropriate and how such a retrieval can legitimately take place."[26] Moreover, contemporary American culture emphasizes pluralism, equality, and the right of the individual to make free choices. Hence the relevance of a religion, its practices and the interpretation of its texts are decided by the individual.[27] Rothenberg acts on the basis of these general American principles when he reinterprets Judaism.

The reappropriation of tradition may take different forms. Liebman provides three major categories for the analysis of reappropriation: selectivity, transformation, and transvaluation.

SELECTIVITY denotes "the selection or emphasis of certain themes and the de-emphasis or ignoring of others." This process is illustrated, for example, by the way in which the followers of the ultra-Orthodox Rabbi Kook in Israel have "reappropriated Judaism in an ultranationalist, xenophobic form."[28] Likewise, Rothenberg's reconstruction of Jewish tradition is highly selective. *A Big Jewish Book* concentrates on the marginal and the repressed aspects of Judaism and de-emphasizes liturgy and observance.

TRANS*FORMATION* designates the "retention of structurally recognizable features of traditional symbols, while changing certain aspects of its *form* [italics are mine]."[29] The fast of *Tishah b'Av*, for instance, the day on which Jews mourn the destruction of the temple, may be reinterpreted to embody also the commemoration of the Holocaust. Rothenberg's entire oeuvre involves transformation in a general sense, but one also can single out a more specific type of transformation. In his event poems, he makes use of "reduction." He composes poems out of condensed ritual instructions, thus transforming ritual into a poem. Furthermore, transformation is also constitutive to translation, which Rothenberg employs artfully.

TRANS*VALUATION* describes the "retention of the forms of traditional symbols while imposing new meanings on the traditional symbol."[30] In other words, a tradition is given new *value*, as for instance, in the case of the Ḥanukkah festival. Rothenberg's use of gematria (Jewish number mysticism) falls under the rubric of transvaluation. In the poetic sequence "14 Stations" and in his book *Gematria*, the poet employs number mysticism as a kind of chance operation rather than as an exegetic device (in accordance with Jewish tradition).[31]

One may ask how these various forms of reappropriation are related to the previously mentioned "appropriative strategies" of the avant-garde. While Liebman's categories can be applied to *all* forms of reappropriation in many different contexts other than literary, the term "appropriative strategies" refers to specific literary devices. The appropriative strategies analyzed in this book can be regarded as a literary subcategory of Liebman's terms. Rothenberg utilizes the appropriative literary strategies of the avant-garde in order to select, transform and transvalue Jewish tradition.

Methodology

Researching Rothenberg's oeuvre entails many methodological problems. There is, first of all, the immense, almost epic breadth of Rothenberg's work and its inclusiveness. It comprises various types of writing: poetry, anthologies, poetics, magazine publications, translations, ritualistic theater plays, and adaptations of plays. Moreover, the poet makes use of many different poetic forms—prose poems, concrete poems, long and narrative poems, dialogue poems, and poetic sequences.

Rothenberg's interests range from "archaic," "primitive," and "oral" poetry to the most current avant-garde experiments. He regularly spends time in Europe, especially in France, Italy, and Austria, but also in Eastern Europe, Japan, and Mexico, where he gives readings and joins poetry festivals. The two anthologies, *Poems for the Millennium*, demonstrate his sweeping knowledge of modern and contemporary poetry and his will to expand his own poetics continually. Each anthology explores new territory, as Rothenberg proves once more in *A Book of the Book* (edited with Steven Clay), an assemblage of diverse written and visual materials reflecting on the role of the book in a digital age.[32] A selection of Rothenberg's recent poems and sound-files of his readings are also available on the Internet.[33] The Special Collection at the University of California, San Diego (UCSD) owns a large number of tape recordings of Rothenberg's performances. Many of his readings are accompanied by music, some by theater.

Second, Rothenberg's work leans toward mixed media. For example, the poet has cooperated with Klaus Schöning of the *Westdeutscher Rundfunk* in Cologne on the production of radio sound plays.[34] Moreover, his poetry was adapted for the theater and performed by experimental theater groups, such as The Living Theater, The Bread and Puppet Theater, and the Center for Theater Science and Research (Luke Theodore Morrison).

Art and mixed media also permeate his poetry in the form of collages, drawings, postcards, nostalgic photographs, and photomontages. The anthologies include pictorial material, and

Rothenberg's own poetry has a strong imagery. For a while, the poet was professor of visual arts and poetry at the UCSD. On the whole, his writing invites the interaction of different types of media. For that reason, Rothenberg frequently collaborates with creative people working in a variety of fields. These persistent collaborations spring from his notion of the avant-garde as "the work of individuals acting together—an effort somehow in common."[35] Rothenberg has worked with visual artists (Eleanor Antin, Allan Kaprow), photographers (Laurence Fink), painters (Ian Tyson, Arie Galles), and composers and musicians (Charlie Morrow, Bertram Turetzky). Furthermore, the poet cooperates with anthropologists (Diane Rothenberg, Stanley Diamond, Dennis Tedlock), ethnomusicologists (David McAllester), philologists (Charles Doria, Harris Lenowitz) and literary scholars (George Quasha, Michael Benamou, Pierre Joris), and many more. These excursions into other disciplines nurture the intertextuality of Rothenberg's work.

Third, his poetry abounds in overt and covert allusions, partial, full-blown and crypto-quotations, epigraphs, mottoes, and dedications to poets and friends. Exhibiting intertextuality in all its possible facets, Rothenberg's poetry avails itself to the study of the poetic possibilities of intertextuality. Some poetry is inspired by texts from his anthologies and frequently alludes to them. At the same time, Rothenberg's assemblages themselves display an intricate net of cross-references supported by bibliographic information and annotations. This complicated structure of interconnections is representative of his oeuvre as a whole.

Ideally, his work should be studied like the Talmud, that is, in its totality. For instance, the only way of knowing all the Talmudic rulings about the observance of the Sabbath is "to read the whole thing through."[36] As with the Talmud or the Bible, both of which are non-systematic, there is no one single passage or part of the work where one can find summarized the poet's opinion on one particular issue. Since Rothenberg's work emphasizes process, it is difficult to pinpoint his poetics. In his writing, the poet continually reveals new aspects of his subject matter—sometimes in the most unexpected places, for instance, in commentaries or annotations sprinkled throughout many books and magazines. Naturally, the reader can feel overwhelmed by this diversity.

Fourth, the concept of intertextuality implies that the

boundaries of Rothenberg's own writing are not fixed. Furthermore, the author's literary output of poetry and book projects grows yearly. The impulse toward change is also manifest in the poet's re-publication, revision, and reworking of his own books. Rothenberg tends to publish the same poems in different formats, for example in pamphlets, broadsheets, artists' books, limited editions, and poetry collections. These different publications might differ with respect to title, design, or theme.[37] Some poems, such as the early "installations" of *Poland/1931*, were published in finely crafted, beautiful books that include special visual material. An appropriate interpretation has to take into account these variants.

Several of Rothenberg's anthologies, *Technicians of the Sacred*, *Shaking the Pumpkin*, and *A Big Jewish Book*, have been revised and updated, in the process of which texts were added or removed, prefaces appended or rewritten, and commentaries changed. Another characteristic instance of rewriting pertains to *The Notebooks*.[38] Its poems have undergone curious transformations: after first being published in *The Notebooks*, they reappeared in the form of prose commentaries to various anthologized texts in *A Big Jewish Book*; some of them were reprinted as poems in *Vienna Blood*, but they were left out of the revised anthology, *Exiled in the Word*.[39]

And finally, Rothenberg's poetics is deliberately antisystematic. In 1967 he proclaimed that we were entering a "post-logical phase"[40] (Charles Olson). The application of post-logical thinking is apparent in the poet's "definition" of his key term *poesis*. Rothenberg constantly reformulates the signification of this concept. At one point it is interpreted as a

> language process, a "sacred action" (A. Breton) by which a human being creates & recreates the circumstances & experiences of a *real* world, even where such circumstances may be rationalized otherwise as contrary to fact. (*BJB*, xxxiii)

Yet every new context—and there are many—reveals a slightly new meaning, and this new meaning does not cancel out previous definitions, but adds another dimension to the richness of the term. *Poesis* thus becomes an all-embracing concept. For example, it marks "a primary human process," which "persists as process, as preparation: it is evolving, contradictory, not fixed or rigid but 'with an infinite capacity for taking on new forms'" (*BJB*, xxxiii, xxxiv). Of course, this process could also be described in terms of deconstruction. According to this view, Rothenberg endlessly defers the meaning of *poesis* and thus undermines the concept itself. Yet, it seems to me that the poet's primary concern lies with broadening the referential frame of *poesis*, rather than in any deconstructionist activity.

Disinterested in consistency or hard definitions, Rothenberg wholeheartedly embraces contradiction. He shares "Blake's continuous desystematization, or Whitman's contradictions, Olson's 'will to change,' or Duchamp's 'I have forced myself to contradict myself,' etc." (*JR*, 516). Thus, Rothenberg rejects the notion of "a number of mutually exclusive categories" that might be set up in order to get his work under control. He contends that his stance is "irreducible" (*JR*, 546). On the basis of these assertions Rothenberg claims poetic license: "So I would hope, as a poet, to be able still to use my full powers—& as long as I do that, I can't 'adhere in any strict sense' to anybody else's sense of boundaries" (*JR*, 546).

Moreover, the infusion of contradiction may energize a text, which is why Rothenberg claims "VISION & CONFLICT AS THE ESSENTIAL CHARACTERISTICS OF THE POEM [capitals are his]" (*JR*, 529). The idea that the poem is "a high energy-construct and, at all points, an energy-discharge" goes back to Olson's seminal essay on Projective Verse.[41] Rothenberg reformulates this concept and connects it with Blake's proverb "Without Contraries [*sic*] is no progression."[42]

Let me draw another parallel with the Talmud. The poem with conflict/contradiction at its center resembles the Talmud, which presents the "'contradictory' propositions of the schools of Hillel & Shammai, etc.: not to eliminate conflict but to recognize its presence at the heart of discourse" (*BJB*, 452). Interestingly enough though, Rothenberg does not only emphasize contradiction, but also its opposite—synthesis. This is why some critics have called him a great "synthesizer." Consequently, Rothenberg's poetics harbors two contrary impulses pulling the poem in opposite directions—toward conflict and synthesis.

What emerges from the above survey is that Rothenberg's inclusive oeuvre poses formidable methodological problems to the researcher. This is further aggravated by the lack of thorough investigations of his poetry. To this day Rothenberg's oeuvre has only been studied partially and rather superficially. There is not one single book or thesis solely devoted to his poetry. If Rothenberg receives some attention in doctoral dissertations, it is usually in connection with ethnopoetics, performance, or Holocaust poetry.[43] Even though the concept of ethnopoetics may also be applied to his Jewish poetry, this is hardly considered in doctoral dissertations to this day. Generally, Rothenberg is perceived as a writer of subversive poetics, an original anthologist, the founder of the discipline of ethnopoetics, and a translator of Native American poetry. A number of interviews with Rothenberg are available, but these fall under the category of poetics as the poet expounds his own views in conversation.[44]

It is conspicuous that Rothenberg's anthologies receive more attention than his poetry. Most reviews concentrate either on his ethnopoetics and total translations, or on poetics and performance—and all these aspects certainly deserve treatment—but informed comments on Rothenberg's poetry are rare. Similarly, the adaptation and transformation of Jewish traditions in his poetry has been almost completely ignored, which is the more surprising as the poet openly admits that "the Jewish instance" is his own "main main" (*BJB*, xxxiv).

This situation reflects the general state of research regarding Rothenberg's writing. With the exception of consideration in the studies by Marjorie Perloff, Henry M. Sayre, and Sherman Paul, which all deal with aspects of postmodern poetry and art, Rothenberg's poetic experiments have been mostly overlooked in academic circles.[45] Only recently, have some critics begun to peruse Rothenberg's literary strategies and to interpret his poetry in the context of postmodernism. Among them, Paul Christensen, Frederik Garber, Hank Lazer, Peter Middleton, and John Zalenski provide useful analyses and interesting ideas in their recent articles on various aspects of his writing.

However, one will have to look hard and long to find Rothenberg's name mentioned in any anthology of contemporary American poetry or in any mainstream poetry magazine, with the one fortunate exception of Paul Hoover's anthology of *Postmodern Poetry*.[46] Lazer observes correctly that Rothenberg's "work is absolutely unrepresented and unacknowledged in the Norton Anthology used in most universities, indeed in all other 'major' anthologies of American literature and modern poetry."[47] By contrast, his poetry is included in "outsider" anthologies, such as Eliot Weinberger's collection, *American Poetry Since 1950*, and Douglas Messerli's monumental compilation, *From the Other Side of the Century: A New American*

Poetry 1960–1990.[48] The latter is astonishing because it contains a diverse selection of Rothenberg's poetry from the indicated three decades. Not only does Messerli incorporate poetry that has not been previously anthologized, but he also integrates translations and even a short "theater piece." This way, Messerli, the editor of Sun & Moon Press, shows his recognition of the poet's wide-ranging work. However, the audience for this kind of anthology is a small group of poets interested in experimental writing.

Among writers and critics, not many are acquainted with Rothenberg's poetry. Critical comments tend to run along the following lines: "I knew about Rothenberg for years, knew his anthologies and magazines and translations, respected his energy and intelligence, but somehow never read much of his poetry."[49] This negligence may be due to the fact that Rothenberg's innovative literary strategies are very subtle. Few as substantial articles about his poetry are, they most often come from friends and colleagues and from critics of the "Pound tradition." While such criticism is astute, its distribution through the little magazines of the avant-garde (e.g., *Kulchur*, *Vort*, *Parnassus*, *Sulfur*) is low.

The deplorable neglect of Rothenberg's poetic oeuvre—and especially its Jewish aspects—may have several reasons.[50] First, in the oral poetry movement Rothenberg allied himself with David Antin, Jackson Mac Low, John Cage, and others who chose to be outlaws of the American poetry scene.[51] In consequence, their oral performance poetry has not received much critical attention besides that in the movement's own little magazines, *Vort*, *Alcheringa*, and *New Wilderness Letter*, the latter two of which were coedited by Rothenberg. Oral poetics views itself as a "counter-poetics" opposing the formalist "establishment" that flourishes in the *Kenyon*, *Hudson*, *Sewanee*, and *Partisan* reviews, at university and in MFA writing classes. Following the example of Pound, Olson, and Duncan, Rothenberg frequently employs obscure allusions, which demand patient uncovering. But at the same time, his poetry intentionally sets itself apart from "academic poetry."

Second, Rothenberg believes in the necessity of literary and cultural subcultures. Hence his own poetry finds appreciation by a group of friends and associates, but tends to get ignored by academic publications: "Rather than beat his head against closed doors, Rothenberg created his own channels of cultural communication—his own magazines, his own small press, his own anthologies."[52]

Third, the study of American-Jewish poetry is still in its infancy. Until very recently, critics of Jewish literature have focused exclusively on American-Jewish novelists, while "the poets have been largely disregarded."[53] This may be owing to the fact that poetry invariably has a smaller readership. Besides, it is more difficult to read poetry discursively or thematically. Harold Bloom suggests that the relative neglect of American-Jewish poetry is related to the fact that

> [t]here are no Bellows or Malamuds among them, though there are a few signs that this melancholy estimate some day may need to be revised upward. . . . [T]here are a number of good poets, in several generations. But no poet with the high individuality of the major sequence of modern poets . . . seems likely to emerge from among them, any more than a single American-Jewish poet of undoubted major status has established himself in a century now more than two-thirds gone.[54]

Since 1972, when Bloom first voiced his dreary evaluation, many Jewish poets have objected to his opinion, most vehemently Jerome Rothenberg. The latter responded to Bloom's assessment with a ferocious article in the magazine *Sulfur* and with the programmatic poem, "The Covering Cherub & The Academy of Dada."[55] The critic and the poet fundamentally differ in their views of literary history and their notion of a canon. Bloom interprets the history of modern poetry in terms of the anxiety of influence—a history of struggle between strong precursors and aspiring latecomers.

On the basis of his theory of the anxiety of influence, Bloom makes the argument that American-Jewish poetry can never to be "strong" because it lacks Jewish predecessors. (Obviously Bloom ignores Yiddish and American-Yiddish poetry.) Since the "fathers" of American poetry are for the most part Protestant and sometimes even notoriously anti-Semitic (Pound, Eliot), the Jewish poet is left without models; there are no Jewish texts for misprision.

But why should American-Jewish poets limit themselves to WASP poetry? Rothenberg finds models for poetry everywhere—among the international literary avant-garde, in "primitive" poetry, and in ancient and medieval Jewish texts—and he fashions these forms in such a way that they suit his own purposes. Rothenberg resolutely disagrees with Bloom's Freudian perspective, which interprets literary history as a contest between poetic fathers and sons. In sharp contrast to this view, Rothenberg's own way of relating to poetic predecessors involves actively *embracing* the poetic forefathers rather than rejecting them. The knowing absorption of the work of one's predecessors (for instance, "the Dada fathers") takes place by means of appropriation, derivation, and imitation.

However, the "fathers and mothers" of Rothenberg's countertradition are left out of Bloom's canon. The latter's survey of American-Jewish poetry deliberately omits Gertrude Stein and the Jewish Objectivists, such as George Oppen, Louis Zukofsky, and Charles Reznikoff.[56] To balance out such negligence, Rothenberg provides, in *A Big Jewish Book*, a catalogue of approximately fifty contemporary American-Jewish poets, proving that notable American-Jewish poetry *does* exist, but that it has been widely ignored (*BJB*, xlii–xliii n. 5). Their experimental Jewish poetry receives inspiration from international avant-garde movements and places itself in line with the Pound-Williams-Olson tradition as opposed to the Eliotic strand of modernism, which informed the formalist readings of the New Critics as well as the canon constructions of Harold Bloom.

With the exception of treatment in Jonathan N. Barron's and Eric Murphy Selinger's collection of essays and a recent book by Norman Finkelstein, the theoretical challenge posed by American-Jewish poetry has not been met adequately.[57] Few as the studies of American-Jewish poetry are, they often fall into the trap of a purely thematic approach. For instance, R. Barbara Gitenstein's *Apocalyptic Messianism and Contemporary Jewish-American Poetry* contends itself with paraphrasing Gershom Scholem's work on Jewish mysticism.[58] For the most part, Gitenstein is busy hunting for references to his books in the texts of contemporary poets. Although her study assembles a lot of interesting material, it lacks a convincing overall thesis and fails to appreciate the literary (or, for that matter, oral) character of the poetry it discusses. Gary Pacernick provides a survey of American-Jewish poetry in his two books on the subject, but he approaches poetry mostly on a formal and thematic level.[59]

Most studies of this type fail to do justice to the complexity of Rothenberg's poetry inasmuch as they ignore its experimental character and its place in the general context of American avant-garde poetry. In his new book, the British critic Stephen Wade devotes one chapter to American-Jewish poetry, yet his interpretations are very tentative, while other portions of his study, especially those on the historical and social background of American-Jewish writing, are worth considering.[60] In addition, several recent doctoral dissertations deal with American-Jewish poetry in a general sense; they suggest various models for analysis.[61] Furthermore, the following two recent anthologies of Jewish literature at least include some texts by Rothenberg: Steven J. Rubin's collection of American Jewish poetry and a new Norton Anthology dedicated to Jewish literature in America.[62]

For study in this book, I will select only those texts in which the poet clearly makes use of Jewish tradition and that strike me as either typical of his poetry or as particularly interesting compositions: *Poland/1931* (and its various illustrated versions), *The Notebooks*, *Vienna Blood & Other Poems*, *Khurbn and Other Poems*, *Gematria*, and a few poems from *Seedings & Other Poems*. For quotations, poetry collections, which are easily available, are preferred over chapbook editions or artists' books. Yet relevant material (e.g., illustrations) from rare editions will be considered as well. Moreover, the Jewish assemblages *A Big Jewish Book* and *Exiled in the Word* must be taken into account, since they are instrumental to the way in which Rothenberg constitutes a countertradition. Working within the framework of a literary subculture, he often reads and performs for a circle of like-minded people. His large correspondence in the archive of the UCSD testifies to the author's avidity in communicating with other poets, artists, and thinkers.

Rather than examining Rothenberg's work chronologically and book by book, this book proceeds systematically. It must, therefore, of necessity isolate—somehow artificially—various aspects of Rothenberg's writing: the concept of totality, the notion of the destruction and renewal of language, various possible responses to the experience of loss, and the use of appropriative strategies. Among the latter, the most dominant strategies are collage/juxtaposition, translation, and palimpsest. Employing these literary devices, Rothenberg produces different types of poems, such as long poems, narrative poems, prose poems, poetic sequences, concrete poems, gnomic poems/riddle poems/minimal poems, found poems, and event poems.

The allusive features of Rothenberg's work necessitate a method, that—unlike formalist readings—takes into account the poems' diverse references to anthropology, ethnography, Jewish mysticism, and the history of religion. Drawing on theories from the field of sociology, anthropology, Jewish studies, and ethnic studies, my purpose is to place Rothenberg's writing in a larger context to reveal the contemporary relevance of his poetry.

Furthermore, my approach fuses various perspectives and theories rather than limiting itself to one single literary model. Different theories may be used in such a way that they complement each other. This method also has the advantage of spurning dogmatism and one-sidedness. Today, we are forced to be eclectic, since the only way of dealing with the vast amount of information that confronts us daily is "to pick and choose." Hence, I will freely select and combine those literary and nonliterary theories that suit my argument. For pragmatic reasons, I will avoid lengthy theoretical debates. Take, for example, the distracting controversy concerning the various implications of the attributes "American-Jewish," "American Jewish" or "Jewish American." In adopting the hyphenated version, I interpret American-Jewish literature as one specific manifestation of hyphenated cultures in contemporary America. But I am also aware that

> there are problems in the use of the adjectives here, just as the term "Anglo-Irish" is fraught with difficulties when applied. But the preoccupation with what exactly is implied by varying terms seems to obfuscate an already complex literary critical practice.[63]

Finally, one may ask whether is it acceptable for a German researcher to study the rewriting of Jewish tradition. Or, in other words: Is a non-Jew entitled to write about Jewish literature? Dieter Lamping responds to this grave question by pointing to the circumstances under which such an investigation may take place. He reveals that his own research is propelled by the awareness of the loss of Jewish literature in Germany.[64] Similarly, I am prompted to search for Jewish writing in other cultures and literatures. This leads me to the study of American-Jewish literature. This book analyzes the reappropriation of Jewish tradition by employing theories that can be understood and applied by any researcher—whether Jewish or not.

Yet this is not to cover up the fact that I am writing about the "Other" and that in doing so I am necessarily an outsider. In the context of current debates about ethnicity and identity politics, some critics would maintain that no outsider has the right to speak of a culture not his or her own. Although this contention is understandable from a postcolonial perspective, it also raises questions. One problem is that the descent concept of ethnicity (i.e., "you have to be born Jewish in order to write about Jewish literature") can be misused to "aggrandize and to wrap a cloak of legitimacy and authenticity around the speaker who invokes it."[65] Furthermore, emphasizing the harsh boundaries between different cultures may give too much weight to difference. Carried to the extreme, there would be no more room for human empathy. Werner Sollors therefore concludes:

> critics should not give in to such demands for biological insiderism. Taken to its radical conclusion, such a position really assumes that there is no shared history and no human empathy, that you have your history and I have mine—in which case it becomes quite pointless to give lectures on ethnic literature.[66]

It is possible to acknowledge difference and yet to be empathetic. Like Rothenberg's own work, which is much concerned with writing about the "Other," this book aspires to understanding and empathy, while recognizing its own limitations. In the future, others may examine Rothenberg's poetry from *inside* the experience of being Jewish.

A Brief Overview

The two main parts of this book examine Rothenberg's reappropriation of Jewish tradition with reference to religion (part I) and history (part II). Since "questions of loss & separation"[67] run through the poet's entire work, the theme of loss and recovery functions as the overall framework to the different chapters. The following short survey only concentrates on this key issue. Each chapter also makes a more complex argument in which a number of different issues are interwoven, but this cannot be summarized briefly.

In part I, chapter 1, "Rothenberg's Reappropriation of Jewish Mysticism," Rothenberg claims that important aspects of Jewish tradition have been suppressed. The recovery of the repressed, heretical, and marginal strands of Jewish mysticism will be demonstrated by one specific example: the appropriation of Abraham Abulafia's ecstatic kabbalah by the "counterculture kabbalists." On the basis of mystical texts Rothenberg legitimizes his "transgressive" poetics.

According to chapter 2, "Rothenberg's Reappropriation of Jewish Ritual," contemporary American-Jewish culture struggles with the loss of community. Rothenberg's rewriting of rituals, paralleled by endeavors in the Jewish renewal movement, strives for the recovery of community, holism, continuity, and meaning, all of which ritual may provide.

According to chapter 3, "A Jewish Poetry of Names, Numbers, and Letters," deconstruction proudly proclaims the loss of the unity between signifier and signified; Rothenberg mourns it. His experimentation with amulet poems (Jewish magic), numerology, and gematria (Jewish number mysticism) aims for the recovery of a primal language in which word and thing are unified. In this context the connection between poetry and the process of naming is revealed.

Part II, chapter 4, "Imagining History," deals with preliminary theoretical issues, such as memory and history. Moreover, it answers to critiques that accuse Rothenberg of ahistoricism.

Chapter 5, "*Poland/1931:* Evading Nostalgia," discusses how the loss of traditional Jewish culture in Eastern Europe caused by modernization, immigration, and the Holocaust motivates Rothenberg's attempt to re-create the past in his imagination. This chapter investigates the ways in which the poet invokes his ancestral history without resorting to nostalgia.

Explored in chapter 6, "Confronting the Holocaust: *Khurbn* and '14 Stations,'" Rothenberg's Holocaust poetry suggests that there can be no redress for the loss of six million Jews, among whom were members of his own family. The poet rejects any attempt to find meaning in the events of the Holocaust. This is manifest in his arbitrary use of gematria. This exegetical method usually presupposes a hidden, mystical meaning, but in his Holocaust poetry Rothenberg subverts this device by utilizing it to undermine meaning.

The conclusion, "A Jewish Ethnopoetics and Experimental Jewish Poetry," proposes that Rothenberg's Jewish ethnopoetics is based on the preoccupation with the Jewish Other. Furthermore, it locates his experimental Jewish writing in the context of contemporary American and American-Jewish poetry.

Rothenberg's Biography

The argument in this book does not rely on biographical data. It holds with the poet in denying

> . . . autobiography
> or that the life of a man
> matters more or less
>   "We are all one man"
>   Cezanne said
> . . .
>
> (*P*, 119)

However, a certain amount of biographical information may illuminate the poet's religious and cultural background. Even though Rothenberg logically belongs to the second generation, he exhibits many traits typical of the third generation. Such incongruity arises from the fact that the bulk of Jewish immigrants from Eastern Europe arrived between 1880 and 1920 (Rothenberg's father came to America at the end of this immigration period).[68] This group is often spoken of as the first generation. The children of these immigrants, the second generation, went through the American educational system between 1920 and 1945, and were rapidly Americanized. In retrospective, this period presents itself as the time of assimilation. One of the foremost Jewish poets from that generation is Louis Zukofsky (b. 1904). Although both he and Rothenberg chronologically belong to the second generation and both had Yiddish as their first language, their approach to Jewish tradition and identity is very different. Since Rothenberg was born much later (b. 1931), his rewriting of Jewish tradition took place under historical and social circumstances that commonly are associated with the third generation. Because of these terminological ambiguities, Chaim I. Waxman suggests a distinction between chronological and sociological generations. The sociological generation is determined by a shared experience during a certain historical period.[69]

Consequently, it is necessary to specify in what sense one speaks of the "first," "second," and "third" generation of American Jews. I consider Rothenberg to be part of the third sociological generation (as characterized by Marcus L. Hansen). The following biographical sketch focuses on Rothenberg's Jewish education and upbringing in order to illuminate his cultural background, on the basis of which he begins his quest for a suitable Jewish tradition.

Jerome Dennis Rothenberg was born on 11 December 1931, in New York City (Brooklyn), as the second child of Morris Rothenberg and Estelle (Esther) Lichtenstein, Polish-Jewish immigrants from Ostrow-Mazowiecka (sixty miles northeast of Warsaw) who had come to the United States in 1920. Together with his brother Milton, who was eight years older, he grew up in Brooklyn (New York City). In Poland, Rothenberg's grandfather had been a ḥasidic follower of the Rebbe of Radzymyn (*BJB*, xlv). He had sent Rothenberg's father to the

> Slobodka Yeshiva in Vilna. There my father broke from the religion and returned in secular clothes and determined, as I understand it, to lead a secular life. His principal language was Yiddish, and in later life he would read the Bible and Talmud—in the original and in Yiddish translation—as a form of recreation.[70]

Due to his religious upbringing, Rothenberg's father knew "Hebrew and Aramaic quite well," but hardly spoke any Polish.[71] Despite his rejection of traditional Judaism, Rothenberg's "father was willing to speak about them [the mysteries of religion]" to his son, who remarks retrospectively: "I think I shared with him a sense of the poetry and a mistrust of the dogma."

Yiddish was Rothenberg's first language. Besides primary education in public schools, he received a Jewish education at Yiddish and Hebrew schools, to which his parents sent him, even though they were "confirmed non-believers." Out of "deep affection" for his Orthodox grandmother (the mother's mother), who had come to live with the family just a few months before Rothenberg was born, he decided to have his bar mitzvah, about which he recalls: "The bar mitzvah training was largely taken up with sounding and chanting the liturgy but there was also some attempt at comprehension." Rothenberg's interest in "the mysteries of the religion"—as he calls it—however, came out in his late teens. Moreover, around the age of fifteen he became intrigued with poetry, his head

> filled with Stein & Cummings, later with Williams, Pound, the French Surrealist, the Dada poets who made "pure sound" three decades earlier. Blues. American Indian things from Densmore. Cathay. Bible, Shakespeare, Whitman. Jewish liturgies. Dali & Lorca were ferocious possibilities. Joyce was incredible.[72]

In 1952 Rothenberg received a BA from City College (New York). It was during his college years that he met David Antin. Delmore Schwarz, who taught workshops at the Ninety-Second Street "Y" in New York, was his first poetry teacher. After leaving college, Rothenberg attended the University of Michigan for a year of graduate study, to avoid being drafted. He wrote his master's thesis on Smart's hymns and graduated in 1953.[73] In 1952 Rothenberg married Diane Brodatz. Together they went to Germany, where Rothenberg served in the United States Army for almost two years (1954–1955); the young couple lived in Mainz.

On returning to America, Rothenberg utilized his knowledge of German and translated and edited his first book, *New Young German Poets*, under the encouragement of Lawrence Ferlinghetti.[74] During the 1960s the Rothenbergs lived in New York, where he taught English Literature at the Mannes College of Music from 1961 to 1970. His son Matthew was born in 1965. Rothenberg founded the publishing company Hawk's Well Press in 1958, and edited two journals: *Poems from the Floating World* (1960–1964) and *some/thing* with David Antin (1965–1968). Moreover, he became active in the New York poetry scene. From 1972 to 1974 the Rothenbergs lived on the Allegany Seneca Reservation in western New York State. Rothenberg's wife, an anthropologist, was writing a thesis about Quakerism among the Seneca.[75] The experience of living among Native Americans certainly had an impact on Jerome Rothenberg's perception of his own Jewish identity.

Accepting a teaching post at San Diego State University and later at UCSD, Rothenberg moved away from New York in 1976. He taught extensively at UCSD from 1976 to 1986, and was visiting professor at various other universities. After that, he held for two years a tenured appointment with the State University of New York in Binghamton. In 1988 Rothenberg became professor of visual arts and literature at UCSD. As a poet and anthologist, he has received numerous awards and research fellowships.

Stages in Rothenberg's Writing

Rothenberg's biography needs to be complemented with a description of the various stages of his work. Looking back over his almost forty years of writing, one can distinguish four different strands of poetry related to the poet's preoccupation with deep image/surrealism, oral poetry, Jewishness, and dadaism. However, Rothenberg has continually expanded his range and absorbed more materials into his work. Each new issue gets assimilated into his earlier concerns and thus adds to the multilayered character of his texts. I will isolate four individual strands of his writing—four "ideal-types" (Max Weber). My assumption is that Rothenberg's oeuvre can be structured according to stages, and that one or two important books that epitomize a certain tendency in his writing may represent each stage. Since the beginning of a new phase is never clear-cut (the writing of a "new" type of poetry naturally precedes the publication of the first significant book), the provided dates are only approximations. Each stage led to new associations and friendships with other writers, artists, and thinkers. Yet in this brief overview, many names will have to remain unmentioned. This survey maps the emergence of certain concerns that continued to inform Rothenberg's poetry.

Post-Surrealism and Deep Image (1960–1967)

In the early 1960s, Rothenberg coined the term "deep image." Subsequently, he and the poet Robert Kelly became known as the proponents of "deep image."[76] Deep image poetry is visionary poetry. In a letter to Robert Creeley, Rothenberg defines "deep image" in terms of perception and vision: "The deep image is the content of vision emerging in the poem." Such vision draws on the imagination and "the power to freely associate perceptions—probably the main link . . . with the Surrealists."[77] Beth Fleischman emphasizes this connection:

> Rothenberg coined the term deep image to describe a concrete detail drawn from the poet's unconscious that operates in a context of powerful feelings and evokes a similar context in the reader when it appears in an imaginatively conceived poem. In his words, the deep image is "an exploration of the unconscious region of the mind in such a way that the unconscious is speaking to the unconscious."[78]

This comment hints at Rothenberg's preoccupation with surrealism. Retrospectively, the poet himself characterizes this period as "post-Surrealist."[79] Rothenberg's poetry of the early '60s absorbs surrealist poetics by using mixed media and chance operations and by drawing on the unconscious and dreams, the imagination and the fantastic. The French surrealist Tristan Tzara, who was also a member of the dada movement, is one of Rothenberg's avowed poetic "fathers." Moreover, his early poetry, especially in *White Sun Black Sun*, reveals the impact of surrealism.[80] *Poems for the Game of Silence* includes a sequence entitled "The Gorky Poems," which thematizes the paintings of the painter Arshile Gorky.[81] It also indicates the pivotal importance of Stein's work for the early Rothenberg. Her writings assisted the poet in balancing his surrealist impulse toward depth with attention "to the solid verbal elements on the surface."[82] This becomes especially clear in "A Steinbook & More,"[83] where "Rothenberg experiments . . . with combining highly charged, emotional language . . . with Stein's methodology."[84] The poet's openness toward experimentation is already apparent in the 1960s. One of its routes leads into concrete poetry as exemplified by Rothenberg's translation of Eugen Gomringer's poems in *The Book of Hours and Constellations*.[85] Since then, concrete and sound poetry have nourished Rothenberg's own poetic experiments with magic formulae and sound.

Oral Poetry and Ethnopoetics (1964–1985)

Rothenberg's contribution to the counterculture lies in his propagation of oral poetry. What led him and his fellow poets to the study of oral literature was the search for other approaches to poetry than those of New Criticism. The countercultural impulse drove them to seek non-Western models of literature that were to revitalize poetry and bring about the conflation of art and life. By virtue of its close connection with performance, oral poetry—its translation and recitation—catered to these needs:

> the oral recovery involves a poetics deeply rooted in the powers of song and speech, breath and body, as brought forward across time by the living presence of the poet-performers, with or without the existence of a visible/literal text. (Rothenberg, *Symposium of the Whole*, xiii)

In the early stages of this oral poetics movement, Rothenberg worked together with David Antin, Rochelle Owens, and Jackson Mac Low. The exploration of the communal function of poetry and ritual took two directions in Rothenberg's work: First, it strengthened his links with theater, for instance, in his translation and transformation of tribal rituals in *Ritual: A Book of Primitive Rites and Events.*[86] Second, it motivated the preoccupation with anthropology and ethnology. Gary Snyder introduced Rothenberg to the anthropologist Stanley Diamond, with whom he then collaborated on a number of projects. The study of tribal cultures and texts eventually led to the publication of his first major anthology of "primitive" poetry, *Technicians of the Sacred* (1968), through which Rothenberg made a name for himself; the book was reviewed enthusiastically. Rothenberg's research into oral poetry continued with the magazines *Alcheringa: A First Magazine of Ethnopoetics* (1970–1976), which he edited together with the anthropologist Dennis Tedlock, and his own *The New Wilderness Letter* (1976–1982). Preoccupied with oral poetics, Rothenberg published two subsequent anthologies, *Shaking the Pumpkin*, a collection of Native American poetry, and *Symposium of the Whole*, a collection of theoretical texts on "primitive" literatures and cultures following a conference on ethnopoetics in 1975. The publication of this anthology in the mideighties marks—for the time being—the end of Rothenberg's writing on American-Indian cultures. During a period of twenty years the poet became known as a promoter of Native American and oral poetry, anthologist, translator, and poetical theorist recognized for his writings on ethnopoetics.

His collaboration with McAllester resulted in the experimental translation of "Frank Mitchell's 17 Horse Songs"[87] following the principles of "total translation," according to which "everything in these song-poems is finally translatable: words, sounds, voice, melody, gesture, event, etc., in the reconstitution of a unity that would be shattered by approaching each element in isolation."[88] Total translation grows out of a total and informed response of the poet/translator to the original text. This total response involves the body and all the senses. Rothenberg's translation of this cycle of Navajo poems presents "analogues" in English to the "non-sense" vocables of the Navajo:[89]

Go to her my son N wnn & go to her my son N wnn N wnnn
  N nnnn N gahn
Go to her my son N wnn & go to her my son N wnn N wnnn
  N nnnn N gahn

Because I was thnboyngnng raised ing the dawn NwnnN go
to her my son N wnn N wnn N nnnn N gahn
("The Tenth Horse Song of Frank Mitchell," *TS*, 224–25)

Rothenberg's life among the Seneca and study of Native American poetry also impinged on his own writing. *A Seneca Journal*, for instance, demonstrates the facility with which he assimilates poetic devices from other poetries.[90] Some of the distinctive features of Seneca poetry, such as its minimal structures, the utilization of silences, and the use of comic elements, have correspondences in his poetry from that period. Through his double role as anthropologist and Jewish poet, Rothenberg explores the link between shamanism and Jewish mysticism.

Jewishness (1970–present)

In the preface to the revised version of *Technicians of the Sacred*, Rothenberg recalls how his interest in archaic poetry eventually led him to investigate European oral poetry, which he had ignored until then.[91] Choosing to take a "Jewish inroad" into European texts, the poet decided to approach European oral culture through its hidden and suppressed Jewish traditions. This enterprise materialized in the anthology *A Big Jewish Book*, but also in several chapbooks, such as *The Notebooks* and *The Pirke & The Pearl*.[92] This increased preoccupation with Jewish texts falls into the period during which Rothenberg lived among the Seneca. The year 1974 brought the publication of the overtly Jewish poetry collection *Poland/1931*, following an earlier deluxe version of "ancestral poems." Parts of this book were also published individually, such as *Esther K. Comes to America*.[93]

In the early 1970s the poet developed a friendship (and correspondence) with the editor and poet David Meltzer who lived in San Francisco. Both shared an intense interest in kabbalah and Jewish magic. At that time Meltzer, Rothenberg, and a group of poets publishing in Meltzer's kabbalistic journal *Tree* strove for the rediscovery of suppressed Jewish mystical traditions.[94] Besides translating kabbalistic texts, these poets also wrote their own poetry drawing on Jewish mysticism. Such an eruption of kabbalistic poetry among the Jewish counterculture would not have been possible without the books of Gershom Scholem and Raphael Patai, which provided essential historical and mystical background knowledge to Rothenberg and his fellow poets. The "Jewish" period in Rothenberg's writing may be divided into three phases:

1970–1978 early phase	Exploration of Eastern European Jewish culture and "suppressed" Jewish traditions
1978–1987 middle phase	Experimentation with number and letter mysticism
1987–present	Addressing the shoah

While the early phase is marked by the general discovery of mystical and marginal Jewish texts and the exploration of ancestral roots in *Poland/1931*, the middle phase, during which Rothenberg published *Letters & Numbers* and *Vienna Blood*, entailed further experimentation with number mysticism.[95] "Abulafia's Circles" points toward two upcoming concerns of his poetry: dada and the Holocaust.

The shoah hovers already over *Vienna Blood* in a number of poems addressing the subject of anti-Semitism. Following a trip to Poland to visit the former home of his family, Rothenberg began to write poetry that openly deals with the shoah. The publication of *Khurbn and Other Poems* significantly contributes to the corpus of American-Jewish Holocaust literature.[96] However, Rothenberg had been aware of Holocaust literature much earlier. He included Holocaust poems by European Jewish authors in *A Big Jewish Book*, but only hinted at the subject in his own poetry. Since the late 1980s he openly addresses the shoah, first in *Khurbn*, and most recently in the cycle "14 Stations." In the latter sequence he continues his poetic experiments with number mysticism, which also prevail in the book *Gematria*.

Dadaism (1983–present)

Rothenberg's admiration for dada also originates in the 1960s. In the book *That Dada Strain*, he presents his view of the history and significance of dadaism. According to Rothenberg, dada stands for resistance against authority and established literary traditions. Dada is taken to be part of the "Great Subculture," which shares the subversive impulse of the Jewish mystics. Subversion entails the destruction and inversion of conventional aesthetic values; its ultimate end is self-annihilation: "The true Dadas are against Dada" (Tzara as frequently quoted by Rothenberg) (*DS*, vii). Yet "the collapse of language" (*DS*, ix) as it prevails in dada writing also prepares the ground for a renewed poetic language. *That Dada Strain* begins with a series of portraits of the "Dada fathers"—Hugo Ball, Kurt Schwitters, Tristan Tzara, and Francis Picabia, but ends with a poem dedicated to the shamaness Maria Sabina. Since the shamanistic experience implies a journey from dismemberment to recovery and healing, this becomes an apt metaphor for the poetic process: its linguistic elements pass through the stages of atomization and recomposition. Rothenberg's own poetry and poetics fluctuate between the two poles of destruction and healing.

Since the publication of *That Dada Strain*, Rothenberg has continued to work with dada texts, most directly in his translation of Kurt Schwitters in *PPPPPP*.[97] Furthermore, his recent anthologies of modern and postmodern poetry contain large entries on dada and neo-dada. What makes dadaism so attractive to Rothenberg is its marginality in the American literary context and perhaps also the curious observation that some of its proponents, such as Tristan Tzara or Marcel Janco, were in fact Jewish. The merging of different kinds of marginality characterizes these poets as "multiple outsiders."

Writing the "Jewish Poem"

Throughout this introduction, mention has been made of "Jewish poetry." But, one may ask, what is Jewish literature and what is Jewish poetry? Is a poem "Jewish" because a Jew wrote it, or because it deals with Jewish themes, or because it has certain qualities that might be characterized as "Jewish"? Rothenberg himself has variously commented on the concept of "Jewish poetry" as in "Poland/1931: 'The Fish:'"

> lazy & alive remembering
> our mothers' pictures in the grass
> this is the jewish poem
> not being jewish much less
> being polish
> much less being human
>
> (*P*, 15)

Does a poem become "Jewish," if someone calls it so by saying "this is the jewish poem"? An absurd idea, which however contains a grain of truth. It reminds us of the fact that there are different ways of reading a text. Reading it as Jewish literature is one among several possibilities. What we make of a text depends as much on us as on the text itself: "None of this precludes the possibility that a work can inhabit several literary traditions simultaneously. Its characterization as Jewish will depend upon the reader and all of the circumstances of reception."[98] That is why Rothenberg suggests in the above passage that this poem may also be read in terms of its "Polishness" (it is set in Poland and evokes Jewish life in Poland) or just as a human piece of writing. One reading cancels out the next: "the jewish poem / *not being* jewish *much less* / being polish / *much less* being human" [italics are mine]. This way Rothenberg ironically undermines all attempts at definition.

The problems he raises are indicative of the discussion of Jewish writing. In her introduction to the book *What is Jewish Literature?* Hana Wirth-Nesher summarizes various approaches to the subject and comes to the conclusion that "there is no consensus nor is it likely that there ever will be one about defining the subject under study."[99] There are certain open questions that are intricately linked to the definition of Jewish poetry: Who is a Jew? What is Jewish identity? It is impossible to answer these questions conclusively, for Jews do not agree about any of these issues. Moreover, Jewish identity is not fixed. On the contrary, it is being created continually—just like other identities in America. Hence some contemporary American-Jewish writers compare their own search for identity to that of other American ethnic groups: "In the 1990s it is clear that the newest generation is beginning to compare its people's literature of ethnicity and difference with that of Black American writing."[100]

Dieter Lamping suggests that the continuous process of constructing a Jewish identity might be called "Jewish discourse."[101] This definition of Jewish literature is attractively simple: Jewish literature involves Jewish discourse; Jewish discourse in the twentieth century addresses questions of Jewish identity. Moreover, this concept is broad and flexible enough to accommodate historical change. Although Lamping limits his analysis to Jewish literature in German, it can easily be applied to American-Jewish literature. I would argue that one aspect of Jewish discourse involves the rewriting of Jewish tradition as demonstrated by Rothenberg's work.

Being very much aware of the problematic issues raised by notions of "Jewish poetry," Rothenberg nevertheless ventures his own explorations of the subject. He characterizes "Jewish poetry" as ancestral and exilic. Ancestral poetry involves memory. This is already implied in the above poem in the verse "remembering / our mothers' pictures in the grass" and is taken up by another motif in *Poland/1931*—"writing their mothers' names in light."

The latter quotation occurs at the end of "Connoisseur of Jews," a Steinesque poem, in which Rothenberg satirizes definitions of Jewishness: "just as there are jews & locomotives / & jews & jars" or "jewish locomotives / & jewish hair / & just as there are some with jewish fingers" (*P*, 13). The poem foregrounds the grammatical and musical features of the words "jew" and "jewish." On the basis of similar sounds it links "Jews" and "jars" (alliteration) and "oranges" and "jars" (assonance). At the same time, it explores playfully the grammatical usage of "jew" and "jewish" as nouns and adjectives in a number of absurd examples. What this list shows is that the words "jew" and "jewish" can be used to name *anything*—hair, fingers, alphabets. Taking the naming activity to the extreme, Rothenberg reduces it to absurdity. Naming is a double-edged sword, which can also be used to discriminate against people. The lines "the moon's face burnt onto their arms" and "men who ride the train to lodz" allude to the Holocaust. We are reminded that the Nazis might have thought of themselves as "connoisseurs of Jews." Their act of naming—calling something "Jewish"—was racist; its aim was to separate Jews from non-Jews.

But naming does not necessarily have to be discriminatory and exclusionary. For instance, names are instrumental to memory:

> if there are still men who ride the train to lodz
> there are still jews
> just as there are still oranges
> & jars
> there is still someone to write the jewish poem
> others to write their mothers' names in light

(*P*, 12)

The last two verses of the poem "Connoisseur of Jews" do not specify whether or how the act of writing "the jewish poem" and writing "their mothers' names in light" are related. Does the last line provide us with a definition of what it means to write a Jewish poem (i.e., "writing the Jewish poem means writing their mothers' names in light")? Or, does it contrast two different ways of writing Jewish poetry: ethnic poetry ("to write the jewish poem") versus ancestral poetry ("to write their mothers' names in light")? The latter type of writing, "ancestral poetry" in Rothenberg's sense, involves naming as an act of memory.

In a letter to the Jewish poet and editor Howard Schwartz, Rothenberg voices his reluctance to define Jewish poetry solely in terms of theme: "I'm also not sure that Jewish poets have to be represented with (thematically) Jewish poems, any more than French poets, say, with (thematically) French poems—but that's a different matter."[102] He suggests that Jewish poetry might rather be described in terms of a certain energy: "the Jewish side of *poesis* is itself a point worth making—not only as theme [ancestral poetry, etc.] but in the energy of a large number of poets." (*BJB*, xxxix).

Rothenberg's (projectivist) concept of the poem as a field of energy centers on conflict; the exilic condition may represent one such form of conflict. Furthermore, the poet asserts that Jews and poets alike share the experience of exile—a point of view that is also held by other writers. Marina Tsvetayeva's universalizing dictum ("all poets are jews") was passed on by Paul Celan. For Rothenberg as poet and Jew, exile takes many forms. First, exilic writing entails the acceptance of marginality:

> admitting to being a poet or admitting to being Jewish is in some sense quite liberating. Like coming out of the closet, say. And the thrill comes along with the liberation, you know, but there's also the sense that you can end up in a very threatened position—as a Jew or as a poet deliberately accepting the position of marginality. (*RI*, 16)

Second, drawing on his notion of the Jews as nomads, as "a primal people," Rothenberg converts the anti-Jewish stereotype of the "Wandering Jew" into a positive image. He characterizes Jews as "supreme wanderers—even before & after the forced diaspora—the Jews' historical & geographical range has been extraordinary" (*BJB*, xxxvi) Such wandering may carry Jews beyond the bounds of their own culture and lead to the expansion of their cultural range—precisely the goal of Rothenberg's poetics.

Third, he identifies Jews "as mental rebels, who refuse consensus" (*BJB*, xxxv). Both poets and Jews belong to a minority that resists oppression. Rothenberg takes this idea even further and applies it to humanity as a whole:

> It is my belief, spoken throughout these pages, that "exile" is central to our fate as humans, that it is political as much as spiritual, and that its corollary (once deeply Jewish) is a dream of liberation & a message, precisely, of *resistance*. (Rothenberg, *Exiled*, 14)

Resisting the oppression of the unredeemed present, Rothenberg portrays "the Jew" as a utopian dreamer:

> the poet man who seeks the precious light,
> passes the day beside a broken door
> no one can enter. Hold it shut,
> the god cries & the Jew rolls over
> in his endless sleep.
>
> ("Prologomena to a Poetics," *S*, 70)

What does "the Jew" dream of? Of redemption? Of the messiah? Rothenberg draws another parallel between Jews and poets: both are waiting—for inspiration, liberation, and redemption. In *Poems for the Millenium*, he quotes Edmond Jabès: ". . . the difficulty of being Jewish . . . is the same as the difficulty of writing. For Judaism and writing are but the same waiting, the same hope, the same wearing out."[103]

Fourth, as marginalized people, Jews and poets represent the Other. Being in exile means being in the role of the outsider, the Other. The Jewish condition of exile is exemplified by Rabbi Simeon bar Yoḥai, who refused to accept the failure of the Jewish rebellion against the Romans in 132–135 c.e. In its aftermath, he was forced to hide from his persecutors in a cave for twelve years. Rothenberg's poem about Bar Yoḥai alludes to Jewish difference: "you fled to hating / 'even the best of gentiles.'"[104] Even in a secularized world, ethnicity—New Ethnicity—relies on the symbolization of difference.[105] The poem reflects on the boundaries between Jews and non-Jews. While boundaries are necessary for the construction of identity, they may also bring about exclusion and misunderstanding:

words in your exile
hurt because you made them
not fit not be what
the others heard
(they said) the Jew is
stubborn in his hole
drove you
to see your Jew's face
other's face of exile
(Rothenberg, "5/76," *The Notebooks*, 43)

In his essay on American-Jewish poetry, John Hollander proposes that Jews and poets share the experience of being misunderstood. The misinterpretation of their identity/texts indicates their exilic condition:

> If poetry is like Jewishness, it is that both know very well what they are, and though with a lot to say on nearly everything, they cannot easily explain that. Both poetry and Jewish identity are forever condemned to being misunderstood, to being wrongly interpreted.[106]

Yet misinterpretations of Jewishness have gone far beyond the literary plane. Jewish history is permeated by "misunderstandings" in the form of anti-Judaism and anti-Semitism leading to persecution and murder. Therefore, Rothenberg makes a point of it that Simeon Bar Yohai is *driven* into a cave. The cavern itself represents a primeval space and evokes the universal human experience of birth and death. It is the place where the particular experience of a persecuted Jew is brought to the universal plane. Rothenberg points out that according to gnostic and kabbalistic sources, exile is a cosmic principle. It originates in the separation from the divine that occurred at the beginning of creation: "The result was 'exile' (*galut*), which later came to define not only the Jewish experience as such, but a universal condition: human, existential, ultimately gnostic" (*BJB*, 154). In accordance with the gnostic view, separation and loss are at the basis of life and cannot be overcome in this world. This explains the birth/death imagery at the end of the poem:

at world's center
you would say—o universal
Jew fierce rabbi brother—

we are all one man
the cry of vision covers
our last escape
from otherness   from birth
cry when we first saw light
(Rothenberg, "5/76," *The Notebooks*, 43)

Rothenberg adduces the same argument in an earlier poem, "Portrait of a Jew Old Country Style." It concludes with the following proclamation:

'We are all one man'
Cezanne said
I count the failure of these jews
as proof of their election
they are divine because they all die
screaming
like the first
universal jew
the gentiles
will tell you had some special deal
(*P*, 119)

Rothenberg shuns easy polarizations or facile solutions, which is why the poem does not close with an image of universal harmony. Each concluding line switches perspectives and leaves the reader perplexed. We do not even know which voice belongs to the Jew or the "gentile," the "insider" or the "outsider." This shifting of positions is characteristic of Rothenberg's writing. The poet perpetually steps inside and outside of his own culture (and other cultures). But this way of continually recreating a sense of exile advances the exploration of identity:

> I should say that my own strategy . . . is to try to situate myself, partly by a truth, partly by a fiction, in a culturally specific situation—no, mixed situation, both American and Jewish—and to play those games of inside or outside in relation to other cultures. Specifically in my own poetry. (*RI*, 57)

The following study observes Rothenberg "at play" with the material of Jewish tradition. The poet is very much aware that "partly one is dealing with a reading of material from which a separation has occurred."[107] The challenge for him is to overcome this distance through the reappropriation of Jewish tradition and thus to contribute to the construction of an American-Jewish identity.

1
Rothenberg's Reappropriation of Jewish Mysticism

The Revival of Jewish Mysticism in the Jewish Counterculture

The first part of this book investigates Rothenberg's reappropriation of Jewish religion, more specifically of mysticism, ritual, and magic.[1] Religion, for Rothenberg, has many connotations that are not positive. The word "religion" is derived from the Latin *religio* and means "to be bound." Rothenberg contends that "Church & Synagogue" in conjunction with "repressive political states" have the power to bind and repress people (*BJB*, xxxvii). For him, the problem with the general concept of Western religion and the sacred is that it can be used to underscore power structures and to support a monoculture.[2] In that sense the poet is even "anti-'religion' as a fixed & inflexible set of beliefs perpetuated by an organized & powerful institution & hostile to more fluid views of the matter at hand."[3] Consequently, Rothenberg keeps at a distance from institutionalized religion and refuses to be bound by its laws and dogmas. He asserts: "our tendency has been to pull away from religion *as such*"[4] [my emphasis].

However, this skeptical attitude toward religion does not prevent the poet from studying and instrumentalizing myth, ritual, and the sacred. While he repudiates institutionalized religion and theological systematization on the one hand, he is eager to reappropriate the sacred on the other:

> I obviously feel an attraction to the world of ritual and myth, though with a sense too that in any given instance it comes out of a systematized religious context. So, on the one hand, the richness of myth and ritual and on the other their association, in more complex and repressive political states, with religion as an instrument

> of that repression. I am probably proposing two ritual contexts, maybe three: the primitive or shamanic, the religious or priestly, and whatever we're into on our own. . . . I don't want to drift back into anybody's religious system, believe me, but I feel a need for those values, including poetry, and for their survival among us. . . . And from those very old and tribal cultures I begin to get some sense of what it means to live in a state-of-myth in which the numenous, the sacred, enters into daily acts. . . . I was trying to deal with that and at the same time to avoid a reinstitutionalization. (*RI*, 2)

Surely, Rothenberg's preference lies with "primitive and shamanic religion" rather than the "religious or priestly." Shamanic "religion" is associated with small, tribal, anarchistic communities rather than "complex and repressive political states." Rothenberg's fascination with shamanism is motivated by his search for origins and the roots of a powerful poetic language: "But the shaman is . . . deeper into history and psyche, and absolutely essential to an understanding of powers (including those of language) that we're *all* about to lose" (*RI*, 22). Presenting his "vision of the Jewish mysteries" in *A Big Jewish Book* (*BJB*, xl), Rothenberg foregrounds—among other things—the shamanic elements throughout Jewish history. In this view, the ecstatic kabbalah of the Jewish mystic Abraham Abulafia, which exhibits yogic and shamanic traits, takes on a new significance.

In *A Big Jewish Book,* Rothenberg sets out to trace a subterranean, spiritual tradition of *poesis* dating back to "the older shamanism & the general pattern of ancient Near Eastern religion" (*BJB*, xxxvii), continuing through Christian, gnostic, rabbinic, messianic, and kabbalistic movements up to the libertarian revolts of the modern age (Shabbateanism, Frankism, Zionism, revolutionary politics, and the poetics of the avant-garde). This statement postulates that there *is* an underground realm of suppressed and lost Jewish traditions waiting to be retrieved.

It is worth noting that Rothenberg's undertaking shows similarities with certain developments among German Jews at the beginning of the twentieth century. At that time a group of young intellectuals and writers strove for the recovery of mystical Jewish traditions as an alternative to the rationalism of the *Wissenschaft des Judentums*. Martin Buber and Gershom Scholem were important proponents of the search for a Jewish countertradition. Rebelling against his assimilatory, bourgeois German-Jewish background and "the leading figures in *Wissenschaft des Judentums*,"[5] Scholem began his quest for lost knowledge. He devoted his life completely to the study of kabbalah, which had been depreciated and neglected by nineteenth-century Jewish thinkers in the apologetic attempt of trying to portray Judaism as a rational, ethical religion. In reaction to this, Scholem was determined to embrace kabbalah, this "despised and abused Judaism," against "the prevailing antagonism toward it in his cultural surroundings. . . . He refused to accept the verdicts of his elders and his teachers concerning what was worthwhile and what was not."[6] Through persistent labor Scholem produced almost an entire library of scholarly works on various aspects of the kabbalah. His research originated a whole new discipline in the realm of Jewish studies—the study of Jewish mysticism.

It is to the philosophical and scholarly works of Buber and Scholem that Rothenberg and his colleagues turned for information and interpretations of the kabbalah. Striving to create a Jewish countertradition in the American context, their activities coincided with the emergence of the Jewish counterculture and the explorations of other poets, such as Robert Kelly and Robert Duncan. I therefore call Rothenberg, Meltzer, and Hirschman the "counterculture kabbalists." Since their ideas can be taken to be representative of one of the strands of the Jewish counterculture, I will first give a brief overview of the major issues and trends of the Jewish counterculture.

The Jewish counterculture, which evolved out of the broader protest movement of the 1960s, only gathered force toward the end of that decade. It was characterized by an overtly Jewish stance responding to the first stirrings of a New Ethnicity. Many of its central ideas were closely related to existing countercultural attitudes toward politics, drugs, ritual, institutionalized religion, and spirituality. The Jewish counterculture began in reaction to the Black Power movement, which asked white civil rights activists, many of whom were Jewish, to go home and found their own institutions.[7] The Six-Day War in the Middle East in 1967 raised "a gut attachment to Israel"[8] among a great number of American Jews—even those who felt alienated from their Jewishness or who had been critical of the State of Israel. Longing for a renewed and authentic spiritual and communal Jewish life, which the young generation could not find in their parents' synagogues, many young Jews began to search for "roots" along different avenues.[9] One may distinguish three major strands of the Jewish counterculture: one revolutionary and political, the second, psychedelic and spiritual, and the third, antinomian and heterodox (the latter is most relevant in the present context).

First, there was the political activist branch of the Jewish counterculture, which strove to combine radical politics with the awareness of Jewish peoplehood.[10]

Second, the bohemian and spiritual branch of the Jewish counterculture organized itself into the *havurah* movement (*hevrah* is Hebrew for "fellowship"), approximately in the time from 1967 to 1973.[11] This movement, which existed mainly among Conservative Jews, attempted to revitalize spirituality through the formation of egalitarian Jewish study and prayer groups. Its own publication, the journal *Response*, was highly successful. Other Jewish counterculturalists were drawn to two charismatic rabbis: the former Lubavitcher, rabbi Zalman Schachter, and the singing rabbi Shlomo Rabbi. The latter founded the San Francisco-based *House of Love and Prayer* in 1967, which acted as a hippie commune and a center for Jewish dropouts. Many followers of Carlebach eventually became newly observant Jews in the *teshuvah* movement (*teshuvah* is Hebrew for "return/conversion"). By contrast, Zalman Schachter, after his early involvement with the *havurot*, was instrumental in the development of the esoteric strand of Jewish Renewal/New Age Judaism in the 1980s.

One may distinguish one further third strand—the heterodox and unaffiliated fringe, or, in other words, the "counterculture kabbalists." It is with this group of poets and writers that Rothenberg can be identified. Their dissident voices are assembled in Rothenberg's anthology *A Big Jewish Book* and Meltzer's kabbalistic journal *Tree*. Even though all the various streams of the Jewish counterculture showed an interest in Jewish mysticism and were enchanted by the writings of Martin Buber, Gershom Scholem, and Elie Wiesel (Wiesel on Ḥasidism and the Holocaust), only Rothenberg and his poetic colleagues thoroughly reclaimed magical, heretical, polytheistic, and heterodox Jewish traditions and gave them central focus. While the *havurah* and *teshuvah* movements were prone to struggle with the theological strictures of their respective denominations, the counterculture kabbalists had no such worries. Their anarchic urge fundamentally rejected any religious authority, thus paralleling Scholem's earlier, self-declared "religious anarchism."[12]

For many young American Jews, their entry into Jewish mysticism came through the writings of Martin Buber, in particular his philosophical treaty, *I and Thou*, and his various collections of spiritual anecdotes, *Tales of the Hassidim*, *The Legends of the Baal Shem* and *Tales of Rabbi Nachman*. These books contain edifying stories about the charismatic leaders of Ḥasidism—a popular, mystical movement, which arose in eighteenth century Eastern Europe in opposition to the enlightenment. Contrasting Buber's approach to history with that of Scholem, David Biale argues that the philosopher's reading of his sources was subjective and ahistorical; Buber "claimed to put the Jew back in touch with his history by rewriting historical sources on the basis of contemporary experience."[13] Surely, his books did exactly this for the generation of the Jewish counterculture, in whose writings he is mentioned frequently.

But even as early as 1958, Buber's writings were admired by young American-Jewish poets, such as Rothenberg and Antin, who published together a translation of his very early stories in *Tales of Angels, Spirits & Demons* (German: *Erzählungen von Engeln, Geistern und Dämonen*). On the dust jacket of the booklet the translators praise "Buber's achievement, both as philosopher and narrator, [which] lies in his reconstruction of the spirit of wonder and joy with which the ancient beliefs and legends were infused."[14] Emphasis is placed on the reinvigoration of the present through the past. This corresponds to the way in which Rothenberg later absorbs historical material and molds it into his own contemporary, poetic vision. Buber's early influence on Rothenberg is also manifest in his deep image poetics, where the poet employs a kabbalistic metaphor from the philosopher's writings: the image of the kernel and the husks.[15]

Despite this early preoccupation with Buber, Rothenberg's overall knowledge and vision of kabbalah is largely derived from the historical writings of Scholem. According to Biale, the latter's theory of a counterhistory implies ". . . that there is a continuing dialectic between an exoteric and a subterranean tradition. The true history lies beneath the surface and often contradicts the assumptions of the normative tradition."[16] Scholem's account of Jewish tradition is dialectical. The historian sees a continuous conflict between *halakhic* (normative) and kabbalistic Judaism, between myth and rationalism, between "restorative and apocalyptic messianism."[17] This dialectical approach allows Scholem to balance out the disruptive, revitalizing, and irrational forces—the power of kabbalah—with the rationality of legal Judaism; he insists that both are interdependent. Moreover, the scholar always keeps a certain distance from Jewish myth and magic, which, in their more extreme forms, appear to him as "crude." Many of his writings deal with the speculative and theoretical aspects of kabbalah rather than its praxis.

By contrast, the counterculture kabbalists became intrigued with practical kabbalah (i.e., magic and meditation) and myth (i.e., storytelling). Rothenberg's rewriting of Jewish tradition exemplifies this new perspective. False messiahs, nihilists, and heretical mystics become the heroes of his poem "Abulafia's Circles"; *A Big Jewish Book* contains plenty of magic, gnostic, mythical, iconic, and heterodox materials. Consequently, Scholem's delicate dialectic balance gets tipped over toward the "irrational" or "post-logical" side. The poetic impulse/*poesis* of contemporary American-Jewish poets, such as Rothenberg, Hirschman, and Meltzer, runs down all the fences around the "secret garden" of kabbalah.

A Suppressed Bible: *A Big Jewish Book*

The act of recovering a countertradition really involves invention. This is beautifully invoked by a dream Rothenberg tells at the beginning of *A Big Jewish Book*. The poet relates that in his dream he found himself in "THE HOUSE OF JEWS," where he was asked to name a dark room in that house and decided to call it "CREATION": "But CREATION—*poesis* writ large—appeared to me first in that house" (*BJB*, xxxi). It is the history of this creative urge and its impact on language that Rothenberg designates as *poesis* and that he delineates in his Jewish anthology:

> I'm interested in the career of language as it goes through the history of the Jews: those language explorations that are part of the traditional culture and involve a kind of poetry or a number of language processes that are shared with poets per se. (*RI*, 20)

Tracing the history of what might be called a "Jewish poetics" involves the appropriation of known as well as suppressed texts. Rothenberg's creation of a Jewish countertradition takes place in the Poundian tradition of rewriting, which was carried further by Robert Duncan.

In the late 1950s Duncan and Rothenberg began a literary correspondence that affected the young poet's poetic development.[18] Retrospectively, Rothenberg admits that he "was able to draw and learn from him [Duncan] in a very direct way" (*RI*, 53). Duncan, who claimed to have been raised in a theosophic family where he was surrounded by hermetic and occult literature, had already been reading the *Zohar* and had alluded to it in his book *The Letters* (1953–1956). Through his friendship with Duncan, Rothenberg was introduced to Scholem's writings.[19] The correspondence with Duncan covers the grounds of poetics and mysticism (Duncan also frequently quotes Buber).

What makes the rewritings of Duncan so instructive in the present context is the high degree of poetic self-consciousness and the very deliberateness of the poet's choices. Compelled by his personal situation as a homosexual poet and his marginal position as theosoph, Duncan creates his own countertradition. He finds his literary lineage in gnostic and hermetic writings and especially among a number of female poets, such as H.D., Marianne Moore, Edith Sitwell, and Gertrude Stein.[20]

Likewise, Rothenberg constructs his identity as a Jewish poet on the basis of a Jewish tradition that differs significantly from the canon of normative Judaism. Fundamental to Duncan's and Rothenberg's activity of rewriting is the idea that one may *select* one's literary ancestors. Michael A. Bernstein argues that such choices are unavoidable because today, there is no generally accepted reading community or literary authority to which the poet may appeal. Hence contemporary writers are compelled to construct their own canon.[21] According to Bernstein, the poet's ability to justify his or her choices is a sign of the poet's relevance. Rothenberg accounts for his selection criteria in the preface to *A Big Jewish Book*. His detailed introduction shows how much self-awareness is involved in constituting a Jewish countertradition. While some critics expose the "manipulative" side of such an attitude toward tradition, Bernstein praises its innovative character and stresses its impact on future writing:

> then one of the surest indices of a potentially new voice is the enrichment/subversion it can bring to the established heritage of his own mentors, his capacity significantly to add to the horizon of

"pre-texts" already marked out as canonic by the prior selection of his teachers.[22]

Surely, Rothenberg expands the "horizon of Jewish pre-texts" immensely. He presents us with a corpus of Jewish texts, which has the following three functions: First, it broadens the notion of Jewish literature. Second, the texts may be employed as models in the construction of a Jewish poetics. Third, it provides a "poetic quarry" or an "alternative library" from which Rothenberg draws material for his own writing. Jed Rasula calls this phenomenon "compost library" and ascribes disturbing effects to it, such as "devastation of the ordered social library, with all the subterranean energy of compost."[23] While the discovery and exploration of Rothenberg's assembled materials threaten the canon, such activity inspires the poet. Therefore, many quotations, themes, and literary devices find their way into his poetry by means of appropriation. Through an active dialogue with his sources and predecessors Rothenberg is able to "derive" poems (Duncan's term). An abundant number of examples of derivations can be found in the poetry of the counterculture kabbalists.

As a general principle one could say that Rothenberg tries to be culturally specific in his own poetry, in which he tends to situate himself in just one or two cultures. In most of his anthologies, however, he strives toward expansion and universality. In that sense *A Big Jewish Book*, with its "ethnic" focus, is an exception. Yet, this particular instance allows Rothenberg to appropriate from "the inside":

> Part of the attraction was that I could enter into it as a direct participant in a way that I couldn't, say, with the American Indian poetry. . . . With *A Jewish Book* [*sic*], I felt that anything I did was from the inside. I also felt that the Jewish anthology as such—that kind of ethnically centered configuration—was itself a debased form, but a form that had, if one went at it in a total way, all sorts of lovely possibilities.[24]

But even here, where ethnicity puts a limit to the number of texts to be incorporated, the editor's tendency toward inclusion remains untrammeled. For Otherness also exists within the Jewish fold. The Other is that which—throughout history—has been repressed and excluded from normative Judaism, for example, the hidden history of the "Hebrew Goddess." Rothenberg draws heavily on Raphael Patai's exploration of this subject. Only by embracing the suppressed, can one achieve wholeness and a "total" Jewish identity. Duncan, who envisions a community among all the living, speaks of such a "symposium of the whole." Not surprisingly, Rothenberg repeatedly cites and interprets Duncan's declaration:

> To compose such a symposium of the whole, such a totality, all the old excluded orders must be included. The female, the proletariat, the foreign; the animal and vegetative; the unconscious and the unknown; the criminal and failure—all that has been outcast and vagabond must return to be admitted in the creation of what we consider we are.[25]

The goal of Rothenberg's Jewish countertradition is precisely to create a Jewish symposium of the whole is. By modeling his anthology *A* Big *Jewish Book* [my emphasis] deliberately on the Bible, which contains many books written in different times and places, Rothenberg creates a library for the Jewish countercanon. He calls the various sections of this anthology "books." Moreover, its three main parts correspond to the tripartite division of the *Tanakh*: *Torah* becomes "Ways," *Nevi'im* "Visions," and *Ketuvim* "Writings."[26] Rothenberg employs this structure to trace a movement from myth (first part of anthology) to history (second part) to language and poetics (third part).

The first part consists of two "books": "A Book of Powers" and "A Book of Worlds." Both deal with notions of the godhead and creation. Rothenberg takes this as an opportunity to introduce a number of important kabbalistic concepts (e.g., the ten sefirot, Luria's theory of *ẓimẓum*). The running theme of the first book is the kabbalistic theory of the emanations of God. In this context, Rothenberg comments on what he conceives to be the "image-making impulse" in Judaism: "the Jewish enterprise develops a range of phanopoeia (image-making) as fantastic as any going in the ancient Near East" (*BJB*, 21). It is this impulse that undermines the monotheist doctrine and pulls Rothenberg and other "mad Jews" toward heterodoxy, dualism (gnosticism) and pluralism:

> wonders of the old books we both read
> those martyrs to the images
> mad Jews whose words
> splintered the ONE into di-
> versity who

robbed of freedom
dreamt it back to life
high spirits

(Rothenberg, "from 'the notebooks' 10/75 a letter to Meltzer for his 3rd visit to Milwaukee," *BJB*, 66)

Thus, in the attempt to demonstrate a continuous tension between subterranean impulses and official doctrines, Rothenberg presents some texts that approach the borders of monotheism and others that clearly transgress doctrinal boundaries.

"A Book of Worlds" continues the reflections on the process of creation. Rothenberg explores the theological and mystical concept of nothingness and then introduces the *Sefer Yeẓirah*, the golem, and various kabbalistic theories about the creation of the world through the Hebrew alphabet. Main focus is given to Jewish creation symbols. The text suggests a movement from the sky (astrology—Jewish sun-worshippers) to the earth and the Garden of Eden. We learn about the symbol of the Tree of Life, the menorah, *Adam Kadmon* (the archetypal man), and the serpent.

The second part of the anthology, entitled "The Visions," again consists of two subsections, "A Book of Beards" and "A Book of the Wars of Yahveh." As Rothenberg explains in the preface, "beard" is the Hebrew world for patriarchs or elders—an appropriate title for a book that covers the times of the Hebrew patriarchs up to the Talmudic period (200–600 c.e.). This section is dominated by allusions to the Jerusalem temple, its services and rituals. Tracing the ongoing repression of the goddess (Ashera, Anat), Rothenberg draws heavily on Patai's *The Hebrew Goddess* and *Man and Temple*.[27] Further emphasis is placed on the patriarchs, the kings, the prophets, and the rabbis. During each time period, the poet reveals the persecuted Other: the pagan idolators, Baal and Ashera, the Canaanite shamans and heretics, such as Jesus, and other Jewish apostates, and they all find a place in this anthology.

The next section, "A Book of the Wars of Yahveh," has the same title as a lost book of the Bible and shows Rothenberg's intention to retrieve a lost tradition.[28] In this portion the poet recovers the tradition of rebellion and its "voices in anger & pain, rebellion & madness, hatred of other & of self" (*BJB*, 277). The book deals chronologically with Jewish history, the upheavals under the Romans, and the subsequent exile. It contains many stories about rebellious Jews, that is, magicians and messiahs, and concludes with a number of contemporary poems and translations from the Yiddish, most of which are related to history and politics.

The last part of the anthology, "Writings" ("A Book of Extensions," "A Book of Writings"), concentrates on language and poetics. Its Jewish texts contribute to "the recovery of forms of language & 'language happenings' that our conventional poetics has long ignored" (*BJB*, xli). "The word" is shown to extend beyond the page. The texts included in "A Book of Extensions" either emphasize sound (sound poetry, magic incantations, etc.) or visuality (magic script, numbers, etc). Both tendencies present ways of making words tangible.

In all this, the subversive push of Rothenberg's Jewish anthology is evident. By reading old Jewish texts in a new way and by searching for analogies "with contemporary forms of poetry & art, to isolate structures not usually included in the conventional anthologies or not thought of as poetry *per se*" (*BJB*, xl), Rothenberg transvalues these texts. They are turned into paradigms of a Jewish poetics. Some critics remark on this "secular" transvaluation in Rothenberg's work and censure him for instrumentalizing religion:

> Kabbalah, merkaba mysticism, Jewish gnostical writings and their associated iconographies and literatures, are the materials not so much of art as of religious commitment, meditation, and practice and contemplation, teaching devices that are "self-secret" in the sense that they are to be understood, as with most mystical teachings, in the context of spiritual dedication. Rothenberg presents them . . . in isolation, wrenched from the spiritual endeavors which in a sense they embody.[29]

Rothenberg is accused of lacking "spiritual dedication" because he utilizes religious texts poetically. Michael Heller remarks that the poet's translations of Jewish texts "look too much like the contemporary stuff."[30] Yet, it is exactly this surprising ability to bring the past into the present that appeals to other readers and inspires other writers. Rothenberg transvalues the assembled texts by shifting focus from Jewish norms toward Jewish rebellion. Resistance to authority is considered to be essentially Jewish.

A Big Jewish Book also perfectly demonstrates the selectivity involved in reappropriation. By choosing a large amount of heterodox Jewish materials, Rothenberg constitutes a counter-tradition. As expected, some critics attack him for misrepresenting Judaism and Jewish mysticism.[31] Interestingly enough though, similar reservations were expressed about Scholem's construction of a Jewish counterhistory. Scholem strove for a total Jewish historiography because he was under the impact of early Zionism. Freed from the need to be apologetic or defensive about any aspect of Jewish history or thought, Jewish historiography would thus be "normalized": "All manifestations of Judaism—even 'the question of the Jewish underworld of the eighteenth and nineteenth centuries: thieves, robbers, and the like' would be open for review."[32]

The similarities between Scholem's and Rothenberg's perspectives are intriguing. Not only does Rothenberg characterize the subterranean tradition as "a world of Jewish mystics, thieves & madmen,"[33] but he also argues that due to

> a long history of life under the gun, Jews have tended in their self-presentation . . . to create an image that would show them in the "best light" & with the least possibility of antagonizing their oppressors. By doing so we have often denied ourselves the assertion of a full & multi-sided humanity, choosing to present an image that was gentle, passive, sensitive, & virtuous, & that in its avoidance of complication tended to deny negative emotions or experiences & to avoid claims to ideas & personalities that our antagonists had staked out as their own. (*BJB*, xxxvi)

Here the poet explains why in the past many Jewish self-portrayals were apologetic. However, there is a crucial difference between Scholem's and Rothenberg's points of view: the latter does not write as a Zionist nor from the land of Israel. On the contrary, his diaspora perspective makes him very much aware of the "tragedy of Palestine."[34] Thus, his claim to a total Jewish tradition does not rest on Zionist beliefs. Rather, it grows out of the poet's opposition to the "Jewish orthodoxy, with its concept of the single immutable vision & text, & with its hostility to innovators and counter-culturists among its own people" (*BJB*, xxxvi). As Jewish poet and anthologist, Rothenberg tries to reintegrate "the sinister & dangerous sides of existence" and to make known that "the actual history of the Jews was as rich in powers & contradictions as that of the surrounding nations" (*BJB*, xxxvi).

Half a century after Scholem (Scholem began his kabbalistic

studies during World War I), American-Jewish poets—Rothenberg among them—draw on the scholar's work, while at the same time radicalizing it. No longer is normative Judaism viewed as a necessary balancing factor in the dialectics of Jewish tradition. On the contrary, it appears as a force blocking creativity. The fact that Rothenberg feels entitled to address the "dark sides" of his tradition without apologetic inhibitions is a sign of poetic rebellion. In joining his chosen Jewish predecessors, Rothenberg himself becomes a participant of a tradition that "carries with it a poetics of the open as against the closed, the free against the fettered, the transgressive and forbidden against the settled."[35]

Abulafianism Among the Counterculture Kabbalists

The issue of discipleship is raised by an intriguing phenomenon, which will be examined in the following subchapter—"Abulafianism." This term was coined by Gitenstein to designate the fascination of a group of Jewish poets with the mystical writings of Abraham Abulafia, a medieval kabbalist.[36] Rothenberg, Meltzer, and Hirschman were greatly inspired by Abulafia's work. Other poets, such as Jackson Mac Low, Hannah Weiner, Stuart Perkoff, and the artists Wallace Berman and Bruria Finkel shared their fascination with Jewish letter mysticism.

Altogether, Abulafianism, which emerged in the late 1960s, marks an early instance of the reappropriation of kabbalah in postwar American-Jewish poetry. What renders it an expressly "Jewish movement" is its use of Hebrew, which introduces a new feature into American-Jewish poetry whose only precedents are found in the visual arts. Already in the 1950s, Berman, a California painter and friend of the kabbalistic poets, produced occult collage works integrating large Hebrew characters.[37] However, in the context of Abulafianism, such a general interest in Hebrew letter mysticism would take on very specific forms.

Examining Rothenberg's rewriting of Jewish mysticism in the context of Abulafianism demonstrates that the poet was not alone in his attempt to construct a Jewish countertradition. Moreover, Abulafianism provides the foil against which Rothenberg's specific take on the subject can be foregrounded.[38]

Meltzer, Hirschman, and Rothenberg shared a background in the Jewish neighborhoods of New York (the Bronx and Brooklyn) before they eventually moved to California. All of them were raised in secular families. Their sudden interest in Jewish mysticism and kabbalah can be understood in the context of the Jewish counterculture and its search for a valid Jewish spirituality. Abulafia's teachings promised ecstatic mystical experiences and poetic inspiration. His work was to contribute to their construction of a Jewish countertradition. Even though other kabbalists and printers had suppressed Abulafia's esoteric texts and visionary accounts, they circulated as manuscripts and survived as a secret tradition until the 1960s.[39]

In retrospect, Abulafianism was triggered by two factors: the poets' reading of the *Sefer Yeẓirah* (The Book of Creation) and Scholem's discussion of Abulafia's kabbalah in his groundbreaking work, *Major Trends in Jewish Mysticism* (1941).[40] Once again, Scholem's work sparked the discovery of suppressed Jewish tradition, and again, Duncan was instrumental in introducing other poets to Scholem's writings (Meltzer became familiar with it through Duncan in 1964). *Major Trends* contained a chapter on Abulafia's mystical theories and several substantial passages translated from the original Hebrew sources.[41]

Abraham Ben Samuel Abulafia, a thirteenth-century Jewish mystic, developed a theory that Scholem called prophetic or ecstatic kabbalah. It attempted to induce ecstatic and visionary states. In order to attain trances, during which the mystic receives visual or aural revelations, various techniques were employed.[42] These techniques are based on Abulafia's philosophical and psychological assumptions. He imagines that our five senses, through which we perceive the natural forms of the world, prevent us from beholding other, divine dimensions. The divine world is hidden from us because our consciousness is blocked by the natural images filling our minds. To use Abulafia's metaphors, "seals" are imprinted on our consciousness and blind us to other dimensions; "knots" entangle our minds. In order to achieve freedom from such entanglements, Abulafia employs a meditative technique. His method involves the contemplation of abstract objects—the Hebrew letters.

According to Abulafia, the Hebrew characters consist of pure and abstract forms that lack reference to the mundane world. Hence he employed the Hebrew alphabet for his "science of the combination of letters" (*hokhmat ha-ẓeruf*). One technique, "skipping and jumping" (*dillug* and *kefiza*), involves the associative transposition of Hebrew letters according to certain rules. This method seeks to bring about an expansion of consciousness. If adapted to art, the letters may set off associations, not unlike automatic writing.

Another ecstatic technique concerns specific ways of transmuting the letters of the names of God. According to certain combinatory rules, the consonants and vowels of the Hebrew names of God are transposed. For instance, the consonants of the name *Adonai*, 'DNY (אדני), are split up into pairs of two consonants each, which are then alternately combined with the five Hebrew primary vowels. The last two consonants (N and Y) in the name *Adonai* would then generate the following sounds: NOYO, NOYA, NOYEI, NOYI, NOYOO etc. (נֹיֹ נֹיָ נֹיֵ נֹיִ נֹיֻ).[43] Words are broken down into letters and then recombined in such a way that their semantic function is destroyed. Carrying no verbal meaning, they become pure sound. Hence, Abulafia draws parallels between the permutation of letters and music. The overall abstraction process is supposed to lead to spiritualization; the pronunciation of nonsemantic words divests the mind of any meaning. This emptiness of the consciousness then prepares the mystic to receive visions from God.

Once the counterculture kabbalists were introduced to Abulafia, they arranged to translate some of the original texts. Apparently the close friendship between Meltzer and Hirschman and their intense written correspondence was the catalyst for this project. Bruria Finkel, an Israeli-born American artist, prepared the literal translations from the manuscripts, which were put into verse by Hirschman and published in Meltzer's journal *Tree*.[44] The intention of these publications was to make Abulafia's writings available to an interested English-speaking readership. By juxtaposing Abulafian texts with contemporary poetry, Meltzer hoped to create an American-Jewish version of the kabbalah: "My Kabbalah the English-American Kabbalah received via translation into language complexly reduced from Kabbalah's primary source: Hebrew."[45]

While the *Tree* journal would provide a forum for heterodox Jewish texts from the past and present, the small press Tree Books was to issue monographs by marginal Jewish writers and from the realm of Jewish mysticism and magic. Both means of publication were important for the dissemination of Abulafianism. Retrospectively, it appears that the printing of visionary texts by Abulafia had a domino effect. The ensuing Abulafia craze culminated in two subsequent anthologies by Meltzer with Jewish mystical texts, and in various translations by Lenowitz and Rothenberg from the original manuscripts for the anthology *A Big Jewish Book*, and a great number of poems alluding to the ecstatic kabbalah.[46]

Of particular relevance was the translation of passages from Abulafia's *Sefer ha-Ot* (The Book of the Letter).[47] This text represents Abulafia's only surviving prophetic work.[48] It was published in Hebrew in the nineteenth century by the Austrian scholar Adolph Jellinek, but only became available to a modern readership through Hirschman's translation. In the *Sefer ha-Ot*, Abulafia records his ecstatic visions. This text is characterized by an extremely complex poetic structure, which partly accounts for its appeal to contemporary poets.

Several years after the Tree translations, Lenowitz and Rothenberg set out to render a passage into English from Abulafia's *Sefer Ḥayyei ha-Olam ha-Ba* (Book of the Life of the World to Come); sometimes the book is also called *Sefer ha-Iggulim* (The Book of Circles).[49] This work, which exists in manuscript form in the British Museum, contains mandala-like circles of Hebrew letters and words for meditative instruction. Rothenberg reproduces several of these in *A Big Jewish Book* to evoke their powerful visual effect and mysteriousness. These images, then, are juxtaposed with his translation and a useful commentary. He provides exact reading instructions and explains how Abulafia derived these circles and what function they have:

> Abulafia's poetry of permutations . . . here takes the form of nearly 200 circles, consisting of a discourse on meditation, a set of instructions for specific permutations, & the permutations of the letters themselves. . . . In this way the disciple is led into the circle, must follow their message as an act of concentration. (*BJB*, 405–6)

The purpose of his lengthy commentary, not all of which is reproduced here, is to bridge the gap between the medieval, esoteric text and contemporary poetry. For the same reason, Rothenberg points to the similarities between the two. He asserts that

> [i]n touch with Yogic currents from the East, Abulafia's intention here seems clearly mantric; but his practice of a systemic & con-

crete poetry also closely resembles the 20th-century lettrism of Isidore Isou, the asymmetries & nuclei of Jackson Mac Low, & the blues kabbala improvisations of Jack Hirschman, all of whom he may have influenced. (*BJB*, 406)

These comments and the translations themselves reveal that Rothenberg lays no claim to an academic rendering of the text. Rather than striving for academic accuracy or comprehensibility, these versions are composed in the *spirit* of Abulafia, a spirit that for poets like Hirschman and Rothenberg resonates with surrealism and lettrism and other trends in poetry. When the translations of the counterculture kabbalists come over as strange and unfamiliar, this is not incidental. For the poets deliberately exploit the obscurity of the medieval text and Abulafia's esoteric language as, for instance, in the following translation:

LOWER RIGHT
outer rim: last of the middle . last of the first . first of the last . middle of the last . first of the middle . middle of the first . middle of the middle . first of the first . last of the last
middle rim (large letters): permutations of the name "72"
inner rim: **whatever has my name I made it for my honor formed it worked it truly & concerning this the name informed**
inner spokes: **his prophets (be he blest) / about his name / by 3 / ways / of creation / of skies / & earth / & man**
(Rothenberg, trans., "Abraham Abulafia, *From* LIFE TO THE WORLD TO COME: CIRCLES," *BJB,* 401)

Rothenberg transforms a visual image into an experimental text. His translation incorporates references to the actual shape of the circle in the manuscript—its rims and spokes—and to the original Hebrew words and phrases. For example, in the first passage, each phrase is separated by a period, in the last part, each "spoke" of the circle, which consists exactly of one Hebrew word, is represented by a phrase in English and marked by a slash. (By the way, the extremely esoteric first section gives instructions for the permutation of the letters of the Name of God, Rothenberg explains.)

Because of the lack of syntactic cohesion—a result of Abulafian transpositions and Rothenberg's rendering—the overall effect of this text is perplexing. But this is the crux of this difficult exercise: by disrupting our reading habits, the text provides a contemporary, literary example of the effects of the Abulafian technique. Rothenberg's defamiliarizing version breaks the "seals" of our minds by assaulting preconceived notions about poetry. However, rather than experiencing an opening toward the divine influx, the contemporary reader will be induced to stop and think about this unfamiliar use of language—which is precisely the kind of effect avant-garde writing tries to achieve. In this subtle way Rothenberg puts a spiritual text to poetic use.

Thus, the medieval "pre-text" supplies material for contemporary explorations of new writing. The poet allows himself to be inspired by the "strangeness" of medieval writing, rather than merely projecting his own poetics onto a medieval text. Michael Bernstein reminds us that in the Pound tradition, translation, poetic practice, and poetics are interlinked.[50] Rothenberg integrates translation into his own poetry in such a way that "translation," the Other, can no longer be distinguished from his "own" writing. His translations demonstrate the fusion of his own voice with that of the text that is to be rendered. For him, the function of translation is therefore to merge the Other with the "self/own" in a "single creative enterprise." Hence, Rothenberg calls "such processes—both of translation and collage—'othering.'"[51] The Other is brought into the poem by means of translation and collage. Both appropriative strategies are used abundantly in "Abulafia's Circles."

Why were the counterculture kabbalists so strongly attracted to the figure and work of Abulafia? Besides the poeticity of his work, his appeal arises from two general tendencies among them: a certain distance from Orthodoxy and a bohemian lifestyle. Alienated from institutionalized Judaism, they could identify with Abulafia, the outsider, who also was at a distance from the Jewish authorities of his own time.[52] The mystic's prophetic writings are potentially heretical, since they emphasize individual visionary experience over the established Jewish tradition. Realizing this, the rabbis put Abulafia under a ban, considering him a heretic. He was even accused of claiming messianic status, which is one of the reasons the Abulafian tradition was repressed.[53]

Naturally, such a marginalized character fascinated poets who were rebelling against the political, religious, academic, and artistic establishment. The poem "Abulafia's Circles" portrays the mystic as mad messiah, shaman, and poet and puts him into one line with other Jewish heretics and subversive poets. Abulafia's kabbalistic world could be taken to represent some kind of oppositional mystical culture—a counterculture. His esoteric theory was just right to provide a suitable jargon for an allusive and esoteric discourse among a group of friends.

Furthermore, there are several elements in Abulafia's teachings that suited the bohemian lifestyle of the counterculture kabbalists. They saw an affinity between Abulafia's beliefs and their own issues and found ways to combine them. The following excerpt from Hirschsman, for example, references the antiwar movement, occultism, Yiddish studies, kabbalah, drugs, public revolt, Zen Buddhism, the Beat movement, homosexuality, existentialism, suicide, and the Abulafian meditation:

> Pacific Venice last wave from Viet
> yiddishist returned to the kabbala
> John has fled in rosicrucian glory
> peyotl public gong relations aflute
> Wallace makes violent static messages
> where are all the bohemians gone?
> Allen first gut an guru of the fall
> out to innocent streetboy terror and
> nightly chants of syllables abulafian
> my promise to suicided Jack Epstein[54]

Another source of affinity lay in the lack of extreme asceticism in the Abulafian method. This is unusual as "radical asceticism is a widely used method for attaining ecstatic states."[55] Because it assumes that the inner struggle takes place between the imagination and the intellect, and not between the body and the soul, Abulafia's kabbalah does not require physical denial. Similarly, Hirschman, Meltzer, and Rothenberg nurture a kind of mysticism that includes the sexual experience and interprets it in terms of the *unio mystica*. This notion is especially relevant to Meltzer's writing on Abulafia, in which he frequently joins letter mysticism and sexual intercourse. Sexual ecstasy is compared to the mystical occurrence of speech and light visions—Abulafia blended with "Jehovic tantric stirrings."[56]

The inducement of trances through letter permutation must have appealed to poets who had their roots in surrealism (Rothenberg, Hirschman) and the Beat culture (Hirschman, Meltzer) and who likewise were set on the exploration of new states of mind through drugs, meditation, or shamanism.

Moreover, there are remarkable parallels between Abulafian meditation and yoga as regards breathing instructions.[57] This resonates with the adoption of Far Eastern practices among some Westerners beginning in the 1960s and continuing to the present day. The fascination with different states of mind also fueled the preoccupation with "madness." What the "madman" and the vatic poet aspiring to prophesy share is scientifically labeled a "hallucinatory" experience; drugs may also cause it. Hence Meltzer and Hirschman often speak of the mystical experience in terms of drug-related imagery, such as cracks or blasts.[58]

The considerable knowledge of Abulafia's life and work that was acquired by Meltzer, Hirschman, and Rothenberg affected their poetry in many ways. Most obvious are the great many allusions in their poetry to Abulafia's biography and writings. These references may vary from straightforward quotation to covert hint. Legendary events from the mystic's biography as reported by Scholem are mentioned in Meltzer's poem "Abulafia"[59] and in Rothenberg's "Abulafia's Circles."

Typically, Rothenberg selects for his poem the most spectacular parts of the story, for instance, Abulafia's quest for the mythical river Sambatyon or his fabulous visit to the pope (*VB*, 71–72). The legend claims that Abulafia traveled to Rome to convert the pope in the belief that he himself was the messiah. Scholem suggests that "urged by an 'inner voice,' Abulafia went to Rome in the summer of 1280 with the intention of calling Pope Nicholas III to account for the sufferings of the Jews and to persuade him to ameliorate their lot."[60] However, when Abulafia arrived in Rome, he learned that Pope Nicholas III had just died. The Franciscans then imprisoned Abulafia for twenty-eight days. After his release he traveled through Italy. In *The Book of the Letter,* Abulafia himself alludes to his experience in Rome:

AND BEHOLD THE
MESSENGER WAS
CALLED BUT HE
DID NOT COME
FOR THE 12
STOPPED ENTRY
AND YDVD
ARRANGED WITH
THOSE WISE IN

WAR TO DEFEAT
HIS ENEMIES
TOTALLY BEFORE
THE ADVENT OF
HIS REVELATION
[Hirschman's emphasis]
("From: The Book of The Letter" *Tree*, 145)

Rothenberg cites another version of these events in *A Big Jewish Book*.[61] He also introduces "A Book of Extensions" with a quotation from Abulafia's prophetic book in Hirschman's translation. In this passage the kabbalist characterizes himself as "Zechariahu the Messenger" (the names "Raziel" and "Zechariahu" were Abulafia's pseudonyms):

And Adonai said to
Zechariahu the Messenger,
Raise your voice
with the tongue
of your pen
write
the word of God, this book with
your three
fingers
("Abraham Abulafia: *From* The Book of the Letter," *BJB*, 383)

All these passages depict Abulafia as a visionary with prophetic claims—a man who is on an arduous mission, a man with a disturbing message. But it is exactly this quality of being a "trouble-maker" that appeals to the counterculture kabbalists. Rothenberg claims Abulafia as a "model therefore, of the poet/rebel in language & in life, common to Jewish & other marginalities within the monolithic nation-state."[62] In Hirschman's perspective, the mystic's marginal position is emphasized by the fact that

> Abulafia . . . was never admitted into the great rabbinic canon of the Jews because in fact he was the Jew's first truly modern poet/ visual artist saw the abstract musical beauty of the letters of the Hebrew alphabet (Hirschman, cited in *BJB*, 406)

The notion of Abulafia as a poet is essential to his appreciation by the counterculture kabbalists, who often compare poets and mystics. One of the most intriguing parallels pertains to the use of letter permutations in medieval meditative practice and in contemporary avant-garde poetry.

Beginning with the futurists (e.g., Velimir V. Khlebnikov), poets have employed permutation as an experimental device. For example, permutations feature in Gertrude Stein's poetry and in the texts of those who write in her "tradition" (e.g., Language Poetry); permutational operations also mark a great number of sound and concrete poems; they were used abundantly in the 1960s by experimental composers (Cage, Mac Low), choreographers (Merce Cunningham), playwrights (Mac Low and the Living Theater) and happening-makers (Alan Kaprow). Being aware of these tendencies, the counterculture kabbalists explore this subject in various ways. Rothenberg includes an Abulafian permutation chart in *A Big Jewish Book*.[63]

Moreover, one of his own poems in *Poland/1931* is appropriated from an Abulafian manual. Its instructions concern the preparations that should precede the performance of letter permutations. Abulafia recommends that the mystic adept

> adorn his house with nice decorations, the most important that he has, and with kinds of spices which have a nice fragrance. He also should have shrubs and fresh grass in the house. These are very good because, having secluded himself, his vegetative soul, which is connected with his vital soul, shall find pleasure in all these things. He should then advance to playing music . . . and . . . he should make music with his mouth and voice, [chanting] psalms of song and of the desire for the Torah, in order to give pleasure to the vital soul. . . . Then, at that time and afterwards, sit and take ink, pen and paper in your hand and start to permute letters, quickly and in great passion . . . , because all this is necessary in order to separate the soul, to cleanse it from all the forms and material things which previously were part of it.[64]

In the following palimpsest (overwriting of another text), Rothenberg assimilates this passage to his own poetics and interprets it in terms of current avant-garde activities, happenings, and events that were popular in the 1960s. (Note that in the modern poem "desire for the Torah" becomes "The Book of Law," a subtle indication of contemporary antinomianism):

> WORD EVENT
>
> He sits in a house whose walls are decorated with fresh vegetables, praying & singing psalms, & reading from *The Book of Law*.

> Then he begins to move the letters that he sees, until they make new words & sounds.
> Quickly he jumps from word to word, letting the words form thoughts in any order.
> Finally he drops the words out of his mind: word by word until he thinks of nothing.
> Freed from thought, the consonants dance around him in quick motion. Forming a mirror in which he sees his face.
> (*P*, 73)

At least two readings of this poem are possible. If one knows Abulafia's teachings, one can imagine that the text describes a mystic who transmutes letters until he reaches a trance. Otherwise, one might think the poem's protagonist an experimental poet, who shifts around words and letters in the process of composition or in the performance of sound-poetry. By creating texts with such double meanings, Rothenberg subtly turns the mystic practitioner into a poet. Thus, the mystic *is* a poet and the poet *is* a mystic.

A friend of Rothenberg's, the avant-garde poet Jackson Mac Low, composes poems by employing "non-intentional methods," i.e., permutations and chance operations. From 1967 onwards, he performed "word events" precisely like those outlined in the above poem. Mac Low first read Scholem in the early 1950s and was especially impressed by the exposition of the teachings of Isaac Luria and Abraham Abulafia.[65] Subsequently, his own poetic experiments utilized some of the techniques described by Scholem. Mac Low elaborates:

> In 1961 I also began producing "Word Events": performances in which speaker-vocalists freely improvise without scores with the sounds of the letters in a particular word, phrase or name. They not only say or sing the separated letter sounds but also regroup them into words (mostly other than those in the original "seed"), of which they also may make phrases and sentences.[66]

The score for such a word event takes the form of a poem.[67] To the extent that such a "permutation poem" or mantralike chant approaches the effect of music, it demonstrates the connection between Abulafian meditations and music. Hence, Rothenberg relates Abulafia's practice to

> the mystical poetry of our own time
> on loops of tape

white noise that contains
all colors

(*VB*, 77)

In "History Seven," Rothenberg seems to cite another text by an anonymous Abulafian disciple, the author of *Sha'are Ẓedek* (Gates of Justice):[68]

> "During the second week the power became so strong in me that I couldn't manage to write down all the combination of letters wch [*sic*] automatically spurted out of my pen. . . . When I came to the night in wch [*sic*] this power was conferred on me, & Midnight had passed, I set out to take up the Great Name of God, consisting of 72 Names, permuting & combining it. But when I had done this for a little while, the letters took on the shape of great mountains, strong trembling seized me & I could summon no strength, my hair stood on end, & it was as if I were not in this world. Then something resembling speech came to my lips & I forced them to move. I said: "This is indeed the spirit of wisdom." (*P*, 137)

However, the "quotation" is not completely accurate. If one compares this passage to Scholem's original translation, one notices that Rothenberg, in fact, transforms the text in a very cunning manner. He tricks the reader into thinking that the text is a simple quotation, whereas really, we are dealing with a palimpsestous reappropriation. Most indicative of Rothenberg's overwriting strategy are *unmarked* omissions. It can be shown in several places that these changes have the function of lessening the original's realistic and rational element. For instance, compare the end of the passage (Rothenberg's omissions and changes are marked in the original text by bold and italics script, in the table on the following page).

This example is very telling. It divests the speaker in the historical report of his rationality and skepticism, which, however, are exactly those features that constitute him as a real historical character and a reliable source. His self-doubt concerning the mystical experience ("Was it really a divine audition?") is movingly human, but Rothenberg omits it. As a result, the reduced text conveys the impression that the mystical adept is neither skeptical toward the mystical event, nor afraid of going mad, but confidently interprets his experience. What emerges from the palimpsest is the image of an "omnipotent," magician-like speaker untroubled by self-doubt.

Furthermore, Rothenberg's version suggests that the vision-

SHA'ARE ẒEDEK (SCHOLEM'S TRANSLATION)[69]	**"HISTORY SEVEN" (ROTHENBERG'S PALIMPSEST)**	**DESCRIPTION OF APPROPRIATIVE DEVICE**
At once I fell down, for I no longer felt the least strength in any of my limbs.	—	Text omitted by Rothenberg. Omission is not marked.
And behold, something resembling speech ***emerged from my heart and*** came to my lips	Then something resembling speech came to my lips	Omission of a pious interpretation. Omission is not marked.
and ***forced*** them to move.	& I forced them to move.	Insertion of another agent.
I thought—perhaps this is, God forbid, a spirit of madness that has entered into me? But behold, I saw it uttering wisdom.	—	Text omitted by Rothenberg. Omission is not marked.
I said: 'This is indeed the spirit of wisdom.'	I said: 'This is indeed the spirit of wisdom.'	Exact quotation.

ary force rests *inside* the speaker. This is achieved by ignoring the reference to the supernatural, extra-human force. In the original, the passive construction, "*something* . . . forced my lips to move," [my emphasis] asserts that an *external* force assumes power over the adept. However, by introducing a human agent, as in Rothenberg's "*I* forced them [my lips] to move," [my emphasis] the mystical experience is "psychologized" and the divine element is removed. What remains is an inspirational event arising from the "visionary consciousness,"[70] which Rothenberg claims mystics and poets share.

All the texts of Abulafianism have in common a peculiar Abulafian imagery—knots, seals, black ink, white flames, blood, mirrors—metaphors and symbols drawn from the sources. Yet at the heart of this stock of images are the black shapes of the Hebrew letters and their appearance in a mystical vision. Abulafia and his disciples report such abstract letter visions as a result of their ecstatic technique and take them as the mark of mystical enlightenment. In the writings of the counterculture kabbalists, the Hebrew letters acquire a personal and spiritual meaning. Hirschman asserts: "I associate them [the letters] with the inmost meaning of my life, the visible bridges between past and present, as well as prophetic events of the future."[71] Just like the medieval mystic, Hirschman employs the ecstatic kabbalah in order to gain letter visions, but his revelations come in the form of poetry:

> He sees them
> small, a roachcrawl [*sic*]
> over the body of a Daleth
> holy as a big old psalm[72]

Similarly, the experimental poet Hannah Weiner claimed to be able to see letters on her forehead and in the air. In *The Clairvoyant Journal* she transposes her visions of English words into writing by using different kinds of script. Capital letters, italics, and normal typography are employed to convey the different voices that Weiner sees/hears in her vision. Here is a short excerpt from Weiner's book:

> MEET [*sic*] OUT OF THE FREEZER in pink letters about 18 inches off the floor *negative red letters* it's not HIGH ENOUGH Neither are the *negative* words about 10 inches off the bedroom floor The words in the living room are eye level higher I can't stand it TABLECLOTH 45 degrees the bedroom must be the least BEAUTIFUL *honest* room *enough* COUNT 1 2 3 COUNTING says forehead.[73]

Although Weiner suffered from schizophrenia, she was able to transform hallucinatory experience into experimental writing. Rothenberg, who calls Weiner a "poet-mystic" (*BJB*, 410), views her poetry as the contemporary embodiment of the ecstatic kabbalah: "the words are / circles / Abulafia & Hannah Weiner" (*VB*, 72).

Despite the lack of religious framework in which these words and letters can be embedded, the Hebrew characters are employed to create powerful artistic effects. That is why the counterculture kabbalists depict the visual quality of the Hebrew letters on bookcovers, and title pages, and in collages, photographs, and drawings. Abulafianism favors the letters of the Tetragrammaton—*Yod*, *He*, *Vav*—as well as the letter *Aleph*, which, according to Abulafia, plays a major role in the permutations of the names of God. Even though Rothenberg, Meltzer, and Hirschman did not know Hebrew fluently, the ancient language held a strong fascination for them. The notion of Hebrew as the "Holy Language" is closely related to the search for origins, which also propelled Scholem, Kafka, and Walter Benjamin several decades earlier. Hebrew could be conceived as "an Ursprache that provided access to a perilous and challenging realm."[74] It is this dark and mysterious power of the sacred language that Rothenberg evokes in a poem dedicated to Berman. The California painter chose *Aleph*, the first letter of the Hebrew alphabet, as his personal symbol and employed it frequently in his art. In the following poem, Rothenberg recounts his own letter dream, in which the alphabet is personified as it is in Abulafia's visions:

11/75
(a dream)
in memory of Wallace Berman
the Alphabet came to me
in a dream
he said
"I am Alphabet
"take your light from me
& I thought
"you are numbers first before you are sound
"you are the fingers' progression & you end in the fist
"a solid mass against the world
but the Alphabet was dark
like my hand writing these words
he rose
not as light at first though issuing from light
but fear a doubled headed body
with the pen a blacker line at center
A began it but in Hebrew not a vowel
a choked sound it was the larynx stopped the midrash said
contained all sound
sound of Alphabet initial to all speech
as one or zero
called it WORK OF CREATION in my dream
a creature more than solid more than space or distance
& he said
"all numbers & all sounds

"converge here
but I knew it   said
that I would count my way
into the vision
grooved thus with numbers & with sound
the distances to every side of us
as in a poem

(*VB*, 40–41)

In Hebrew all letters have a number value. *Aleph*, the first letter of the alphabet, is equal to "zero" or "one." It plays a central role in kabbalistic speculations on the creation of the universe.[75] Some of these ideas are exposed in the *Sefer Yeẓirah*, the Book of Creation. However, in his dream, Rothenberg names it "WORK OF CREATION," thus hinting at his own "creation dream." The poem delineates the origin of the letter *Aleph* (א), the first letter of the alphabet, growing from a dot into a "doubled headed body" (*VB*, 41). This image also refers to the kabbalistic creation myth, according to which the universe emanates from a small dot. However, Rothenberg tells us, at the beginning is sound: "sound of alphabet initial to all speech" (*VB*, 41). Music, which is essential to his "primal poetics," necessarily relies on numbers for its rhythm and for the concept of the musical scale. These ideas feature prominently in Pythagorean number speculation.

Thus, various notions are fused in Rothenberg's poem, which briefly evokes a sense of unity: "'all numbers & all sounds / 'converge here" (*VB*, 41). Yet this wholeness immediately evaporates into "the distances to every side of us / as in a poem" (*VB*, 41). Evidently, the poet is not ignorant of the distance that separates him from "origins" and from the medieval mystical texts he reappropriates in his poetry. What remains, however, is the rebellion of the poetic countertradition, "the fist / 'a solid mass against the world" (*VB*, 40).

"Abulafia's Circles": Shamans, Tricksters, and Transgressors

In our account of Abulafianism, Rothenberg's poem "Abulafia's Circles" (*VB*, 69–90) has been mentioned frequently. It can be taken to represent the poet's own take on Abulafia.

For even though the counterculture kabbalists share many

interests and approaches, each of them gives a different focus to the material. Meltzer seems most interested in the subversive and spiritual possibilities of Abulafia's teachings and in transferring these to the present; his poems connect Abulafian ecstasy with tantric spirituality, and sexually implicit imagery. Like Rothenberg, he appends notes to his poems to provide the reader with some contextual information. By contrast, Hirschman uses his Abulafian "insider" knowledge without assisting the reader with any clues. His fascination is with the most esoteric and occult aspects of kabbalah; his own poems are equally hermetic. Since Hirschman studied Japanese calligraphy for a short time as a young man, the visual character of the Hebrew letters especially appeals to him.

Both Hirschman and Meltzer are engrossed with the parallels between mystical and drug-induced states of mind, while Rothenberg interprets Abulafian meditation practices on the background of shamanism. Moreover, he goes furthest in exploring the similarities between kabbalistic teachings and contemporary poetics. In doing so, he employs the widest range of poetic and appropriative devices. Since his interest in the ecstatic kabbalah arose a few years after Meltzer and Hirschman first "discovered" Abulafia's work, he had the advantage of being able to draw on the texts and materials they had assembled. His poem "Abulafia's Circles" is the last significant product of countercultural Abulafianism. It appeared together with Lenowitz's translation of the sayings of Jacob Frank as one of the last issues of Meltzer's journal *Tree*.[76]

"Abulafia's Circles" comes over as the grand finale of Abulafianism because of its sheer length (approximately twenty pages). Rothenberg employs the "American genre" of the long poem, which has been described as inclusive and exploratory.[77] This form enables him to transcend the confines of the lyric and to incorporate historical material. The "transgressive" tendency of this loosely defined and open genre is just right for the exploration of antinomianism to which the poet aspires. Since the long poem has the capacity to assimilate many different modes of writing and a lot of disparate material, it can become a medium for collage—one of Rothenberg's favorite appropriative strategies. "Abulafia's Circles" is a poetic vision that blends many different voices and time periods into a seamless collage.

This poem reveals that Rothenberg's reappropriation of Jewish mysticism takes into account contemporary spiritual and poetic issues. Like other experimental writers, he defies normative systems and finds religious or aesthetic alternatives in subversion, anarchism, and antinomianism. The shaman, the trickster, and the transgressor manifest these impulses. Not only are the central characters in the poem associated with these mythic types, but the role of poet himself is associated with being a shaman, trickster, and transgressor. In his poetry, and also in his rewriting of Jewish tradition, Rothenberg employs shamanic, tricksterish, and transgressive poetic devices.

As previously stated, Abulafia's meditative methods reflect "those types of approaches which Mircea Eliade, the scholar of comparative religions, would designate as 'shamanistic.'"[78] Rothenberg, who is acquainted with Eliade's monumental study, *Shamanism: Archaic Techniques of Ecstasy*, dwells on the connection between shamanism and certain types of ecstatic mysticism.[79] Therefore, it is precisely the role of the visionary shaman and healer that Rothenberg attributes to Abulafia, the "wise man" (*VB*, 75). Just as the shamanistic initiate undergoes an imaginary stage of physical dismemberment, the Hebrew words are torn apart and atomized into single letters. Without the destruction of language—in Abulafian terminology, the "untying of the knots"—no vision can occur; no shamanic healing power is attained without the visionary dissection of the shaman.

Thus, in Rothenberg's view, destruction and renewal are inextricably linked. In the final part of the poem this comparison is taken further. Rothenberg correlates the "collapse of language" in the Abulafian meditation praxis with the revolutionary activities of dada and other avant-gardes, all of which involve "collapse & reconstruction—that led them to invent new languages (like Ball's wordless poetry)" (*DS*, viii). Rothenberg sees these "new languages" taking form in sound poetry (e.g., Hugo Ball) and in nonintentional, chance-generated poetry (e.g., Mac Low). He also suggests that the new languages might be found in the shamanist chanting for they give an entry to "what poets in our own culture have long pursued: an entry to what the Yaquis so beautifully call 'enchanted world' or 'flower world'" (*DS*, ix):

> the letters sing o Abulafia
> whose meanings
> fail us
> flowers spun from

the four colors of the glow
colors of the alphabet

(*VB*, 77)

Shamans attain trances by exerting themselves in ecstatic dance accompanied by drum music or by taking hallucinogenic drugs. The Abulafian practitioner achieves similar states by shuffling around letters; metaphorically speaking, he makes the letters dance. Resulting from permutation practice, the Abulafian adept is reported to have visions of Hebrew letters standing around him or her as if they were human beings. Rothenberg turns this strong image into a scene of ecstatic, shamanic dance:

circles
everywhere
the bodies mass around the flame
begin the round dance
& explode
red alephs
yellow yods
blue hum of ayins

(*VB*, 77)

Yet Rothenberg and the counterculture kabbalists were not the first modern Jews to be fascinated by Abulafia's technique. As a young man, Scholem himself was drawn to such experimentation for a short time, only to leave it behind soon for his studies of theosophical kabbalah.[80] In his subsequent research, he laid special emphasis on the distinctness of Jewish mysticism. Eschewing the approach of comparative religion, Scholem was concerned with demonstrating the Jewish specificity of kabbalah rather than showing its similarities with other kinds of mysticism.[81]

The counterculture kabbalists, by contrast, are particularly attracted to those aspects of kabbalah that can be universalized. Rothenberg's focus on the analogies between the ecstatic kabbalah and shamanism is illustrative of this comparative and syncretistic approach. Rothenberg is less interested in setting up boundaries between different kinds of mysticism than in revealing certain underlying human primary needs, which are believed to be at the roots of spirituality and religion. Even though his search for origins takes the poet into kabbalah, he does not limit himself to this perspective.

The figure of the shaman fascinates Rothenberg because it can function as an archetype of the visionary poet:

> The shaman does those things that poets do; the shaman uses language as poets use language but does it within a culturally specific context in which the language is able to function in a meaningful, significant way: curing, healing, defining reality for himself and others. I do not see what there is to disagree with about that connection to shamanism, at least the yearning for it, here and now. (*RI*, 23)

Both shaman and poet project their visions into language toward the ultimate goal of healing. Their language is considered to be powerful because it is able to initiate "change." In all that, the shaman is—like the prophet—a figure with a significant social role. By comparing the shaman and the poet, then, Rothenberg attempts to "recover" a more central position for poetry and the poet in contemporary society.

Not only does Rothenberg portray Abulafia as a "Jewish shaman," but he also suggests that he may belong to a long line of shamanic tricksters. In anthropological literature, much has been made of the similarities and differences between shamans and tricksters. Of course, the trickster is a common motif in Native American and American literature, and thus reminds us that Rothenberg writes his Jewish poetry in the context of American literature. Although the trickster has many features, I will only examine three aspects in the present context: the trickster as a shape-shifter and clown, thief, and transgressor. "Abulafia's Circles" consists of three parts, each of which deals with a different Jewish figure—Abulafia, the Jewish shaman; Jacob Frank, the false messiah; and Tristan Tzara, the dada nihilist. All these characters are associated with the trickster.[82]

This long poem contains a multitude of different voices; among them are Abulafia, Hitler, Jacob Frank, Hannah Weiner, Ossip Mandelstam, Hans Arp, Richard Huelsenbeck, and Tristan Tzara. Rothenberg uses various devices to merge their voices in a fantastic, surrealist vision. For instance, he marks the beginning of many verses with inverted commas, suggesting direct speech or quotation, but it is not always clear who is speaking and whether we are dealing with an "authentic" citation or a pseudoquotation (invented by Rothenberg). Further confusion arises from the fact that some verses are enclosed by quotation marks, whereas others are not. Here is an example:

they will sell new knives
to wives & daughters
"o the lives of Jews are hard"
(the song goes)
"even the messiah sits
"in shit
"beside the sewers   screws
"an eye toward heaven
lady fades
the sun in darkness shuts
his only lid

(*VB*, 82)

By means of such trickery, the poet concocts a text in which the voice permanently shifts, just as the trickster changes his shape. The narrative turns into lament (perhaps adapted from Yiddish) and continues with a song (or a pseudosong invented by Rothenberg); perhaps the song is sung by the false messiah himself, but strangely, the last line of the "song" blends in with the ensuing narrative, in which someone is said to see a vision of a "lady." This way the poet creates a fluid imagery with a hallucinatory effect.

At the same time, Rothenberg exhibits his own tricksterish mentality, for not only does the poet resemble the shaman, but also the trickster. Shaman and trickster may transform their shapes.[83] The trickster, in particular, is known for his elaborate disguises and his tendency to cover his tracks.[84] This is exactly what Rothenberg does in his seamless collages. The poet also disguises invention. Pretending to "discover" a suppressed tradition, he really invents it. Much of his Jewish countertradition is tricksterish invention in disguise.

William J. Hynes proposes that the trickster is a "situation-inventor," who has "the ability to overturn any person, place, or belief, no matter how prestigious."[85] Subversive, like the sacred clown, the trickster entertains and parodies the sacred: "As sanctioned parodist of the sacred and of its language . . . the clown is the embodiment of his culture's ability to sustain ambivalence and contradiction."[86] It is exactly this role that Rothenberg assigns to himself when he rewrites Jewish tradition. He affirms "the poet as sacred trickster (juggler/jongleur/shaman)—[with] a role forever public."[87]

"Abulafia's Circles" certainly is humorous, but it also contains satirical passages, such as a parody of a speech by Hitler: " 'these people are so dirty / '(pheh) / 'I Hitler Shitler / 'smelling so smartly of wagnerian highs" (*VB*, 75). However, this fairly obvious case of mocking is matched by many other instances in which it is much more difficult for the reader to appreciate Rothenberg's disrespectful appropriations and disguises. For often they are concealed like the deeds of a thief.

The trickster is also known to be a thief.[88] Rothenberg, who takes up Scholem's suggestion not to exclude from Jewish history "thieves, robbers, and the like," includes into his poem the Jewish gangster Bugsy Siegel and the mafia (*VB*, 73) and calls Frank's followers "Jewish gonnifs / [who] march with him / on roads to Warsaw;" "*our leader!* / say the thieves / *our little g-d*!" (*VB*, 81). According to Scholem, Jacob Frank had a "powerful personality, which was compounded of limitless ambition and cunning;" he was "a mixture of despotic ruler, popular prophet, and cunning impostor."[89] Lenowitz describes Frank as "a first-class confidence man."[90] Not surprisingly therefore, Rothenberg portrays him as a thief. Yet this is an ambivalent gesture because really we find delight in the trickster's clever exploits, including his stealing.

But this transvaluation of "theft" is not incidental. The postmodern poet, in fact, often operates as a "thief," just like his mythic predecessor Hermes.[91] Appropriation *is* stealing! Collaging and palimpsestous writing (e.g.,"Word Event," "History Seven") are forms of theft. As such, they can generate different responses from the reader: criticism for improper quotation, misleading presentation, and lacking originality and "authenticity," but also admiration of the poet's artistry and cleverness. Moreover, as Lewis Hyde suggests, theft implies "substitution" and "'[s]ubstitution' is the precondition of signification."[92] By appropriating mystical texts then, Rothenberg creates new meaning.

Tricksters are also necessary breakers of taboos.[93] Hence trickster tales are filled with transgressions, such as incest, rape, and various other kinds of impurity (excrement, blood, corpses, and organs of sexuality). Precisely such breaking of ritual and religious taboos was practiced by the followers of the false messiahs Shabbatai Zevi and Jacob Frank. Their transgression and final apostasy (conversion to Islam and/or Catholicism) was justified by their followers with the seductive theology of the "holiness of sin." According to this belief, the messiah had to descend into the abyss of sin in order to redeem the divine in the sparks that had fallen into utter darkness in the primordial catastrophic act of creation. The pseudomessiahs Zevi and Frank and their followers committed appalling breaches of the Jewish law, for example, by pronouncing the Ineffable Name of God, desecrating the Jewish festivals, eating forbidden fats, and practicing polygamy and incest. Rothenberg selects some of these shocking acts of transgression and presents them in "The Secret Dream of Jacob Frank," the second part of "Abulafia's Circles," which begins in the following way:

remembered
he is your counterpart   the other
Jew transgressor
of their law
moves to the performance of
your dream
the synagogues he stalks thru
scrolls thrown down
this madman   nihilist
once mounted
pissed 'gainst the parchment
howling

(*VB*, 78)

Jacob Frank, who defiles the Torah scrolls, embodies the spirit of antinomianism. At the same time, Rothenberg's description of the act of profanation alludes to the subversive performances of dada and their attacks on the "sacred" institutions of art.

In the poem, Jacob Frank is characterized as the "counterpart" calling to mind Scholem's notion of a nonapologetic Jewish historiography that should also include its dark Other. Following his own prescriptions, Scholem began to research the suppressed history of Shabbateanism and Frankism. In his essay "Redemption Through Sin," which years later was followed by his massive biography on Shabbatai Zevi, the historian outlines the principles of Jewish antinomianism.[94]

Much has been said about Scholem's interpretation of Shabbateanism. Suffice it here to remark on only aspects (mentioned by Alter): The historian shows those aspects of Judaism that are surprising or taboo:

> Scholem shows us Jews casting off all bounds, entering, so they thought, into a new world of unlimited freedom where, according

to the Sabbatian maxim, "the abrogation of the Torah is its true fulfillment."[95]

This apt characterization of Scholem's enterprise also applies to Rothenberg, who likewise is fascinated with the history of Jewish antinomianism.[96] The poet includes Shabbatean and Frankist texts in his Jewish anthology. Moreover, he reprints a passage from a novel by Isaac Bashevis Singer that deals with Shabbateanism and that inspired his own poem "Satan in Goray."[97]

However, Rothenberg appropriates Scholem's work to take it beyond its bounds. The scholar's overall portrayal of Shabbateanism and Frankism is always dialectically balanced. On the one hand, he empathizes with the Shabbateans and their sincere longing for liberation and redemption; on the other hand he exposes their fatal fall.[98] By contrast, Rothenberg abandons the paradox and wholeheartedly embraces contradiction and antinomianism. Hence, *all* Jews portrayed in "Abulafia's Circles" are—in a certain sense—transgressors: Abulafia figures as self-proclaimed messiah; Frank as blasphemer, false messiah, and apostate; Tzara as nihilist and communist. Significantly, Rothenberg speaks of Abulafia and Frank as "unresolved messianic figures" (*VB*, 89) rather than as "false messiahs." The term "antinomian" does not appear in any of his comments on Shabbateanism or Frankism.

Although the poet is aware of the demonic side of Frankism, the fascination with transgression is overwhelming. It climaxes in the third part, "The Holy Words of Tristan Tzara," which portrays the Jewish dadaist as the ultimate symbol of antinomianism. Dada nihilism proclaims its self-destruction and Tzara—a communist!—is made to announce the end of any utopian messianism: "god dada / messiahs are passé" (*VB*, 88). In his commentary Rothenberg asserts: "he [Tzara] made no messianic claims" (*VB*, 90). The poem also contains fragments from Tzara's 1918 dada manifesto, which Rothenberg interprets elsewhere as an

> irritation—a disgust—with solutions altogether ("no more solutions! no more words!") & with prescriptions (old or new) for making art. At the heart of Dada was a pullback from the absolute, from closed solutions based on single means: not a question of technique, then, but a way of being, a state-of-mind, of "spirit." (Rothenberg, *Poems for the Millennium*, vol. 1, 289)

According to Rothenberg, it is this spirit of resistance and negation that unites mystics, messiahs, and dadaists: Abulafia, Frank, and Tzara—all are involved in Tzara's "great negative work of destruction. Sweeping, cleaning. The cleanliness of the individual affirms itself after the state of madness, the aggressive complete madness" (*VB*, 90). The same quotation by Tzara is echoed in the poem:

"messiahs are passé
"the word we dream is
"dada
"dada sweepeth out
"dada teareth linens
"rips clouds & prayers to shreds

(*VB*, 85)

Destruction takes many forms: Abulafia, the shaman, demolishes the syntax and semantics of language, just like a contemporary avant-garde poet; Frank rebels against ritual taboos and religious laws; Tzara profanes the "sacred" institution of art and breaks all its rules.

In accordance with the doctrine of the "redemption through sin," Rothenberg reinterprets transgression in terms of liberation. One may in fact argue that antinominism permeates his general approach to Judaism and poetry. For instance, thematically, Rothenberg favors those streams of Judaism that are heterodox, while normative Judaism is equated with the monolithic mainstream. Methodologically, he appropriates Jewish mysticism toward poetic ends and thus could be said to "profane" kabbalah. Moreover, Rothenberg underwrites a transgressive poetics whose appropriative strategies involve "disguise" and "theft." Some of these trickerish devices are apparent in "Abulafia's Circles"; others will be brought to light in other parts of this book.

Conclusion

We have investigated Rothenberg's reappropriation of Jewish mysticism in *A Big Jewish Book* and in his involvement with Abulafianism. These two aspects of his work grow out of the search for the suppressed aspects of Judaism, for spirituality outside normative Judaism, and for a Jewish poetics. In part, this "recovery" of a Jewish countertradition leads to a focus on antinomian Jewish movements. Shabbateans, Frankists, and other transgressors, such as Jewish image-makers and goddess worshipers, gnostics, heretics, thieves, charlatans, and magicians—they all are included in a Jewish symposium of the whole. They all contribute to the history of the Jewish creative impulse. They all play a role in the history of a Jewish *poesis* and poetics.

In "Abulafia's Circles," the shaman and the trickster/transgressor are the paradigm of the poet. Shamanism becomes associated with the notion of a powerful language. This shamanic language has the power to heal because it has gone through the purifying and liberating process of destruction and renewal. Trickery and transgression, on the other hand, are necessary appropriative strategies, which Rothenberg applies in his rewriting of Jewish tradition.

Despite its marginality, Abulafia's teachings and methods inspired the poetry of the counterculture kabbalists. Through Abulafianism the Hebrew language acquired (for a while) a special status among a small group of American-Jewish poets. For them, Abulafia's writings became an object of mystical and magical study. This had an impact on the imagery of their own poetry, while their avant-garde experiments were underscored by Abulafia's permutation technique.

Through united efforts, the counterculture kabbalists (with Rothenberg among them) derived a Jewish countertradition, which radicalizes Scholem's earlier position. By re-reading the works of Jewish mystics, messiahs, and heretics in terms of poetry or poetics, Rothenberg transforms and transvalues Jewish tradition. It is a mark of our time that the counterculture kabbalists feel entitled to address the "dark sides" of Jewish tradition without apologetic inhibitions and *outside* the land of Israel. This may indicate the growing self-confidence of diasporic Judaism in multicultural and ethnic America, where there is a relative lack of anti-Semitism.[99] And certainly, Rothenberg's rebellious stance is characteristic of the avant-garde whose only permanent value is the belief in constant change.

2

Rothenberg's Reappropriation of Jewish Ritual

Ritual, Ethnopoetics, and Avant-Garde Primitivism

The poetics of change also permeates Rothenberg's approach to Jewish ritual.[1] For what interests him most are those aspects of ritual that invoke change and transformation.

The 1960s and 1970s saw an upsurge of ritualistic stances. During this period, ritual was a major factor in avant-garde art, experimental theater, performance, and countercultural Judaism. By way of introduction, I will briefly explore one specific movement among the American avant-garde: the discipline of ethnopoetics, which is associated with the oral poetry and performance movement. Rothenberg's activity in ethnopoetics impinged on his reappropriation of Jewish rites.

Although Rothenberg may be considered "the father of American ethnopoetics,"[2] the ethnopoetic core group is larger. It comprises poets, such as Gary Snyder, Simon Ortiz, Armand Schwerner, Nathaniel Tarn; anthropologists, for instance, Dennis Tedlock, Stanley Diamond, and Victor Turner; and the critic Sherman Paul, who wrote several books and articles about the movement.[3] If one takes into account the partial overlap of ethnopoetics with oral poetry and performance, one also has to include MacLow, Antin, Kelly, Owens, Clayton Eshleman, Diane Wakoski, and Anne Waldman as well as various musicians, composers, and performers (this list is not exhaustive).

Rothenberg coined the term "ethnopoetics" in the late 1960s.[4] He elaborated his ethnopoetic perspective further in subsequent anthologies and invited others to participate in a discourse on ethnopoetics in the magazine *Alcheringa*. Its first issue maps out the ethnopoetic program. Importantly, the overall goal of *Alcheringa* is not academic, but poetic and human: "to combat cultural genocide in all its manifestations."[5] This also implies furthering poetic diversity. Paul Christensen notes that ethnopoetics developed "a host of strategies for absorbing primitive and Third World traditions into contemporary poetic expression."[6]

Ethnopoets like to speak of "*re*-covery." Their goal is to rescue "ritual possibilities in our own lives for which the older ones in some general sense can serve as models or reminders" (*RI*, 55). As Diamond remarks, the underlying assumption of this thought is that the artist or poet is "perpetually recovering his primitivism."[7]

But what is primitivism? From an ethnopoetic vantage point, primitivism denotes the utopian recovery of "primaries." For Snyder, "primitive" is not a word that means past, but *primary*, and *future*."[8] Rothenberg dreams of a communal life in a tribal society where the poet's/seer's role is socially more integrated. In "primitive" cultures the tribal poet speaks to a small community of people for whom his or her work has significance: "I suppose the best and historically earliest situation for the poet is in relation to some rather small and limited community for whom he is *the* poet, rather than the large and nameless, faceless society."[9] While Rothenberg admits being "susceptible in turn to a nostalgia for the sacred," he also realizes that it might be impossible to recover a "primitive" society.[10] For him, tribalism mostly "remains a kind of metaphor."[11] This metaphor is employed in creating a poetics.

What makes ethnopoetics such a fascinating and controversial subject is its paradoxical nature. On the surface, ethnopoetics supports and defends diversification. However, in searching for primaries Rothenberg really is looking for a unifying human poetics and (what Finkelstein calls) the "underlying structural unity of the mythic imagination."[12] Rightly, the latter suggests that this tendency represents the "universalizing strain of Judaism."[13] Again, particularism and universalism are interconnected. Yet some critics point out that all too often the balance tips toward the universal and then the ethnopoetic material stands in danger of losing shape.[14]

The longing to overcome division runs through Rothenberg's whole work. In the introduction I have referred to this concept as "totality." To a large extent, it is this dream of unity that propels the ethnopoetic movement. The search for the primitive aims at a unification of experience. In his essay, "New Models, New Visions: Some Notes Toward a Poetics of Performance" (1977), Rothenberg argues that the resurgence of performance in all the arts is motivated by the search for origins. Performance is perceived as very ancient and even said to precede human existence, as ritual can be shown to have evolved out of animal behavior.[15] What the poet finds in ancient and tribal ritual is the unification of experience in some kind of "total art:"

> This dream of a total art—and of a life made whole—has meant different things and been given different names throughout this century. "Intermedia" was a word for it in its 1960s manifestation—also "total theater" and "happenings"—behind which was the sense of what the nineteenth-century Wagnerian consciousness had called *Gesamtkunstwerk* and had placed—prefigured—at the imagined beginnings of the human enterprise. (Rothenberg, *Symposium of the Whole*, xii–xiii)

Rothenberg refers to such "total art" as a dream. Both the anthropologist Victor Turner and the critic William Spanos recognize the romanticism of this dream. Yet while Turner seems sympathetic to Rothenberg's romantic striving "to regain wholeness, hence identity, through seeking 'a fundamental human nature,'"[16] Spanos responds with skepticism. He insists that the abolition of time in the search or recovery of some paradisal state or golden age is a sign of escapism.

Yet, there are also supportive voices. Eliot Weinberger, for example, draws attention to the poetic character of Rothenberg's holism. He suggests that the poet strives for and succeeds in presenting a coherent vision, an alternative way of looking at the world: "we cannot deny that Rothenberg, as so few others, has managed to construct a world. . . . Not Utopia, but a model of the world to set against the world."[17] Ethnopoetics may very well be romantic, but—just like romanticism—it brings about innovation and experimentation. The explosive and creative potential of Rothenberg's approach finds ample evidence in his appropriation of Jewish ritual.

Ritualization in the 1960s and 1970s: Some Motivations and Functions

Judaism is a ritualistic religion. Hence, anyone who strives for a contemporary renewal of Judaism necessarily will have to address the issue of ritual.[18] The Jewish counterculture became the breeding ground for ritual experimentation. Even though Rothenberg and his avant-garde friends are not directly affiliated with this aspect of the movement, they hold similar concerns. Both react to a sense of estrangement and loss, or, as Olson put it: "Man is estranged from that with which he is most familiar."[19] Rothenberg suggests that the response to the various types of estrangement "is a recovery/discovery of lost powers & possibilities."[20] His own poetry and the ritual experiments of the avant-garde run parallel to the attempts of the Jewish counterculture to revitalize ritual. After briefly reviewing some basic approaches to Jewish ritual renewal, I will explore possible motivations for ritualization and analyze some of the issues that are shared by the avant-garde and the Jewish counterculture.

Especially fascinating are political TRANSFORMATIONS of Jewish ritual. In the late 1960s Arthur O. Waskow, a Jewish political activist, had the idea of employing the Passover meal politically. His "freedom seder" addressed the current political agenda of the Left (Civil Rights movement) in terms of Jewish liberation rituals. One of these "happenings" aimed to expose the Presidency's Pharaonic oppressive power by reenacting the nine plagues, which involved "pouring blood on the fences [of the White House], releasing cockroaches and rats onto the front lawn."[21] Although Waskow claims that such spectacles have their roots in the symbolic actions of the prophets, their theatricality was, in fact, fueled by the shock methods current in the performance art of the period. For example, Waskow was very much aware of the activities of the Bread and Puppet Theater and The Living Theater, both of which employed ritual in the service of radical politics.[22]

Moreover, the Jewish counterculture also placed new emphasis on older rituals (TRANSVALUATION). *Havdalah*, a short ceremony performed at the end of the Sabbath, was developed into an entire service.[23] SELECTIVITY and transvaluation play a role in restoring rituals that presumably were lost, such as the celebration of the new moon, which took place during the time of the first temple. Finally, there are also cases of straightforward ritual INVENTION. Jewish feminists developed many new rituals for women, for example birthing rites, rituals for the sanctification of menses and menopauses, and a blessing ceremony for Jewish girls to complement the circumcision ritual for boys.

In sum, the last thirty years have seen much Jewish ritual creativity, sparked by the Jewish counterculture/Jewish Renewal. Some of its creative efforts are reflected in the *Jewish Catalogues* and in the journal *Menorah: Sparks of Jewish Renewal.*[24] How can this recrudescence of ritual be explained? Why did rites suddenly become so popular?

My suggestion is that ritual spoke to several pressing needs of the young generation. Ritualization responded to the longing for a recovery of community, totality, meaning, and continuity.

First, the performance of a ritual creates—momentarily—a community of equals (Turner calls this *communitas*).[25] It helps to overcome the sense of alienation and fragmentation, which is a byproduct of modern life. The use of ritual in happenings, theater, and performance had the goal "to entertain, to have fun, and to create what Victor Turner calls 'spontaneous communitas,' the dissolution of boundaries shutting people off from each other."[26]

Along these lines, Richard Schechner, the former director of the avant-garde theater troupe *The Performance Group*, suggests that they were at their best when they managed to invoke "a sense of genuine community in the theater."[27] New rituals have the function to generate a sense of community, while at the same time avoiding ossification. When asked to speak about the achievement of ethnopoetics, Turner himself makes the connection with *communitas*: "Ethnopoets are concerned with what I call *communitas*, with breaking down all social distinctions and status roles, political and other hierarchies, and segmentation into competing corporate groups."[28]

But, as Turner observes, every "anti-structure," or *communitas*, eventually evolves into new structure. Hence, even the practice of ethnopoetics might one day lose its marginal and subversive status and become academically institutionalized. Likewise, the initial experimentalism and anarchism of the counterculture was followed by a careful re-institutionalization. It first took the form of "normative communitas"[29] in the shape of communes centered around ritual performance, such as *havurot* and theater troupes. This was then followed by the return to "structure" or institution proper, when, for example, former members of the *havurot* set out to found their own synagogues.

Second, ritual speaks to the need for wholeness. Both the avant-garde and the Jewish counterculture were striving to overcome what was conceived as a split between life and art, life and religion, body and mind. Ritual, which essentially is intermedial, can serve as a means for unifying the senses and intensifying perception.[30] From a holistic vantage point, the attractiveness of ritual lies in its "experiential" character; ritual is experienced through the body rather than the intellect: "rituals persuade the body first."[31] Ritualism among the avant-garde and the counterculture involves the body in many different ways: in self-lacerating performances, in shamanistic healing sessions, in experimental theater and performance art, in body art, and in the physical presence of the performing poet (an important tenet of the oral poetry movement) among others.

Waskow, who argues that Judaism is now entering a new stage, also propagates the return to the body and to a more holistic kind of Judaism. He declares that contemporary Judaism seeks to unify the "word-Judaism" of the rabbis with the "body-Judaism" of biblical times. The goal is "to learn to synthesize the body and the word, and bring them together in a more holistic Judaism for the whole person, the whole community, the whole earth."[32] Such new holism motivates an interest in cycles—life cycles, seasonal rites, etc. It also leads to a new appreciation of the Jewish calendar and of women's rites among Jewish counterculturalists. Rothenberg's own approach to history, which is cyclical and synchronous rather than linear, ties in with this trend.

Moreover, both ethnopoetics and the Jewish counterculture strive to recover the suppressed sides of our culture and humanity. These submerged elements might be variously described. Rothenberg and Snyder speak of "wilderness," which the latter equates with "the Great Goddess Artemis."[33] This touches on a crucial aspect of holism: the "return of the goddess" among poets and artists in the 1960s and 1970s. Rothenberg and many of his literary friends, for example Tarn, Snyder, Meltzer, and Kelly, share a strong interest in the goddess cults of ancient, tribal, and Eastern cultures. The goddess signifies the repressed side of the divinity, the nourishing and destructive mother, nature, and the earth. Concurrently, the Jewish counterculture began to rediscover the feminine side of God, the Shekhinah.

This countercultural turn to the body goes hand in hand with the return to the earth and to "earth people." For example, *The Living Theater* celebrates the Native American as the archetypal Natural Man.[34] Ethnopoets and Jewish counterculturists seek to learn from "primitive" cultures a respectful way of treating the earth. Snyder intends to learn ecology from the Native Americans of California, while Waskow sees the need for Jews to recover their ancient roots as agrarian people.[35] In the 1970s, followers of the neo-ḥasidic rabbi Shlomo Carlebach set up a tofu factory in Israel and today Jewish Renewal groups propagate eco-Kosher food products.[36]

Third, ritual provides a sense of continuity. It fulfills this role even if it is secular, newly devised and only performed once. The central criterion is that ritual constructs continuity and covers up discontinuity.[37] Through ritual, one may appear to tap back into tradition, at least *some* kind of tradition. This link with the past is essential to Judaism, even if it is merely constructed. Similarly, by drawing analogies between contemporary poetry and medieval Jewish texts, Rothenberg constructs new continuities and a new poetics.

Fourth, ritual satisfies the need for meaning. The performance of a ritual confers meaning on an activity or experience.[38] In case of the happening, for instance, this meaning may not be obvious. Participants are expected to construct their own meanings. One of these meanings might be aesthetic. Riv-Ellen Prell, who studied the use of ritual in the countercultural *havurah* in Los Angeles, observes that

> [a]esthetics in general, particularly music, Hebrew (whether or not it is understood), and to some extent body movement, worked together to integrate the forms of prayer. . . . Hence, members experienced the maximum integration—the sense of themselves as interiorizing and reproducing Judaism through aesthetic media.[39]

The emphasis on aesthetics in the performance of a ritual renders an activity meaningful even without a belief system. What unites the avant-garde and Jewish Renewal groups is the overall neglect of traditional frameworks for the performance of their rituals and the focus on aesthetics as a source of meaning.

Ritual and Contextualization/Decontextualization: Jewish Event Poems

In his anthologies and some poetry collections, Rothenberg includes passages of so-called "events," which he describes as the "mythless activities of our own time" (*TS*, 513). In other words, events are rites without mythical embedding. Nevertheless they produce similar effects as ritual. Rothenberg further elaborates:

> And ritual—at least as performance—has entered *all* the arts in an unprecedented way . . ., often with no mythic pretensions, unless it can be said to be leading to a new mythology derived from its activities & from other materials & images at hand.[40]

Although contemporary avant-garde events are mythless, they may eventually generate new myths. What these new myths are is difficult to tell. (Perhaps a look at contemporary New Age publications can give us some ideas.)

Rothenberg recalls that by the end of the 1960s, the term "happening" had degenerated into a commercial expression. Hence other, more neutral words, such as "event," "activity," "doing" came to substitute for "happening."[41] The term "event" was also frequently employed by members of the fluxus movement to describe their activities. Since many of Rothenberg's friends were, in fact, associated with fluxus, he gives attention to their events in the commentary of *Technicians of the Sacred* (*TS*, 514–19). The poet's own ritual experiments are also indebted to fluxus practices.

For Rothenberg, "event" is an umbrella term, which has the function to correlate traditional ritual and avant-garde performances. Exploring the similarities between tribal and avant-garde ritual, he includes several "Books of Events" into *Technicians of the Sacred* and *Shaking the Pumpkin*.[42] The goal is to emphasize or point out the similarities between "primitive" and modern material.

In the 1960s, Rothenberg was in touch with experimental theater, happenings, and performance. Like so many other avant-gardists, he experimented with ritual.[43] In preparing his assemblages Rothenberg cultivated the skill of appropriating traditional rites and transforming them into contemporary poetry. Most frequently, he applies an appropriative strategy that might be called "reduction" or "condensation." Transforming found material, creates Rothenberg "event poems."[44] (Really, they are "found poems," but since the poet frequently overwrites the found texts, we may also call them "palimpsests.")

"Composing" an event poem entails an act of discovery.

When anthropological or religious material is read from the point of view of an ethnopoet, exciting things can happen. First Rothenberg becomes attentive to the "poeticity" of a particular text. Then he "lifts" (Rothenberg's phrase) the material from its original context and rewrites it in such a way that its poetical character is brought out. Most often, the transformation of found material involves reduction. The omission of words can have an aesthetic or semantic function. For instance, the previous analysis of "Word Event" demonstrates that Rothenberg fundamentally changes the meaning of his "pre-text" by making very small alterations to it.

By applying such subtle, appropriative strategies, the poet produces a series of Jewish event poems, which I will discuss now. The relevant poems are published in *Poland/1931* (*P*, 72–74) and "The Book of Extensions" (*BJB*, 398–99, 439–78). Even a brief glance over these texts reveals Rothenberg's proclivity toward the extraordinary. For the great bulk of his Jewish event poems deals with unusual and strange rituals. The poet admits that he is "most interested in those [rituals] that deal with extraordinary, momentous & critical events rather than everyday ones."[45] Here Rothenberg differs from Alan Kaprow, whose happenings focus on the ordinary. Rather than making an event poem out of the Orthodox daily morning prayer, the poet appropriates kabbalistic, magic, and folkloristic rites. He shares this liking for the supernatural and the weird with surrealism. Rothenberg's material comes from Jewish mysticism, folklore, history, and anthropology. While the sources are listed in the annotations at the end of *A Big Jewish Book*, the event poems in *Poland/1931* are presented without explanation.

Rothenberg's *Jewish* event poems focus on those aspects of ritual that have parallels in other religions and cultures: meditation techniques, mantras, body movements, modes of speech (whispering, shouting, singing, etc.), and the use of sound from nature. By contextualizing or decontextualizing Jewish material, Rothenberg demonstrates the universal features of Jewish rites. At the same time, he transforms his pre-texts in such a way that similarities with contemporary avant-garde events are revealed.

The poet contextualizes poems in two different ways: first, by taking up the Jewish tradition of commentary; second, by arranging poems contextually (building assemblages). Here, I will mainly concentrate on the former aspect.

In Judaism, the tradition of commentary is an ancient one.[46] In fact, the entire oral Torah, that is, the Talmud and most of the rabbinic writings, constitutes some kind of commentary on the biblical text. Similarly, much of the kabbalah is commentary. Traditional rabbinic commentary has the function to interpret the ritual law so as to enable Jews to follow the biblical prescriptions in their present life. But commentary also serves to illuminate "dark" passages in the sacred scriptures or to fill out the "blanks" of the text. For instance, the rabbis may wonder why God did not accept Cain's sacrifice. Part of their commentary may then be a story, a *midrash*, which provides a reason for God's action. Commentary often involves the reinterpretation of the law in a variety of ways.

Thus, commentary plays an essential role in the rewriting of Jewish tradition; the rabbis have developed it into a highly sophisticated tool. Sometimes religious innovation disguises itself in commentary. For instance, a kabbalist may pretend to adhere to tradition because he interprets a sacred text, such as the Hebrew Bible, and in doing so follows established, hermeneutic rules, but really this is nothing but a "pretext" for innovation. Scholem draws our attention to the explosive character of mystical commentaries. The kabbalist may reinterpret tradition in terms of his personal experience and thus introduce a new element into this tradition.[47] This is also Rothenberg's strategy. Bringing to bear on the Jewish rituals his experience as a contemporary poet and his knowledge of anthropology, he rewrites them by means of "reduction" and commentary.

Surely, Rothenberg is not the only one to annotate his texts. His friends Meltzer, Tarn, and Kelly likewise append their poems with explanations. But, to my knowledge, Rothenberg is the first to entitle his notes "commentary" and to take them to a new level by making them an integral part of his anthologies. Rothenberg's commentaries take many different forms. Sometimes they simply explicate the text or provide background information. More often, however, they reinterpret the text in terms of contemporary poetics. Frequently, the commentary consists of several numbered quotations. Sometimes Rothenberg juxtaposes these citations without any apparent interference, while in other cases he fuses quotations to his own expositions. The overall effect is that of assemblage. It blurs the division between "primary" (main text) and "secondary" (commentary) texts. As Perloff writes:

> Since it is often difficult to know where a given text ends and the editors' commentary begins, or again, at what point that commentary blurs into a commentary by some other critic or scholar, the collage anthology becomes, in an ironic sense, the "seamless web".[48]

In typical postmodern fashion, the hierarchies between texts are dissolved. In the following example the length of the commentary by far exceeds the event:

> RAIN EVENT ONE
> Whisper until it rains.
>
> **COMMENTARY**
> (1) The Hebrew word for magic—*kishuf*—literally "murmuring" or "muttering."
> (2) "If you see a generation over whom the heavens are rust-colored like copper so that neither rain nor dew falls, it is because that generation is wanting in whisperers. What then is the remedy? Let them go to someone who knows how to whisper." (Talmud: *Ta'anit* 8a.)
> (3) "In oriental countries in general, the Jews have acquired, for one reason or another, a special reputation as rainmakers." (Raphael Patai, *The Hebrew Goddess*.) (*BJB*, 470–71)

The event itself is synthesized from various sources. Rothenberg gives us a further clue in the annotations:

> "Rain Event One." From multiple sources, e.g., those in the commentary; the connection to "murmuring, muttering" from *The Friday Night Book* (Soncino Press, London, 1933). "Said Rabbi Eleazar ben Perata: Ever since the Temple was destroyed, rain is diminishing in the world." (Talmud: *Ta'anit* 19b). ("Sources, &c.," *BJB*, 621)

This short event is a perfect example of condensation. The poet manages to reduce the complexity of a rainmaking rite into an event of seven words (the title is integral to the event). What is so intriguing about this text and its commentary is the way in which Rothenberg "reconstructs" a Jewish tradition of rainmaking. Certainly, in the Hebrew Bible the lack of rain is often interpreted as an indication of God withholding his blessing (e.g., 1 Kings 17:1).

The saying by Rabbi Eleazar ben Perata also hints at this. However, the interpretation of the Jewish prayer for rain in terms of magic is very much of Rothenberg's own making. He chooses a passage from the Talmud that seems to speak in support of "whisperers" (read "magicians"). Since the Talmudic quotation is given without reference to its larger context, we are forced to understand it in the context *Rothenberg* provides and, in this context, "whisperers" are "magicians." That the Talmud generally forbids magic is completely ignored in this instance.[49] The poet wants to demonstrate that Jews have performed rainmaking rites just like other "primitive" cultures.

The goal of magic is to work transformation. Rothenberg's rain event represents a kind of "speech act," in which whispering causes change. This takes us back to the poet's insistence on orality and performance. Sayre argues that the focus on the breath and voice, "this sort of psycho-, physio-, bio-, cosmological poetics,"[50] originates in Olson's "Projective Verse." He suggests that oral poetics is fond of John Austin's speech act theory; it assumes that speech is a gesture/an event and therefore authentic: "In the 'breath-event' [Sayre's phrase] we discover the new sublime—that is, the old sublime reconstituted in the lyrical self."[51] Following this line of reasoning, the above event may be described as "whisper event." It illustrates Rothenberg's assertion that poetic speech initiates change.

The same can be said about the "Golem Meditation Events." Here is the first one with Rothenberg's appended commentary:

GOLEM MEDITATION EVENTS

(1) Take pure earth from a mountain, strew some of it over your house, & wash it from your body. Knead the earth in running water & form a golem from it. Bury the golem in the ground, then walk around it in a circle & recite the 221 alphabets. Repeat the process 442 times, while concentrating on the Name of God.

Commentary

The "golem" as visual object-of-meditation, linked by Scholem to a series of "yoga practices that had been disseminated among the Jews chiefly by Abraham Abulafia." Part of that hidden, often fragmented tradition described by Gary Snyder as "the Great Subculture which goes back as far perhaps as the late Paleolithic," in which the Jews, like other peoples-of-the-book, continued to share long after the virtual disappearance of the shaman seers.

For more on the golem (as a humanoid creature created by magic), see above, page 98. (*BJB*, 462)

The final reference to other passages in the *Big Jewish Book* typifies the intertextual character of this anthology.

Once more, Rothenberg raises the "skeleton" of the event from a text by Scholem.[52] However, in this instance the commentary provides a minimal amount of explanation and a maximal amount of interpretation. What exactly the golem is we only find out in a parenthetical side-remark at the end of the commentary. The golem-making ritual itself is not explained, either. In cryptic words we are told that the golem may function as an object for meditative visualization. Rather than elaborating on the meaning of the rites, that is, the use of earth and water, the burial rite, the symbolism of the numbers 221 and 442, and responding to the obvious questions any thoughtful reader would ask ("what are the '221 alphabets'"?), Rothenberg presents us with a string of associations: golem, meditation, yoga, Abulafia, shamans, Great Subculture. Although the reader of this book may now be able to make sense of these connections, anybody who has not been initiated into Rothenberg's countertradition will have difficulties in following him. In this example, the poet neglects explanation in favor of innovation and his own "reconstruction" of the continuities of the Jewish subculture.

The observation that commentary might as much obscure a text as clarify it applies to a great many of Rothenberg's annotations. In the flight of the poetic imagination they take us to faraway places. Paradoxically, therefore, contextualization may produce estrangement. That some commentaries hardly touch on the "primary" text itself is a sign of its unfamiliarity. Perhaps, in some instances, the poet intends to reinforce the "strangeness" of the text, and perhaps the reader will be thrilled and inspired by it.

A shortened version of the above "Golem Mediation Event" can be found in *Poland/1931*:

> ALPHABET EVENT (1)
> Recite the 221 alphabets while walking in a circle.
> Repeat the event 442 times.
>
> ALPHABET EVENT (2)
> Do the first Alphabet Event walking backwards.
> Recite the alphabets starting from the end.
>
> (*P*, 72–73)

The first event alludes to the magical teachings of the *Sefer Yezirah* (Book of Creation), an early example of hermetic Jewish letter mysticism, which mentions "221 gates or combinations."[53] In the history of the kabbalah, these teachings were employed in visualizations and magical procedures, such as the creation of a golem.[54] Reciting the "alphabet," a series of letter combinations, over the molded creature, would bring the golem to life. Conversely, by walking backwards and reciting the alphabets (letter combinations) backwards you could destroy the golem.[55]

In the above poems, the poet makes no indication that the "alphabet events" refer to the creation and destruction of a golem. Rothenberg has successfully stripped away all the particularities of the ritual. What is left are instructions for an activity. In the language of the avant-garde one would call this the "score" of an event. Quite often events were scripted in such a way that they could actually be performed by a number of participants. But how can we recite "the 221 alphabets," one may ask, if the poet does not even tell us what they are?

Rothenberg's scores are ambivalent. They fluctuate between the literal and the metaphorical. This way they mirror the ambivalent character of their sources. It is debatable how the theurgic instructions of the kabbalistic sources should be read. Should one assume that they functioned as visualization devices, or are they remainders of an actual magical practice? Similarly, Rothenberg's "alphabet events" can function as the actual score for an event, although it would be rather complicated and involve a certain amount of kabbalistic research and much imagination and patience to apply them; or, otherwise, they may be interpreted metaphorically as statements about the power of the word.

Our example demonstrates that contextualization and decontextualization are closely related. In a way, they complement each other: something is taken out of one context (decontextualized) and transferred into another (contextualized). This process of dislocation may also be called "displacement." If displacement is employed intentionally—as in Rothenberg's work—it may indicate a sense of loss and separation. In fact, the poet is very much aware that "[p]artly one is dealing with a reading of material from which a separation has occurred."[56] He further elaborates: "So, there's a kind of distancing and the distancing is what we really know and have to know to get our bearings. In other words you work out of the circumstances you find yourself."[57]

Here the poet indirectly hints at another paradox: by displacing something, one may actually be able to get closer to it; dislocation may bring the Other closer to us—which is exactly what Rothenberg attempts to do in many of his ritual events. He works "a series of distortions conditioned by the later culture & symptomatic of the obvious differences between the two [cultures, contexts]" (*TS*, 517). For "it's precisely the kind of distortion that can have a value in itself. Like seeing Greek statues without their colors" (*TS*, 514). We are accustomed to seeing Greek sculptures without color, even though we know that originally they were painted. Yet most contemporaries would probably prefer Greek sculptures in this habitual "distorted" state to their authentic form. When presented with the reconstructed "original" statue, our contemporaries might actually feel strangely alienated from the object.

On the basis of such reflections, Rothenberg conducts his experiments with decontextualization. He proceeds by removing traditional rites from their context and by eliminating any cultural or historical particularities. Metaphorically speaking, he strips the texts of their "flesh" and ends up with a "skeleton"—the activity, or event. Or, in his words, "as far as possible, . . . all reference to accompanying mythic or 'symbolic' explanations" (*TS*, 513) is suppressed. This method enables him to emphasize their character as activities so that "the form of the activities is, for the first time, given the prominence it deserves" (Ibid.). We can observe this effect in the above "Alphabet Events" as well as in the following example:

> NAME EVENT THREE
>
> A participant selects a piece of deerskin parchment.
> He cuts it up to make a sleeveless garment, large enough to fall across his shoulders & his chest down to his navel & along his sides down to his loins. He also makes a hat.
> The name of God is stitched into the garment.
> The participant fasts for seven days, then at night he brings the garments to a lake or river, where he speaks the holy Name.
> If he sees a green shape on the way, he begins again. If he sees a bright red shape, he walks into the water to his waist.
> The participant puts on the name.
>
> (*BJB*, 399)

This is a palimpsest of an ancient theurgic ritual from pre-Zoharic times, which was called "putting on the Name."[58]

Rothenberg rewrites the rite in such a way that the cultural specificity disappears. The reader may compare the poet's event to Scholem's exposition:

> A piece of pure deerskin parchment is selected. From it are cut a sleeveless garment, modeled after the *high priest's ephod*, covering shoulders and chest down to the navel and falling along the sides to the loins and a hat connected with the garment. On this *magic* garment the *secret* names of God are inscribed. Then *the adept* must fast for seven days, *touch nothing unclean, eat nothing of animal origin, neither eggs nor fish, but only peas, beans and the like.* At the end of seven days he must go at night to the water and call out the Name—evidently the name written on the garment—over the water. If he perceives a green form in the air above the water, *it is a sign that there is still something unclean in the adept and that the same preparations must be repeated for another seven days, accompanied by alms and acts of charity. "And pray to our Creator that you will not be shamed once again.* And if you see the form in bright red over the water, *know that you are inwardly clean* and fit to put on the Name. Then go into the water up to your loins and put on *the venerable and terrible Name* in the water."[59] [italics are mine]

In this quotation I have marked the passages that contain specific allusions to the Jewish ritual context. Rothenberg omits them—previously I named this strategy "reduction"—and thus he extracts the structure of a mythless ritual, which can also be imagined outside the Jewish framework. For example, one might read it as the description of a Native American rite (mentioning of deerskin, fasting, the vision on the water). Thus, the event poem invites the interpretation of one ritual in terms of another. This illustrates again the poet's fascination with "those intersections that operate at the less explicit—& possibly 'deeper'—level of human experience" (*TS*, 517).

However, presently I would like to dwell on the effect of decontextualization on the reader. By leaving out any explanation of what the green and red shapes might signify, Rothenberg encourages reader participation; we are required to provide our own context. As Michael Castro writes, the "skeleton must be fleshed out by the cooperative and creative efforts of Americans, based on the reality of contemporary American cultural conditions: what's needed and what's possible here, now."[60]

Moreover, an interesting parallel with rabbinic writing offers itself. For the rabbis also stand in the habit of decontextualization. Whenever they comment on a text, they adduce support for their interpretation from a number of other verses, which often are only cited incompletely or with slight distortions. The competent reader is expected to keep in mind the original context of these verses and to apply this knowledge to his or her reading. In the same way, the reader of Rothenberg's palimpsests and collages needs to be sensitive to the way in which they relate to their pre-texts.

Some critics, however, feel offended by Rothenberg's secular use of sacred material. Heller calls the poet a "technocrat of the sacred," because he employs religious and mystical material toward poetic ends.[61] The same critic attacks Rothenberg for viewing his material only from the "outside" when he tries to comprehend it technically with the aim of utilizing it. Heller wonders whether it is really possible to understand the sacred from the "outside."[62] But against this thought-provoking charge it might be argued that for Rothenberg a clear division between the sacred and the secular no longer exists. He regards this binary concept as "Western" and wholly rejects it.[63]

Rothenberg's ritual decontextualizations are paralleled by the experiments of two contemporary directors—Jerzy Grotowski and Felicitas D. Goodman. Both assume that one can find the essence/"origin" of certain rituals because they all resemble each other on a physiological level.[64] To prove this point, both directors decontextualize rituals. Goodman works with trance postures she adapts from ethnographic literature and teaches to her dancers. Participants imitate these ecstatic postures and enter a trance. The trance state is then utilized to derive new ideas for creating masks and choreography (i.e., the participant meets his or her animal spirit in the underworld and receives messages from it). Here, the ultimate goal of decontextualization is the creation and performance of a dance.

Grotowski makes use of a similar technique. He invites trained ritual dancers from various cultures and watches their movements and postures. Then he tries to abstract from them certain basic patterns, which his students are asked to act out subsequently:

> Grotowski's method is to sift through many practices from different cultures for what is similar among them, searching for the "first," the "original," the "essential," the "universal." These are then synthesized into repeatable sequences of behavior.[65]

This remark almost perfectly fits Rothenberg's own ethnopoetic goals. One could easily substitute Grotowski's name with that of the poet and obtain a meaningful statement. Just as Rothenberg's event poems, the director's "exercises and improvisations, whatever their sources, are intentionally drained of their specific cultural meanings."[66] Even more intriguing is the fact that Rothenberg and Grotowski actually made an attempt at communicating with each other.[67] Keeping these similarities in mind, it is not surprisingly that Rothenberg, Goodman, and Grotowski all are accused of practicing "white shamanism" and participating in "Western reification and appropriation"[68] (despite the fact that they are trying to get away from "Western" thought). They may be criticized for not respecting the autonomy of the religious or cultural context from which they lift their material. For as long as the decontextualized structures work as a poem, ecstatic posture, or dance, they continue to exploit their sources.

However, it could be objected that at least in his Jewish event poems Rothenberg limits himself by appropriating material only from his *own* culture. As far as the use of Jewish sources is concerned, he cannot be accused of "stealing" from other ethnic groups. Yet the problem of utilizing religion without being involved in its practice remains. That is why the poet openly admits:

> I am in that way still working on it from the outside, although this time I feel a different kind of outsiderness. But the relation to the "Jewish community" is very strange for many of us who have now gotten into this, and I would here go back to conversations about it I had with people like Meltzer and Hirschman and Tarn, and over in France with Jabès. . . . I think you'd have to be very foolish to imagine that the kind of Jewish poetry that emerges from this process is going to be generally accepted by Jews—it's not. (*RI*, 16)

Observant Jewish readers might find Rothenberg's ritual experiments unacceptable, while others may be inspired by the fresh and flexible approach to tradition. Moreover, in transforming and "distorting" his pre-texts, Rothenberg intensely interacts with his material. One may argue that his continuing preoccupation with Jewish texts is a sign of his engagement with Judaism. Driven by the longing to overcome division and to find unity, the poet draws analogies between Jewish, Native American, and avant-garde rituals.

Jewish Rituals as Theme and Activity

The preceding account reveals Rothenberg as a selective tradition maker. His Jewish event poems do not make much of common Jewish rites, such as daily prayer, the liturgy, and the festivals. This can be explained by the fact that Rothenberg's interest lies not in the normative, but in the transgressive and subversive. Rather than emphasizing the formalized and repetitive aspects of ritual, the poet investigates "the degree to which ritual is involved with processes of change" (*RI*, 56). So even if he does not dwell on magic rites of transformation, change is the leading concept:

> What has come to us, then at ground-zero . . . is the sense of what ritual can be: ritual [& myth] freed from conservative, fixed content & used as a vehicle for change in ourselves or against the preconceptions that have trapped us.[69]

That is why in his talk "Innovation & Disruption as Ritual Modes," Rothenberg gives focus to subversive ritual. The sacred clown, who shares many features with the shaman and the trickster, symbolizes ritual subversion. By producing a "programmed chaos, in which the brain turns upside down & lets order come to birth,"[70] the clown reverses the ritual order. To illustrate this, Rothenberg describes a Yaqui ritual that he witnessed around Easter time. The central characters in the ritual performance are the clowns and the Pharisees who mock Jesus:

> Jesus is a wooden statue or later (in his rebirth) a plastic babydoll, & the Yaqui catholic maestros who defend the church lead a strict, text-oriented ceremony; but the pharisees & especially the chapayeka clowns bring the mythic to life & engage in often open, often improvisatory rituals, including a comic mock scourging of Jesus as an eggheaded old man & a zany clown orchestra getting "drunk" & celebrating the crucifixion on the midnight of Good Friday.[71]

This ceremony could very well be analyzed in terms of the carnevalesque (Mikhail M. Bakhtin).[72] Even more so, Rothenberg's own approach to ritual can be aptly described along these lines. For the poet, subversion constitutes a permanent state of mind. By means of decontextualization, the poet profanes the "authoritative word" of Judaism. This way he expresses his rejection of the privileged patriarchal, authoritative discourse. His counter-discourse is *poesis*. It assimilates everything to its own word.[73] Rothenberg himself compares the rebellious push of contemporary writing to ritual reversal.[74]

There are many ways of undermining the "single vision" of an authoritative religion. The following subchapter analyses Rothenberg's approach to some common Jewish rites. Primary focus is given to thematic aspects and the poet's own involvement in Jewish ritual activities.

Imitative Ritual (Re-Enactment of Myth)

It is noteworthy that Jewish seasonal rites are not given much attention in Rothenberg's work. References to the Jewish calendar or the Jewish year are negligible. Typically, the one instance in which the poet appropriates a seasonal ritual from the past draws on an account by Patai about rainmaking ceremonies in the Jerusalem temple. It outlines the Jewish rite of water libation, which was performed at *sukkot* (Feast of Booths), "a festival of gratitude to God for the bounty of the earth that is celebrated in autumn at the end of the harvest festival."[75] Patai relates these temple ceremonies to ancient Middle Eastern fertility rites and myths.[76] Yet surprisingly, Rothenberg does not dwell on the mythical elements of this ritual. Rather, in a fashion now familiar to us, he strips away all mythical elements. This results in the following score:

RAIN EVENT TWO

1. Covering an altar with green willow branches
2. Walking around the altar with mixed branches
3. Beating the altar with palm or willow branches
4. The lighting of the lamps
5. The torch dance
6. Songs accompanied by numerous musical instruments: repeated blasts of trumpets
7. The process to the well begins at cock-crow
8. The water-drawing: pouring water on the altar
9. Pouring out of wine
10. A tumult with palm branches on the Sabbath
11. Lightheadedness begins: the women watching from a separate place
12. Joy of the house of water-drawing

(*BJB*, 471)

The numbering of the various steps of an activity is a device frequently employed by Rothenberg. It creates the impression of abstraction and emphasizes the quality of the poem as a score or a list.[77] Due to the generalized description of the event there is much room for interpretation. What do the "mixed branches" consist of? How would the torch dance look? Which melodies should be played and on which instruments? But perhaps what matters more than the actual performance of this score is its beautiful imagery, which creates a sense of harmony, and the evocation of an ancient ritual. Since the second temple was destroyed, most of these rituals are no longer performed. After the destruction of the second temple, Judaism underwent significant transformations. Laying out postbiblical ritual and liturgy, the rabbis decided to replace the prescribed animal sacrifice with prayer. Hence, Orthodox prayer memorializes the ancient temple rituals. Reciting the descriptions of the sacrificial rites is taken to fulfill the ancient biblical requirements for sacrifice.[78] Thus, the narration of the ritual activity becomes a ritual itself.

Rothenberg makes a similar point when he claims that "[t]he telling of the myth—i.e., the telling of the telling—is itself a ritual, a cultural performance."[79] Likewise, the event poem performs an act of memory. But at the same time, the text is permeated by the awareness of loss: the loss of the temple as a demarcated sacred place and a center of communal ritual. Rothenberg's yearning for the temple is part of a long history of Jewish exile and finds expression in the memorable section from a poem for Paul Blackburn:

> exiled in Salamanca
> & driven mad by
> Image of the Temple
> ("[for Paul Blackburn]," *The Notebooks*, 49)

Salamanca refers to the town in which Rothenberg lived while he stayed on the Seneca Indian Reservation. The longing is geared toward the "Image of the Temple"; the imagination enforces the power of this image. The poet actually describes myth in terms of image: "Myth here is the expression/projection of such an image, such a world of images."[80] The image is out of reach until it gets projected and enacted. One such enactment may be a poem, another, the performance of a ritual.

It is fascinating that the Jewish Renewal movement has actually taken up one of the practices Rothenberg mentions in his poem: "3. Beating the altar with palm or willow branches." And in fact, there is an Orthodox ritual that has been forgotten for a long time or was only enacted privately at home at the end of *sukkot*. It involves the beating of willows on the ground, uttering prayers and blessings for the healing of the earth. Jewish Renewal groups enacted this ceremony on the Hudson River bank with old and new prayers and combined it with a demonstration against Hudson General Electric.[81] The difference between this revived ritual and Rothenberg's score is indicative. The earth substitutes the altar; it becomes the altar. Therefore, this transvalued and politicized Jewish ritual can be utilized to give perfect expression to the ecological concerns of Jewish Renewal groups.[82]

Prohibition and Tabu

Many of the negative ritual precepts in Judaism deal with purity. From an anthropological point of view, these prohibitions have the function of setting up a distinction between the sacred and the profane. Since he is drawn to a notion of totality that overcomes division, Rothenberg challenges those aspects of Judaism that decree separation. In his criticism, the poet focuses in particular on ritual laws concerned with purity and impurity regarding sexuality and food.

A category of negative laws concerns "family purity."[83] One of the commandments requires that husband and wife have no sexual intercourse during the menstruation period and approximately seven days afterward. During the time of her period, the wife is considered to be *niddah* (literally, "separation"). She must be separated from her husband because she is considered to be impure (*tumah*). This impurity only ceases when she immerses herself—after the prescribed time of five days and seven days—in a ritual bath (*mikveh*).

Rothenberg addresses these rituals of sexual purity in his poem, "The Grandmothers." Despite the plural in the title, which is to indicate the archetypal perspective of the author, this text really gives us only the portrait of one specific, pious old woman. It is possible that in writing this poem Rothenberg remembers his own grandmother. The poem abounds in graphic physical detail. In a manner that might strike the reader as disrespectful it concentrates on the physical frailness of old age. But there is also a tone of warmth, love, and sympathy for the old woman. Thus, the poet confronts us with the transitoriness of the body, while his earthy language helps to avoid nostalgia:

3
past caring a grandmother
bathing checks mucus in her eyes dough
on her hands shit between
asshole & water dirt under her fingernails
her false teeth backed with gold
wax in ears snot in nose lice at pubis
still seeking to be pure the residue
of past bleeding buried with her sons
but fresh in mind she yawns from
drowsiness sometimes or belches after meals
in pain her legs feel heavy a blood spot
whirls before her   inserts a soft
white woolen cloth the cock's remembered
length inside her that returns in whiteness

(*P*, 17)

The last four lines refer to a test that Orthodox women are required to perform in order to examine whether the menstrual bleeding has really stopped. Even though the old woman no longer is obliged to fulfill the laws of *niddah*, her identity as a woman is determined by the memory of these precepts and by the knowledge that "no woman will ever be clean" (*P*, 16). Central to her memory is the image of blood ("a blood spot / whirls before her"), since according to Jewish law blood renders a woman impure. Lenowitz proposes that the fluidity of blood represents chaos and confusion that are difficult to control: "the control of fluid is the most difficult control to achieve since fluids are so instantaneously responsive to gravity and so irredeemably commingling."[84] Hence blood represents desire, which the ritual law tries to control. Jews are fighting a battle against blood:

> They are always the same, with the same problem of graduating chaos-fluid-blood; They engage the fluids, again and again, with heroism, especially in the bloody desires of their lives; lust for sex, for food, for taste, for blood itself.[85]

On the other hand, blood represents the mystery of life—and it seems to be a mystery from which men are cut off:

4
the men by custom wait outside
her door even the young boys grandchildren
for whom the alphabet flowers in hebrew
'have respect for the body of a grandmother
'have respect for the vessel of blood
'emptied   bearer of offspring from her damp nostrils'
in the small rooms where the grandmothers
sleep they are still women
still withdrawn   glowing   in the mystery
that forbids us to drink from her cup
keeps her mattress in the center of the room
forever keeps her blood away from us
as softly the curtain flutters on her wedding night
something between a woman & a man

(*P*, 17)

One function of the ritual law is to make distinctions. In doing so it enforces gender identity, but also decrees separation ("the men . . . wait outside," "forbid us to drink from her cup"). Any state of division is characterized by a lack of wholeness/totality. On the one hand, Jewish ritual law underscores the periodical separation of husband and wife; on the other hand, this law is said to enhance marital relations, once the wife has regained ritual purity. Rothenberg reflects on this ambivalence in the last verse of the poem, which might be read in two different ways: as a general statement about the Jewish ritual law separating men and women in many different ritual contexts, or a metaphor suggesting that women and men share a secret with each other, that is, "there's something between them." The poet withholds a direct comment about these laws of ritual purity. By simply presenting a selection of Jewish rites and customs, he leaves it up to the reader to ponder their meaning and validity.

In modern times the various strands of Judaism permanently renegotiate the significance and interpretation of the ritual law. Lenowitz proposes that Rothenberg participates in this process, even if he struggles with the Jewish law (*halakhah*) or ultimately rejects it. Just the fact that he bothers at all indicates a certain "adherence" to tradition: "I should say that for all of us awareness of the system presented in the Code is adherence, whether we follow the rules as given, re-interpret them or choose to oppose them altogether."[86]

The "Code" refers to the *Shulḥan Arukh*, the standard code

of Jewish law dating from the sixteenth century, from which Rothenberg draws material for the series "From THE CODE OF JEWISH LAW" (*P*, 64–71). The poem consists of ten numbered sections and lists a variety of ritual precepts. Since each section holds a poem in its own right, one might also speak of a series or a mini-assemblage. To provide some variation, the poems are composed in different styles. There is a clear emphasis on dietary ordinances, laws of purity, and commandments for the Sabbath. On the whole, the series deals with the fear of blood and impurity in Judaism. Impurity is associated with forbidden foods, body secretions, and sex.

The last section/poem, combines the imagery of blood and milk. One of the basic rules for kosher food is that meat and milk dishes are not to be commingled. Mixing milk and blood is a transgression that results in impurity:

10
your hands are full of blood
because you think of it
& touch it
you make it hard by
sleeping on it
. . . .
the milk from your own body
running down your leg
staining the sheets with dishonor
yellow & stiff
by morning
that has made you a murderer
someday will raise
the midnight lament for
the temple   demanding
repentance to hold
the circumcised babe by its leg
smile at the iron-toothed mother
but turn from the shame of
your flesh   in love
& the pursuit of peace

(*P*, 70–71)

Here, blood and milk, symbols often associated with women, are employed to represent male sexuality. Blood alludes to desire (is it the same desire that causes violence?); semen produced in nocturnal emissions is referred to as "milk." In the rabbinic Jewish tradition, the involuntary discharge of semen causes impurity.[87] Spilling the seed in vain therefore is a sin:: "the milk from your own body / . . . has made you a murderer." Rothenberg simply states this in the voice of the *Shulḥan Arukh*. He refrains from intrusive comments about the rationality of this belief, but simply presents the material in a way that reveals its bizarre character and ambivalence.

Blood and semen are associated with murder ("your hands are full of blood"). Yet one of the chief purposes of the Torah is to protect life. However, Rothenberg leaves it open as to how this goal may be achieved. The last three verses of the poem permit two mutually exclusive readings. They may allude to the Orthodox observance of all precepts against sexual impurity ("the shame of / your flesh"); their ritual observance is motivated by the wish to become holy and to demonstrate one's love for God ("in love / & the pursuit of peace"). But the passage may also refer to the opposite, that is, someone turning away from the habit of being ashamed because they pursue love in a different way. In the first place someone is ashamed, in the second someone rejects the feeling of shame. The two interpretations represent two possible Jewish paths pointing in opposite directions—one toward observance, the other away from it. Both claim to act for the sake of love. Rothenberg leaves the Code of Jewish Law at that.

Despite such occasional digressions into *halakhah*, which, by the way, are not common in Rothenberg's writing, the overall thrust of *Poland/1931* is toward the acceptance of blood and "fluidity, sex, violence, etc., with all its felt dangers."[88] For the poet, such acceptance of the body and desire involves the transgression of the ritual law. In fact, Rothenberg virtually cultivates impurity. This happens on several levels. The acceptance of the body and suppressed desire finds expression in many sexually explicit passages, which even have a tendency toward the pornographic. Like the dadaists, Rothenberg aims for the "release of suppressed and repressed urges in the secular and aesthetic."[89]

Furthermore, the desire for food—even forbidden foods—also plays a prominent role in *Poland/1931*. For instance, the speaker of the poem "The Wedding" lusts for Polish sausages which certainly are not kosher: "poland / let us tread thy markets where thy sausages grow ripe & full" (*P*, 3). Rothenberg incorporates in his poems a great variety of ethnic, kosher, and forbidden foods. Archival sources reveal that he thoroughly researched Jewish food laws and Eastern European customs. For example, he noted down a number of ethnic foods, which might be unfamiliar to the American reader: "roast squab & egg-noodles, egg-cookies & brandy, coffee with chicory, a head of a carp wrapped in cabbage leaves, three macaroons (hidden in her stocking)."[90]

In addition, Rothenberg prepared lists of forbidden and clean foods, which he excerpted from Jewish codes and manuals of observance. He remarks that it is prohibited to eat "food cooked by a non-jew even if 'fit to be served at the table of a king.'"[91] The implications of this precept are all too obvious: Jews and non-Jews are prevented from sharing meals together. Rothenberg tells us that, from an anthropological perspective, the sharing of food originates in a "pre-human situation where groups of primates come together and enter into ritual-like activities around a common food gathering site" (*RI*, 56–57). Sharing a meal is therefore a communal act. *Halakhic* attempts at preventing the communion between Jews and non-Jews obviously conflict with Rothenberg's universalist impulse. Hence, rather than abiding by *kashrut* and other laws of purity, the poet practices transgression. Rothenberg professes that in *Poland/1931* he was experimenting with the blasphemous.[92] It is therefore not incidental that the epitaph of the book alludes to defilement: *"And I said, 'O defiled flock, take a harp, & chant to the ancient relics, lest understanding perish'"* (Edward Dahlberg).

The pursuit of impurity is characteristic of much postmodern writing and Rothenberg's poetry can be viewed in this context. His work transgresses boundaries by confounding categories and mixing what is to be kept separate: the sacred and the profane, milk and blood, forbidden and clean foods, Jews and non-Jews. On the literary level, he fuses the lyric with narrative, the event with the poem, and poetry with prose. But these transgressions entail discovery. By mixing various genres, styles, linguistic levels, and forms, Rothenberg participates in the creation of new "hybrid" forms. Literary transgression, therefore, is productive.

Sacrificial Ritual

Interestingly enough, sacrificial rites, which are common in many tribal cultures, hardly feature among the magic and kabbalistic rituals Rothenberg retrieves from Jewish tradition. The main reason for this is that in Judaism animal sacrifice is no longer practiced. The poet's overall attitude toward sacrifice is ambivalent. His *Realtheater Pieces*, for instance, illustrates "both the repulsion and attraction"[93] toward sacrifice. Talking about the use of blood and meat in plays by Rochelle Owens and Carolee Schneemann, Rothenberg asserts that it is "[n]ot just unpleasant but terrifying, terrific, once you got a good look. And that was the 'sublime in the old sense,' as I remembered it."[94] But on the other hand, the question is whether "old sublime" can and should be recovered. While recognizing "the latent power"[95] of sacrifice, the poet also exposes "the violent nature of religion."[96]

Here is a found poem from the Jewish magic tradition, which illustrates this perspective[97]:

WOMEN'S FERTILITY EVENTS

. . . .

(5)
A woman drinks a mixture of wild tea leaves, or a woman
eats a rooster complete with comb & gizzard, or a woman
drinks water seeped in the ashes of a burnt male rabbit.

(6)
A woman swallows the foreskin of a newly circumcised
infant.

(*BJB*, 472)

This "poem" is juxtaposed with a comment from Kaprow's book about happenings: "The line between art and life should be kept as fluid, and perhaps as indistinct, as possible."[98] Rothenberg abides by this principle by scripting this grotesque and gruesome event in such a way that we cannot know whether we are dealing with fantasy or historical reality. Were these magic rites really supposed to be performed? Did women really swallow the "foreskin of a newly circumcised infant"? Instead of factuality there is uncertainty. The poet skillfully exploits the indeterminacy of magical sources to produce a text in which the line between fantasy (art) and history (life) is fluid. Since this device shocks and confuses the reader, the emotional impact of the text is very pervasive. We sense the dark side of ritual. Rothenberg further expands this in the subsequent event. It alludes to the Christian sacrificial theology and its implications for Jews:

BREAD EVENT
Stab a wafer until it bleeds.

(*BJB*, 473)

A brief instruction of great complexity. Once more, the mix of perverted fantasy and historical reality fulfills Kaprow's request of blending art and life. Medieval Christianity held the superstitious belief that Jews secretly desecrated the eucharistic host in order to obtain blood for rites of black magic. This anti-Judaic superstition was then used to justify Jewish persecutions. Hence there is a loaded history behind this statement. By re-phrasing this crude notion as a score for an event, Rothenberg foregrounds the violent side of ritual. The effect is shocking. Ritual can be linked with the destructive powers of the soul. Rothenberg comments:

> The so-called desecration of the Christian eucharist—though more likely a product of Christian than of Jewish imagination—may now be viewed as the central enactment of an ongoing Jewish "guerrilla theater." As with more contemporary instances, the danger to participants & bystanders is integral to the event itself. (*BJB*, 473)

Rothenberg's reinterpretation of the Jewish experience of persecution in terms of "guerrilla theater" matches Turner's assertion that "social conflicts are a form of theater."[99] Yet the characterization of persecution as "theater" must be taken with a pinch of salt. It rests on scathing self-irony.

Rites of Passage

One of the foremost Jewish rites of passage certainly is the circumcision. However, Rothenberg avoids dwelling on this fundamental Jewish ritual. Alternatively, he engages with a much less traditional initiation rite: the bar mitzvah (literally, "Son of commandment"). This ceremony marks the ritual maturity of a Jewish boy at the age of thirteen. Subsequently, he is required to follow the precepts of the Torah. Since this ritual is not decreed in the Bible, it may be handled with some flexibility.[100]

Rothenberg took this situation as an opportunity to design an elaborate ceremony for the bar mitzvah of his son Matthew. The archive holds a detailed description of the celebration, which took place on a Saturday morning (25 March 1977). The poet also wrote several poems to reflect on this special occasion. An interpretation of these texts is worth its while because it recapitulates much that has been said in this chapter. In devising the bar mitzvah program, the poet illustrates his own assertion that so much in ritual and religion is "syncretistic: in art terms, a collage of disparate elements fused into a new configuration."[101] Texts, people, and activities—much that is dear and meaningful to the poet finds a place in this ritual collage.

Rothenberg wrote the following poem for the day of the celebration. It is printed on the program the guests received:

o limen!
lumen!
today the threshold
's crossed!
the light & dark converge
in common worlds!
both praised![102]

Rothenberg interprets the bar mitzvah ritual as a rite of passage. *Limen* refers to the threshold, which the neophyte crosses on the day of the ritual. Liminality, a term coined by Turner, marks the stage when the novice is at the threshold to a new state of being.[103] Liminality involves a period of uncertainty and freedom from "structure." Of course, this liminal sense of openness ties in perfectly with Rothenberg's poetics. The reason he places so much emphasis on the bar mitzvah ritual is that it can be employed to explore the creative and communal potential of liminality. Turner asserts that liminality is accompanied by *communitas*. Even if only transitory, ritual creates a sense of community—and this is what Rothenberg is after. Hence, the poet emphasizes the participatory quality of the celebration. Many of the guests contribute something to the ritual: Torah readings, poems, performances, events, and music.[104] On Saturday four major events are scheduled:

<u>A First Event: Bar Mitzvah</u>
Meditation (Pauline Oliveros)
Shema
Torah reading
Bar Mitzvah & Haftorah blessings
Haftorah reading [reading from the prophets]
Closing Haftorah blessing

Kaddish Gatha (after Jackson Mac Low)
Poems (Clayton Eshlemen, Barbara Einzig, Jerome Rothenberg)
Adon Olam (audience participation)

A Second Event
Short kiddush (wine blessing)
Meal

A Third Event
Music by "A Big Jewish Band"
Performance pieces by Linda Montano, Allan Kaprow, Ron Robboy, Bert Turetsky, Matthew Rothenberg & David Reeves, plus others

A Havdala Event at Dusk: Escorting the Queen[105]

Matthew Rothenberg participates in a number of activities, especially the blessings and the Torah readings. But he also gives a performance on Saturday afternoon and accompanies his father in symbolically escorting the Shekhinah at the end of the Sabbath. Typically, Rothenberg selects a poem by Sabbatai Zevi to conclude the event.[106]

Many of the readings are drawn from *A Big Jewish Book*, which Rothenberg was assembling at that time. The poet introduces miscellaneous kabbalistic readings into the liturgy, for instance, the unconventional and very esoteric piece, "Luria's Poem for the Small Face" (*BJB*, 30–32). Much of the ritual seems to be modeled on Scholem's description of kabbalistic Sabbath rituals.[107] Rothenberg scripts the "Bar Mitzvah Events" in such a way that they come to represent his own Jewish countertradition. The recitation of these texts constitutes a miniature performance of *A Big Jewish Book*.[108]

Similarly important for Rothenberg's "poetics of the sacred" is the fusion of sacred and secular texts. Therefore, the program includes contemporary English and traditional Hebrew texts, secular and religious readings. This way he attempts to overcome the "Western" division between the sacred and the secular. The goal is community, unity, and continuity. Rothenberg takes up this subject in the poem, "B·R·M·Tz·V·H" (*VB*, 33–34), which has a speech for Matthew. It contains various references to Jewish tradition and history. For example, the title imitates Hebrew writing, which commonly does not include vowels.

Moreover, since this is a poem of memory, the text contains plenty of autobiographical allusions placing Matthew Rothenberg in line with his ancestors. The theme is "survival." At the time of his son's birth, Rothenberg was the only "survivor" of his own family; his father, mother, and brother had died, other relatives were killed in the Holocaust: "deaths of other curly-headed / cousins sacrificed / only their photos left to scan thru" (*VB*, 33). This allusion to the murdered family has a disconcerting effect and seems out of place at a happy celebration. But Rothenberg asserts that death and life are very close: "the mystery thus thrust / into our thoughts /—of light & dark" (*VB*, 33). His indebtedness to truth requires him not to ignore the dark sides of life. Survivors must live off memory. Hence Rothenberg constructs ancestral poems around his own memory and fantasizes about his ancestors in *Poland/1931*, "ancestors the imagination made" (*P*, 33).

The poet wishes to pass on these fantasies and memories to his son. He invokes the life of his own mother, Matthew's grandmother, and his father, who died dissatisfied with his new life in America. However, the dead live on in their children's memory. For Rothenberg, their resurrection takes place in the mind, in the imagination: "when all the dead arise / in my mind they sing" (*VB*, 34).

Once more, this demonstrates the concern of his ancestral poetry, in particular, to create a connection with the Jewish past.

Conclusion

Jewish tradition involves passing on the communal memory of a people. In this process ritual plays a powerful role because it creates a sense of continuity. Some anthropologists even claim that a ritual that is only performed once—a "nonce ritual" in Myerhoff's terminology—already constitutes a tradition.[109] Rothenberg's events and rewritings fall within this category. The poet actively participates in what Meyer describes as "the self-chosen recovery of a custom or practice . . ., which may once again become tradition if he or she succeeds in passing it on within the family to the next generation."[110] His strategy of rewriting and appropriating Jewish ritual adds to the tradition of Jewish writing. Contextualization creates new perspectives, while decontextualization deeply transforms and transvalues traditional Jewish pre-texts. Both approaches generate texts that become part of the Jewish countertradition and counterpoetics.

Most central to Rothenberg's Jewish subculture are rites of transformation, change, and subversion. The poet finds these in the mystical and magical Jewish tradition rather than in Orthodox ritual observance. Like the Jewish counterculture and the avant-garde, Rothenberg employs ritual to blow "life into ourselves" (*RI*, 55). The goal is to recover community, holism, meaning, and continuity by means of rite.

Rothenberg's involvement with ethnopoetics motivates him to focus on the universal aspects of Jewish ritual. This means that he favors ceremonies that have parallels in other cultures or in contemporary avant-garde performance. At the same time, the poet explores and exploits the poetic character of ritual patterning. Rites are turned into event poems. On the one hand, this may be criticized as a profanation of sacred material. On the other, the appropriation and displacement of sacred rites allows for new meanings to arise and inspires new poems. Certainly, Rothenberg's appropriative strategies imply rebellion against authority. Yet they also reveal a need for some kind of "primal" tradition. Thus, they respond to the needs of the counterculture and the avant-garde of the 1960s and 1970s.

3

A Jewish Poetry of Names, Numbers, and Letters

IN THE PREFACE OF *A BIG JEWISH BOOK*, ROTHENBERG STATES THAT he intends to focus on the suppressed side of Judaism, "especially the mystical & magical side of the Jewish tradition" (*BJB*, xxxvii). The poet appropriates Jewish mystical and magical traditions in order to create a Jewish poetry of letters and numbers. This chapter investigates three kinds of poems drawing on Jewish tradition: amuletic, numerological, and gematric poems.

Most of Rothenberg's amulet poems are based on a found text or imitate a real Jewish amulet. His numerological poems play with the symbolism of numbers, while the gematria poems utilize the Jewish discipline of gematria. These diverse Jewish poems might be analyzed in terms of ancient genres, such as the charm and the riddle. Basically, amulets are recorded charms; numerological and gematric poems share the features of a riddle. Both charm and riddle essentially involve naming. Magic incantations employ the powerful names of supernatural forces in order to bind and manipulate the Other. Likewise, riddles bind us; their puzzling element blocks our mind, until we find the answer. The answer to a riddle tends to be a name. By naming the subject of a riddle we recognize the Other and thus are freed from the blockage.[1]

For Rothenberg, naming resrepresents the poetic act per se. Since in his view naming is pivotal to poetry, it also plays a significant role in the construction of his poetics of the sacred. The poet recalls that for him, "a sacralized view of the world was tied, somehow, to a clear sharp language of names and nouns, dream names included."[2] Such a poetics aims at healing and the recovery of meaning. Rothenberg's Jewish poetry of letters and numbers attempts to re-empower poetry by taking it back to its assumed origins in charms and riddles. The language of amulets and charms shows the working of powerful words. Magic names are efficacious because they are words that act and bring about change. These concepts fit perfectly into Rothenberg's poetics.

Amulet Poems

Amulets are objects "supposedly charged with magical power . . . to ward off misadventure, disease, or the assaults of malign beings;" they are empowered by magically charged material or an authorized person, by the performance of a magic rite or the appropriate magic formulae or incantation.[3] In Jewish culture, the writing on the amulet is of particular significance. Fundamental to an understanding of Hebrew amulets is the fact that in most cases Jewish magic is name magic: "[t]he literature of Jewish magic was predominantly an anthology of magical names."[4]

Jewish amulets are part of the popular religion as opposed to "official Judaism." Historians observe a permanent conflict between Jewish theology regarding the use of amulets/magic and the actual practice. Theodore Schrire maintains that Jewish amulets belong to a partly suppressed, oral tradition. The knowledge of the formulae and names of God and angels was often passed on orally. Charging an amulet magically may require the recitation of a charm. Hence amulets often display an oral style.[5] It comes as no surprise then, that Hebrew amulets suit Rothenberg's Jewish countertradition. Since Jewish amulets often employ incantation, they may be compared to tribal texts. Furthermore, they are also visually attractive. The poet takes advantage of this feature in his translations of amulets.

Rabbinical Judaism makes many distinctions between permitted and forbidden magic. There are also laws concerning the use of amulets, for instance, prophylactic amulets are allowed, while curative ones are prohibited.[6] Naturally, Rothenberg does not trouble himself with such normative distinctions, which is why *A Big Jewish Book* also includes Jewish amulets from heretic traditions, such as Samaritan and Shabbatean exemplars (*BJB*, 395–96, 335). Obviously, the poet's interest in Jewish amulets is artistically and poetically motivated.

Apart from many references to magic rites, incantations, invocations, and charms, *A Big Jewish Book* contains various depictions and transcriptions of Jewish amulets. Each represents a type: a protective amulet, a devotional plaque with divine names, a talisman, an amulet against the evil eye, a charm against the female demon Lilith, and an amulet against all evils.[7] There is also a Samaritan amulet, which Rothenberg translated himself. In transforming the charm into a concrete poem, he proceeds as in his "total translations" of Native American chants. An oral structure is represented visually so that the end product looks like a concrete poem rather than an ancient text.[8] Rothenberg also emphasizes the analogy between the two forms in the title of his rendering:

(Samaritan Hebrew, traditional)
CONCRETE POEM: "YHVH GREAT GOD"

Y H V H G R E A T G O D Y
H V H G R E A T G O D V H
V H G R E A T G O D V H V
H G R E A T G O D Y H V H
G R E A T G O D Y H V H G
R E A T G O D Y H V H G R
E A T G O D Y H V H G R E
A T G O D Y H V H G R E A
T G O D Y H V H G R E A T
G O D Y H V H G R E A T G
O D Y H V H G R E A T G O
D Y H V H G R E A T G O D

(*BJB*, 395)

This translation foregrounds the shared features of the Samaritan amulet and concrete poetry. It emphasizes the nonsyntactic relationships between words, employs the transmutation of letters, focuses on the properties of each single letter (it is possible to read this amulet by spelling out the name of each letter), and is written in a geometric form (here, in a square). Rothenberg gives the amulet a shape that impels us to read it like a crossword puzzle. His geometric rendering invites vertical, diagonal, and even reversed readings and accents the visual properties of amulets.

Moreover, the separation and recombination of the consonants of the Tetragrammaton, YHVH, is typical of Jewish amuletic writing. While some combinations appear to be meaningless, the poem also contains semantic meanings, such as "YHVH Great God," "eat" and "go." The word GOD has the anagram DOG. In Hebrew, this inversion does not produce a blasphemous word, but the English "concrete" version has this semantic possibility. Rothenberg seems to be very much aware of it. For in a different context he cites exactly this instance as an example for "anagrams, or rearrangements of the letters of a word to form a new word or word series, as 'god' to 'dog' in English" (*BJB*, 431).

Furthermore, Rothenberg integrates various Jewish amulets into his book *Poland/1931*.[9] I will call these texts "amulet poems." Reproductions and translations of amulets are distributed throughout the poetry collection and are complemented by Rothenberg's own imitations of amulets. Many of these texts consist of spells against demons or the evil eye and therefore may be classified as protective amulets. But the poet also includes recipes for making amulets. Note, for example, the instruction, "Take a chain, a hook & the figure of a bird. / Make a talisman of leather" (*P*, 6), or, the command to tie various substantive elements "to the neckhole of the shirt with a white twisted cord" (*P*, 75). Indeed, the latter prescription concerns the preparation of an amulet and is appropriated from Talmud *Shevuot* 15b, but—as usual in his poetry—Rothenberg disguises his sources. The reader cannot know whether this text is found or made up by the poet. In "The Numbers (1)," we are simply given a list of strange magic ingredients:

> Then he said: Take seven prickles from seven palm trees, seven chips from seven beams, seven nails from seven bridges, seven ashes from seven ovens, seven scoops of earth from seven door-sockets, seven pieces of pitch from seven ships, seven handfuls of cumin, & seven hairs from the beard of an old dog, & tie them to the neckhole of the shirt with a white twisted cord.
>
> (*P*, 75)

Left to our own devices, we may discard the text as bizarre nonsense, marvel at an exotic piece presumably gathered from anthropology, folklore, or history of religion, or we could just delight in the surrealist juxtapositions and the grotesque imagery of this list.

As in many other instances, the interpretation of Rothenberg's amulet poems requires attention to context. Each amulet may be analyzed in relation to the texts that frame it. For instance, a Hebrew prophylactic amulet against the female demon Lilith, comes directly after the poem "She," in which the same Lilith is praised as the Hebrew goddess (*P*, 81).[10] This subtly suggests that Lilith is first summoned and then expelled.

Furthermore, by placing prophylactic Jewish amulets next to his own poems, Rothenberg performs a protective ritual. As Kevin Power rightly remarks, "[t]he amulets serve to concentrate the power of word, image, or story and as such closely link Rothenberg's submergence into his Jewish roots with his interest in 'primitive' verse."[11] The amulets have the function to create the impression of authenticity and tradition. Even if we cannot decipher them if we do not read Hebrew or are not familiar with magic formulae, the amulets are there to exercise some kind of visual and aural power. The reader resembles the user of an amulet and is charmed by its charged language and materiality without really understanding its meaning.

Amulets hold the poet's fascination because they illustrate name magic, and name magic can be associated with poetry. Gertrude Stein, one of Rothenberg's early influences, suggested that poetry is constituted by the act of naming. The common denominator between magic and poetry is a "passion for the names of things that Gertrude Stein saw as the basis of all poetry" (*TS*, 457). This passion certainly prevails in Stein's own poetry of names and permutations. Likewise for Rothenberg, naming represents a central aspect of poetic creativity. He claims "that giving a name to something is a fundamental act of poetry."[12] Rothenberg's dream about "THE HOUSE OF THE JEWS" illustrates this idea. The poet has the task to name a dark room and decides to call it CREATION.

Just like Adam, who named the animals in paradise, "the poet is a namer and what he names is the most / subtilized ether."[13] These words by Armand Schwerner aptly describe Rothenberg's poetics. In return, Rothenberg dedicates to his friend a poem about naming and knowledge:

> animals & people in a world we knew
> soon to be wrested from us by invasion
> of some darker mind
> knowledge by which we named our animals
> or named ourselves
> for animals
> a language shared
> pleasure

fulfillments
in a world of nouns

("11/75 for Schwerner as introduction
to a series of poems about the world
earth foremost in our thoughts,"
The Notebooks, 23)

In "primitive" thought, according to Theodore H. Gaster, "the name of a person is not a mere verbal appellation but an essential component of his being (like his shadow or voice)."[14] Rothenberg alludes to this concept in connection with the biblical creation myth. However, the invasion "of some darker mind" seems to have destroyed the primordial unity between name and knowledge. What remains is the pleasure of nouns. It is a "pleasure" that can still be felt in poetry today. Rothenberg asserts "that a language in which names convey real information may be superior because of that to one whose proper nouns, etc. have been stripped of all significance."[15]

Along the same lines, Hugh Kenner proposes that, essentially, poems are lists. Literacy begins with the making of lists. The power of a list rests on the specificity of its names/nouns. And "[t]o think of the poem as a list is to gain a new respect for its hidden power. A poem specifies, specifies. It does what can stir deep fear: it names, names, names."[16] Rothenberg explores this effect of poetry in his amulet poems. The poem "She," for instance, merely catalogues the names of Lilith, which are also her attributes:

2.

She Matronit
She Dancer
She Northerner

She in the Night
She Agrath
She Igrath

She Ishtar
She Tail of the Comet
She Child

She Charmer
She Crooked
She Serpent

She Stiff Necked
She Stick
She Lilith

She Liar
She Thorn
She Screech Owl

She Stranger
She Alien Crown
She Heaven

She Howler
She Hole
She the Hole for the Dead

She Dazzler

(*P*, 80)

Rothenberg assembles these names from the literature about Lilith, especially from Patai's book.[17] The latter speculates that this mythic figure is derived from the ancient goddesses of the Middle East—Agrath, Igrath, Ishtar—whose attributes were transferred onto the myth of Lilith. According to Jewish folklore, this she-demon is believed to secretly copulate with men at night in their sleep and to conceive demon-children by them. But she is also said to hate children and be intent on killing newborns. This is why the custom developed to fix amulets against Lilith to the beds of infants and mothers in childbirth. According to Patai, however, the she-demon underwent remarkable cultural transformations. In medieval kabbalism she reemerged as God's royal consort and thus became, once more, a kind of goddess.[18]

While the first part of Rothenberg's poem (not reproduced here) dwells on the positive and beautiful sides of the Hebrew goddess, the second section (see above) lists her dark and threatening attributes. It exploits the suggestiveness of Lilith's names and their imagery. Rothenberg fashions the list in such a way that it becomes a poem. The basic structure of the poem is very simple: "She" + "Name of the Demon/Goddess." The stanzas are tercets; there is no punctuation. The names are capitalized, even if they are mere attributes, such as "howler" (Rothenberg turns it into "She Howler").

This lucid structure draws attention to juxtaposition. (An unbroken list of names would not have the same effect.) The reader is prompted to search for analogies or associative principles between the three names that occur in each stanza. For instance, the second line might expand on the image of the first line, as in "She Ishtar [from Star] / She Tail of the Comet." But then, the third verse is perplexing—"She Child." Alternatively, the three lines might be quite unrelated except for sound patterns which bind them together: "She in the Night / She Agrath / She Igrath." The stanzas are joined through alliteration, consonance, assonance, and imagery. An image invoked by the last verse of a strophe is taken up and elaborated in the following verse: "She Serpent // She Stiff Necked / She Stick / She Lilith." Here, Rothenberg plays on the association between serpents and sexuality and serpents and magic; the phrase "stiffnecked" comes from the Bible, where it designates rebellion against God (Deut. 9: 6, 13 refers to the Israelites as *am kishay oref*, stiffnecked people).

Taken together, these images suggest that Lilith symbolizes revolt against God and men. Thus, by subtly manipulating his material, the poet generates complex symbolic meanings in minimalist forms. Jewish amulets employ names in various ways. They designate the owner of the amulet and invoke the mystic names of God and angels in many forms and permutations.[19]

What is striking about these various transmutation techniques is that they concur with procedures used in modern poetry. Futurism provides a prominent example. Khlebnikov's *zaum*/beyond sense poetry utilizes permutation to focus the reader's attention on the magic quality of language—its sound and materiality. The purpose is "to reclaim a power for poetry by reaching back beyond (*za*) intellect (*um*) to the roots of language."[20] Similarly, Rothenberg searches for the roots of poetry in magic. Magic incantations, which are written down on amulets, often contain nonsemantic words. This phenomenon also prevails in the Native American chants. Among the many explanations that have been ventured to account for these "meaningless" syllables, the poet seems to favor Bronislaw Malinowski's interpretation.[21] The latter claims that in the course of time the meaning of these magic words was lost. But their power remains and it is revealed in "a very considerable coefficient of weirdness, strangeness and unusualness."[22] This coefficient of weirdness, which shows in "phonetic, rhythmic, metaphorical and alliterative effects, with its weird cadences and repetitions"[23] has the function to set magic language off from everyday language and to mark its sacred character. It is this strangeness that Rothenberg examines in the following amulet poem:

AMULET

pishon nohsip	gihon nohig	hiddekel lekeddih	euphrates setarhpue
euphrates setarhpue	hiddekel lekeddih	gihon nohig	pishon nohsip
hiddekel lekeddih	gihon nohig	pishon nohsip	euphrates setarhpue
pishon nohsip	hiddekel lekeddih	gihon nohig	euphrates setarhpue

(*P*, 63)

As regards the strange names in this concrete poem, Rothenberg only gives us one clue. At the bottom of the page a note specifies "The rivers of Paradise." And, in fact, at least one name is recognizable—that of the river Euphrates. Moreover, the attentive reader may notice certain patterns. Like the Samaritan amulet above, this poem may be read in a vertical, horizontal, diagonal, and reversed way. We are encouraged to search for nonsyntactic relationships between the elements of the poem. To produce the second word in each set, we need to read the first name backwards: "pishon" becomes "nohsip." (Palindromes are frequently used in magic.) Pishon, Gihon, Hiddekel, and Euphrates are the names of the four rivers of paradise (Gen. 2:11–14).[24]

In his poem, Rothenberg reproduces only the first eight lines of this amulet, which he appropropirates from Schrire's book. Despite the relative simplicity of the pattern of this text, it produces alien, defamiliarizing words. It is intriguing that permutations and transpositions in concrete poetry can have very similar effects. Implicitly, the poet draws attention to the similar use of language in magic and in experimental poetry. Elsewhere he explicitly comments on this phenomenon. For example, in his anthologies, Rothenberg wishes to reveal the "primitive" roots of sound poetry by juxtaposing ancient and contemporary texts. He argues that

> a poetry without words had existed, traditionally, in different times & places: magic formulas from the old Greeks & Hebrews,

from Russian peasant cultures & many others, throughout the Indian Americas, & so on.[25]

In fact, sound poetry and concrete poetry are closely related; many concrete poets performed their poems as sound poems. According to Rothenberg, this movement began with the dadaists: "Wrote Hugo Ball of his own first soundings (1915): 'I now noticed that my voice, which seemed to have no other choice, had assumed the age-old cadence of the sacerdotal lamentation'" (*BJB*, 387).

It is precisely this sacred effect that Rothenberg seeks to convey in his amulet poems. Northrop Frye claims that even if we do not understand the words, charms lead us back "to some kind of mythological universe, a world of interlocking names of mysterious powers."[26] He calls such enchanting poetry "charm poetry" and maintains that prior to the twentieth century most poetry was charm poetry. Its power relies on the fact that "ordinary processes of response are short-circuited."[27] By contrast, riddle poetry is conceptual and visual. It became prominent with the onset of modernism. Eliot's appreciation of the metaphysical poets and the imagist movement were the first stirrings of this modernist tendency.[28]

Rothenberg, however, does not limit himself to one type of poetry, but experiments with both, charms and riddles. For amulets mark a point of intersection of the two modes of writing. Deciphering an amulet comes close to solving a riddle. Activating the magic potential of an amulet involves reciting the charm with its sound patterns, strange words, and irregular rhythms. Thus, amulet poems manifest the visual and the rhythmic properties of letters and words. They illustrate, to speak with Rothenberg, "the old, creative functions of the 'letters' (Hebrew etc.) working somewhere between sight & sound."[29]

In primitive thought, signifier and signified—name and thing—are one. The name has power over the object. This notion is based on the belief that magic names are words of power. In the magic worldview, knowing the name of someone or something gives you control over the creature, person, or object. The respective object or being can then be impelled to obey the magician's command. This is why many amulets against Lilith comprise her names.

A Jewish legend relates Lilith's confrontation with the prophet Elijah. Realizing the prophet's superior power, the demoness promises to disclose all her names, if he lets her go. Furthermore, she swears that anyone who invokes these names will be protected from her.[30] Traditional Jewish amulets therefore often include this story together with the various names of the she-demon. Here is an example from "History One:"

> She told him she was Lilith & that if he let her go she would teach him all her names. The names she wrote down were
>
> LILITH ABITR ABITO AMORFO
> KKODS IKPODO AYYLO PTROTA
> ABNUKTA STRINA KALI PTUZA
> TLTOI-PRITSA.
>
> He told her he was Elijah.
>
> (*P*, 123)

Rothenberg presents this amulet in such a way that we are inclined to read it simply as a story about a woman by the name of Lilith and a man called Elijah. The two characters do not necessarily have to be legendary or mythical. However, the strange names create confusion. How is one to pronounce the name "Ptrota"? What language is it? Only the names "Lilith" and "Kali" (possibly the Hindu goddess) are recognizable. The other words seem to result from letter manipulation. They are, in fact, Lilith's traditional names employed in amulets.[31] Yet more important than this factual information is the observation that these names have no "meaning," but only a function.[32] In this particular story, the function of the names is to exercise power over Lilith. By revealing her names, she gives Elijah control over herself. The names are a source of power. Since the narrative demonstrates this concept neatly, the story serves as a metaphor for the empowerment of language by the act of naming.

The poet attempts to infuse contemporary poetry and poetics with an archaic, magic concept of language. While poststructuralism presupposes that there is no bond between signifier and signified and that the signifier is radically cut off from its referent, Rothenberg seeks a poetry and poetics that reunifies the two. The poet insists "on the closeness between thing and word ('signified' and 'signifier' . . .)."[33] The aim is to recover what seems to have been lost to contemporary language philosophy—the notion of a magic bond between word and thing. In contrast to Language Poetry, Rothenberg admits that his "own interests make the 'mystical' and 'magical' . . . a part of any larger poetics I might still hope to build" (*RI*, 49). He strives for a "poetics of the sacred" in which word and thing are reunified and which aims

> (while bound to fail) to heal the break between reality and language. Some such aim has been a central project to our work as poets; it has been a key both to our search for a primal poetics and to our search for the sacred.[34]

Once more, the push of Rothenberg's poetics is toward healing—healing the split between thing and word, "the break between reality and language." In order to achieve this admittedly utopian goal, the poet explores the power of words. The implied magic notion of language re-empowers poetry and enables it to regain its ability to charm and enchant. Even though Rothenberg and the Language Poets share a concern with the materiality of language, which they explore by undermining syntactic structures while at the same time experimenting with other ways of patterning a poem, they are divided on the subject of language philosophy. Despite deconstruction, Rothenberg still believes in the power of the word. His interest in name magic provides sufficient evidence. Moreover, the poet's emphasis on orality, recitation, charm, and chant is characteristic of exactly the kind of "phonocentrism" that Derrida rebukes. Sayre observes:

> The mythology of speech's priority, as Derrida has pointed out time and again, is based on a metaphysical faith in the spoken word and its seeming ability to unify signifier and signified, inside and outside, self and world.[35]

It seems, however, that Rothenberg does not feel answerable to Derrida or to philosophy in general. Rather, he concentrates on his role as a poet. For him, "the poet's work, like the shaman's, may be carried on primarily through language and use that as the vehicle with which to drive toward meaning, toward a (re)uniting with the world."[36] Thus, the poetics of the sacred and the appropriation of magic are signs of a push toward meaning. Such meaning may be nondiscursive and nonsemantic, as in the "meaningless vocables" of chants, or esoteric and weird, as in amuletic writing. We may have to struggle with it, but it is meaning nevertheless because it has a function. The poet tends toward a functional understanding of "meaning." Regarding the effect of magic spells, he claims that "the meaning contained then is how it's made to function."[37]

Keeping his distance from deconstruction, Rothenberg demonstrates an experimental alternative to Language Poetry. Peter Middleton aptly sums up the poet's innovative approach:

> Rothenberg has managed to mark out a possible poetic practice that extends beyond either the New American Poetry or Language Poetry, although it has elements of both. . . . Not because he achieves some bridging synthesis however, but because he shows that it might be possible to imagine a poetic practice that is performative but does not need the authority of a first person to speak and so can imagine a poem that is not a history of its negotiations with the subjectivity of authorship, and yet can go outside any supposedly constraining condition of a language known in the terms of philosophy, linguistics and literary theory.[38]

Although Rothenberg does not reject the lyric, "the authority of a first person to speak," he also explores other forms of poetry. His amuletic, numerological, and gematric poems, for instance, do not rely on the lyric voice. Some of these poems examine the materiality of language, while others use new/old means of composing and structuring a poem.

Numerological Poems

Earlier I mentioned that the Hebrew consonants also operate as numbers: א is 1, ב is 2, ר is 3, etc. This convention relates words and letters to numbers. And in fact, numbers are also essential to the creation of poetry. The poet puts it this way: "And I have lain awake . . . & counted numbers in sequences that play on mind & body until the rhythm of numbers, letters, shapes, & forms is inescapable—as still another source of naming" (*VB*, 68).

Numbers may be taken as a "source of naming" because they can be used to describe the properties of an object. The Pythagoreans, who sought to unify all the various phenomena of the universe by numerological correspondence, first expanded this thought. Pythagoreanism speculates that numbers—not names—are at the root of everything. Rothenberg comments:

> A "poetry of number" . . . was once the limit of the poetry we could see, not only that "numbers" was itself the working term for

"verse," but that it linked *all* arts & science together: a great unifying & synthesizing concept with roots into the Orphic-based, inspired & sacred mathematics of the Pythagoreans.

(*VB*, 68)

The poet places special emphasis on the "unifying & synthesizing concept" implied in Pythagoreanism. His own poetry of number utilizes numbers as a concealed unifying principle. This poetry is part of a broader trend, which Perloff delineates in the following way:

> *numbers* have increasingly been replaced, either by a free verse where lineation as such seems to be the only criterion for poetry, or by *number* as a generative device: the artist derives his or her text from, say, the Fibonacci series (1, 2, 3, 5, 8, 13 . . .) or from a mesostic rule or from alphabet series or from lipograms (texts where one letter is proscribed).[39]

In those cases where the underlying structure of the poem is disguised, it comes over as a riddle. However, Rothenberg also employs numbers openly in his "numerological poems." In that case we need to find out what the respective numbers signify.

The term "numerology" indicates that Rothenberg's poetry of numbers belongs to an old type of poetry, which was particularly popular in the Middle Ages and the Renaissance.[40] Although his numerological poems do not constitute a major genre of his work, I will take a brief look at the sections with number poems in *Poland/1931* and *Vienna Blood* ("Numbers & Letters").[41]

The following poem entitled "Numerology" consists of two parts, which are labeled (a) and (b), perhaps in allusion to Pythagorean geometry. There are no stanzas. Many lines comprise only one word or a numeral. The numbers are not spelled out, but given as numerals to underscore their properties as numbers in relation to other numbers. They seem to be ordered according to some kind of pattern. Moreover, certain words (cipher, empty, spaces, cloud, sky, holes / hole, shadow, rock) and numbers are repeated in different ways:

1
7-7-7-7-7
shadow
1
shadow cipher sky

1
spaces
9-9
shadow
9
numbers
9
1-1-1-1-1
2
cipher
empty

(*VB*, 61)

A permutation or substitution principle seems to be at work. But what is disconcerting about this list is that it is difficult to comprehend how the numbers 1, 2, 7, and 9 and the words cohere. Yet if we make an effort, we can find certain patterns. For instance, numbers tend to be repeated five times (7-7-7-7-7, 1-1-1-1-1), or the equation 2 + 7 = 9 may explain the occurrence of these numbers in the poem. But the question still remains: What is the point of this? Why does Rothenberg choose the numbers 2, 7, 9 rather than, for example, 1, 7, 8, or any other series of numbers? These reflections lay open the arbitrariness conveyed in this poem. The beginning of the poem is obscure as well:

(a)
the man of numbers
cries too loud
he is a cipher   empty
his spaces
are yours
they open up through him
a cloud & sky
beyond him
centered in the holes they make
I call out
1!
2!
7!
9!
falling against his shadow
on the rock

(*VB*, 60)

We may wonder about the identity of the "man of numbers:" is this a poet waking up at night and counting the rhythm of his poem as suggested by Rothenberg's earlier remark? Or does this poem refer to Plato who drew on the teachings of Pythagoras? Perhaps the keywords "shadow," "rock," and "cloud" allude to Plato's cave parable. However, the clue lies in the word "cipher." For cipher means "zero" and "empty."[42]

Now, the image of the "man of numbers" begins to take shape: the man is a cipher—a zero! Hence the references to emptiness and the image of a hole in the middle! By further investigating the meaning of the word "cipher," we find that it designates encryption techniques. The *Encyclopaedia Britannica* defines "cipher" as "any method of transforming a message to conceal its meaning" and tells us that "[a]ll ciphers involve either transposition or substitution, or a combination of these two mathematical operations—i.e., product ciphers."[43]

This information may suggest that Rothenberg actually encrypted the poem. Even if we cannot decipher the code, this text illustrates the puzzling effect of encryption techniques. Similarily, certain types of gematria work like a secret code. They involve the substitution of one letter for another or one letter for a number according to an esoteric system.[44] The product of gematria or encryption displays unusual letter and word combinations. Rothenberg draws the reader's attention to these permutations and to the mystery of numbers.

In the next poem, Rothenberg adapts the methods of Hebrew number mysticism to the English language. Since this poem has obtrusive rhymes, which are reminiscent of a lullaby, it is subtitled "Song." The poet allocates a number value to the first seven letters of the English alphabet so that A is one, B is two, etc. However, the prescribed mathematical operations do not work out [the numbers in italics are mine]:

NUMEROLOGY "A Song"

One	*[1]*
Number one	*[1]*
And one	*[+ 1]*
And a one	*[+ 1]*
A.	*[1]*
And an A	*[+ 1]*
A A A	*[1 1 1]*
And a three	*[+ 3]*
Three & C	*[3 + 3]*
A & B	*[1 + 2]*
Into three	*[3]*

And four	*[+ 4]*
Into D	*[4]*
Into G	*[7]*
B & E	*[2 + 5]*
Minus three	*[− 3]*
Minus D	*[− 4]*
And me	
And divided by me	

(*VB*, 62)

A peculiar logic prevails in this poem. Its purpose is to mislead the reader into thinking that this list can be treated like a mathematical problem. We will find it difficult to calculate the sums. The last few lines of the poem can be numerically rendered in the following way: $2 + 5 = 7$; $7 - 3 = 4$; $4 - 4 = 0$. The number zero is somehow connected with the speaker.

Unexpectedly, psychology comes into the equation of the poem and throws it out of balance: "And me / And divided by me." Which number equals "me"? Perhaps zero? But it is impossible to divide anything by zero. If we substitute "me" by the number zero, we get "And zero / And divided by zero," but mathematically the equation 0:0 is invalid. Alternatively, we may equate the personal pronoun "me" with any other number resulting from the complex and arbitrary calculations, but the results will remain indeterminate. Numerology in its popular form also tries to predict character traits on the basis of calculations involving birth dates and other personal numbers. Yet despite such speculations, human beings remain a mystery. Easy calculations and categorizations are destined to fail. Rothenberg himself makes a connection between numbers and the issue of identity when he comments on a poem by Maria Hebrea. This text might actually have served as a model for his numerological song. It employs logic in the same inscrutable way:

THE NUMBERS

2 are 1
3 & 4 are 1
1 will become 2
2 will become 3

Commentary

The entry through alchemy, in the figure of Mary the Jewess, said by some to be the mother of the art. Of her verbalizations only

> these formulas survive, reminiscent of E. E. Cummings' description of the poet's strategy: to hold that 2 times 2 *is* 5. Or Edmond Jabès of a *poesis* specifically Jewish: "The number '4,' he said, is the number of our ruin. Do not think I am mad. The number '4' equals 2 times 2. It is in the name of such obsolete logic that we are persecuted. For we hold that 2 times 2 equals also 5, or 7, or 9. You only need to consult the commentaries of our sages to verify. Not everything is simple in simplicity. We are hated because we do not enter into the simple calculations of mathematics." (*The Book of Questions*, page 92). (*BJB*, 422)

Maria Hebrea's formula characterizes numbers in terms of transformation rather than along the lines of fixed, mathematical conventions. Rothenberg claims that the role of the alchemist and the poet is to bring about metamorphosis and to confuse the minds of those who are set on their "obsolete logic." Others, however, may feel threatened by the unfamiliarity and unpredictability of this approach. That is why poets and Jews often experience rejection for being different and for thinking differently. The Talmud has a logic of its own, which is not self-evident to the uninitiated reader. Poetry, likewise, subverts and exposes the habitual use of language.

Thus, once more, Rothenberg equates poets and Jews to confirm Tsvetayeva's assertion that "all poets are jews." Poets and Jews are shown to be marginal subverters who use numbers in their own, idiosyncratic way. In the Jewish mystical tradition, this is done by linking numbers and letters and speculating on their esoteric properties. The poet is drawn to this

> verbal/visual tradition, a sense of language & reality, that went very far back; the idea of language as an instrument in forming . . . the entire universe, the possibility of describing reality itself through the elemental or constituent forms of language, the relations that this assumes between the alphabet & the structure of the world as such.[45]

And, since in gematria the alphabet and numbers are related, one might also claim that, according to the Jewish mystical tradition, letters and numbers are the "building blocks of the universe." Rothenberg asserts exactly this:

> there was of course a whole mysticism of sacred numbers, magic numbers, number symbolism. But I think what I was particularly interested in was how, in one line of the Jewish mystical tradition, letters & numbers converged, because the same symbols (the let-

ters of the alphabet) were used for both. They were both the building blocks of the universe (a kind of mystical algebra) & a means for showing associations between words and phrases and utterances whose letters/numbers added up to the same sum. These associations then were something to consider: to accept, reject, or simply meditate on.[46]

Gematria Poems

The above quotation refers to Rothenberg's experiments with gematria. Scholem defines gematria in the following way:

> *Gematria* . . . is one of the aggadic hermeneutical rules for interpreting the Torah. . . . It consists of explaining a word or a group of words according to the numerical value of the letters, or of substituting other letters of the alphabet for them in accordance with a set system.[47]

The poet appropriates this method from Jewish tradition in order to generate a Jewish poetry of number. However, his use of gematria diverges from tradition. A method rooted in a religious context is appropriated with the aim of composing poetry rather than underscoring religious teachings. In the following, the nontraditional aspects of Rothenberg's Jewish poetry of number will be analyzed with an eye to contemporary poetry.

Rothenberg interprets the result of gematria operations in terms of his own poetics rather than in a traditional Jewish context. His gematria experiments are affected by avant-garde experimentation with chance operations and non-intentional methods as well as surrealist, tribal, and concrete poetry. Exploring gematria over a period of twenty years, the poet developed his skills in using this technique. In the course of time, he produced various types of gematria poems and worked shorter gematrias into longer poetic series and sequences. This subchapter investigates these various forms.

One could say that Rothenberg's gematrias constitute a new "Jewish" genre and a new poetic genre. I will interpret their significance in two ways: First, like the numerological poems, they demonstrate the return of number into contemporary poetry. Perloff contends that some of the most innovative contemporary poetry today displays numerological patterns and hidden constraints. These have to be distinguished from traditional meter. In fact, they constitute an alternative to the New Formalist return to metric structure. Drawing on Perloff's observation, one may suggest that Rothenberg's gematria poems reveal the "return of the (numerical) repressed."[48]

Second, I will argue that Rothenberg's gematrias resemble riddles. In fact, these gnomic poems *are* riddle poetry. Their effect is derived from juxtaposition. The juxtaposition of images also plays a considerable role in riddles, where one thing is imagined in terms of another. For instance, the traditional ice riddle describes water and ice as mother and daughter: "My mother brought me forth, / then shortly I her daughter / brought her forth again."[49] The riddlic disguise suggests a metamorphosis of the daughter into the mother. This imagery acts as block element for the reader to overcome. The reader needs to find a similarity between the two elements, that is, the subject of the riddle (mother, daughter) and the disguise (giving birth).

Thus, solving a riddle and trying to see the correspondence between the two parts of a gematria equation involves the same problem. Both gematria poems and riddles induce a process that is both sensual and cognitive, which engages perception and thought.[50] The overall impulse is the search for meaning, and—as I shall argue later on—meaning is gained through naming.

In Jewish tradition, gematria has hermeneutic, didactic, and mnemonic functions. It features in talmudic, legendary, and kabbalistic literature. Here, we will focus on its hermeneutic aspects. Gematria is employed in the exegesis of the Torah in order to show mystical or hidden connections between different words or passages. The purpose is always to support the authoritative tradition as in the following example:

> The Holy Ari Zal teaches that when eating bread one should dip the bread in salt three times since three times Hashem (God's name) 26 equals 78, the Gematria for both salt מלח (78) and לחם bread (78).[51]

The validity of such interpretations derives from a special conception of language. For gematria "presupposes the divine, or at least a non-conventional, nature of the Hebrew language, which ensures the significance or the numerical relations."[52] That is to say that gematria rests on the notion that God imbued Hebrew, the holy language, with particular power and meaning, since God himself was speaking Hebrew when he created the world. Hence "the individual letters and their combinations are not subjective, conventional symbols. They are objective."[53] The discovery of meaningful, hidden relationships between words, then, is possible because meaning is inscribed into the words and letters; it is intrinsic. According to this doctrine, everything in the Torah is meaningful.[54]

Likewise, Rothenberg is preoccupied with the semantic as well as the nonsemantic meaning of words, letters, and sounds, and he demands that permanently new meanings must be brought to the fore. But the poet discards notions of a divine source of meaning. On the contrary, he is interested in exploring how humans construct meaning and what function it has for them. In order to do so, he appropriates the ancient, exegetic strategy of gematria. In his hands, gematria becomes a generative device for producing poems. To use the jargon of the avant-garde, gematria works as a "constraint" for a chance operation. Constraints are generative, which means that they determine, "not what is already fixed as a property of the text, but *how* the writer will proceed with his composition."[55] Rather than supporting a religious doctrine or authority, Rothenberg employs gematria to underscore his own poetics. As we shall see, he even employs gematria to question and undermine traditional Jewish concepts. By using gematria for what the author of the introduction to the dictionary calls "arbitrary personal ideas" and not remaining "within the limits of the legal and spiritual boundaries of Torah,"[56] the poet opposes the rabbinic authorities. Rothenberg employs gematria toward artistic and subversive ends.

The poet's earliest experiments with gematria date back to the 1970s. They grew out of the collaboration with Lenowitz. Sifting and reading through Jewish texts in preparing *A Big Jewish Book*, Lenowitz chanced on many startling, traditional gematrias. Rothenberg got interested in the poetic character of these word and phrase equations and integrated several of them in his anthology (*BJB*, 429–31). Twenty-five short pieces are spread out over two pages and accompanied by an elaborate commentary that explains the functions and various forms of gematria.

This allows Rothenberg also to explore the semantics of the space of the page on which the poems appear (an approach he later develops further). Here is an example:

Messiah *The Devil*
Snake. Fat-ash.

This Pope
This garbage.
(Rothenberg, Lenowitz, "25 Gematria," *BJB*, 430)

The gematria equaling "messiah" and "snake" is infamous, for it was already used by the Shabbateans to justify that their messiah, Shabbatai Zevi, had to transgress the law and become unified with evil (the serpent). Although traditionally gematria is not supposed to be employed to make new discoveries, the Shabbateans and some kabbalists bent this rule in their rereading of Jewish tradition.[57]

Rothenberg does the same. In the above example he juxtaposes three provocative gematrias. This produces a bizarre effect. For instance, the opposition of the noun phrases "messiah" and "the devil" evokes traditional notions about good and evil. But this easy polarization is undercut by the fact that the messiah rather than the devil is equaled with a snake. Moreover, the grotesque juxtaposition of the devil with fat and ash is perplexing. "Fat-ash" can be related to "this garbage" (fat and ash *are* garbage). And, of course, the juxtaposition of the pope with garbage is irreverent. The more we ponder these gnomic poems, the more we realize their extraordinary cleverness. Like concrete poems, these "constellations" can be read in different ways. We might associate the titles (snake—This Pope—The Devil), or recombine its elements (Messiah—This garbage—Fat-ash, etc.).

Recognizing the combinatory potential of the material, Rothenberg finds a way of playing this off in the medium of cards. In collaboration with Lenowitz and Karl Young, he creates twenty-seven gematria cards using the same material. These cards were, in fact, published one year before the anthology. Like playing cards, the gematrias are kept in a little cardboard box. Each card has writing on one side and an image on the other. The design grew out of the collaboration between Rothenberg and Young, the owner of the Membrane Press. It was Young who suggested putting illustrations at the back of the cards.[58] The pictures are fragments from a photomontage by Eleanor Antin (*Poland/1931*) and an elaborate chart from a medieval kabbalistic manuscript. Two cards of the set display full reproductions of these two illustrations; they provide a kind of map for the user. On a separate, folded sheet Rothenberg explains different kinds of gematria.

The writing on the cards always consists of two parts: one word or a short phrase written in all capital letters—the title—and below it, another word or phrase written in sentence case. Thus, the gematric equivalence is represented by juxtaposition. The advantage of putting these correspondences on cards is that it allows the reader to mix them and read them in a random order. We may also arrange them in piles, single out the ones we do not like or do not understand, and select our favorites. Furthermore, the reader may spread the cards out in space and find her own correspondences, opposites, and paradoxes. Here is a simple example:

THE SOUL OF ADAM	FIRST ADAM
Lilith.	Hell is open.

(Rothenberg, Lenowitz, *Gematria* 27)

It becomes an illuminating exercise. Certainly, as Rothenberg notes, these associations are "something to consider: to accept, reject, or simply meditate on."[59]

From a secular perspective, however, gematria is an intellectual game, in which different elements—words, letters, numbers—are shuffled around (like cards) until some amazing connection offers itself. It resembles a jigsaw puzzle. The concrete poetry movement also put the idea of poetry as a game forward. Gomringer, whose work Rothenberg translated, envisions poetry as a *denkspiel*. The poet knows and makes the rules of the game. Concrete poetry is characterized as a constellation (of stars).[60]

Doubtless, Rothenberg writes his gematria poems with this background in mind. Gomringer's metaphor of the poem as a constellation of stars is taken up by Rothenberg in one of the illustrations included in the gematria game pack. It depicts a chart by a seventeenth-century Christian kabbalist who viewed the stars in a peculiar way. He projected the image of magic letters onto the night sky,

> where patterns of stars (points joined by "lines") can be read as letters, groups of letters read as words, etc. In the process the sky becomes a massive concrete poem, whose words or "messages" are constantly transforming. (*BJB*, 420)

Adding this image to the gematria cards, Rothenberg hints at the poetics of concrete poetry. For him, concrete poetry addresses the "question of making the words cohere in a given space. . . ."[61]

What makes Rothenberg's minimalist poems cohere is an invisible set of gematric rules, an underlying pattern of letters and numbers. From a traditional Jewish perspective, there is a hidden, divinely guaranteed meaning that unifies the diverse parts of a gematria equation. These secret connections then could be symbolized by the illustrations on the back of the cards. The parts of the puzzle all fit together. Although we are not able to see everything at the same time, we are assured that there is an overall picture.

Reading through the cards, the reader makes astonishing discoveries. Sometimes the image and the words interact in a humorous way. For instance, one card displays a part of Antin's collage with a photograph of Rothenberg's head on it. Turning the card around, we find the following words: "THE HEAD / I make you happy." For the reader, there is no way of knowing whether such coincidences are intentional or not.[62] We are left to our own devices in looking for connections and analogies between the two parts of the poem, especially in those poems where the correspondences are less obvious. This way the reader is made aware of her active participation in the construction of meaning. At the same time, she may share some of the thrill that Rothenberg, Lenowitz, and Young must have felt in putting the pieces together.

Not only are these poems part of a puzzle, but each individual gematria makes up a riddle. For instance,

REBEKKA

This.
12.

(Rothenberg, Lenowitz, *Gematria* 27.)

Here, the reader's task is to find the factor that unifies the name "Rebekka," the number 12 and the demonstrative pronoun "this." Translated into the standard format of the riddle, the problem could be expressed in the following way: "I am related to Rebekka and to the number 12 and to 'this.' What am I?"

The block element of this riddle lies in the difficulty of linking Rebekka with the number 12. This number may allude to the 12 tribes of Israel. But how can they be associated with Rebekka, who had only two children—Esau and Jacob? However, it was Rebekka's son, Jacob, who became the father of the 12 tribes of Israel; *he* had 12 children. She thus can be said to be the grandmother of the 12 tribes of Israel. Yet the pronoun "this" introduces another nonsensical element. The word is just there to block our understanding.

Anyway, the "solution" of a gematric riddle matters less than the cognitive and imaginative process set off in the mind of the reader by juxtaposition. Indeed, many riddles employ juxtaposition. Dr. Johnson, who disliked riddlic conceits, aptly characterizes the phenomenon as "a combination of dissimilar images, or discovery of occult resemblances in things apparently alike"; "[t]he most heterogeneous ideas are yoked by violence together."[63] Yet, it is precisely this idea of "bringing together . . . two more or less remote realities"[64] that the surrealists pursued. In composing his gematria poems, Rothenberg draws on surrealist poetics as much as on certain models he finds in tribal poetry.

A brilliant example for the second type are African Bantu riddles. Rothenberg presents them in *Technicians of the Sacred* as "Bantu Combinations." Here are two examples:

> The little hut falls down.
> Tomorrow debts.
> . . . .
> We are the fire that burns the country.
> The Calf of the Elephant is exposed on the plain.
>
> (*TS*, 16)

While in the first combination the connection between the two lines is fairly obvious, the correspondences in second one are strained. Rothenberg annotates these riddles with a revealing commentary:

> this juxtaposition of images turns up all over in the art, say, of the riddle—of which several of these "combinations" are, in fact, examples. . . . In all these the interest increases as the connection between the images becomes more & more strained, barely definable. . . .
>
> Not subtlety, but *energy*: the power of word & image. For it's right here that the light breaks through most clearly. (*TS*, 455)

It is exactly the surrealist effect of the "riddlic fire"[65] that Rothenberg examines in his gnomic gematria poems and in other earlier, minimalist experiments. In *Sightings*, *Further*

Sightings and the "Midwinter Poems" (*Seneca Journal*), the poet develops the art of juxtaposing images.[66] He insists that simply setting apart an image or an insight can make a poem: "What's happened, simply, is that something has been sighted & stated & set apart (by name or description). . . . It is this double sense of sighted/sited that represents the basic poetic function . . ." (*TS*, 453). The following example from oral literature illustrates such "sighting":

A Bushman Poem for the Blue Crane

A splinter of stone which is white.

(*TS*, 15)

Rothenberg then observes how images are developed into larger structures. Significantly, the following comment also expands on the poetics that pervades his gematria poems:

> But even here there is nothing naïve . . . about the "sightings," save their clarity & the sense that, starting now, the plot (as Cage would say) is-going-to-thicken. Thickens, in fact, while we're watching; for the "single perception" of an image like *a splinter of stone / which is white* can as easily be sensed as two perceptions, & placed against the subject (*blue crane*) as two or three. (*TS*, 454)

A similar "thickening of the plot" takes place in many gematria poems. Here is a piece that juxtaposes concepts rather than images:

THE WORLD/THE YEAR/THE SOUL

Evening.
Morning.
Noon.

(Rothenberg, Lenowitz, *Gematria* 27)

The more we think about this poem, the more complex grow the relationships between its different elements. Evening, morning, and noon are time attributes. Likewise, "the world" and "the year" mark time. But how is the concept of the soul related to this list? What does it correspond to? To evening, morning, noon, or just to the noon? Why is the soul associated with the noon? Questions over questions. They are due to the tripartite structure of the title set off against a poem of three lines. The result is the "thickening of the plot." Invariably the reader will be impelled to "combine" the poem's diverse parts "in search of meaningful combinations" (*BJB*, 420).

In his most recent gematria poems Rothenberg expands minimalist poems into larger series.[67] The thickening of the plot increases complexity. Yet before examining the specific texts, it is necessary to make some preliminary remarks about the entire book *Gematria*. In the "POST/FACE," Rothenberg provides the reader with valuable background information:

> In the foregoing poems I have been working from the over three hundred pages of word lists that make up Gutman G. Locks's *The Spice of Torah—Gematria* (Judaica Press, New York, 1985), which offer easy access to the numerical value of every word in the first five books of the Hebrew Bible. . . . I have proceeded in these works in several different ways: by using one word or word-phrase as title and others (numerically equivalent) as poem; by using the gematria number as a title & constructing poems of single lines and/or stanzas of two or several lines that fall under or add up to that number; & in the selection titled "Beyond Gematria," by using freer selection of words brought to my attention by gematria, but combining & adding to them with considerably more freedom of choice. (*G*, 165)

These three types of gematria poems are found in the three main parts of the book under the subtitles "Gematrias 12 x 22," "More Gematrias (1–100)," and "Beyond Gematria." The expression "12 × 22" suggests number symbolism. For instance, there are twelve tribes of Israel and twenty-two letters of the Hebrew alphabet. The poems are distributed over the pages in the book in such a way that "More Gematrias (1–100)," which are numbered from one to 100, begin on page 100. Altogether, the structure of this poetry collection is intricate and flexible. As we shall see, Rothenberg gives himself much room for variation. The first part of the book, "Gematrias 12 × 22," contains 12 long gematria sequences. They are simply entitled "First Gematria," "Second Gematria," "Third Gematria," etc. However, some of these sequences also have subtitles suggesting a theme, such as "Together," "Lot in Sodom," "In the Shadow," "Among," "Dreamers," etc. Each of these sequences consists of 22 "sets."[68] The sets are separated by lines, and each one may contain up to three numbered gematria poems. One can therefore speak of "two-fold" and "three-fold" gematrias.[69]

Rothenberg utilizes this elaborate structure to generate a complex net of meanings. Actually, the entire book is an experiment in plot-thickening strategies. However, in interpreting these, we encounter a terminological and formal problem. How shall we refer to the different parts of the series? Are they lines, verses, stanzas, poems, or, more vaguely, "pieces"? Designating the different pieces as "poems," suggests a certain autonomy between the different parts of a series. By contrast, to speak of "stanzas" or "verses" implies a greater sense of coherence among the various elements. But what do we really mean when we claim that something "coheres"?

To say the least, our notions of "what coheres" are necessarily biased and inextricably related to our beliefs about what constitutes a poem. The crucial questions are therefore: Can a poem consist of just one line (plus title) or one word (plus title)? Can a poem have many verses that are completely unrelated, as, for instance, in chance-generated poetry or surrealist writing (e.g., *corpse exquisite* compositions)? Is it then still a poem?

As noted earlier, Rothenberg maintains that it is possible to make a poem out of a word and a title. Having demonstrated the poetic energy of Rothenberg's minimalist poems, I will accept this presupposition. Consequently, every text that juxtaposes an image or a concept may be considered a "poem." It constitutes an autonomous entity, which, however, may become part of a larger structure, such as a series or sequence.

Finally, the reason we have trouble in finding the appropriate descriptive terminology and generic categories for Rothenberg's gematria series is that these sequences are innovative, which makes it difficult to apply preexisting terms and concepts. Like other postmodern writers, the poet undermines traditional notions of what constitutes a poem. His gematria sequences expose the arbitrariness of classification. To appreciate Rothenberg's gematria poems it is more important to examine how they are generated and what effect they produce on the reader than to categorize them.

Locks's massive list of words and numbers—318 pages altogether—supplies Rothenberg with many found poems, which the poet then "puts together" in a variety of ways. He recalls:

> With a sense that poems could be made with such minimal juxtapositions (one word set against another word etc.) I opened the *Spice of Torah* book and found the pages filled with little poems that I could extract, or to increase the range, other combinations that I could discover by adding numbers together. Once started I could keep it going on and on.[70]

The poet employs gematria—essentially an exegetical method—as an aleatory device, not unlike the "non-intentional" methods used by Cage or Mac Low.[71] The latter's writing influences especially the gematria experiments. Rothenberg observed Mac Low's use of aleatory methods over a period of thirty years, and selected many of his texts to be included in his anthologies. The first poem in the book is also dedicated to his friend:

A GEMATRIA FOR JACKSON MAC LOW

CHANCE

Made it happen.

(*G*, 11)

Being acutely aware of avant-garde experimentations, Rothenberg gives them a "Jewish turn" by using gematria as a chance operation "opening up new channels of associations—as Jackson Mac Low ('The Friendship Poems'): 'O blessèd chance continue to happen to me! / For I wd never plan so well—I wd have died of my planning' " (*BJB*, 619).

Gematria works as a constraint determining which words and phrases may be collocated. Generally, non-intentional methods for generating poems minimize authorial interference.[72] Fred Muratori asserts that "because these poems resulted from chance operations, it would be dangerous to offer 'interpretations' or to suggest that some universally acceptable exegeses lie waiting to unfold."[73] By contrast, I believe that interpreting Rothenberg's gematria poems is very illuminating. But, of course, this analysis need not be "universally acceptable." Since the poetic use of aleatory devices *always* involves the complex interaction between chance and choice, interpretations of poetic interferences are of great interest.

Rothenberg, in particular, makes his presence felt in many ways, first and foremost through selectivity, translation, spacing, and juxtaposition. It goes without saying that the process of composing gematria poems involves selection. Out of an immense list of phrases, the poet chooses those that suit his purposes. He selects many nouns because they offer themselves for minimalist juxtaposition. There are also a large number of words with sexual connotations or phrases that may take on sexual meanings, if they are placed in a new context. Here is an example:

GEMATRIA 316

The man
was aroused.

The rod
heated up.
("Fifth Gematria: 'Among,'" *G*, 46)

Indeed, the gematria dictionary lists the phrases "the man," "was aroused," "the rod," and "heated" under the entry for the number 316. All these phrases have the same number value and therefore may appear in the same poem. Yet it is Rothenberg who changes the verb "heated" into "heated up" and who rearranges the phrases to derive a sexually explicit poem.

One way of transforming biblical material then, is to give it a meaning that diverges from the original context. Sometimes it is quite comical how Rothenberg exploits the colloquial or idiomatic potential of a word:

"AND FRAIL WITH LONGING"

As she spoke
I dug it.
("Fifth Gematria: 'Among,'" *G*, 47)

This poem contains a short narrative. In a few words, Rothenberg sketches out a story. At the same time he defamiliarizes a biblical passage. In the original context of the Hebrew Bible (which is difficult to reconstruct here), the phrase "I dug it" probably refers to an action, for example, the digging of a cistern or a grave. It will certainly not signify "I understood" or "I liked it" as the idiom of the Beat generation suggests. By reinterpreting the biblical phrase in terms of contemporary speech, the poet manages to bridge past and present in a humorous way.

Another way of giving the material a contemporary flavor is to juxtapose biblical language with a modern title. Rothenberg freely invents titles as in the following set:

PORNOGRAPHIC POEM (1)

A breast
will be glorified.

PORNOGRAPHIC POEM (2)

Goats
will be slain.

PORNOGRAPHIC POEM (3)

What is it?
What is it?
("Third Gematria: 'Lot in Sodom,'" *G*, 36)

This three-fold gematria poem has a humorous effect as well. It plays on the possible reaction of the reader who might be wondering why this poem deserves the title "pornographic poem." The question is thrown back at us: "What is it [a pornographic poem]? What is it?" The repetition—a further point of interference by the poet—adds emphasis to the question that exposes the reader's own pornographic expectations.

Besides making up his own titles, Rothenberg also adds dedications. Some poems are written for poet friends and allude to a central aspect of their work. The dedication tells the reader to look for associations between the gematria poem and the respective poet's writing. Especially beautiful and memorable is the gematria that serves as an epitaph to the entire poetry collection:

For Edmond Jabès, in memory

The desert
speaks.

(*G*, n. pag.)[74]

A curious inversion takes place in this gematria. The desert, a frequent motif in Jabès's writing, is usually associated with silence. However, the assertion here is that it speaks. This gnomic poem then states a paradox, which in turn alludes to the paradoxical character of Jabès' work—the poet who writes about silence cannot stop writing/speaking.

Here is another dedication for Reznikoff, who wrote Holocaust poetry and published a collection of poems with the title *Testimony*, to which this gematria alludes[75]:

TESTIMONY
for Charles Reznikoff

The light.
The terror.
("Fourth Gematria: 'In the Shadow,'" *G*, 39)

Furthermore, Rothenberg does not limit himself to Locks's list of words and phrases. Based on his knowledge of Yiddish and Hebrew, he also makes up his own gematrias:

THE NAME (1)

The Book.

THE NAME (2)

There.

[345]
("21," *G*, 108)

In square brackets Rothenberg informs us that in this poem all the Hebrew phrases have the number value 345. The respective entry in Locks's dictionary, however, only contains the expressions, "her name" (שמה), "to Sephar" (ספרה), and "there" (שמה). So how does the poet derive the noun phrases "the name" and "the book"? Rothenberg simply transmutes the Hebrew consonants. By putting the last consonant, ה, at the beginning of a word, one obtains two new noun phrases: "her name" (שמה) becomes "the name" (השם), and "to Sephar" (ספרה)—"Sephar" is a place name—becomes "the book" (הספר). This letter transposition is relatively straightforward, since in Hebrew the phrases "her name," "the name," and "there" are anagrams, just like "to Sephar" and "book." However, in order to exploit these similarities, one needs some familiarity with Hebrew. Although Rothenberg uses the biblical words in English translation, he is aware of the underlying Hebrew consonant patterns.

The poet also has other sophisticated ways of manipulating gematria. In the previously cited "POST/FACE" he mentions various methods of composing gematria poems. Some of his rules are arbitrary. Rothenberg tells us that the hundred poems in "More Gematrias (1–100)" are generated by "using the gematria as a title & constructing poems of single lines and/or stanzas of two or several lines that fall under or add up to that number." What this means is that we cannot simply postulate that the words/phrase in each line or stanza will have the same number value as the title.

For various reasons, then, it is difficult to monitor the process by which the poems are derived. At first, we need to translate the English phrases back into Hebrew, and that will often give us several Hebrew alternatives and, consequently, various number values to choose from. Second, since Rothenberg may add up the number values of different lines or stanzas to derive a number that equals the title, it is almost impossible to trace back this process. Here is an example:

3
GEMATRIA 105
Man,
the blasphemer.

Man
the bald locust.
("More Gematrias (1–100)," *G*, 101)

If we scrutinize the list of words under the entry for the number 105 in Locks's dictionary, we will find none of the words of this poem. In a second step, we may try to translate some words back into Hebrew, for example "man" is אדם (האדם) or אנוש (האנוש) which have the number value 45 (50 with definite article) or 357 (362 with definite article). If we disregard the second translation, אנוש, because its number value is higher than the number given in the title of the poem, we may subtract 45 (50 with article) from 105 and end up with the number 60 (55 with article). Our hypothesis is now that the elements of each stanza add up to the same number value 105. But the phrases "the blasphemer" and "the bald locust" are not listed by Locks under the entry for the number 60 (or 55). This simple control mechanism then does not work. We are unable to verify how this poem was generated.

This example is instructive in several ways. It demonstrates that even though the poet seems to lay open his compositional procedures, he does not always allow us to watch him at work, particularly not in cases where he "tampers" with chance. We have no way of tracing the exact process by which Rothenberg derives his gematria poems. While the poet can be shown to abide by his constraints strictly in some cases (we are able to "check up" on it), this does not necessarily have to be the case. Despite gematria functioning as a *constraint*, Rothenberg may resort to poetic license. It is, therefore, indicative that the procedural *rule* for the composition of gematria poems is already arbitrary (see above). However, in a way this arbitrary approach parallels the traditional use of gematria; the rabbis devised a large number of gematric rules—one treatise lists seventy-two different rules, which may be handled quite flexibly.[76] To bend the rules is part of the game.

As we saw earlier, new meaning can be created by means of juxtaposition. Juxtaposition may involve a conscious use of space. In his long gematria sequences, Rothenberg explores the semantic possibilities of the page. By filling space semantically, he makes two-fold and three-fold gematrias cohere. The single parts of each set may interact with each other in diverse ways. They may complement or expand each other,

NIGHT (1)	NIGHT (2)
The melons.	& they rolled.

("Fifth Gematria: 'Among,'" *G*, 45)

constitute a kind of parallelism (as in the Psalms),

AMONG (1)	AMONG (2)
Spiritum descended.	Breath trickled down.

("Fifth Gematria: 'Among,'" *G*, 44)

appear completely unrelated (surrealist juxtaposition),

LAUGHTER (1)	LAUGHTER (2)
Their blood into his nostrils.	The window numbered.

("Sixth Gematria: 'Gematria,'" *G*, 53)

or contradict each other,

IN THE MIDST (1)	IN THE MIDST (2)
In the morning.	In the grave.

("Twelfth Gematria: 'Imagination,'" *G*, 90)

Some of the three-fold gematrias visually form a triangle. They often present a kind of "argument" that sometimes can be roughly equaled with thesis (1), antithesis (2) and synthesis (3):

IN A DREAM (1)	IN A DREAM (2)
To pronounce it unclean.	Sweet unto me, dear.

IN A DREAM (3)

It shall be circumcised.

("Third Gematria: 'Lot in Sodom,'" *G*, 32)

But there are also other ways of creating coherence. The following three-fold gematria poem, for instance, "adds up" images allowing the reader to experience its metamorphosis. This text presents a memorable instance of plot-thickening:

20

MOSES (1)

The legs.

MOSES (2)

The hoofs.

MOSES (3)

A bearded
vulture.

[345]

("More Gematrias (1–100)," *G*, 108)

However, the thickening of the plot goes beyond the "micro level" of single, two-fold and three-fold gematrias. For Rothenberg integrates these into larger structures. On the "macro level" (the level of the series or sequence), the poems cohere as well. Sometimes the title of a sequence indicates a theme that is shared by some poems. For instance, "Lot in Sodom" alludes to forbidden sexuality, and many of the sets in this sequence concern this issue.

Alternatively, sets may be connected by rhyme or sound:

GEMATRIA 428

I have sinned
into freedom.

IN SODOM (1)

A garden.
A wall.

IN SODOM (2)

At what time
shall we come?

("First Gematria," *G*, 22–23)

These two sets are linked in several ways: by rhyme (free-*dom*/Sod*om*), by syntactic parallelism (*into* freedom, *in* Sodom), and by semantics. In a simple reading, one may suggest that the walled garden stands for the Garden of Eden, which, however, is felt to be a kind of prison from which humanity got released by "the fall of man." Or else, the phrase "to sin into freedom" may allude to the Shabbatean doctrine, which takes the sexual transgression of the ritual law as a sign of freedom and redemption. Thus, the above verse arrangement cleverly summarizes the Shabbatean credo.

However, the connection between different sections is not always apparent. If we cannot find a way of associating a number of sets, we may read each section as a separate episode, for ultimately, each poem is autonomous. Sometimes, however, the episodes unexpectedly cluster into larger units of meaning as in the next example. To illustrate this, I shall take a closer look at the "Sixth Gematria: 'Gematria,'" which is particularly interesting because the subtitle alludes to the procedure of gematria itself. The first thing to notice is that each set is assigned a letter so that the twenty-two sections make up G/E/M/A/T/R/I/A/G/E/M/A/T/R/I/A/G/E/M/A/T/R. This device emphasizes the special status of this series, which, by the way, occurs in the middle of the cycle (the sixth out of twelve sequences). And, in fact, the sequence begins with a set entitled "gematria:"

GEMATRIA (1)

To spy out.

GEMATRIA (2)

I will bless them. G

GEMATRIA (3)

Shut.

("Sixth Gematria: 'Gematria,'" *G*, 50)

That the term "gematria" can be correlated with the verbal phrase "to spy out" is quite astonishing. For composing and reading gematrias, means spying out for meaning. The second gematria reinforces this idea with the assertion "I will bless them." In other words, we may hope for good results. However, the third gematria is disturbing. The monosyllabic verb "shut" challenges the hope for meaning. It puts an end to exploration. But who decides whether something is "closed" for meaning? God? The poet? The reader?

The continuation of the sequence may give us a clue. There are certain recurring themes: the image of the divine patriarch, and the rebellion against him, and allusions to some kind of fall. The following three sets elaborate the "fall" from an orthodox belief in God:

WE HAVE COME THROUGH
for D. H. Lawrence

From Eden. A
From his bosom.

YOUR FATHER(1)	YOUR FATHER (2)
Bore the loss of it.	In pain. T

FOR A WITNESS (1)	FOR A WITNESS (2)
Heat in the garden.	Unclean R to your mind.

("Sixth Gematria: 'Gematria,'" *G*, 56)

This sequence ends with a reference to uncleanliness. Taking into account the title of this passage—"Gematria," one may suggest that this impurity is actually caused by Rothenberg's subversive use of gematria. For in his hands, gematria becomes an instrument of the fall; it is employed to rebel against God, the father. The three-fold gematria mocks Moses as a "bearded vulture." Other poems question the existence of God, or—from a gnostic standpoint—the existence of a good creator:

WITHOUT GOD

Without terror

("Fourth Gematria: 'In the Shadow,'" *G*, 38)

GOD

is not.

("Ninth Gematria: 'God,'" *G*, 70)

A NUMBER (1)	A NUMBER (2)
Nothing but God.	Our oppression.

("Tenth Gematria: 'Nations,'" *G*, 82)

These are exactly the kind of gematrias the Orthodox publishers of *The Spice of Torah—Gematria* would rather were not revealed. However, Rothenberg brings them into the light to give voice to his own conflicts with Judaism. It is evident that he uses the biblical material and the gematric method for his own purposes. One of his stated intentions is to exploit coincidence:

> Unlike the traditionalists of gematria, I have seen these *coincidences/synchronicities* not as hermeneutic substantiations for religious and ethical doctrines, but as an entry into the kinds of correspondences/constellations that have been central to modernist & "post" modernist poetry experiments over the last century & a half [italics are mine]. ("POST/FACE," *G*, 165)

Thus, the poet directly opposes the Orthodox concept of gematria, which maintains that "[t]he point of such numerical analogies is *not to find coincidental equivalences* between words"[77] [italics are mine]. Opposing this prescription, Rothenberg deliberately dwells on the notion of coincidences. He correlates coincidence with synchronicity and argues that gematria demonstrates the working of coincidence/synchronicity.

Rothenberg's notion of synchronicity goes back to the writings of Carl Gustav Jung, according to whom synchronicity is marked by "spontaneous, meaningful coincidences of so high a degree of improbability as to appear flatly unbelievable."[78] Jung's characterization of synchronicity as an acausal connecting principle perfectly describes gematria. If a "particular pattern has a meaning or a value for the individual who experiences it,"[79] we are dealing with a case of synchronicity. In this view, the reader of a gematria poem encounters synchronicity whenever she succeeds in making sense of the gematric equation. Moreover, Rothenberg relates the notion of synchronicity to the way in which poems explore the space on the page:

> whatever occurs within a space determines the meaning of that space. As a principle of composition ("synchronicity" in Jung's term elsewhere), it forms a common link between such otherwise different modes as chance poetry, collage & montage, automatic writing, "deep" image, projective verse, etc. . . . (Rothenberg, *Poems for the Millennium*, vol. 1, 771)

The poet proposes here that whatever appears on the same page is meaningful. Readers of such poetry habitually assume that what appears in the same space has to be somehow related. This takes us back to our earlier discussion of juxtaposition and spacing. In order to appreciate these strategies, it is essential to assume that there is a connection between the diverse elements on the page. The reader's task, then, is to discover the covert relationships between the words. To find what makes the poem cohere and to name that special link, or to recognize a similarity or analogy, is to solve the riddle.

The final part of Rothenberg's gematria book comprises longer poems, which involve choice to a greater degree. They are inspired by the vocabulary of the Bible, but are not strictly chance/gematria-generated. In contrast to the minimalist gematrias, many of these poems have syntax. On the whole, the "Beyond Gematria" poems are "slightly more traditional."[80] They have the general appearance of free verse rather than of the "constellations" of concrete poetry. This is indicated by regular stanzaic patterns, which is why I call them "stanzaic gematria poems." These poems contain certain motifs and recurring words and phrases that also figure in Rothenberg's "14 Stations." The poet's experiments with gematria culminate in this cycle of Holocaust poems. It takes up many of the themes and leitmotifs touched upon in the "Beyond Gematria" section.

The following biblical words and phrases, for instance, echo the Holocaust cycle: "streaked dainties," "flashing light," "your mistress / conceived," "& those I will kill," "& the fat ones," "She saw streaks & bones," "bright spots / in the grave," "& hooks & jewels," "THIEVES / With solemn manners. / Hooks set in squares."[81] On the one hand, these short phrases testify to Rothenberg's continuing preoccupation with the body and physicality. Allusions to the animalistic side of man are easily extracted from biblical verses about sacrifice (the Torah prescribes animal sacrifice and describes in detail the physical features of the sacrificial animals). On the other hand, the recurring light imagery may be associated with the kabbalah, according to which light was a major factor in the creation of the world. Besides, mystics often describe their spiritual experiences in terms of light and darkness. Flashing lights or "flashing spots" allude to the suddenness of the mystical illumination. Yet, the overwhelming sense of Rothenberg's "Beyond Gematria" poems is one of darkness and threat; they are "darkly evocative, ominously beautiful."[82] Undoubtedly, the Holocaust hovers over these poems:

all over
the night sky,
glowing
as an oven fills with darkness,
the jews inside their cities
lost in sleep

("Gematria Five," *G*, 150)

Thus, the most powerful poems of this last section address the shoah. They carry on themes from *Khurbn* (1986) and further develop subjects that emerge in the minimalist gematrias and the gematria sequences. Once more, the poet draws the picture of a gnostic creator God who oppresses humanity and demands sacrifice. The following poem concludes in the following way[83]:

3
from his youth
she bound him

afterwards
they turned aside
& went

his streams
their vineyards

an apparition
that was at the end

sold in the gutters

"show me"

"I will turn aside"
("KHURBN GEMATRIA [266]," *G*, 156–57)

Significantly, the poem ends with the image of someone turning aside. Who is turning away? God? The poet? Perhaps both. God apparently turns aside from his people's suffering during the Holocaust. As a reaction, the poet turns away from God and comes to reject the notion of divinely inspired meaning.

Though most of Rothenberg's gematria poems are propelled by the search for meaning (for meaningful combinations), there are also alternative ways of utilizing gematria. Gematria may be employed to question the possibility of meaning and our ability to make sense of this world. In "14 Stations" Rothenberg most openly explores this other aspect of gematria.

Conclusion

Rothenberg's amuletic, numerological, and gematric poems constitute a Jewish poetry of letters and numbers. One might even claim that the gematria poems represent a new "Jewish genre," that is, a type of poetry that grows directly out of Jewish tradition. The poet appropriates Jewish letter and number mysticism and adapts it to contemporary poetry; numbers and letters are used to create poetic patterns. These patterns might be overt and visual as in amulet poems and concrete poetry, or covert and numerical as in the numerological and gematric poems. Rothenberg's experimental texts share traits with modern and postmodern poetry (concrete poetry, futurist and dada sound poetry, surrealist poetry, and poetry produced by chance operations). They also illustrate the return of number into poetry.

At the same time, Rothenberg's poems of numbers and letters involve naming in a crucial way and illustrate the poet's belief that naming is a poetic act. Thus, in his poetry naming and name magic take various forms. On the one hand, amulet poems are charm poetry. They are characterized by the "coefficient of weirdness"—aural and visual devices, which Rothenberg exploits poetically. The binding power of amulets is traditionally believed to rest in the mighty and secret names they employ. These magic names can affect the reader in many ways, even if they are not understood semantically. Therefore, Rothenberg employs amulet poems to convey a certain kind of sacred effect. The numerological and gematria poems, on the other hand, demonstrate a different aspect of naming. Functioning as riddles, they bind the reader until she has solved the riddle by naming the solution.

Like riddles, Rothenberg's gematria poems are composed by juxtaposing images or concepts. Gematria functions as a generative device, which provides underlying, hidden patterns, creates coherence, and inspires the poet's imagination. On the background of his knowledge of tribal and surrealist poetry, Rothenberg explores the effect of juxtaposing biblical words and phrases. Reading these juxtapositions is like solving a riddle. The basic assumption thereby is that widely diverse elements that appear in the same space (on the page) are somehow related and that it is possible to specify their relatedness.

There are two ways of accounting for the fact that gematria unexpectedly produces meaningful correspondences. Traditional Judaism explains this phenomenon with reference to God as the source of meaning who empowers the language of the Torah in a particular way. Alternatively, Rothenberg holds that gematria illustrates Jung's concept of synchronicity—it reveals sudden acausal relationships, which nevertheless are meaningful to the reader. Rather than following the exegetic rules of traditional Judaism, Rothenberg utilizes gematria as a method for composing new poems. Many of his gematria poems, in fact, undermine Jewish tradition.

Being fully versed in contemporary avant-garde experimentation, Rothenberg tries to take poetry back to its origins in charms and riddles. The aim is to re-empower language and to create meaning. Such meaning may very well be nondiscursive and preverbal, arbitrary and non-intentional, but it is meaning nevertheless. It affects the reader with its mystery, energy, and poetic spark. Moreover, the magic notion of language, which underlies Rothenberg's fascination with names, presupposes the unity between word and thing, between signifier and signified. The poet asserts that his poetics of the sacred strives to "heal the break between reality and language."

Therefore, Rothenberg conceives a kind of poetry that bases itself on premises that differ from poststructuralist language philosophy and poetry. The enchanting quality of his charm poetry and his poetics of the sacred question the validity of deconstructionist assumptions with regard to poetry. By contrast, Rothenberg does not discount the possibility of some kind of healing and meaning through the language of poetry.

Part II
Reappropriating History

4
Imagining History

Rothenberg's "Jewish Turn"

Rothenberg's reappropriation of Jewish tradition was propelled by what might be called his "Jewish turn." There are various reasons for his interest in his Jewish ancestry. First, the poet recalls that his Jewish poems "were a response to the Viet Nam war":

> a desire violently to disassociate myself from any kind of naive American identification. And at that point, after having denied in some ways the ancestry, I wanted very much to take hold of it, as if what it was that pushed on toward those denials in America no longer made sense.[1]

Where American consent decreases, notions of descent gain new significance.[2] The attack on the melting pot ideology voiced by Nathan Glazer and Daniel Patrick Moynihan in their book *Beyond the Melting Pot* (1963) was followed by the revival of theories of the "power of descent affiliations."[3]

On a personal level, Rothenberg confronted the question of ancestral continuity through the birth of his son. He tells us that his first Poland poems "go back to about '65 or '66. Following the birth of my child, my son—which may have something to do with that. . . . It creates in fact the question of continuities."[4] The issue was raised once more at Matthew Rothenberg's bar mitzvah.

Furthermore, personal encounters, such as Rothenberg's meeting with Celan and his correspondence with Duncan prompted the poet to rethink issues of Jewish identity. In the following remark the poet acknowledges Duncan's formative influence:

> Probably the ancestral poems go back to a few years before 1966. . . . But I think the first indication I had that I should possibly

> be going in that direction was a conversation with Duncan back around 1959 or 60. . . . I think it was in a conversation at that point that he was dropping all sorts of hints to me about the possibility of. . . . That I was giving up too much in ignoring the Jewish identity, which was something that must have been with me in a very deep sense since my first language was Yiddish and not English. . . . Anyway, there was a poem in *White Sun*, a poem about a Leni Riefenstahl movie but really a Jewish poem, which I never thought too much of but Duncan immediately and generously saw what I could do. But I think I pretty much dismissed it at that point as impossibility.[5]

However, a few years later, Rothenberg *did* actually move into the direction indicated by his friend, when his "Jewish turn" came as a reaction to the political situation and his personal circumstances.

One of Rothenberg's first Jewish poems was "Satan in Goray" (1965), an experimental piece dedicated to the eminent Yiddish writer Isaac Bashevis Singer.[6] It employs words from the English translation of Singer's novel *Satan in Goray*, which powerfully evokes the history of Shabbateanism in the story of a Jewish town that comes under the control of Shabbatean demagogues. This intriguing book inspires Rothenberg's first experimental Jewish poem. The poet sets himself the task to compose a pastiche of Gertrude Stein by closely following "the structures of a poem of hers called 'Dates,' while substituting a more heated vocabulary drawn from Singer's novel, *Satan in Goray*" (*RI*, 46). Rothenberg's imitative version has twelve parts, just like Stein's poem. Some passages are perfectly modeled on her text—they contain the same number of words, the same number of syllables, similar sounds, and the same number of verses. The exchange of a few words turns Stein's eighth stanza "Wet yes wet yes wet yes sprinkle. Wet yes wet yes wet yes sprinkle"[7] into "Fat yes fat yes fat yes idol. Fat yes fat yes fat yes idol" (*P*, 8).

By skillfully employing the novelist's vocabulary, Rothenberg retells Singer's tale and invokes the theology of Shabbateanism. "Fat" and "idol" allude to Shabbatean antinomianism; "fat" refers to the ritually forbidden foods the Shabbateans consumed, while the word "idol" hints at Shabbatai Zevi's conversion to a different religion. Rothenberg appropriates Singer's emotive and associative vocabulary to revisit memorable scenes of the novel. His take on the story is humorous. Compare, for instance, Stein's poem to Rothenberg's version:

STEIN	ROTHENBERG
11	11
Pass over.	Pass over.
Pass over.	Pass over.
Pass.	Pass.
Pass.	Pass.
Pass.	Pass. (G. Stein)
	Pass water.
("Dates," *The Yale Gertrude Stein*, 199)	("Satan in Goray," *Poland/1931*, 9)

Rothenberg carries further Stein's word game of splitting the proper noun "Passover," (Jewish festival) into the verb "to pass over." Then he adds another variation—to "pass water." Not only does this phrase allude to the passover story (the passing of the Red Sea), but it also trivializes it through travesty, for "to pass water" has the rather banal meaning of "relieving oneself." Surely, the comical effect of this ambiguous reference is welcome by Rothenberg who comments: "what otherwise would have been a sentimentality emerged as something else."[8] To stress the unsentimental quality of this poem, Rothenberg performed the piece as a sound poem in collaboration with Charlie Morrow:

> In performance it [the first line of the poem, reading "sect"] was repeated at least twenty times, in a myriad [*sic*] of voices, accompanied by a syncopated 4/4 percussion, and transformed into sound poetry or a chant:
>
> Se e e ct t t t
>
> Se e e ck k t t[9]

This experiment also set the tone for many other poems in *Poland/1931*. "Satan in Goray," which utilizes emotional "Yiddish" vocabulary in a nonconventional way, put Rothenberg on a new track. Realizing the possibility of submitting Jewish material to the writing strategies of the avant-garde, he began to compose a variety of "ancestral poems." The second part of this book takes a closer look at some of these poems and explores the way in which the poet utilizes experimentation to evade nostalgia.

Rothenberg's new orientation toward Jewish history and tradition came to the fore during a period in which American-Jewish culture was in a process of change.[10] One response to these events was the emergence of a Jewish counterculture. Both the Jewish counterculture and the poet's personal path exemplify Hansen's law of the "third generation return":

> The Jewish counterculture may therefore be seen as a "third-generation return," which grows out of a particular set of historical circumstances. One of its most basic features is the collective search for meaning through the often explicit and conscious process of "constructing" a Jewish identity.[11]

In the 1970s the construction of Jewish identity took different avenues. Originally the Jewish counterculture had strongly identified with the State of Israel and developed an interest in Israeli culture, but the Yom Kippur War gave rise to critical voices in the movement. While some members of the Jewish counterculture became somewhat disillusioned with Zionism and shifted their focus towards the Diaspora, especially to the plight of Soviet Jewry, others became peace activists.[12] Thus, more attention was given to Eastern Europe. A useful indicator of attitudes among the *havurah* branch of the Jewish counterculture is the journal *Response*. For instance, *Response* 20 reveals the year 1973 as a turning point at which earlier interpretations of Israeli history became problematic.[13]

The growing engagement on behalf of the Soviet Jews was accompanied by a revived interest in Ḥasidism, resulting in the so-called neo-ḥasidic movement. Moreover, this new fascination was reinforced by the growing awareness of the impact of the Holocaust. The murder of a large portion of Eastern European Jewry and the destruction of their *shtetl* culture left the third generation with a feeling of double loss. Many American-Jewish families that originated from Eastern Europe had lost relatives in the Holocaust. But the memory of the *shtetl* had not yet completely faded. Many third-generation Jewish Americans—Rothenberg among them—had vivid memories of their Yiddish-speaking grandparents.

Among the ḥasidic enclaves that had survived the shoah and immigrated to the United States, where they continued to live in segregated communities, were the Lubavitcher Ḥasidim. In contrast to other ḥasidic groups, the Lubavitchers developed a strong missionary activity among Jews, with the goal of "converting" secular Jews back to observance. Within one generation the Lubavitchers established centers across North America, spreading an awareness of ḥasidic culture among contemporary American Jews. Klezmer music, dancing, and the singing of *niggunim* (ḥasidic wordless melodies) attracted the ethnically and spiritually interested third generation.[14]

Moreover, the study of Yiddish language, folklore, and theater found a secular following at universities and Jewish community centers (although the number of people involved in Yiddish Studies should not be overestimated). Yet the more significant generational recrudescence of Yiddish culture only occurred at the end of the 1970s with the formation of the klezmer groups Kapelye and the Klezmer Conservatory band.[15]

The sense of loss, which had motivated the young generation's turn toward the recent past, found emotional redress in imagining the world of the *shtetl*. Buber's *Hassidic Tales* became one of the major triggers of this neo-ḥasidic revival. In addition, Ḥasidism was popularized by Carlebach, the "roving rabbi with a guitar and stories of the Hassidic rabbis,"[16] who used his personal charisma in spreading the word. Of great import was also the revival of the art of storytelling by Wiesel's performance of mystic tales at the 92nd Street "Y" in New York City, "where Elie Wiesel—with disheveled hair, piercing eyes, and an exotic French accent—mesmerized audiences by retelling midrash and hasidic tales."[17] Moreover, Wiesel's Holocaust writings were germinal in furthering the growing recognition of the terrible destruction of the shoah.[18]

Rothenberg and other nonaffiliated and heterodox Jewish poets did not directly participate in this neo-ḥasidic revival in the context of the Jewish community. Nonetheless, the turn toward the diaspora and Yiddish culture is also present in their writing.

Some critics attack neo-Ḥasidism for being inauthentic. Peter E. Gordon contends that neo-Ḥasidism romanticizes the past. It creates a new type of individualized Ḥasidism, which emphasizes universality and "inward spirituality" over communal religiosity, while at the same time rejecting Jewish legalism.[19] Yet others may object that the discourse of "authenticity" does not really touch the core of the problem. Any reappropriation of historical material will necessarily involve selection and distortion and thus confound the "authentic" and the "inauthentic." Therefore, one should rather strive for an aesthetic evaluation of neo-ḥasidic products and develop an understanding of their social and cultural function.[20]

History as Memory and Story

That neo-Ḥasidism resorts to certain aspects of the Jewish past is not incidental. The attempt to construct a Jewish identity invariably leads to the past, for the remembrance of the past is an essential part of Jewish ritual and liturgy. If poetry is to participate in the construction of Jewish identity, it must be concerned with writing "poems including history" (Pound).[21] Hence the final two chapters of this book investigate how Rothenberg develops his own strategies for "including Jewish history" into the poem.

An analysis of this sort requires certain terminological reflections. As Yosef Hayim Yerushalmi points out, "meaning in history, memory of the past and the writing of history are by no means to be equated."[22] It may sound like a truism, but we need to be reminded that historiography and history are two different concepts. Both should be distinguished from the notion of memory.

Yerushalmi insists that the concept of history goes back to the Jews of biblical times. Unlike Herodotus, who is commonly taken to be the "father of history," they were looking for an ultimate and transcendent meaning in history.[23] The bulk of Jewish historiography, on the other hand, only emerged in the modern era, in connection with the *Wissenschaft des Judentums*. It based its investigations of history on purely secular grounds and accepted only immanent causation as an explanation. Yet historiography does not appeal to all Jews: "Many Jews today are in search of a past, but they patently do not want the past that is offered by the historian."[24]

An alternative way of relating to the past is through memory. We may differentiate two types of memory: collective and personal memory.[25] In Judaism, collective memory plays a pivotal role. Not only is the Bible full of injunctions to remember and not to forget, but the rabbis of the postbiblical period gave Jewish memory a more permanent form in ritual and liturgy.[26] However, with the rise of Jewish historiography in modern times a separation occurred between collective memory and historiography. Yerushalmi, therefore, contends that historians cannot "restore" Jewish memory once it is lost, nor can historiography substitute for memory.[27]

It should then come as no surprise that Rothenberg is concerned with memory and myth rather than historiography. The workings of memory involve selectivity and imply constant change, which suits Rothenberg's poetics of change. Moreover, memory is closely linked to the experience of loss. David G. Roskies ascertains that loss is actually the "*precondition* of renewal." This principle, stated with regard to modern Yiddish literature, also applies to contemporary American-Jewish poetry. Roskies insists that history must die first before it can be reused in literature.[28]

Being geographically and culturally displaced, many American Jews, whose families emigrated from Europe, feel the loss of their ancestral roots. Nowadays only a small minority of American Jews grows up with Yiddish as their first language. Poland, which for Rothenberg represents the place of origins, only exists in the memory. What form this memory may take is suggested in the poem "Poland/1931: 'The Fish:'"

POLAND/1931 'The Fish'

the dead fish has no eyes
says my son, poland
has no eyes
& so we live without associations
in the past we live
nourishing incredible polands
lazy & alive remembering
our mothers' pictures in the grass

(*P*, 15)

The poet compares Poland, the old homeland, to a dead fish. The past is "blind" like a dead fish. Perhaps this metaphor also implies a reversal: those who cannot see are the descendents of Eastern European Jewish immigrants. Their children suffer the "death" of Poland. "[I]ncredible polands" and fantastic dreams substitute for it. Rothenberg experiences this separation from the past as a kind of exile and compares it to the situation of Native Americans : "So we aren't as far apart as you might think, because we're all in some way, to some degree, exiled from the *ancestors*. We're all trying to keep a hold on history, to know ourselves in time" (*JR*, 547). The following two chapters, therefore, examine how Rothenberg appropriates the past in response to his double loss: the loss of the ancestral Jewish culture in Poland and the loss of relatives and an entire Jewish world through the Holocaust.

Rothenberg attempts to counteract loss by salvaging something from the past. However, the reappropriation of the past and its traditions always involves "creative betrayal." Roskies suggests that the modern Yiddish writers practice "the art of betrayal" whenever they appropriate traditional Jewish culture selectively.[29] Rothenberg follows in the footsteps of the Yiddish writers, who often disguise their artistic betrayal of tradition in ḥasidic stories, which, on the first sight, appear to be traditional.[30] Because stories can bear a powerful message, Rothenberg illustrates his own approach to loss by relating the following tale:

> The Baal Shem Tov used to go to a certain place in the woods & light a fire & pray when we was faced with an especially difficult task & it was done.
>
> His successor followed his example & went to the same place but said: "The fire we can no longer light, but we can still say the prayer." And what he asked was done too.
>
> Another generation passed, & Rabbi Moshe Leib of Sassov went to the woods & said: "The fire we can no longer light, the prayer we no longer know: all we know is the place in the woods, & that will have to be enough." And it was enough.
>
> In the fourth generation, Rabbi Israel of Rishin stayed at home & said: "The fire we can no longer light, the prayer we no longer know, nor do we know the place. All we can do is tell the story."
>
> And that, too, proved sufficient.
>
> (Cited by Rothenberg, *BJB*, n. pag.)

The mystic fire is lost, and we are left with nothing but stories. Yet at the same time, we are reassured—against despair—that even this "proved sufficient." Despite loss, there is affirmation, for stories give meaning.

Rothenberg introduces his own narrative of the Jewish countertradition, *A Big Jewish Book*, with this tale. Anyone who has read Scholem's *Major Trends* will recall that this same story appears at the end of the study. The scholar of kabbalah closes his book by reflecting on this ḥasidic tale, which he heard from Shmuel Yosef Agnon. He interprets the story as a symbol of the history of Jewish mysticism itself, which underwent formidable transformations. Scholem comments: "You can also say that it [the anecdote] reflects the transformation of all its values, a transformation so profound that in the end all that remained of the mystery was the tale."[31] In the German version of the book, Scholem employs the word "*Geschichte*" to refer to both, "story/tale" and "history" because in German this term comprises both meanings. He thus intimates a connection between history writing and storytelling, that is, he emphasizes the significance of narrative for the writing of history.

Typically, Rothenberg appropriates Scholem's tale without giving us the source. Yet by placing it at the beginning of his anthology (it appears after the preface), he indicates his intention to carry on the story of Jewish tradition, and he is not alone in this endeavor. For, as Scholem correctly foresaw: "The story is not ended, it has not yet become history, and the secret life it holds can break out tomorrow in you or me."[32]

Memory requires the mediation of the imagination. The overall function of the imagination in this process is to "energize" the (re)collected material. Olson envisions history writing as a process in which "energy" is passed on. That is why he demands that scholars—"learned monsters"—pass on the "energy" of a historical text rather than diminish it: "What is worse, they do not know how to pass over to us the energy implicit in any high work of the past because they purposely destroy that energy as dangerous to the states for which they work."[33]

Olson makes this remark in his germinal essay, "The Human Universe," which Rothenberg quotes frequently because it ties in with his overall poetics. Taking up Olson's notion of the poem as a "high energy-construct," Rothenberg proposes that the poem is energized by *poesis*/image-making/mythmaking.[34] In this line of thought, the inclusion of history into the poem can only be successful if it gives off some kind of "energy":

> In that energizing—that first, deceptively simple, act of *poesis*—something strange happens, whether to the world at large or to our sense of it. Remaining here-and-now, the world begins to lure us with a feeling, an intuition, of what the poet Robert Kelly speaks of as the not-here/not-now.[35]

The energy of the poem generates some kind of emotional movement; it pulls us toward something that emerges through the power of the imagination—the memory of the past.

The mythic imagination, however, does not only impinge on

the composition of literature, but also on the interpretation of Jewish history. Yerushalmi emphasizes the fact that for hundreds of centuries Jews have been drawn to a mythic view of history. Most prominent in this context was the Lurianic kabbalah, which provided a convincing explanation of exile:

> Jews were spiritually and psychologically prepared for that which the Lurianic Kabbalah offered them—a mythic interpretation of history that lay beyond history, and that seemed to endow the individual with the power to participate actively in hastening its messianic liquidation.[36]

While this approach to the past indicates a premodern mindset, quite a few contemporary Jews still favor such a mythic model of history over historiography. Rothenberg is one of them. Yet what distinguishes him from medieval people is that he uses myth consciously. The self-consciousness of this act marks postmodern reappropriation.

The Problem of Ahistoricism

Rothenberg does not take "history" at face value. This is demonstrated by a handwritten, visual, concentric poem that precedes "A Book of Histories."[37] In the middle of this image we see a kabbalistic or occult chart in the shape of a flower with petals; the "petals" apparently contain names of God; they are assembled around a ring of Hebrew letters.

Here is the full text of Rothenberg's poem ("transcribed" from the concentric circles):

> a history of the Jews is first a history of subscriptions second a history of coming to the barn last & making a relief of it third a history of unsuited buttons & fourth isn't a history at all but a testament of needless occurrences [pictogram of a hand] in much the same way i asked him to write about it carelessly at first but changing to regret i was in the same position as those unlettered tribes i had no way of keeping it in mind [pictogram of a circle with spikes and a spot in the middle] nineteen thirty one is not a different matter [pictogram of the star of David] i regret the strain it puts on our resources to find ourselves in a place where it puts a strain on our resources [pictogram of person on a globe] but because i escaped first i was thereafter known as henry the first which was indeed to be my name [pictogram of the star of David]

> others were similarly named for occurrences but the order of their resources was less than useful [pictogram of a plus sign] soon they stopped resorting [pictogram] not soon enough [pictogram] not soon enough [pictogram] soon they stopped winning edging weaving learning scoring or resorting [pictogram] i learned each one myself in approximately the same sequence [pictogram] he learned approximately & also in approximately the same sequence [pictogram] this made us practically brothers but we didn't mind [pictogram] this made us approximately those who practically brothers didn't mind [pictogram] approximately this practically didn't mind that brothers didn't mind [pictogram] i told him first to make a suitable history of the jews second to be in sequence third to be always resourceful & fourth not at all [pictogram] he was remiss on only one of the aforementioned points but soon thereafter the plan was scuttled [pictogram]
>
> (*P*, n. pag.)

This text is more than a decorative riddle. For this strange poem addresses pressing questions about history and history writing. Most importantly, it asks how to define "a history of the Jews" and how to write it. Immediately, we are struck by an overwhelming sense of irony. The text pokes fun at any reader who seriously tries to make sense of the circular writing: "i regret the strain it puts on our resources to find ourselves in a places where it puts a strain on our resources"—which is quite untrue. The author has no regrets because he chose this mandala-like form for a good reason. It represents a cyclical notion of history and thematizes the repetitiveness of history. The repetitions take on Steinesque forms: "this made us practically brothers but we didn't mind . . . this made us approximately those who practically brothers didn't mind . . . approximately this practically didn't mind that brothers didn't mind."[38] This device successfully confuses the reader; our eyes lose the lines and the train of thought we were trying to follow: "i regret the strain it puts on our resources to find ourselves in a places where it puts a strain on our resources." Ironically, the reader then resembles "those unlettered tribes" and the writer of this poem, who employ pictograms because we have "no way of keeping it in mind."

Evidently, of course, this poem is a parody that disparages the certainties of historiography. Alternatively, the poem portrays Jewish history as some sort of a joke in suggesting that it is "a history of coming to the barn last & making a relief of it third a history of unsuited buttons." Indeed, this travesty questions the existence of "Jewish history" altogether—or history in general for that matter—by flatly denying it: "it isn't a history at all." Yet despite these negations, the speaker/writer of this "anti-history" cannot help writing "a history of the Jews," which is an amusing self-contradiction.

Eventually, he tells us how to write a history of the Jews[39]: "make a suitable history of the jews," "be in sequence," "be always resourceful," and [be] "not at all." These vague and capricious instructions leave us with more questions than answers. What is "suitable"? Does "sequence" imply linearity, that is, a chronological view of history? Why should a historian of the history of the Jews be "resourceful" and in what way? And, of course, the fourth recommendation undercuts anything said previously. For its syntactic referents are indeterminate. We may derive a number of sentences that contradict each other, such as "be always resourceful," and "not at all"; or "to make a suitable history of the Jews," and "not at all," which may mean "make something not at all suitable," or "make no history at all." This is an inconclusive combinatory game.

These various devices indicate a deconstructive act. Although Rothenberg generally keeps at a distance from deconstruction, in this particular instance he acts as a deconstructor. He questions several basic principles of historiography, such as linearity ("sequence"), thematic coherence ("a suitable history"), and the appropriate use of sources, which is replaced by "resourcefulness" ("be always resourceful"). As an alternative to historiography, the poet brings to bear his own *postlogical* stance by making ample use of contradiction.

"A Book of Histories," which follows the introductory poem, is arranged according to such a postlogical order. To find coherence among various pieces of this compilation of quotations is extremely difficult. Even the fact that the book consists of seven sections (and seven is a sacred and symbolical number) is misleading. The divisions of the sections of the book are arbitrary nevertheless.

Bits and pieces from a variety of Jewish sources are jumbled together: quotations from the Talmud, novels, mystical books, history books, cookbooks, books on Jewish magic and superstition, etc. Hence, some critics describe "A Book of Histories" as collage.[40] Yet, it is almost impossible to find *any* common denominator between the different fragments in "A Book of Histories." Instead there is a rag bag that includes texts about mysticism, food, clothing, recipes, narratives pieces from Yiddish novels, descriptions of ḥasidic life, magic prescriptions, and Jewish laws and customs, among others. The different fragments of each "book" do not constitute one single narrative. This way history becomes a series of stories. Or else, one may compare the fragmented narratives to the scenes of a film as Sherman Paul notes: "These collages are filmic, and in many instances the verbal record could be read aloud and accompanied by images projected on a screen."[41]

Mention should be made that this "book" had a predecessor called "The Materials," which, to be precise, is no book at all, but a collection of cards.[42] Rothenberg recalls: "the *histories* were larger chunks left over from the note-taking that was a part of my research for *Poland/1931*."[43] Before eventually including these fragments in *Poland/1931*, Rothenberg experimented with their performance. In the early 1970s, he randomly shuffled the cards and read out the quotations on the cards, "assisted by folk singer, klezmer band, taped sound collage, clips from Chaplin's IMMIGRANT, slides of old photos & posed stills like those in Esther K."[44]

That the fragments of "A Book of Histories" were originally used in an aleatory way further emphasizes the fact that any sense of overall unity in this "book" is indeed constructed. On the one hand, there is the arbitrariness of history writing, on the other, the unquenchable human need to turn the arbitrary events into a story in order to extract *some* kind of meaning from the past. This persistent search for meaning opens the doors for a mythical reading of history.

In his dialogue with Rothenberg, Spanos focuses on the contrast between myth and historicity and criticizes the poet's

> tendency to minimize man's historicity. On both the cultural level of literary history, what you say seems to me—I may be exaggerating—to emphasize universals, organic, to be sure, but universals nonetheless—inclusive/timeless paradigms or models (myths)—at the expense of historical differentiation. Historicity loses its priority to form, tends to get absorbed . . . into a timeless structural whole in which change is, in fact, extension from a fixed and stable center.[45]

Rothenberg is censured for his preference of timeless, mythical paradigms and the neglect of historical differentiation. But as a poet, he thinks naturally in terms of similarity rather than difference. Therefore, his approach to history also centers on universals. According to Spanos, this perspective involves a cyclical, ahistorical notion of time, and Rothenberg's poetics of collage feeds on it:

> I'm uneasy about the accompanying commitment to a poetry of collage that is insistently committed to a synchronic sense of time, which to me implies a desire to abolish history or at any rate the consciousness of man's historicity.[46]

As we shall see in the following chapter, collage and assemblage play a prominent role in the poet's reappropriation of the past. For Rothenberg, collage is a strategy that allows him to bring the past into the present, while at the same time producing a sense of simultaneousness:

> So, I see the process in time as non-linear & multichronic (including but not dominated by dream-time), though synchronic & simultaneous in consciousness: i.e., the mind bringing together a large number of elements from culturally & spatially separated chronologies. . . . The idea has been to intensify our present consciousness—our sense of past & future not as distant & ourselves as alienated, but as open to our immediate & useful apprehension. (*JR*, 538)

The poet rejects a strictly linear view of history—the perspective of historiography—because it seems limiting. He contends that the purpose of assimilating the past to the present is "to intensify our present consciousness." And such intensification, one may add, counterbalances the sense of loss arising from displacement.

However, Rothenberg's alleged love of circularity is not prevalent in all of his writing. In a deconstructive reading, Garber demonstrates how the poet's praxis undermines his poetics. The observation is apt that Rothenberg's storytelling in itself implies a certain linearity.[47] Moreover, the notion of a suppressed Jewish countertradition and counterhistory presupposes linearity. Therefore, on the one hand, I agree with Garber who correctly claims that "Rothenberg reads the history of the Jews as markedly linear and continuous."[48] On the other hand, however, Spanos is right in drawing attention to the concepts that are implied by Rothenberg's poetics of collage. Apparently, the two critics focus on different aspects of the poet's work. Both perspectives are conducive to my own analysis, which investigates Rothenberg's storytelling as much as his collages. Indeed, his collages tell stories.

Since some of these stories draw on Jewish myths, this takes us back to Yerushalmi's argument about the ahistoricity of a mythical interpretation of history. Apparently Rothenberg's interest in myth is motivated by contemporary needs, in particular the need for meaning. As Yerushalmi observes, this perspective can be very attractive:

> Of course there is something compelling about that large portion of the rabbinic universe in which ordinary barriers of time can be ignored and all the ages placed in an ever-fluid dialogue with one another.[49]

In fact, this view is so compelling that modern and postmodern poets return to it. One of Rothenberg's favorite quotations by Pound asserts that "all times are contemporaneous in the mind." Sometimes the poet leaves out the modification "in the mind" with the purpose of making the statement even more general.[50] For the idea that "all times are contemporaneous" is fundamental to the concept of collage. Curiously enough, this contemporaneous sense of time does not only appeal to parts of the avant-garde, but also to Jewish traditionalists. Yerushalmi comments: "Jews who are still within the enchanted circle of tradition, or those who have returned to it, find the work of the historian irrelevant. They seek, not the historicity of the past, but its eternal contemporaneity."[51]

One could argue with Yerushalmi that, from a modern point of view, much rabbinic thought has to be deemed ahistorical.[52] Nevertheless, this way of thinking constitutes a significant Jewish tradition, and it is Rothenberg who reappropriates this rabbinical tradition. For a better appreciation of this approach, we may consider Ivan G. Marcus's hypothesis that postmodernism really represents some kind of neomedievalism: "some features that modernists claim ended with modern times have reemerged, albeit in a transformed way."[53] While Marcus's analysis is concerned with political factors, I would argue that some of Rothenberg's postmodern, appropriative strategies actually resemble certain medieval writing practices. Palimpsests, commentaries and glosses (notes), imitation practices (pastiche), forgery and apocryphal writing, plagiarizing (theft) as well as the "misquotation of sources, substitution of intuition for available evidence, misrepresentation of presented material"[54]—they all are medieval strategies. Like a medieval writer, Rothenberg tinkers with his sources.

A distinctive difference according to Marcus, however, between the medieval and the postmodern (neomedieval) approach pertains to the consciousness involved in the use of appropriative strategies:

> Postmoderns or Neo-Medievals are conscious of being moderns in search of a more meaningful way of life. Neo-Medievalism, in other words, reflects not only an affinity for tradition but also discontent with being modern.[55]

Likewise, the use of Jewish myths in the interpretation of the past results from a conscious choice. Members of the Jewish counterculture, for example, rabbi Arthur Green, actively strove for the "re-mythologization" of life with the goal of "re-entering the world of myth, in which the constant confrontation with sacred Presence is of the very fabric of daily existence."[56] Rothenberg's Poland poems involve such remythologization. In the Esther K. narrative, for instance, secular history is overlaid with myth—a young Jewish woman becomes identified with the Shekhinah in exile. Rothenberg draws on mythic images because they affect him in a special way.[57]

Consequently, the poet employs the kabbalistic myths of exile and return, separation and reunification. Yet unlike the mythic interpretations of exile ventured by the Lurianic kabbalah, Rothenberg's mythology does not constitute a new belief system. Nor is it singular. For in a postmodern age, many interpretations of history compete with each other. But this is a situation that the poet embraces by combining various mythologies—"Jewish, Indian, experimental."[58] As a result, the Shekhinah and the trickster, Esther K. and Leo Levy, cross paths and meet. In spite of the comical aspects of this unlikely encounter, Rothenberg's *poesis* contributes to the contemporary interpretation of the Jewish past. By employing stories and myths in order to recapture the past, the poet tentatively creates meaning.

5
Poland/1931: Evading Nostalgia

History Enters the Poem as Memory: Ancestral Poetry

how could I
bring them to life for you
except the poems pictures
I began around
their deaths your life
fathers mothers grandmothers
set there as titles
ancestors the imagination made
the shades all poetry
recalls back to Ulysses in the pit
voice of David out of Sheol
orphic Jew my master
de profundis

(Rothenberg, "B·R·M·Tz·V·H," *VB*, 33–34)

As we saw earlier, for Rothenberg writing Jewish poetry means writing ancestral poetry. This enterprise is intimately tied up with memory and the imagination ("ancestors the imagination made"). The recovery of the poet's ancestral past takes shape in *Poland/1931*. The book summons images of the past; photographs and other tokens of memory inspire "the poems pictures," which are dedicated to the poet's ancestors—"The Mothers," "The Grandmothers," "The Fathers," "The Brothers." That is why an early version of *Poland/1931* contains two reproductions of old photographs: one of three young men posing, and another of several girls lying on the grass.[1] "[R]emembering / our mothers' pictures in the grass" (*P*, 15), Rothenberg imagines what kind of conversation his mother might have had as a teenager: "together we sat / together we told the bushes the names of our loves" (*P*, 13).

Memory relies on the imagination. Finding your ancestors entails a creative process. Since the ancestral past is not simply *found* but *made,* Duncan and Rothenberg construct their poetic predecessors. Acknowledging that the past "is also something we discover and create,"[2] Rothenberg invents Jewish mothers, fathers, and grandparents.

The project of writing an ancestral poetry could be understood in terms of ethnicity or "ethnic poetry." Rothenberg, however, clearly distances himself from such a perspective. He insists that *Poland/1931* is not about an ethnic quest: "I play off against it [ethnic poetry] or pretend to it in *Poland/1931,* but I don't think that such an ethnic self-investigation is what the work is about for me" (*RI*, 20). This statement indicates "Rothenberg's complex Jewish refusals and identities."[3] For on the one hand, the poet admits that his Jewish work helped him to get "the big genetic one out of my system,"[4] which implies the relevance of questions of ethnic identity. On the other hand, Rothenberg's perspective on issues of Jewish identity is antiessentialist.[5] Hence, a sense of irony and playfulness pervades the book. Rothenberg proposes that "*Poland/1931*, was unmistakably Jewish; but ironic also, since it accepted (on the surface) a degree of chauvinism & sentimentality I would otherwise deny."[6]

Thus, in *Poland/1931*, the poet performs a difficult balancing act: he strives to write an ancestral poetry of memory ("writing their mothers' names in light"), while at the same time trying to avoid nostalgia. Frederik Jameson argues that we postmoderns have lost a sense of history, which we can only claim back indirectly by creating objects that resemble in their make-up the objects of the past that brought about certain feelings.[7] A collection of ancestral poetry could easily become such an object. As an object of "symbolic ethnicity" such a book would be, according to Gans,

> characterized by a nostalgic allegiance to the culture of the immigrant generation, or that of the old country; a love for and a pride in a tradition that can be felt without having to be incorporated into everyday behavior. The feelings can be directed at a generalized tradition, or at specific ones.[8]

In this context, the word "feelings" is significant. For as Gans rightly remarks, nostalgia for the old country/history has the function of supporting a *feeling* of identity.[9] Rothenberg intentionally evokes the nostalgic potential of ethnic art and writing. It produces the *feeling* of sentimentality or nostalgia. Yet any such easy emotional response is undermined by Rothenberg's subversive strategies. Whenever the poet creates an ethnic feeling of Jewish identity, he also immediately subverts it by playing with the symbols and images of nostalgia. The objects of nostalgia are displaced, transformed, and transvalued.

For instance, Rothenberg pastes a photograph of his mother into a photomontage and thus transforms her into "MME. Shekinah," "Mrs. L. L. nee E.K.," who advertises her services as a "Jewish Soul Healer & Adviser: Removes Evil Spirits and Bad Luck from your home // What your eyes will see Your heart will believe" (*P*, 82). The "pre-text" for the photomontage is an actual pamphlet of a psychic reader, which Rothenberg modifies slightly.[10] Attentive readers will associate the clairvoyant with Esther K., who featuresfeatures in the subsequent narrative. Esther's telephone number is given as "Tef. Poland 0-1931." This humorous device marks the parody, which "of course, is very much a part of Rothenberg's stock-in-trade."[11] By displacing dearly cherished and nostalgic images (Shekhinah and mother), the poet employs parody in order to undermine nostalgia.

It is hilarious how Rothenberg parodies Jewish folksongs in "The Seven Melodies of Esther K." (*P*, 94–96). In a performance with the Klezmatics, the poet actually sang one of these melodies in a sentimental voice accentuating its burlesque character.[12] The comic provocation of this song arises from its bizarre juxtapositions and crude imagery:

Variation on a Jewish Love Song
(The Sixth Melody of Esther K.)

In love with a gypsy
how beautiful
my days are my feet
begin in Vilna
& carry me to Havana.
He rubs my pudenda
& stuffs it with his frankfurter.
I will follow his motorcycle
up the Great Wall of China.

(*P*, 96)

What is striking about this poem other than its obscene imagery is that it alludes to a historical reality: just before World War II, there really was an immigration of Jews from Vilna to Havana.[13]

A similar antinostalgic effect is achieved by the presence of comical and grotesque elements in poems such as "Cokboy," where Baal Shem becomes "the veritable CO[C]KBOY, creator god, say, like Atum, and asserts his patriarchal authority by shows of sexual prowess taken directly from the accounts of Coyote, the trickster."[14] As Rothenberg remarks, comic displacement portrays the "Baal Shem at the end of *Poland/1931* as a kind of cowboy (which he pronounces cock-boy) and the locals, because he's got a shtreimel on (the big hat that the Hasidic Jews wear), figure he's from Mexico, and so on."[15]

Of course, such scenes are very funny. Like many other Poland poems, the explicit sexuality of the text affirms physicality and sensuousness. Striving for the recovery of the repressed, Rothenberg portrays many of the Jewish characters in *Poland/1931* as sensuous and lustful; there are "pictures in it / of rabbis with hardons unheard of" (*P*, 114). Other poems actively seek defilement. Defilement in Rothenberg's ancestral poems involves the transgression of ritual and sexual taboos as well as the treatment of certain taboo subjects. The poem "Murder Sutra, Inc." (*P*, 114–16) conjures up the names and biographies of Jewish gangsters involved in Murder Inc., "Lepke Gurrah 'Dutch Schultz' / Rothstein Lansky Siegel" (*P*, 115). Rothenberg addresses a taboo, and some may criticize him for inviting anti-Semitism. Yet the poet accepts this risk for the sake of his overall goal to salvage a repressed Jewish world. All this said, Rothenberg does not present the crimes approvingly, but lays open their horror: "the flesh / retreats from these as other / killers Jews" (*P*, 116).

These "tough" poems illustrate Rothenberg's struggle to evade sentimentality. This is also apparent in a letter to Schwartz. The latter asks Rothenberg for the permission to include four Poland poems in his Jewish anthology. Yet Rothenberg is uncomfortable with this choice for the following reasons[16]:

> the three short poems . . . are misleading anecdotal & out of context, can easily be sentimentalized as genre pieces, re-countings, etc. I would certainly have preferred one longer poem, where I really take off on my own, to the 3-poem combination . . .—viz.,

one of the longer "testimonies," or the Murder Inc. Sutra or others from the Esther K. section, or even the opening "Wedding" poem but not all by itself, etc. I'm probably a little wary of Jewish anthologies as muddling the issue of my poetry by juxtaposing with too much of the nostalgic stuff that's now running rampant.[17]

Evidently, the poet is anxious not to be mistaken for a sentimental writer. Nostalgia is not a viable option for Rothenberg, who always approaches the past by trying to relate it to the present. Equally, the present leads him to the reappropriation of the past. This makes the use of collage and assemblage very appealing.

Collage by definition always involves "the juxtaposition of disparate materials without commitment to explicit syntactical relations between elements and without a consistent authorial voice as ordering principle."[18] The author may blend material from diverse historical periods and cultures, a practice that goes back to the modernists.

Many critics characterize *Poland/1931* as a collage. However, I would rather describe the design of the book in terms of assemblage. *Poland/1931* is built up out of a number of interrelated sections, some of which were also published separately: in the Unicorn editions of *Poland/1931*, *Polish Anecdotes*, *Esther K. Comes to America, 1931*, or in *A Book of Testimony* (Tree Books).[19] The poet himself suggests that *Poland/1931* has "the nature of assemblage as it works itself out both in the book as a whole & in the separate sections."[20]

According to William S. Seitz, the term "assemblage" was originally used by Jean Dubuffet to describe "all forms of composite art and modes of juxtaposition"; it denotes "'the fitting together of parts and pieces,' and can apply to both flat and three-dimensional forms."[21] Likewise, Rothenberg assembled and appropriated various memorabilia for the composition of *Poland/1931*. The poet recalls that the inspiration for the book goes back to an earlier project, the making of

> a kind of Poland box, an ancestral box of poems and pictures, pieces of cloth and amulets and little bits of grain and stones: like a bigger version of the first Unicorn edition. (The pictures in the book are a gesture in that direction—and some day I would want to fill them out.)[22]

Around the same time (1969–1970), Rothenberg's friend, the artist Eleanor Antin, was experimenting with a similar idea.

She created "movie boxes" resembling "glass-and-aluminum display cases of still photos commonly used in movie theater lobbies at that time to advertise coming attractions."[23] Although Rothenberg's "Poland box" did not materialize, the concept of assembling and arranging material came to inform the book.

Some critics wish to stress the fragmentary quality of *Poland/1931*, while others emphasize the coherence of the book. Garber, whom I cited earlier, proposes that *Poland/1931* has a linear narrative, which starts off in Eastern Europe and ends in America with Cokboy visiting a Native American reservation.[24] Others go even further in suggesting that the book "traces a specific autobiographic journey."[25]

Surely, the notion of the book marking a journey or a quest is appealing because it can be easily connected with issues of Jewish identity and "the search for a usable past" (Roskies). Nevertheless, I prefer to imagine this journey in a circular way with the poems, stories, and images "circling" around the date 1931, the year of the poet's birth. Several poems evoke life around that time in different places: "The Wedding" (Poland), "The Fish" (Kansas, where Jewish immigrants open up stores), "A Gallery of Jews" (Poland and America), "The Paradise of Labor" (in an American city), etc. This circular model corresponds to Rothenberg's general notion of history and eschews oversimplification. Certainly the various texts and images in the book point in many different directions and connect in many different ways. A linear reading is too limiting and it ignores Rothenberg's predisposition to create "whole networks of connections" (*JR*, 527)—just like in his anthologies. Therefore, I will analyze the overall structure of *Poland/1931* in terms of "assemblage," while I regard the individual pieces in this collection as "collages."

In this book, I have commented several times on Rothenberg's preference for collage. We saw that Rothenberg utilizes surrealist collage principles in many of his experiments with juxtaposition. He exploits what André Breton calls the "the fortuitous encounter upon a non-suitable plane of two mutually distant realities."[26] But the poet also composes collages in which the diverse material is perfectly fused ("seamless web") and that have a visionary effect. These collages can be described as "synthetic" or "organic." And such homogeneity is in fact intentional as Rothenberg tells us:

the poem has brought together, fused, the diffuse input in a single structure. I don't know if that "works"—I certainly have to keep the process going—but I hope the breaks aren't too visible: that the collage, as it develops, doesn't keep the fragments separate but joins them, makes a "good tight fit." Or to paraphrase what a hasidic rabbi said of prayer: POETRY IS COPULATION WITH THE SHEKINAH. (*JR*, 546)

Thus, different historical time periods are brought onto the same plane and synthesized into one piece. Collage functions as a kind of "memory space."[27] Autobiographical material provides the poem with "concrete particulars" and Luminous Detail (Pound). The poet pays much attention to concrete particulars, whenever he tries to include history into the poem.[28] Just like Pound, Rothenberg takes great care to be specific. As a result, his poems overflow with Luminous Detail. In a letter to Kelly, Rothenberg divulges his concern with the specifics of Jewish history and culture:

It is without question the direction of my own thought & work—toward that final synthesis—but I'm also increasingly aware, as you must be also, that any such synthesizing should rest on a base of accumulated particulars & shouldn't dismiss, without first probing, the experience of those who emerge directly from it, growing up *per accidens* in a milieu that makes one *that* without a choice about it. The culture thing, like someone else's topos, has long struck me in that sense, & I feel it, though as part of a dialectic, in a way no less strong than Olson on the question of history as a new localism, etc. However that is, I don't want to evade it, not at once or not again (as earlier we all did) by a quick (& too welcome) escape from the burden which it also carries.[29]

According to Rothenberg, a larger synthesis of Jewish culture and history rests on "accumulated particulars." Yet the poet implies that these particulars are not just arbitrarily selected, but somehow given to Jews through their ancestry. At the same time, he insinuates that generally you do not choose to be Jewish, but are born Jewish ("the experience of those who emerge directly from it, growing up *per accidens* in a milieu that makes one *that* without a choice about it"). Hence the cultural specifics of the world of his ancestors have to be included into the poem.

Rothenberg views these historical, cultural, and biographical particulars as a kind of burden. What makes them a burden? Is the knowledge of the past a burden? Is acquiring that knowledge a burden? Or else, does the poet refer to thematic or formal limitations placed on him by tradition? Certainly, the writing of ancestral poetry requires much knowledge and attention on the poet's side. He acknowledges that the task of assembling and including concrete particulars into poetry is demanding.

His approach can best be observed in the poem "Portrait of a Jew Old Country Style." The text has three parts. At first, I will take a look at the second section. It is written in a straight column and a prosy style and contains details from Rothenberg's own family history. All the information is autobiographical:

> my grandfather the baker son of bakers
> YOSEL DOVID ben SHMIEL
> who was a hasid at the court in Rizhyn
> came to U.S.A. circa 1913
> but found the country godless
> tho he worked in leather
> shoes were the craft all our friends
> got into first
> like his brother-in-law we called
> THE UNCLE
> I remember in a basement shop
> somewhere "downtown"
> bent over shoes he stitched
> how many years would pass
> till nineteen-fifty maybe
> when I saw him last
> his lungs gone in east bronx tenement
> . . . .
> my grandfather had died
> in nineteen-twenty
> on the night my parents
> ran to warsaw
> to get married my father
> left for the U.S.A. the next day
> no one told him of his father's death
> he would never be a talmudist
> would go from shoes
> to insurance
> from insurance back to shoes
> later an entrepreneur & bust

(*P*, 117–18)

The specificity of this passage is remarkable. We are given very exact information, for example names ("YOSEL DOVID ben SHMIEL"), dates (1913, 1950, 1920), and place names (Rizhyn, U.S.A., "downtown," an East Bronx tenement, Warsaw). Mentioning names, dates, and places gives substance to the past and fleshes out the abstract skeleton of history with autobiographical detail. Moreover, we get an insight into the life stories of several men of the Rothenberg family—the grandfather, the uncle, the father. The above passage sketches the character of each, before they are blended into one mythic "portrait of a Jew old country style." The conflation of autobiographical material with archetypal elements becomes transparent toward the end of the above passage:

"jews don't wear beards"
(she said) no
not in golden U.S.A.
the old man had fled from
to his Polish death

(*P*, 118)

The speaker remembers his religious grandmother scolding him for wearing a beard like a religious Jew, which is an irony in itself. But who is "the old man" fleeing from America? The reference is not entirely clear. Does it allude to the poet's grandfather (father's father), who returned to Poland after the failed attempt to settle in America?[30] Or does it perhaps invoke *any* old (Jewish) man, thereby implying a universal perspective? Both interpretations are possible. For this particular way of intermingling the autobiographical and the fictive is characteristic of many of Rothenberg's poems, in which he intends to bring "concrete particulars" to a more general level.

The poet, who has never seen a photograph of his paternal grandfather, imaginatively takes advantage of this situation.[31] On the backdrop of the assembled fragments of the life story of his grandfather and other male members of his family, Rothenberg draws a "portrait of a Jew old country style." Yet this portrait is radically unsentimental:

visitor to warsaw
        old man with open fly
    flesh girls could suck
            mothers would die to catch sight of

sometimes would pass your door
            his song was
      a generation is a day, time floweth

. . . .

he tells them
      all we touch is love
      & feeds us
this is a portrait of a jew old country style
the gentile will fail to understand
the jew come on better days will run from it
how real
the grandfathers become

(*P*, 117)

This first part of the poem tears down the ancestor's halo. Fighting nostalgia for the "old country" and its "old people," Rothenberg sketches out the picture of a lecherous old man who has sway over women. We may speculate on the reasons for his allure: perhaps he is rich with "money . . . pinned to caftan" (*P*, 117), or far-traveled and exotic ("visitor to warsaw"), or he simply has the mentality of a seducer ("love brings him to the words he needs" [*P*, 117]). If this is the portrait of a Jew, it is not the most flattering: "the jew come on better days will run from it / how real / the grandfathers become." By using the plural, "Rothenberg avoids the trace of autobiography by introducing us to composites, to plural prototypes."[32] Hence *Poland/1931* contains a number of poems about Jewish archetypes, such as "The Mothers," "The Grandmothers," The Fathers" and "The Brothers":

> the poet dramatizes the lives of mothers, grandmothers, fathers, brothers, among others. Instead of using the monologue form, Rothenberg tells the stories of these people from a point of view that shifts between the third and first person, and he creates a unique mixture of racy narrative details, nonstop rhythms, and elusive syntax. The one thing that distinguishes these characters, besides the fact that they are so energetic, so reeking with sensuality, they seem bigger than life. Even the grandmothers dance on tables and are obsessed with their bodies.[33]

Autobiographical information then is used to construct archetypal Jewish ancestors. The significance of this approach lies in the fact that memory works in a similar way: the imagination transforms recollections (autobiographical material, etc.) into an image; and it is this image that Rothenberg evokes in his poems. In the process specific people or historical personages are turned into mythic or legendary types. Paradoxically then, autobiographical elements are used for non-autobiographical purposes. Thus, Rothenberg utilizes autobiographical information, while he openly denies autobiography, as in the last verses of "Portrait of a Jew Old Country Style":

> for which reason I deny autobiography
> or that the life of a man
> matters more or less
>   "We are all one man"
>   Cezanne said
> I count the failures of these jews
> as proof of their election
> they are divine because they all die
>   screaming
>   like the first
>   universal jew
>   the gentiles
>   will tell you had some special deal
>
> (*P*, 119)

The third part of the poem is marked by a different style, "an unpunctuated, uncapitalized free verse of great syntactic liberty and fluidity that conveys the interpenetrations of many levels of experience."[34] The lineation imitates the movement of Hebrew from the right margin of the page to the left producing "a kind of reverse version of Williams's stepped verse—moving from right to left, like Hebrew."[35] Most importantly, however, this passage switches from the earlier "autobiographical mode"[36] (second part of the poem) to something else, perhaps a kind of "universal mode" (third part of the poem), when the speaker of the poem announces the denial of autobiography. Rothenberg shares this point of view:

> and I think simply that there are other things in the world that are more interesting than my personal, psychological development. . . . I find such things as the history of a people, for example, more interesting than most personal histories.[37]

In other words, he rejects the notion of poetry as autobiography, since it restricts the poet's use of material:

> I don't think poetry *is* autobiography. Poetry may be autobiographical, but to say that a poet must be restricted to things out of

> his personal experience, things from his psyche in the trivial "confessional" sense, seems to me to put limits on poetry, put limits on any writer or artist.[38]

The poet does not accept such limits. As we shall see, he draws his material from a great number of sources; autobiography and his personal family history are only one element of this. Rothenberg radically affirms universalism: "the life of a man / matters more or less / 'We are all one man'" (*P*, 119). But who is the "one man" Cezanne mentions? The poem associates him with "the first / universal jew." This contradiction in terms assumes the particular to be universal. But this paradox ties in with Rothenberg's postlogical approach. Simple categories are broken down. As in much contemporary writing, autobiography and fiction can no longer be neatly separated.

To sum it up then, the use of concrete particulars has several functions: First, autobiographical Luminous Details stimulate the reader's curiosity. Second, the specificity of the material makes the poem interesting and reveals the particularity of the Jewish culture and history. Third, since this autobiographical material is lifted from Rothenberg's own ancestral history, it allows the poet to create a substantial link with the past.

These observations also hold true for other aspects of *Poland/1931*. Its texts and images explore the interplay between autobiography and prototype, between personal memories and general notions of the past. The Unicorn edition of *Poland/1931*, for instance, contains the reproduction of a map of Ostrow-Mazowiecka, the town where Rothenberg's parents first met each other.[39] Its Yiddish annotations designate different places in the *shtetl*, such as "*der magistrat*," "*di algemayne shul*," "*alter bet hamidrash*," "*nayer bet hamidrash*," "*di yeshiwe*," "*di gimnazje*."[40] Yet the poet withholds a gloss or commentary. We are therefore inclined to take the sketch to be representative of any *shtetl* in Eastern Europe.

Since all the photographs in the Unicorn version are untitled, the people in them remain anonymous to the general reader. Only the author and his "initiates" know that these pictures are drawn from Rothenberg's family archives and portray his father and mother in diverse groupings. Because of these photographs, the Unicorn edition has a special value for him. The poet writes to his publisher:

> Certainly I don't expect any subsequent version of *Poland/31* [*sic*] to match the impact & very special quality of this one. I feel it very

> deeply as an extension of myself: rather a reconnection with a past I've had to struggle to get a grasp of, even if only in the mind. For this the basic design you offer goes far toward enhancing that reality, & I remain ever thankful for it.[41]

This particular edition is meaningful to the poet because it provides a space for memory. Since he cares about the layout of the book, he inists "that photos should be printed on mat surface, as truer to the originals & the period, etc."[42] Rothenberg strives for verisimilitude to facilitate memory. The appearance of authenticity reinvokes the past. Hence, the poet appropriates visual and written material from his family's memorial book (*Yizkor* book). Many such books about former Polish towns were around at that time:[43]

> Yizkor books were written after the Holocaust as memorials to Jewish communities destroyed in the Holocaust. They were usually put together by survivors from those communities and contain descriptions and histories of the shtetl, biographies of prominent people, lists of people who perished, etc. They are often embellished with photos, maps, and other memorabilia.[44]

By integrating some of these elements into *Poland/1931* in a number of different ways, Rothenberg attempts to create his own memorial book. The New Directions edition of *Poland/ 1931* contains other illustrations. Among the family items is a black-and-white postcard of a young woman with a slight smirk on her face (*P*, 100). This is Rothenberg's mother, Esther. The card includes a loving note in Yiddish from the poet's mother to her husband, who had already gone to America, while she stayed in Europe.[45] Yet while Yiddish readers are able to decipher the message, others may feel distanced by the foreign language and script. The same effect is produced by a nostalgic postcard with imperial emblems and Russian and Yiddish writing. This piece is

> from the back of an old postcard carrying a family photograph on the front, but the writing is a Yiddish translation of the opening lines of "Poland/1931: 'The Wedding'"—from the start to the words "mad poland." (The "scribe" for this was Eleanor Antin's mother, who got tired of doing the writing at that point and wouldn't go on.)[46]

Clearly, the poet takes great care to incorporate his family and friends in this work of memory; he inscribes their presence into the texts and images of the book.

The New Directions edition of *Poland/1931* also includes "pseudo-documents" besides "authentic" memorabilia. The book is illustrated by film stills from a fictive silent movie. While the New Directions edition only contains one "still" from this fictive film (see page 28), the artist's book *Esther K. Comes to America, 1931* is accompanied by a series of black-and-white photographs from this imaginary film. Rothenberg recalls: "They were originally shot for a performance version of Poland/1931."[47] The interplay between these stills and the text deserves a detailed interpretation to reveal the intricacies and ironies of the design. I will focus on two examples.

The last photograph in *Esther K. Comes to America, 1931* adds meaning to the poem that otherwise would not be there. Let me explain: The photograph depicts a man in a dark room, perhaps a basement. His face looks dismal; he does not wear any ritual clothes or culturally specific attire; his hair is long, but we cannot see its color. In the background on the left side of the man, there is the vague image of another person who seems to look at the observer or at the man in the picture. The scene is mysterious and dark. Is this the dark room of CREATION that appears in Rothenberg's dream? Is the man in the dark Rothenberg himself representing "the universal Jew" or Cezanne's "one man"? Is the shadow in the dark a manifestation of "shades" made by the imagination (*VB*, 33)? We cannot view the characters clearly. The mystery of Jewish identity is not lifted. After pondering the roles and poses taken by Rothenberg and his collaborators, we return to the beginning—the dark room of creation.

Since *Esther K. Comes to America, 1931* is modeled on a movie script, the back cover informs us of the collaborative efforts that went into it:

Written & directed by Jerome Rothenberg

Photography: Laurence Fink

Cover montage: Eleanor Antin

Design consultant: Lynn Braswell

Cast: Kathy Acker, Cyrelle Foreman, Leonard Neufeld, Jerome Rothenberg

Once more, Rothenberg invites friends to participate in his project. The writer Kathy Acker with her partner, Leonard Neufeld, and the folk singer Cyrelle Foreman appear together with Rothenberg in the cast of this fictive film. Acting out roles, their normal identity is disguised. The cover of the book shows a display box with photographs from a fictive Yiddish film entitled *Jerome Rothenberg's Esther K. Comes to America (1931)*. The three stills from the "film" display: a rabbi and woman, their faces half hidden behind a coat; a bourgeois man with his wife; a woman dressed in black with a mournful look, her face is hidden behind a veil. The reader is motivated to match these "film stills" with the poems/stories of the book.

That the artist Eleanor Antin designed this "movie box" is not unimportant. Apart from collaborating with Rothenberg on his Poland project, she also experimented in her own work with different ways of approaching the past. Like other woman artists and performers, Antin produced a variety of works in which she takes on different personae or selves; she becomes a king, a gypsy woman, Florence Nightingale, and the black ballerina Antinova.[48]

On a small scale, Rothenberg engages in a similar activity. Like Antin, he tries to appropriate the past by dressing up as a character from the past. He asserts that his Poland project involves "a kind of *participation mystique* in something very old."[49] However, dressing up also carries overtones of trickery. The trickster poet loves to shift shapes. His fictive film cast demonstrates the sincere desire to overcome the distance from the past, but also the impulse to play with it. Both tendencies are representative of the poet's overall approach to history.

Rothenberg notes that the goal of his Poland project was to create

> a presentation of the Eastern European Jewish world from which I had been cut off by birth, place and circumstance, and to which I no longer have any way of returning, because it doesn't exist in that place any longer.[50]

The poet bemoans the loss of the Yiddish literary tradition, which according to the yiddishist Brad Hill, was for the most part extinguished "in the Holocaust, through Soviet repression, and by linguistic and cultural assimilation in western Europe and the Americas."[51] In the 1960s, when the poet began to investigate his ancestral past, he developed an interest in modern Yiddish poetry. Rothenberg recalls:

> I was curious as to whether the literature had developed along the lines of other European languages and literatures. Singer's work . . . was a revelation to me, and when Cecil Hemley, who was Singer's editor at Noonday Press, introduced us, I asked him about (modern or experimental) Yiddish poetry, hoping that there might be something like what he was doing as a prose writer. But he didn't come up with much or was rather discouraging about there being anything there that would be of interest to my own concerns.[52]

Evidence of his preoccupation with modern Yiddish writing can be found in certain sections of *A Big Jewish Book*.[53] Rothenberg was wondering what Yiddish poetry would have been like, if the Holocaust had not happened:

> In the beginning raising for myself the questions, well, if the Yiddish poetry—if the Jewish poetry in this century had developed instead of being cut short, what would the Jewish poetry be? I could create the imagined, the desired, poetry, and with that, an image-of-the-world . . . I imagined myself as *that* poet![54]

Poland/1931 then is an attempt to fill the void with new Jewish poetry. Even though Rothenberg sets off on his own path in the process of re-creating that kind of poetry, he is eager to bind his work to Yiddish culture in one way or another. The translation of "Poland/1931: 'The Wedding'" into Yiddish and its performance in poetry readings represent one such example.[55] One reviewer comments:

> "The Wedding" . . . was read in English, almost as a chant overflowing with feeling. Rothenberg then read the poem again—this time in Yiddish. And this time one heard, even more, the mournful sound of the bell tolling for Poland.[56]

Rothenberg tells a remarkable anecdote about one of these readings in the 1970s. Witnessing the powerful effect of his Yiddish performance, an elderly person from the audience remarked: "I like the original more than the English version."[57] This story foregrounds the postmodern effacement of the distinction between an original and its translation. For Rothenberg does not make a fundamental discrimination between writing a "new" poem (primary process) and translating a poem (secondary process). What matters to him is that both processes involve *poesis*. Utilizing his poetic skills and imagination, he composes a poem that evokes Yiddish through its rhythm, language, and imagery. Toward the end of the poem the "wedding song" takes on the intense tone of lamentation:

> o poland o sweet resourceful restless poland
> o poland of the saints unbuttoned poland repeating endlessly
>   the triple names of mary
> poland poland poland poland poland
> have we not tired of thee poland no for thy cheeses
> shall never tire us nor the honey of thy goats
> thy grooms shall work ferociously upon their looming brides
> shall bring forth executioners
> shall stand like kings inside thy doorways
> shall throw their arms around thy lintels poland
> & begin to crow
>
> (*P*, 3–4)

One could think that this text dates back to the 1930s and was perhaps written by Aron Zeitlin or Yehiel Yeshaia Trunk, but was more sexually explicit than their work.[58] What makes this proposition so intriguing is the possibility of describing Rothenberg's poem as an apocryphal or forged text. Not surprisingly, therefore, Gérard Genette's definition of forgery perfectly fits Rothenberg's purposes: "forgery is an imitation in a serious mode whose dominant function is the pursuit or the extension of a preexisting literary achievement."[59] The poet's goal is precisely to extend the Jewish literary tradition. In that sense, he "forges" an experimental Jewish poetry. Some of his Poland poems could pass for translations or imitations of Yiddish originals. Like forgery, they aim at passing "for an authentic text in the eyes of the reader of absolute and infallible competence."[60]

Of course, the comparison with forgery and apocryphal writing has its limits. For Rothenberg openly admits that "The Wedding" is *his* poem; he does not attribute it to someone else. Yet on the other hand, he enjoys the thought that it could be taken for a translation: "I felt, if it seems all right to say so, that I was translating in effect from a Yiddish poetry that had never been written."[61] I would, therefore, speak of a "forged translation." Despite its limited applicability, the concept of forgery is useful in revealing that "forgery" in *Poland/1931* has the purpose to draw us back into a forgotten world. Moreover, since forgery and pseudepigraphy were common in the Middle Ages, this brief analysis underscores my earlier speculations on the poet's neomedieval writing practices.

Rothenberg's attempt to reclaim his ancestral past involves personal and collective memory. Collective memory is based on tradition rather than experience. Hence, the revitalization of collective memory inevitably relies on sources. It is fundamental to Rothenberg's work to reappropriate such material, "to try in my own way to open to those other possibilities—to question what we get both from experience & from tradition."[62] In order to help his imagination to recreate an image of "the old country," the poet examines a lot of material:

> I'm trying to reconstruct for myself a world to which I am both closely connected—and therefore do not *totally* deny autobiography in some sense—and from which I am at a great distance, with no possibility of returning. Therefore something to be reconstructed by the imagination. The helps to the imagination are whatever sources for that world I can put my hands on, you know, by a process like collage. So I work partly out of reminiscences remembered from my family, partly from old Yiddish novels, partly from letters, histories, pictures of Jewish Poland, photographs by men like Roman Vishniac and others.[63]

Archival material confirms just how much effort went into the composition of *Poland/1931*. Rothenberg widely read about ḥasidic and Yiddish culture, Polish and Jewish history, Yiddish folklore, etc.; he also did research at the YIVO in New York City. His reading resulted in many excerpts and notes, which he intended to include in his poetry. The archive holds his lists, which are full of "concrete particulars" dealing with subjects such as "Clothing & Body Adornment," "Forbidden Foods" and "Clean Foods," other ethnic foods, "Things Forbidden Because They are Dangerous," "Odessa, Gangsters, Etc.," "The Jews of Russia & Poland," and much more.[64]

Moreover, the poet includes material from different historical periods into his Poland assemblage: amulets, concrete poems, incantations, prayers, magic spells, ritual scores, anecdotes, and poems with esoteric kabbalistic material. This device suggests that "all ages are contemporaneous in the mind" (Pound). Since collage brings objects into the present, it helps to overcome historical distance. Rothenberg exploits this prominent aspect of collage, that is, its ability to give a sense of "the *presence* [Rothenberg's emphasis] of the collaged element (for eye & ear)—the reader's recognition of source a variable not imposed but dependent on his own experience."[65]

Collage also presupposes parataxis. Since there is no longer a hierarchy, different genres and materials all exist on the same level.[66] The idea goes back to early modernism. For Rothenberg interprets, this indicates that "the modern poem is open to everything: . . . it becomes the vehicle for 'anything the mind can think.'"[67] Today, the inclusiveness of postmodernism and the related erasure of boundaries enable the incorporation into the poem of any discourse or any kind of material.

Visual collages are based on the same principles. It is therefore not incidental that a collage by Eleanor Antin precedes the text of *Poland/1931*. By assembling and intermingling disparate images from the past and present, Antin creates a collage that functions as memory-space. Similarly, Rothenberg's performances of *Poland/1931* produce a memory-space with the overall effect of "total theater." He utilizes intermedia devices and cooperates with musicians, singers, dancers and composers. In the late 1960s, the poet began to perform his Poland poems in an inter-media setting. The Archive for New Poetry provides ample evidence of his numerous experiments with the performance of *Poland/1931*.[68] It would be wrong to ignore this material because, as Sayre rightly states, "one cannot even begin to appreciate a work like *Poland/1931* until one experiences it in performance."[69]

While the earliest readings of the poems are accompanied by Yiddish and Hebrew songs, sung by Cyrelle Foreman, later performances also include Klezmer music, slides, and a film, that is, Charlie Chaplin's movie, *The Immigrant*. It is vital that these events are advertised as "All-Jewish Dream Fantasy Show."[70] Obviously, Rothenberg's aim is to present the audience with a historical fantasy. Visual and aural means intensify this experience and externalize elements of personal and collective memory. Talking about his collaboration with the composer Charles Morrow, Rothenberg divulges his motivation for these elaborate multimedia performances:

> the work that seems to me most significantly to be a collaboration is a collage piece, a sound collage, which was set up as a kind of overture to a grand "total performance" of the *Poland* poems. . . . The idea at that point was to extend *Poland* into a multi-media

> piece, and largely to satisfy my own desire to be surrounded by visual images of . . . to see with my eyes what the words had to carry in the poems. Well *Poland* is after all a construct of . . . the imagination. . . . I was thinking of supplying visual images from photographs and so on, and with Charlie [Charles Morrow], of adding a possible sound dimension, using pre-recorded materials: music, voices of people talking in Yiddish, polkas, Yiddish vaudeville, scraps of poems. I was even reading off some pieces from the Dutch Schultz deathbed transcription. So, a sound collage which easily intersected, paralleled the collaging in the poems—but here with Charlie in the lead. And the visual things, the slides and film clips, which were an objectification (as the Surrealists spoke of that): an objectification of my own memories, even (to be real funky about it) of my dreams.[71]

Once more Rothenberg resorts to the concept of collage/assemblage. By describing the performance in terms of a "sound collage," the poet expresses again his longing for "totality." For ultimately the vision behind this multimedia project is to blend literary, visual, and sound collage into one "total performance."

History Enters the Poem as Story

The performance aspect of *Poland/1931* is stressed by the oral style of various poems. As an active member of the oral poetry movement, Rothenberg is very much aware of the features of oral poetry. In *Poland/1931* he explores some of the characteristics of oral poetry. Apart from the unobtrusive sound patterns (assonance, consonance, alliteration, and internal rhyme), which are always present in Rothenberg's poetry, and incantatory features, he introduces narrative and dramatic elements into his poems, for traditional oral poetry often tells a story. Inspired by these examples, certain contemporary poets with affiliations to the oral poetry movement set out to utilize stories in their own poetry. This exploration is especially evident in David Antin's improvised talk poems.[72] Equally, Rothenberg introduces narrative components into his anecdotal poems and the two sequences "Galician Nights" and "Esther K. Comes to America."

Roskies proposes that stories foster collective memory, but narratives are also utilized to construct national identities.[73] Occasionally, Rothenberg's contribution to the construction of

Jewish identity and history takes the form of parody. The poet cloaks one of his versions of Jewish history in the bizarre story of Esther K. and Leo Levy, which runs through several parts of *Poland/1931*. This text demonstrates the reemergence of narrative in postmodern poetry. Rothenberg's utilization of narrative elements corroborates Perloff's presentiment regarding poetry that "a narrative that is not primarily autobiographical will once again be with us, but it will be a narrative fragmented, dislocated, and often quite literally non-sensical."[74] The use of narratives has the function to "reclaim for poetry a significance it has lost to narrative over the period since Blake, a transfer of hegemony that is now so entrenched it is rarely questioned."[75] I will now investigate "the return of story" in one of Rothenberg's hybrid poetry sequences.[76]

The title "Galician Nights, or a *Novel* in Progress" [italics are mine] is unexpected as novels are usually associated with prose rather than poetry. Although the title suggests a narrative, the reader will have trouble identifying a straightforward story.[77] For Rothenberg prefers a fragmentary narrative to a linear one.

This sequence can be read as a kind of "mini assemblage" collating prosy pieces, a letter, songs, incantations, and even a hymn. But it also contains hybrid forms. For instance, the first section, "*The Early Life, Loves & Circumstances of Esther K*," displays poetic and prosaic features. This text has long lines rather than the justified margins, which characterize prose. Furthermore, sound patterns, repetition and rhythm mark its poetic quality. Yet at the same time, the text tells a story and utilizes dialogue. Shall we therefore think of it as poetry that leans toward prose, or as prose with poetic elements inserted into it, or as prose tending toward poetry?

In order to (con)fuse and blend rather than to separate and keep apart, Rothenberg creates his own new forms. Margueritte S. Murphy contends that this subversive tendency is the main characteristic of the contemporary prose poem.[78] Undermining genres and literary conventions, the prose poem belongs to a tradition of subversion: "The tradition of the prose poem then, is a convention of subversion: Convention here, I will argue, is rather a convention of subversion, and of subversion of prose conventions."[79] The American prose poem therefore permanently tries to distinguish itself from prose, "[o]r, to borrow a term from Derrida, the prose poem relies on a *différance* from other forms of prose."[80] Since the way in which the prose poem differs from prose constantly changes, it is impossible to pin it down. Some, like Renée Riese Hubert, claim that the prose poem is "undefinable."[81]

"Galician Nights" is the story of a Jewish woman named Esther K. who uses her charm over men to protect herself and her people. As a healer and soul adviser (see Rothenberg's photomontage, page 82), she promises to help her customers "to gain the love of the one you desire." Yet there is more to Esther K. She also represents a manifestation of the "Hebrew goddess," that is, the Shekhinah. The goddess of Rothenberg's "novel" is a down-to-earth woman.

In this narrative Rothenberg presents a clever blend of various historical periods, all of which are related to the name Esther K. It synthesizes different times (Persian empire, Kazar empire, medieval Poland, and modern China) and places (Persia, Turkey, China, Havana, Poland). Such a Poundian layering of time is based on the idea that "all times are contemporaneous in the mind."[82] Besides referencing Kafka's Joseph K., the poem hints at the names of various ancient goddesses, most prominently, the Akkadian Ishtar, and "Easter, named for [a] German goddess with [a] related name."[83] Second, it alludes to the biblical character of Esther, the Hebrew queen in Persia, who, according to the Bible, saved the Jews from persecution: "Circumstances in Persia" (*P*, 90). Third, it plays with the legendary character of "Estherke (Esther K) who was wife of the early Polish emperor Casimir."[84] The poem alludes to the legend in the following way: "Circumstances of King Casimir & the Jewish queen who sat beside him" (*P*, 89). Finally, the narrative also evokes Rothenberg's mother who was also named Esther and came from Poland to America.

These various Esthers then are viewed as emanations of the Shekhinah throughout history. The Shekhinah "progresses" through history. Rothenberg carefully weaves into the narrative a variety of tales, which he himself only learned as an adult: "Circumstances of the legends I never knew that were kept from me in childhood" (*P*, 90). What all these tales have in common is that they tell the story of a "Jewess" who "makes it in the world," that is, who rises to the status of a queen in Persia, the Kazar kingdom, and Poland.

On the mythical level, the narrative stands for the "fantastic career" of the she-demon Lilith, who emerges as God's emanation—the Shekhinah. The sixteenth-century kabbalist Isaac Luria honors her in a hymn, a translation of which Rothenberg includes at end of "Galician Nights."[85] This way the narrative culminates in the lofty celebration of the Hebrew goddess as the Sabbath Bride, whom the kabbalists welcome with their songs.

Yet before this grand finale, we need to trace Esther's rather earthy journey. Indeed, she succeeds in sraising her status by becoming the courtesan of "The Governor." The latter stands for various governors at different historical periods and cultures. The governor is a prototype who takes on historically specific roles, for instance, that of a Persian or Polish king from Jewish history. The first part of the text gives a sketch of the governor and his relationship to the Jews, whom he views with anti-Semitic prejudice. The narrator portrays "the Jew" from the governor's perspective: "The Jew's beard is sleek, so are his eyes sleek & shameless in an otherwise bland face" (*P*, 85). But then he presents the Governor from the perspective of "the Jew." From this viewpoint, the Governor comes over as a pathetic weakling: "He trembles on the balance of a kiss, he dawdles, he grows sick, he waves his arms, he vanishes, he is heard of nevermore" (*P*, 85).

In the second section we meet Esther K., who becomes the governor's courtesan: "My love! cries Esther K. as she undresses" (*P*, 85). Esther K., the promiscuous, archetypal goddess, exploits the Governor's infatuation with her for her own benefits. She surrounds herself with wealth: rich foods ("white honey on her lips" [*P*, 86], "honeycomb," [*P*, 86] "thou eatest tripe & poppy seed" [*P*, 87]) and expensive clothes and furniture ("The mirror swings along its golden chain" [*P*, 86], "thou wearest a rose gown" [*P*, 87]).

The motif of Esther as a courtesan comes out very clearly in the third passage, in which Esther is addressed as a German goddess and celebrated like the beloved in the Song of Songs:

> O Esther K. thou my semitic beauty thou easter excellence
>   thou poor forsaken witness yet plyest thy trade in peace!
> Thou warmest a towel for the Governor.
> Thou wearest a rose gown.
> (A man, once come on business, learneth to stay & bathe with
>   thee.)
>
> (*P*, 87)

But there is a downside to Esther's life with the Governor. Esther, the "Jewess," is alienated from her own people because she gives birth to the child of a gentile, a "white-haired child which smelleth of old laundry" (*P*, 86). Hence, Esther must go into exile, since "for the Jewess who has tasted of the Gentile's honey there is no reunion in her father's tent" (*P*, 86).

In the fourth part, Esther K. receives a letter from China. She is invited to become the wife of a mysterious man whose signature is "L.L." At this point, the narrative grows increasingly fragmented. For example, we are prompted to construct the remaining plot from a chant. In this chant each line begins with the phrase "circumstances of . . ." and is completed by a further part of the story. Here is an example from "The Early Life, Loves & Circumstances of Esther K.":

> Circumstances in a Jewish house.
> Circumstances of Esther K.
> Circumstances of men exchanging wallets in front of the guildhall.
> Circumstances of carts circumstances of leather lines in the hands of the master drivers.
>
> (*P*, 88)

The poem insinuates that some kind of monetary agreement is reached that leads to the marriage between Esther K. and L.L. Eventually, Esther K. travels to America and arrives at Attorney Street ("Circumstances of her noble station on Attorney Street" [*P*, 89]). Attorney Street on the Lower East Side of Manhattan, by the way, has an autobiographical significance for Rothenberg, who "was under the impression at one point" that his father lived there when he first came to America as an immigrant.[86] According to the tale, L.L. from China also seems to have arrived there. Several figures merge with the mysterious L.L., who is now clearly characterized as a charlatan: "Circumstances of Jews in pigtails & of a visit by the false messiah Leo Levy" (*P*, 89). Thus, L.L. embodies Shabbatai Zevi, while Esther K. manifests the Shekhinah. Dreaming of the false messiah, L.L. closely identifies with Zevi: "Circumstances of his dream of Shabtai Tswi's dream of a Turkish heaven. / Circumstances of the Shekhinah leaning on his arm" (*P*, 89).

In passages like these Rothenberg infuses his "non-linear and multichronic" narratives with different interpretive paradigms (autobiographical, historical, mythical). That is, Leo Levy is associated with the poet's father, as well as Shabbatai Zevi, and with the ninth *sefirah*, a kabbalistic emanation. Moreover, the poet also mingles the mystical with the comical.

For instance, Leo Levy's "Angry Song" (*P*, 93–94) is hilarious. It parodies a counting-out rhyme, as it starts off with a short sentence that gets repeated and expanded in each subsequent verse. The end of the poem reeks of bitter satire:

> I hate Esther K. & am angry at her contempt for me which I deserve less than she knows being estranged from me who went to sleep in Jewishtown I feel so sad to be a fornicator of demons & to smell of onions & to see God's pickles with my true blue eye & nothing with my lovely glass eye no this is no way to treat the Lord's anointed because I am ugly
>
> OY OY OY IT'S HARD TO BE A JEW!
>
> (*P*, 94)

Though some readers may welcome this scathing self-irony, others could be bewildered or offended by it. Yet this song illustrates just what extreme measures the poet deems necessary in order to avoid sentimentality. Since these mocking songs are amusing, they help to restore an element of entertainment to poetry. Yet on another level, laughter constitutes a possible response to the experience of loss. Loss creates a vacuum, which can be filled by laughter. It is laughter at pain: "OY OY OY IT'S HARD TO BE A JEW!" The attempt to deal with pain, while at the same time exorcising nostalgia takes the poet into comedy.

Like the kabbalists, Rothenberg employs myth in order to give meaning to history. Frye defines myth as "a certain kind of story, generally about a god or other divine beings."[87] The mythmaking impulse of the kabbalists generated an entire kabbalistic mythology, on which Rothenberg draws selectively:

> The Jewish mythology is something that I've been carrying around since childhood but that has opened & expanded for me over the past twenty, maybe twenty-five years. I was slow to come to it as a resource for my own work, but once into it, it began to shape a good part of my poetry.[88]

A prominent example of the reappropriation of myth is the poet's use of the concept of the Shekhinah. This Jewish figure is multisided and complex. Both Patai and Scholem expound a number of different (if not contradictory) myths, which developed around the Shekhinah. "Shekhinah" literally means "presence." The term was used by the rabbis to explain biblical anthropomorphism. By positing that it was not God, but his "presence" (Shekhinah) that did these things, it was possible to retain the theological concept of a transcendent God. In the course of time, however, the figure of the Shekhinah gathered further significance. Since she was thought to embody the part of the deity that can be perceived through the senses, the Shekhinah was given physical attributes. In the High Middle Ages, the kabbalists conceived her as a personified female, an emanation of God.[89]

Not surprisingly then, Rothenberg taps into the kabbalistic reservoir of images and myths about the Shekhinah. The poet's reappropriation of her myth parallels the growing preoccupation of American Jews with God's female emanation. Selinger distinguishes several stages of American-Jewish interest in the Shekhinah:

> The first grows out of the kabbalistic counterculture of the 1950s, 1960s and 1970s, and is mostly written by men. The second, which comes of age a little later and has lasted rather longer, is a feminist recasting of this figure, often with a progressive communal and spiritual agenda in mind.[90]

It is evident that Rothenberg belongs to the first group of writers, together with Meltzer, Hirschman, and Tarn. In the 1970s, various stands of Judaism—the *havurah* movement, Jewish feminists, and, later on, Jewish Renewal—became attracted to the concept of the Shekhinah. Evidence of this can be found in prayer books, songs, klezmer music, book publications, and feminist thought. This trend came as a reaction to a sense of loss of the feminine in Judaism.[91]

For Patai, the kabbalistic Shekhinah marks the return of the goddess, which normative Judaism attempted to repress. Scholem also suggests that by inventing the Shekhinah, the kabbalists rebelled against the repression of myth and mythology in mainstream Judaism.[92] The Shekhinah represents therefore the reemergence of the goddess and myth.

That the Jewish counterculture picked exactly these elements indicates certain needs, most prominently, a need for a powerful—almost tangible—symbol of God, something that overcomes the abstractions of theology and "makes him a living God in the mind of a believer."[93] As Selinger points out, the Shekhinah could serve as a counterweight to Jewish patriarchy.[94] The explicit sexual imagery and language associated with the Shekhinah accounts for her attractiveness during a period of sexual liberation. Moreover, the Shekhinah's romantic life can be viewed in mystical terms by comparing the *unio mystica* with the experience of sexual union. All these factors stimulate Rothenberg's reappropriation of the myth of the Shekhinah.

Rothenberg eclectically uses different concepts of the Shekhinah in his poetry. Central to his experimentation, however, is the notion of the Shekhinah as the Matronit. This is the name the kabbalists gave to the tenth *sefirah* or emanation of the kabbalistic Tree of Life, who was identified with the Shekhinah. Patai holds that the kabbalistic Matronit displays the contradictory features of a goddess. In fact, she *is* the Hebrew goddess:

> The goddess thus speaks to man with four tongues: keep away from me because I am a Virgin; enjoy me because I am available to all; come shelter in my motherly bosom; and die in me because I thirst for your blood.[95]

In his poems, Rothenberg explores various facets of this goddess. The Jewish mythology of the Matronit suggests that she had her bedchamber in the temple where the King, the male emanation of God, who is equated with the ninth *sefirah*, came to visit her every Friday night to join her in sexual union. Yet with the destruction of the temple, the Shekhinah/Matronit lost her home and husband and was sent into exile, where she suffered sexual abuse by foreigners.[96]

Rothenberg appropriates precisely this myth in "Poland/1931: 'The Bride'" by picturing the violation of the Shekhinah in exile. The poem begins as a lament:

> o Shekinah o thou my defeated flower
> trampled my Bessarabian daisy by the boots of strangers
> cossacks have struck their cocks on thee
> on thy thighs have slept generations of tatars
> what bitter exiles have brought thee to this bed
> to leathern blankets aflake in Polish air
> contamination of lungs o my Slavic moongirl
> my bride where hast thou gone then
>
> (*P*, 26)

In the kabbalah the Shekhinah embodies the people of Israel, who manifest God's presence on earth. Rothenberg takes up this tradition and transfers it to recent Jewish history. The persecution of the Jews in Eastern Europe, which caused their mass emigration to the United States, is translated into the disgraceful image of rape.

But the sexual explicitness of the poet's language has precedents in kabbalistic literature. That is why it could be said that the poet merely "translates" a mystical tradition into the present. Furthermore, Rothenberg's projection of a mythic concept onto modern Jewish history is extremely provocative, and there is no doubt that the poet utilizes this tradition in order to explore and break taboos. Nevertheless, Selinger brings to our attention that the poet's imagery is also undeniably male:

> The risk, the dare of "The Bride" lies in Rothenberg's desire to make his own poetic persona part of the Shekhinah's problem. He may not take part in the physical assaults on her, those marks of her exile, but the language he uses implicates him in it. . . . Rothenberg also understands the cost of all this male release. . . . The book knows this—and at several points it silently hints at an alternative.[97]

The same duplicity informs the next passage in the poem, where the King expresses his longing for reunification with his Bride. The milk imagery evokes a devoted worshiper yearning for the mother goddess:

> & wherefore wherefore hast left thy milk bottles behind
> thy tits will I squeeze upon for wisdom
> of a milk that drops like letters
> sacred alphabet soup we lap up o thou my Shekinah
> do not be thus far from us in our Galician wildernesses
> (*P*, 26)

The style evokes the English of the King James Bible and more specifically, The Song of Songs, in which the lover praises the beauty of his beloved. (That text, by the way, plays a prominent role in the history of Jewish mysticism.) Yet there is an incongruity between the lofty style and the pornographic imagery. In the next section, Rothenberg takes his daring experiment even further:

> in thee the fingers of God shall come together
> shall know themselves in thee o Hole o Holy Mother
> o Shekinah who seeketh thy happy home around the bend

& wilt thou find it now will the memory be gone for thee
gone the forced nights in Polish brothels the whip of the
delighted nobles
on thy ass brought low brought to thy knees in sucking homage
o cunt of God o Goddess o thou egg thou albumen

(*P*, 26–27)

Not only does the poet describe the Shekhinah as mother goddess and a poor abused virgin, but also as a whore. Among the different faces of the Hebrew goddess, one is that of a prostitute. A certain kabbalistic tradition holds that the Shekhinah changes her aspect in exile; she is believed to adopt the features of Lilith.[98] This idea impinges on Rothenberg's depiction of the Shekhinah. For certain portions of the Esther K. narrative portray the Shekhinah as a wanton woman.[99]

"Esther K. Comes to America: 1931" recounts further events in the life of Esther K. Since the narrative is fragmented, the reader gathers from various hints that Esther K.'s relationship with L.L. is a failure: "leading her to first meet / & then lose / Leo Levy" (*P*, 109). Leo Levy is driven by the American dream, but he also symbolizes that dream. The preceding poem, "The Immigrant," depicts America as a place where everything is gold: "you walked on a gold carpet America was gold to you / a gold boat drifted on a lake of gold" (*P*, 107).

Unfortunately however, Leo Levy's American dream fails dismally. Esther K. has to realize that her husband is a loser: "going every morning to the chicken market / [he] pursues his dream of power" (*P*, 108), but really, he is just a self-deluded man, who polishes "his fingernails / with eggwhite" (*P*, 109). Like the false messiah, L.L. makes false promises. His idea of turning Esther K. into a movie star ("to make '1931' as a talking movie"[(*P*, 109]) comes to nothing. Instead, Esther K. experiences sexual abuse from "the priest [who] tormented her & that was one / the governor broke into sighs & that was another" (*P*, 108), and "the Shanghai dog-merchant" (*P*, 108).

The story of Esther K. in America ends in exile. For Esther K. is exiled twice: from Poland and from her husband. Hence, the poem depicts the couple sitting wordlessly in a café in New York:

The Wilderness: but otherwise
name of a cafeteria
where the two lovers drink tea

not speaking to each other
but sharing a world through separation

(*P*, 108)

A dream has turned sour. At the end, we are left with the image of "three half-chewed jelly slices" and "a lemon" (*P*, 110). The poem fades out into melancholy and bitterness, while the experience of exile and separation continues.

Rothenberg portrays America as a place of exile, just like Poland. This takes us back to the poem, "The Bride," which is characterized as the "hymn of Shekinah on her last night from home" (*P*, 27). Yet where is "home"? The poem suggests that it is not a place at all, but a state of being. This state of being is envisioned by the kabbalah and celebrated in this poem: "& know no separation male & female / shall be one in three" (*P*, 26). It is represented by the reunification of the Shekhinah/Matronit with the King, Holy One Blessed Be He, and symbolized by a wedding. The Lurianic kabbalah claims that the unification of these two complementary principles of the godhead can be brought about by every religious act performed with awareness. Such acts of unification contribute to the overall goal of redemption.[100]

Rothenberg is not the only Jewish poet to utilize this myth for an interpretation of history. Tarn wrote a long poem, *Lyrics for the Bride of God*, which draws on the same mythology. It recounts a love story that is interwoven with various goddess myths. Among these, the myth of the Shekhinah plays a prominent role.

By recreating the myth of the Shekhinah, both poets follow Patai's injunction that the myth of God and the Shekhinah should be told in its entirety.[101] Both retell the Jewish myth by fusing it with contemporary elements, such as autobiographical material, historical, and contemporary references. Commanding a variety of poetic modes and styles, both poets use narrative, lyric, and dramatic elements to compose their collages. At the same time, they both appropriate and overwrite their sources. But only Rothenberg repeatedly resorts to comedy and parody.

What concerns me here, however, is that both poets approach the myth of the Shekhinah from a male perspective. It hardly can be denied that the concept of the Shekhinah was invented by men. In the mythological context of the kabbalah, the Shekhinah stands for the passive and receptive principle, which relates to and receives from the male generative principle.[102] Representing the "lowest" *sefirah* of the kabbalistic tree, she depends on the masculine principle, the ninth *sefirah*, which always precedes her. And this is just one point where gender relations inform the structure of kabbalah! Therefore, Selinger rightly puts his finger on it when he warns that the Shekhinah is exiled in the male mind: "She's been exiled, we can see, in his [Rothenberg's] masculine imagination: an exile that only some change in human and American gender relations will be able to cure."[103]

Interestingly enough though, Rothenberg himself reflects on this idea in "9/75 a letter to Tarn to honor *lyrics for the bride of god* at this point in the writing."[104] Here is the poem:

> & seeing the old struggle there
> —even in God the Androgyne division
> conflict of the sexes
> later would pull the world apart—
> the mind evades it almost
> smug in the male imagination builds a house for her
> or sets her up in it
> the House of God
> though if it's HIS house or if it's HER house who would say
> now?
> as the other day a letter from our old friend Clayton came
> "that the Shekhinah is just another one of the 'masks' that
> male origin wears" he wrote
> —I wouldn't doubt it for a minute either
> though that adjustment made the question will still
> remain
> of domicile of building that greater world
> that replication of the *shi'ur koma*
> & the mind the mind will ache from it forever
> throbbing call it habitation
> call it palace "image of the world" they said
> & wrote about the heavens
> seven by their count
> now I have read the *hekhalot* the books of palaces
> before Shekinah GOD THE MOTHER in her exile
> sat outside the town & heard the trains call
> like voices of her angels
> she who first experienced the *galut* poor old soul
>
> (*VB*, 37–38)

This discursive poem gives us an important insight into Rothenberg's approach to myths. The text tackles Clayton Eshleman's question whether the Shekhinah is not just a product of the male imagination. Rothenberg accepts this critical point: "I wouldn't doubt it for a minute." Yet in thinking about this problem, he wishes to go beyond gender issues. Instead he wonders how we imagine "god." To examine this, the poet reflects on the *shi'ur komah*, an ancient Jewish concept attempting to describe the "measure of the body" of God's presence. The kabbalists would employ abstruse calculations, monstrous numbers, and secret names to designate each body part.[105] (Rothenberg cites fragments from these texts in his Jewish anthology.[106]) The poet takes these obscure kabbalistic endeavors as representative of the human mind, which cannot stop to imagine god. Even if "the mind will ache from it forever," there hardly seems to be a way around such imaginings—whatever form they take.

Exploring other conceptions of the Shekhinah, Rothenberg invariably touches on Tarn's poem, which characterizes the Shekhinah as the habitation of God. Tarn dwells on this theme in his introductory poem "The Kitchen."[107] In this scene the woman is "put in her place;" she is set up in a house, "smug in the male imagination." Rothenberg further comments on this image by conjuring a number of associated images, such as the house, the domicile, the building, and the temple, but also the heavenly palaces which early Jewish mystics saw in their ecstatic visions and which they recorded in the *heikhalot* writings. When these texts were produced, a personified notion of the Shekhinah did not yet exist: this was "before Shekinah GOD THE MOTHER in her exile." The poem concludes with the powerful image of exile. The poet pictures the Shekhinah sitting outside the town, "she who first experienced the *galut* poor old soul."

Galut means "dispersion"/diaspora, and the Shekhinah embodies *galut*. Yet the poem gives this concept a surprising turn by proposing that the Shekhinah is displaced in the male imagination. Such displacement in the form of a misunderstanding constitutes just another form of exile. On the other hand, the myth of the Shekhinah also has the purpose to express a longing for reunification and the union of opposites, that is, a yearning for what I have previously called "totality." The totality of the divinity is symbolized by the unity of the sexes. The hermaphrodite is one of its forms. Rothenberg celebrates an androgyne god in a number of texts, most prominently in his poems about the female Christ.[108] Similarly, even "The Bride" praises this concept of the godhead as an ideal: "o hermaphrodite will we not bring thee balm" (*P*, 27). Yet we only get a glimpse of what such "totality" could mean, since for the most part the Esther K. narrative and many other Poland poems concern themselves with the opposite state of being—exile.

The Myth of the Trickster

Rothenberg's use of the trickster figure represents a second major example of his reappropriation of myth. Stories about tricksters exist all over the world, but it is controversial to what extent they share universal traits.[109] Rothenberg gives special attention to one particular type of trickster—the Native American Coyote. For example, in "Coyote Night Poem" a man dreams of Coyote and identifies with him (*VB*, 13–15). But most memorable is Rothenberg's infamous long poem "Cokboy" (*P*, 143–51), which appears at the end of *Poland/1931*. Although the myth of Coyote is not particularly Jewish, I will discuss the poem briefly because it demonstrates the blending of Jewish and Native American myths as well as the conflation of history and myth.

Much has been written about "Cokboy," "one of Rothenberg's finest poems."[110] Many people have seen the poet's captivating performance of this comic piece, in which he makes the audience laugh at his imitation of a deliberately exaggerated Yiddish accent in English ("vot em I doink here / how vass I lost tzu get here" [*P*, 143]) and other humorous passages, while he leads them into the fantastic world with "the distances vanishing in kabbalistic time" (*P*, 145). The poem tells the story of revered ḥasidic rabbi Baal Shem who comes to the American West as Cokboy (cowboy): "saddlesore I came / a jew among / the indians" (*P*, 143).

Like the trickster, the Baal Shem undergoes various transformations. At one time he takes on the form of Coyote, "with cock slung over shoulder" (*P*, 149), while at another time he is reborn as a beaver: "the Baal Shem is a beaver" (*P*, 148). (In 1968 Rothenberg himself was adopted by the Seneca Indians into their beaver clan.)[111] By reappropriating the myth of the trickster and conflating it with Jewish imagery, Rothenberg invents his own American creation myth:

> Whether he is being humorous, ironic, deadly serious, or some combination of the three, Rothenberg is definitely writing his American creation myth, starring an Indian-Jewish-beaver, who is a totally animated sexual creature, a primal Cokboy.[112]

The significance of this myth lies in its ironical perspective. For "Cokboy, Jew of the West"[113] actually originates from Eastern Europe. Gitenstein proposes that

> Further . . . this history is also that of Jerome Rothenberg in his confrontation with the myth of the American West and the fact of the Native American peoples. This special historiography would require the Jew to see the continent and the Native American in a different and un-Western way.[114]

In other words, Rothenberg utilizes the legendary Jewish figure of the Baal Shem to construct a non-Western perspective on Native American culture and history. His approach is to contemplate a marginal culture (Native America) through the eyes of other marginals (the Jewish minority). This perspective of "double marginality"[115] offers itself, since Jews and Indians share certain experiences. Not only do they both suffer a sense of displacement, but they both are survivors. Rothenberg asserts: "I think of Jews & Indians alike as survivors."[116] In addition, Snyder argues that the trickster himself is a survivor. Coyote, for example, never dies, or if he dies, he always comes back to life.[117]

It is therefore significant when Rothenberg portrays Jewish figures as tricksters. Indeed, the poet's list of Jewish tricksters includes Abulafia, Jacob Frank, Tzara, and—now we may add—the "false messiah" Leo Levy. There are multiple reasons for the appeal of the trickster.

First, Coyote is a genuinely American figure, who features not only in novels, films, and cartoons, but also in the poetry of white Western writers, such as Will Staple, Barry Gifford, Ed Dorn, Enrique Lamadrid, Margo St. James, James White, and James Koller. Rothenberg joins the contemporary American trend of drawing on local, that is, Native American, myth and lore.[118]

Second, the trickster stands for suppressed aspects of the psyche which the poet wishes to recover. Of the manifold interpretations of the trickster, Rothenberg favors the archetypal perspective of C. G. Jung.[119] According to the latter, the trickster constitutes an ancient, repressed archetype and is associated with the shadow, which is split off from consciousness, but continues to inform our behavior. It is exactly this primeval aspect of humanity that Rothenberg aims to repossess, "to find a place for what—as animals, children, etc.—we were & are: to be aware of, even to enjoy, the very thing that scares us with threats of madness, loss of self, etc." Coyote's behavior may be repulsive, amoral and shocking: "Coyote appears in the familiar role of primordial shit-thrower, cock-erupter, etc.," but his function is "to satisfy the need for all that in the full pantheon of essential beings." Thus, the trickster helps us to get in touch with our animalistic and vital side.

Third, the trickster ridicules "our ordinary behaviors by breaking (vicariously at least) their hold on us: to punch holes in established authority (= the way things are) so as not to be its forever silent victims." In other words, Coyote represents an active and subversive force. Being a kind of clown, the trickster turns the world upside down. Since he is "the product of a profound & comic imagination playing upon the realities of man & nature," he provides for much comedy. By placing the comic trickster in his concluding Poland poem, Rothenberg uses laughter once again in order to undermine sentimentality. At the same time, it demonstrates the return of the comic in postmodern poetry.[120]

To draw one more parallel with the trickster suggested by Hynes, the poet "manifests a distinctive transformative ability: he can find the lewd in the sacred and the sacred in the lewd, and new life from both." Rothenberg acts just like a "sacred and lewd bricoleur."[121] As this chapter reveals, he assembles a great amount of diverse (if not contradictory) material and transforms it into poetry. This chapter examined how Rothenberg gives coherence and meaning to materials of the past by building them into a narrative.

Conclusion

Poland/1931 is Rothenberg's memorial book. The poet responds to the loss of a close connection with the past and the culture of his Eastern European Jewish ancestors by collecting autobiographical and historical materials and arranging them as an assemblage. His "recollections" take various forms. One is the performance of Rothenberg's *Poland/1931* as a historical fantasy show; another is the book itself and its various versions, which all have the purpose to conjure up memory.

In this process assemblage and collage function as central appropriative strategies. Both exteriorize the working of personal and communal memory. Collaging involves the transformation and synthesis of disparate materials. In this particular case, Rothenberg blends together autobiographical, historical, and mythical elements, which enable him to include "concrete particulars" as well as archetypal figures, such as the goddess and the trickster.

In this chapter, I have examined the story of Esther K. and Leo Levy, which Rothenberg relates in several sections of the book. There is a complex interplay between the narrative and the accompanying photographs and songs. An ironical tone—sometimes joking, sometimes mocking—pervades much of the writing and illustrations. Hence *Poland/1931* illustrates two postmodern trends in poetry: the return of story and the return of comedy/parody into contemporary poetry. Parody in particular functions as an effective antidote against nostalgia. Furthermore, the reintroduction of narrative and comic elements expands the possibilities of poetry. Both aspects also play an important role for the oral poetry movement. It is therefore instructive to examine the oral features of *Poland/1931* and to pay attention to those parts that take on a special flavor in performance.

Performance helps to invoke presence and therefore can be utilized to make the past present. This concept ties in with the overall goal of the book, which is to overcome the distance from the past and to repossess it. Utilizing an array of tricks and disguises, Rothenberg manages to blend past and present, or autobiography, history, and myth.

Thus, the poet projects the myth of the Shekhinah onto recent Jewish history. Since it provides an interpretation of suffering, exile, and Jewish history, this myth has appealed to Jews throughout centuries. Rothenberg links to that tradition by reappropriating and transforming it. However, no longer does the myth of the Shekhinah have the purpose of underscoring observance by positing that every pious deed contributes to the reunification of the separated "male" and "female" parts of the godhead. Yet, although the idea of mystical union (totality) appeals to the poet, the main function of the myth of the

Shekhinah in *Poland/1931* is to give a pattern to history by means of a story, for the interpretation of history through a story or myth provides emotional satisfaction, entertainment, and meaning, while at the same time allowing one to establish a connection with tradition.

6

Confronting the Holocaust: *Khurbn* and "14 Stations"

An Experimental Holocaust Poetry

In spite of his deep awareness of the Holocaust, Rothenberg avoided thematizing it explicitly in his poetry for twenty-five years. Although the genocide of the Jews was a constant presence in his work, "[w]hat was Jewish lurked beneath the surface—or lived inside the words. A witnessing by silence" (*NA*, 140). Not only did the enormity of the event paralyze the poet for a fair amount of time, but Rothenberg was also careful to let the survivors speak first. On the one hand, he felt that he should not talk in place of the victims. On the other, he was unwilling to regard the Jews exclusively as victims. The poet elaborates this view in an important recent essay:

> I do not intend to single out the Jews as victims, as if their lesson is only for us—or the suffering. Nor do I want to see us only as victims, the innocent sufferers, though Auschwitz & the Holocaust are at their most horrible the accounts of innocent suffering. To be only the victim, as the founders of Zionism knew, was to be only partly human—a perception that has led on its negative side to the tragedy of Palestine & to a new state of oppression borne by Jews as now a nation among nations. (*NA*, 139)

For this reason, Rothenberg first reacted to the Holocaust by taking "the legacy of Auschwitz as a call to vigilance against all forms of chauvinism & racism (even held by Jews)" (*NA*, 139).

But this is not to say that his early work was oblivious to the shoah. Notably, in the 1960s Rothenberg was contracted by Herman Shumlin to retranslate and adapt Rolf Hochhuth's controversial play, *The Deputy*, for its Broadway performance.[1] Drawing on historical material and tackling the tacit complicity of the Catholic Church in the Holocaust, *The Deputy* may be regarded as "an extended polemical statement, a dramatization of historical, political, and theological argument."[2]

The poet was given six weeks to shorten and rephrase the play, which had been translated in a rather stilted way.[3] Initially, Hochhuth and Shumlin had made some cuts, but the cuts no longer satisfied the theater director. Hence he returned to the adaptation process, for which he engaged Rothenberg. However, the director and the poet could not agree on their interpretation of the play. While Shumlin thought that this should be "a play against *all* silence and complacency in the face of injustice,"[4] Rothenberg felt that really the piece represented "*[t]he lineaments of a nightmare* . . . —but of a nightmare so total that the mind refuses to believe it"[5] [Rothenberg's italics].

For the poet, this nightmare was linked to the realization that a long history of Christian anti-Judaism preceded the Holocaust, and that Christianity had failed in its mission of imitating the suffering Christ. In his polemical essay, Rothenberg claims that the play "isn't only about silence but about the age-old disparity between Christ and his Church."[6] By persecuting the Jews, Christianity exposed the hypocrisy of its own theology. According to Rothenberg's vision, this conflict was to be embodied in the character of Riccardo, the Jesuit priest, who experiences two aspects of the nightmare:

> that at Auschwitz the world is going through what the Doctor [Mengele] calls "a turning" in which "the idea of life is over," and that the Pope, in whom the agony of the Crucified should be the most acute, is no more involved than the ordinary benevolent statesman, perhaps less.[7]

Apparently, Rothenberg saw the play as a statement about Christian-Jewish relations. Consequently, the behavior of Pope Pius XII during the Holocaust was to symbolize a larger historical and theological problem. In reworking the play therefore, Rothenberg was keen to include symbolic action and exaggerated language in order to portray the nightmare, while Shumlin insisted on realistic dialogue and causality. As a result, the collaboration between the director and the poet was unsuccessful in Rothenberg's eyes and the play was produced without any coherent vision.[8] The play ran for a several months, during which audiences were agitated, while groups of Catholics and Nazis demonstrated daily against its performance.[9]

What was left of Rothenberg's adaptation was criticized for its overuse of vulgarisms.[10] Yet such charges ignore the possibility that in employing obscene language, the poet "wanted to convey by a brutal exaggeration of every word and gesture" the desperation and futility "of a man who's acting and who knows he must fail."[11] Language gives vent to powerful feelings of anger, rage and despair; the poet asserts that he "wanted it [the play] very much *to hurt our feelings*."[12] This passionate and existential approach to questions arising from the shoah and the use of radical literary strategies also characterize Rothenberg's own Holocaust poetry. Likewise, the disturbing comparison between the victims of the Holocaust and the crucified Christ reemerges in his later writings.

Rothenberg produced a small number of poems alluding to the Holocaust before he began to examine the subject more fully in the mid-1980s. There is "Seeing Leni Riefenstahl's TRIUMPH OF THE WILL" among his early poems; "The Wedding," "King of the Jews," "The Connoisseur of Jews," and "The Student's Testimony" in *Poland/1931*; and "Vienna Blood."[13] However, what propelled an intensive preoccupation with the shoah was the poet's visit in 1987 to the former home of his family in Poland. Rothenberg writes of his own experience in the introduction to *Khurbn*:

> I went to Poland for the first time & to the small town, Ostrow-Mazowiecka, sixty miles northeast of Warsaw, from which my parents had come in 1920. . . . I hadn't realized that the town was only fifteen miles from Treblinka, but when we went there (as we had to), there was only an empty field & the thousands of large stones that make up the memorial. (*K*, 3)

In response to this, Rothenberg begins to write Holocaust poetry. (In this book, the term "Holocaust poetry" is employed to refer to poetry that responds to Auschwitz or is caused by Auschwitz. Hence it covers poetry *on* the Holocaust, which in this particular case is also poetry *after* Auschwitz.) Strangely enough, Rothenberg's poetry about the shoah has been widely ignored by contemporary Holocaust anthologies.[14] Nevertheless, its experimental character deserves special attention. For Rothenberg's writing differs from the great bulk of American-

Jewish Holocaust poetry, which tends to be rather conventional.[15] By contrast, the poet utilizes the modernist aesthetic of cruelty and ugliness in order to expose the rupture of the shoah. He believes that the Holocaust brought about a crisis for language and humanity. This is articulated

> in Charles Olson's words, "man" had been "reduced to so much fat for soap, superphosphate for soil, fillings & shoes for sale," an enormity that had robbed language (one of our "proudest acts" he said) of the power to meaningfully respond. (*NA*, 139)

Rothenberg contends that Holocaust poetry must respond to this crisis; it must allow itself to be touched by it. Thus, poetry after Auschwitz is

> poetry that has somehow been touched, transformed, by Auschwitz & the other terrors of our time. It is altered, transformed, down to its roots (its language), & the extent of its transformation is the measure of its test as poetry. (*NA*, 143–44)

In his writing this transformation takes various forms. The diversity of his Holocaust poems illustrates that different modes and styles of writing about the shoah may be equally effective.[16] In debating the benefits of various types of Holocaust representation, one should, however, be cognizant of the danger of instrumentalizing the Holocaust to justify one's own aesthetics or anti-aesthetics. One critic, for instance, insists that Holocaust poetry must always take the following form: "In the best of the poetry the diction is bare; the word is naked, with no embellishments; compression, ellipsis, and understatement barely control an underlying hysteria. Imagery is not literary but realistic."[17] Apparently it is easy to exploit this discussion to put forward certain literary norms as the new poetic "standard" for poetry after Auschwitz. Since it is difficult to eschew such an approach entirely, one should at least be aware of certain hidden agendas which fuel many discussions of Holocaust poetry.

Rothenberg composes two types of Holocaust poetry. There is, first of all, the poetic sequence "Khurbn," the personal lament of the poet who is overwhelmed by the historical reality of the shoah and by its ghosts: "Rothenberg is the central protagonist of the poem. *Khurbn* describes the American Jewish poet's response to the abyss."[18] Since his response also involves reflection, the poems contain various didactic and philosophical passages. They partake in the discourse on poetry and poetics after Auschwitz and ponder many questions posed by the shoah: How could humans commit such atrocities? How can such genocide be prevented from ever happening again? How does the past affect the present? How does it alter our image of God? What is its impact on poetry?

Furthermore, *Khurbn* is a kind of assemblage that incorporates various types of poems: lyrics, prose poems, songs, a curse poem, and even one gematria poem. This diversity illustrates Alvin H. Rosenfeld's assertion that Holocaust literature must necessarily be a "composite literature" because confronting the past depends on many voices, genres, modes, and styles of writing.[19] The various poems in *Khurbn* allow for different voices to emerge.

The poet's other Holocaust cycle, "14 Stations," differs considerably from "Khurbn." It is characterized by the constraint of feelings and a sense of "objectivity," which arises from Rothenberg's compositional method—gematria. As opposed to the playful pieces assembled in his previous book *Gematria*, in "14 Stations," the poet deploys the same procedural device toward a different end.

Taken together then, these two disparate sequences complement each other. They represent a significant vein of experimental, American-Jewish Holocaust poetry and constitute one of Rothenberg's major poetic achievements, which deserves full recognition.

Encountering Celan

Living in Germany in the 1950s, Rothenberg saw the country just a decade after the demise of the Nazi regime. During this period, the young poet developed an interest in contemporary German poetry and began to translate a number of *New Young German Poets*, such as Karl Krolow, Paul Celan, Helmut Heissenbüttel, Walter Höllerer, Klaus Bermer, Heinz Piontek, Ingeborg Bachmann, Günter Grass, Ernst Jürgen Dreyer, and Hans Magnus Enzensberger. Of Celan's poetry, he translated "A Death Fugue," "Night of the Word," "Corona," "Water and Fire," "Life Cycle," "In the Shape of a Boar," "Shibboleth," and "Snowbed."[20] Rothenberg's rendering of the "Death Fugue"—one of its earliest translations into English—is acknowledged and praised by Hirschman:

It first appeared in America in Jerome Rothenberg's momentous *City Lights* translation. . . . I doubt that any of the more political poets of that early flourishing . . . were not in one way or another—then or subsequently—deeply influenced by Jerry's translation. It was the "best" translation of the Beat period, of what was obviously the finest and most authentic encounter with the experience of Nazified Europe.[21]

A few years after this project, Rothenberg actually came to meet Celan in Paris. Their encounter took place in 1967 and was induced by the publishers of Unicorn Books, who encouraged the American poet to attempt some further translations of Celan's work.[22] Yet the younger poet was weary of dealing with Celan's more recent language-based texts and felt a certain "discomfort . . . that I wasn't really serious about translating him at length, while fearing that he probably *only* knew me as a translator"[23] [italics are mine].

Five years after Celan's death, in a poem entitled "12/75 a letter to Paul Celan in memory,"[24] Rothenberg commemorates his meeting with the Jewish poet from Europe. He also talks of his recollections in a short memoir. This text describes the meeting of two Jewish poets from divergent cultural backgrounds. In my interpretation, Celan represents European Jewry, which was almost completely extinguished in the Holocaust; the poet is a survivor.[25] Rothenberg personifies American Jewry in the process of finding her identity and responding to the shoah, for it was only in the late 1960s that an American-Jewish Holocaust literature emerged. This development was motivated by specific events, such as the Eichmann and Auschwitz trials as well as the Six-Day War, which raised the awareness of the Holocaust and stirred the fear of anti-Semitism on an international political level.[26] Rothenberg recalls that in 1967 he had just began to incorporate Jewish material into his poems:

But Celan, although he was kind enough to acknowledge one of my earlier books, would have had no way of knowing about "The Wedding" or "The King of the Jews" or the "Satan in Goray" poem for Isaac Bashevis Singer, which I had then written and had been performing for the first time in London. For my own part, I wasn't yet aware of the turn towards visionary and brilliant judaisms his work had taken in *Die Niemandsrose* and so on.[27]

Yet Celan seems to have been skeptical of the younger poet's Jewish learning. He questioned the legitimacy of American

Jews to translate his poems : "the burden of the conversation fell increasingly on the idea of 'jewishness'—his discovery of his own and his concern about his translators' ability to share or understand it."[28] Alluding to the "cold light of / our meeting" (*VB*, 43), Rothenberg describes this point of friction. At the same time, he hints at the topic of the poem—the difficulty of two Jewish cultures to relate to each other, in spite of being very close. This situation is symbolized by the fact that the two poets do not seem to share a common language. Although they both know Yiddish, the *mame loschen* (the mother's tongue), they fail to use it communicatively:

> you said "jew"
> & I said "jew"
> though neither spoke the jew words
> jew tongue
> neither the mother language
> *loshen*
> the vestiges of holy speech
> but you said
> "pain"
> under your eyebrows
> I said "image"
> we said "sound"
> & turned around to
> silence lost
> between two languages

Rothenberg, "12/75 a letter to Paul Celan in memory," *VB*, 43.

Notwithstanding his translations from many languages, Celan did not know English well enough to have a comfortable conversation with Rothenberg. Similarly, the latter felt not totally at ease with German, although he had been living in the country for two years. As a result their conversation went on hesitantly:[29]

> The talk on both sides was punctuated by questions and clarifications—the need to speak more clearly or more slowly, since what we were doing was a combination of German and English (clear German, clear English, halting German, halting English). It is a common enough experience, but it stands out sharply from that day because at the end of it—as we were leaving the café—I thought to ask him if he spoke Yiddish. His reply was that while he had not been raised as a Yiddish speaker, he learned it during

> the war. I, on the other hand, had grown up in New York City but I had spoken *only* Yiddish to the age of four.[30]

Not only did the two poets have a common language, but this language was in fact a "Jewish" language! This common Jewish language could have bridged the historical and cultural gap between them.

But since this realization comes too late, the poem dwells instead on those moments of silence that reveal the distance between the two dialogue partners. Celan pronounces the word "pain" (his parents died in a concentration camp). Rothenberg, of course, acknowledges the latter's historical closeness to the atrocity and respects the voice of survivors:

> there was also a feeling that turned many of us from a participation in that writing: a revulsion at taking on the voice of those who suffered, of displaying our own feelings in such a way as to overshadow the terror of those times & places.
>
> (*NA*, 140)

This comment mirrors the general reaction of American Jewry to the shoah. Many explanations have been ventured to account for the community's delayed response (twenty-five to thirty years after the events). Early on, reflection was inhibited by the lack of factual knowledge about the historical events.[31] When this changed, a sense of paralysis and guilt took over. Being confronted with unimaginable atrocities challenged American optimism.

Although both poets identify themselves as Jews and confirm their Jewish identity by saying the word "Jew" (*VB*, 43), they find it difficult to communicate. Rothenberg attempts to overcome the distance by moving into the realm of poetry: "I said 'image' / we said 'sound'" (*VB*, 43). While the American poet is rooted in the poetics of deep image, Celan employs surreal images and metaphors. Yet both writers recognize the power of images and sounds. They both respond to the shoah with a scream: "we could not speak without a scream / a guttural" (*VB*, 43). The same cry of desperation and pain continues to permeate Rothenberg's own Holocaust poetry, even though it does not emerge until twenty years after his meeting with Celan. Moreover, both poets share a visionary perspective:

> the tree
> out of the shadow of

the white café was not
"the tree"
roots of our speech
above us
in the sun

(*VB*, 43)

The American poet appropriates Celan's "vision" to illuminate their encounter. The poem is brimful with quotations from the work of the German-language poet. Some passages contain quotations from Joachim Neugroschel's translation of Celan (here, from the poem "Havdalah"), which Rothenberg has slightly transformed and shortened.[32] The quotation marks hint at the appropriation:

"light knotted into air
"with table set
"chairs empty
"in sabbath splendor

(*VB*, 44)

Yet Rothenberg also takes up Celan's imagery—light and air, roots and trees—and invests it with shamanistic and kabbalistic meanings:

the old man stood beside
in figure of a woman
raised his arms to reach
axis of the world
would bring the air down
solidly
& speak no sound

(*VB*, 44)

The imagery here is plainly shamanistic. The kabbalistic Tree of Life comes to stand for the cosmic world tree, which connects the upper and the lower world and enables ecstatic excursions to both worlds. Like the initiatory experience of a shaman, Celan's descent into the abyss of humanity, his confrontation with the shoah, is filled with pain ("but you said / 'pain'"). But in his role as a poet he "bring[s] the air down / solidly"; he molds the formless. Yet in contrast to a shaman who returns from his journeys with a song, this man is silent. Silence is not only a major topic of Holocaust poetry, but, more specifically, it also predominates, Celan's own writing:

> In each of these poems the proximity to silence, that is to say, to poetic expiration, is nearly absolute, yet in each of them there is as well an intimation that some absolute meaning may reside within, or on the other side of, silence.[33]

Rothenberg knows that such silence requires interpretation. Perhaps this happens in the process of translation when

> . . . you forced
> my meaning
> to your poem
> the words of which still press
> into my tongue
> "drunk
> "blesst
> "*gebentsht*
>
> (*VB*, 44)

This strange inversion—"the way you forced / my meaning / to your poem"—intimates a certain closeness between Rothenberg and Celan, despite the fact that in reality their communication was only partially effective and satisfying. A peculiar connection between the work of the two poets is also suggested by the reference to the braided Sabbath candles (alluding to Celan's poem "Havdalah"), which are mysteriously intertwined, just like the work of the two poets. Not surprisingly then, the poem concludes with a Yiddish word from Celan's poem "Benedicta."[34] As Neugroschel explains, *gebentsht* means "blessed":

> *Gebentsht* is the past participle of the Yiddish verb *bentschen*, to bless, to speak the Jewish prayer that ends a meal. It is cognate with the German word *gebenedeiet*, 'blessed, blest,' and both words derive from the Latin *benedicta*.[35]

In the poetic process of appropriation, the words of one poet become those of the other—they "bless" each other implying a certain reciprocity. This complex fusion suggests that the distance between Celan and Rothenberg is momentarily overcome by the awareness of a shared language. The poem ends with a blessing and a prayer.

Khurbn: The Voices of the Dead

Because of the special significance of the Yiddish language—Rothenberg's mother tongue until the age of four—the poet prefers the word *khurbn* to "Holocaust." The Yiddish word *khurbn* carries an emotional weight, which Rothenberg evokes right at the beginning of the sequence. For the journey of the book involves "returning to a single word / the child word" (5).[36] But since "those who spoke it in the old days / now held their tongues" (5), their voices are conveyed through the poet:

> there is no holocaust
> for these but khurbn only
> the word still spoken by the dead
> who say my khurbn
> & my children's khurbn
> it is the only word that the poem allows
> because it is their own
> the word as prelude to the scream
>
> (*K*, 12)

By employing the Yiddish word *khurbn* and giving Yiddish titles to his poems (the above one is entitled "Dos Geshray [The Scream]"), Rothenberg memorializes and "cradles" the language of millions of murdered Eastern European Jews ("how I would take it from your voice / & cradle it" [5]). Like the Hebrew and Yiddish writers of Holocaust literature, he writes "for a lost community," and, as a poet, he speaks for the voiceless.[37] Furthermore, the word *khurbn* brings back Rothenberg's own childhood, when he first heard people speak about the shoah:

> the childword for me (from which I still feel a tightness in the throat & chest) was *khurbn* (*khirbn* in the dialect of where we came from). Holocaust is a Christian word that bears the image of sacrifice by fire. A totality of fire: that is, in human terms, a genocide. The fire I believe is true; the sacrifice a euphemism for the terror. . . . And it seemed to me then & now that the word itself is false, that the questions that it raised were false, that the answers that it seemed to force only increased the sense of pain & madness. *Khurbn/khirbn* was the word I know for it: disaster pure & simple, with no false ennoblement. Nothing left to say beyond the word. No sacrifice to ponder. (And no meaning.) (*NA*, 139–140)

Rothenberg makes his point unequivocally, both in poetry and prose. He thus joins the general debate about the use of terminology regarding the Holocaust. James E. Young observes that "[w]ary of the archaic Christian notion of a Jewish calvary in the Holocaust, many Jewish writers and theologians continue to resist this term altogether."[38] Yet despite these understandable reservations, Rosenfeld reasons that one may use the word because "we have no precise or authoritative terminology than the phrase 'the Holocaust.'"[39] In alternating between the term "Holocaust" and "shoah" (Hebrew for "destruction"), I follow Dieter Lamping.[40]

The poems of *Khurbn* are written under the influence of the voices of the past, which overwhelm the poet when he approaches the geographic location of the Holocaust—places such as Treblinka, which he finds to be only fifteen miles from his parents' hometown. Certain sites appear repeatedly in the book and are given their Polish or Yiddish names: the towns Ostrov-Mazovietsk (3), Miodowa (6), Ostrolenka (6), Ostrova (6), Vyzhkov (6), Lidice (8), Malkin (13); and the streets Miodowa Street (3), Malkiner Street (5); and the concentration camps Treblinka (7), Chelmo (8), and Oshvietsim (11). Names make history concrete and factual.

The sites are specific as well as symbolic: the empty *shtetl*, the forest near the concentration camp, the field of corpses, the burning pits filled with disjointed limbs, and the gas chambers. Rothenberg takes the reader to these places as he confronts their remains in present-day Poland and as they conjure up in him images and voices of the past. The poems proceed from first expressions of terror to images of destruction; it is a descent into the pit, with the poems "Nokh Aushvits (After Auschwitz)" and "The Domain of the Total Closes around Them" at its center. The poem that ends the cycle, "Peroration for a Lost Town," returns to the imagery of the beginning—an empty Polish town that has lost its Jews. However, its inhabitants are as blind and prejudiced as ever. On being asked about the fate of the Jews who lived in this place some forty years ago, they draw on anti-Semitic myths and superstitions. They have no sense of guilt or regret, just excuses, which the narrator reports in a sardonic tone:

> (There was a people once, they said, we called the old believers. A people with black beards & eyes like shrivel raisins. Out of the earth they came & lived among us. When they walked their bodies bent like yours & scraped the ground. They had six fingers on each hand. Their old men had the touch of women when we rubbed against them. One day they dug a hole and went back into the earth. They live there to this day.)
>
> (*K*, 38–39)

Thus, the sequence concludes with a bleak inventory of the repression of history and the persistence of anti-Semitism.

Although *Khurbn* traces a journey and therefore invites a linear approach, I will nevertheless refrain from a chronological reading because it is self-evident.[41] Instead, my analysis accentuates thematic aspects and issues related to poetics.

Khurbn can be viewed as the counterpart of *Poland/1931*. When Rothenberg composed the latter, he intentionally avoided writing about the shoah: "When I was writing *Poland/1931*, at a great distance from the place, I decided deliberately that that was not to be a poem about the 'holocaust'" (3). He makes up for this omission in the 1980s when he actually visits Poland. The irony is that the sense of loss and absence, which stimulated the fantastic explorations of his earlier book, is even further increased when the poet sets foot in the old country. Paradoxically, in this vacuum the shoah becomes an overwhelming "presence:"

> at honey street in ostrova
> where did the honey people go?
> empty   empty
> miodowa empty
> empty bakery & empty road to warsaw
> yellow wooden houses & houses plastered up with stucco
> the shadow of an empty name still on their doors
> shadai & shadow shattering the mother tongue
> the mother tongue's tongue but empty
> the way the streets are empty where we walk
>
> (*K*, 6)

Emptiness seeps through every line of the poem, "Dos Oysleydikn (The Emptying)." The poem reiterates the ethnic food Rothenberg imagined in *Poland/1931*, but everything has changed: "empty honey," "empty rolls," and "empty sorrel soup" (6). Food, objects, and places function as synecdoche; they invoke and mourn the absence of the Jews.

This invocation is epitomized by the belongings of the victims any visitor to the museum in Auschwitz must confront—suitcases, heaps of shoes, hair, and the soap and lampshades made from the bodies of the victims. Here the imagination reaches its limits. It must imagine that these "shoes & those dearer objects / like hair & teeth" (11) once belonged to people. Do these things speak? "I cannot say that they share the pain" (11), the narrator muses. For these objects seem inanimate and "the spirit of the place dissolving / indifferent to his presence / there with other ghosts" (12). Therefore, the poet is driven to raise his voice on behalf of them.

Rothenberg makes it very clear that he does not claim to be an eyewitness to the Holocaust. Hence the speaker of the poem "Di Magilas fun Aushvits (The Scrolls of Auschwitz)" states: "Was he there? No. No more than I was. But the dead have found him & eaten through his skin. He feels them in the morning when he shits: a gnawing pain beneath his heart" (27). The poet responds to the death of his family members and millions of other Jews as a Jew and a poet. In writing this sequence, he reflects on the function of the poet and poetry after Auschwitz.

The Hebrew and Native American traditions of poetry, both of which have a strong impact on Rothenberg's work, stress the communal role of poetry and the poet. In Native American cultures the poet often is a shaman, who communicates with the tribal ancestors on behalf of others. Some shamans are possessed by ancestral spirits and become their instrument.[42] Rothenberg draws on this idea when he views himself as a kind of shaman, that is, a medium for the voices of the dead. This thought was reinforced by his visit to Poland:

> The absence of the living seemed to create a vacuum in which the dead—the dibbiks who had died before their time—were free to speak. It wasn't the first time that I thought of poetry as the language of the dead, but never so powerfully as now. Those in my own family had died without a trace—with one exception: an uncle who had gone to the woods with a group of Jewish partisans and who, when he heard that his wife and children were murdered at Treblinka, drank himself blind in a deserted cellar & blew out his brains. (*K*, 3)

In this sequence of poems, Rothenberg lets his "uncle's khurbn . . . speak through me" (3–4). The central motif of *Khurbn* is therefore the notion of the poet as medium for the dead. This involves the acknowledgement of a horrifying silence:

> an enormity that had robbed language (one of our "proudest acts" he [Olson] said) of the power to meaningfully respond, had thus created a crisis of expression (no, of meaning, of reality), for which a poetics must be devised if we were to rise, again, beyond the level of a scream or of a silence more terrible than any scream. (Rothenberg, *Poems for the Millennium*, vol. 2, 472)

Yet, as Rosenfeld notes, to indulge "in silence is to court madness or death."[43] Hence Rothenberg underlines the need for a new poetics. Such a poetics is to give room to forgotten and disembodied voices. At first they appear to be formless and mute, but eventually they manifest themselves in dibbiks, the spirits of the Jewish folk tradition. Unspeakable and inexpressible suffering haunts the poems in another motif—the image of the lost tongue: "how I have lost / my tongue" (9), "a raw prong stuck through his tongue (19)," and "the girl without a tongue" (19). For the dead have lost their speech, "their words were silences" (5), "the cry you can hear // is no cry" (10), and they have lost their language, Yiddish:

a disaster in the mother's tongue
her word emptied
by speaking
("In the Dark Word, Khurbn," *K*, 5)

Sometimes the silence is broken by a mute cry: The female victims drowning in excrement "have no language for the horror / left to speak" (20), but their voices speak to and through the poet. Silence becomes a scream in the poem "Dos Geshray (The Scream)" (11–12). The human and spiritual power of the helpless shriek is also revealed in a ḥasidic dictum, which Rothenberg quotes elsewhere: "When a man has a reason to scream, & cannot though he wants to—he has achieved the greatest scream."[44]

Indeed, other poets who write about the shoah evoke precisely this kind of scream. The late work of Nelly Sachs provides a prominent example: "Toward the end, when it was apparent that language itself was giving way, her only recourse was to the raw expression of naked pain."[45] Similarly, Rothenberg becomes a mouthpiece for the spirits of the dead. His imagination and poetic sensibility enable him to "hear" the voice of his uncle, which sounds like

a scream
it is his scream that shakes me
weeping   in oshvientsim
& that allows the poem to come
("Dos Geshray [The Scream]," *K*, 12)

The implied poetics proposes that the speaker's emotions—his screaming and his weeping—are not merely an expression of personal grief. They transcend subjectivity because they allow the dead to speak. By means of such a shamanistic poetics—poetry as the language of the dead—the poem is able to reach beyond personal experience; it speaks to the community, the "tribe" of Israel, and to humanity as a whole. Such a poetics also asserts the poet's communal role and his or her responsibility toward history, which is why Rothenberg insists that "[t]he poems that I first began to hear at Treblinka are the clearest message I have ever gotten about why I write poetry" (4).

This strong sense of a connection with the past is symbolized by the concept of the *dibbik/dibbuk*.[46] According to Rothenberg's glossary at the end of the book, dibbiks are the "spirits of those who die before their time & enter into (i.e. possess) the bodies of the living" (111). In a broader definition, Gershom Scholem's proposes that a dibbik

> in Jewish folklore and popular belief [is] an evil spirit or a doomed soul which enters into a living person, cleaves to his soul, causes mental illness, talks through his mouth, and represents a separate and alien personality.[47]

The poet appropriates this tradition, which also features in Yiddish literature, such as in Ansky's play "The Dybbuk." Finkelstein comments that the possession of a woman by the dibbik of her deceased beloved in this play "may . . . be seen as part of a divinely ordained process of purification." Yet in this critic's opinion, the use of dibbiks in Rothenberg's poetry departs from this earlier perspective. For "the ghosts of the Khurbn that possess Rothenberg are the victims of genocide, the most heinous of crimes, for which there can be no rituals of purification."[48]

Moreover, the poet combines the Yiddish motif of the dibbik with the concept of shamanistic spirit possession and spirit communication. Thus Rothenberg imagines legions of dibbiks perched on trees (27); they are "hapless spirits / . . . millions of souls turned into ghosts at once" (13). Some shamanic cultures visualize the souls of the dead as birds perched on trees.[49] These dibbiks are shadowless: "they cast no shadow of their own" (13)—poor ghosts, who come to possess the living, "clusters of jews / who swarm here mothers without hair / black-bearded fathers" (14). Their invasion of the world of the living is described in the poem "Dibbukim (Dibbiks)" (13–14). It pictures how

> the innocent dead
> grow furious they break down doors
> drop slime onto your tables
> they tear their tongues out by the roots
> & smear your lamps your children's lips
> with blood
>
> (*K*, 13)

The dead are calling for revenge. Their initial silence becomes a scream and eventually turns into a curse in "Di Toyte Kloles (The Maledictions)" (33–35). Rothenberg gives the curse the suggestive form of an incantation. Its accumulative structure and the repeated use of the same phrase ("let this and this happen") supports the build-up of emotional intensity and the expression of anger, rage, and desperation:

> Let the dead man call out in you because he is a dead man
> Let him look at your hands in the light that filters through the table where he sits
> Let him tell you what he thinks & let your throat gag on his voice
> Let his words be the poem & the poem be what you wouldn't say yourself
> Let him say that every man is a murderer & that he is a murderer like all the rest
> Let him say that he would like to beat & kill beat & kill let him say that it is nothing nothing nothing
>
> (*K*, 33)

The dead man's voice is very specific. For it is the voice of Rothenberg's uncle who cries out in Yiddish in the darkest part of the poem:

> But the movement of my soul through space & time brings me inside you
> The immeasurable part of a language is what we speak he says who am I? dayn mamas bruder farshvunden in dem khurbn un muz in mayn eygenem loshn redn loz mikh es redn durkh dir dos vort khurbn

> Mayne oygen zaynen blind fun mayn khurbn ikh bin yetst a
> peyger) a corpse to which the light will not return forever
> for whom the light is lost
>
> (*K*, 34–35)

The depth of the despair and suffering in this passage is marked by the use of a Jewish language, which makes it inaccessible to some readers. Susan Gubar notes that "[b]y making the poem be what he would not have said himself, Rothenberg alienates the speaker (and reader) from the text in a form meant to disturb and shock."[50] However, at the end of the book, the poet provides a translation: "your mother's brother vanished in the khurbn and must speak in my own tongue let me speak it through you the word khurbn // my eyes are blind from my khurbn I am now a corpse" (111). This mournful cry leaves the reader stupefied and benumbed. But because this effect is intended, Rothenberg advises us to dwell on the strange, unknown sounds of these words: "I would strongly urge the reader to catch them in their initial incomprehensibility" (111). These words represent the distance between those who died in the shoah and us. At the same time, they demonstrate the problem of endorsing any other perspective than that of the victims.

This corroborates Lamping's theory that Holocaust poetry is characterized by a turn toward the victims. Many poets who write about the shoah let the victims speak through them. Often their speech is choral and communal.[51] That is why Rothenberg visualizes *legions* of dibbiks:

> Once the dibbik was a singular occurrence. It is now repeated many million times as the result of so much early death. Into whom do the dead souls enter? Each one contains a dibbik, or some of them contain a world of dibbiks. (*K*, 27)

However, Lamping notes that such a close identification with the victims only seems to be a viable option for Holocaust survivors. [52] But Rothenberg breaks with this principle. His poetics proposes that this is not a matter of choice. Overwhelmed by the invisible ghosts and dibbiks of the past, the poet describes his experience in terms of possession. Once more, he reflects on the poet's shamanistic role and draws parallels with other artists. Tatsumi Hijikata, for example, a Japanese post-Hiroshima choreographer and writer, also regards the artist as shaman: "Hijikata writes: 'To make the gestures of the dead, to die again, to make the dead enact their deaths again, this is what I want to feel. The dead are my teachers & live inside me'" (27). Rothenberg leaves no doubt that these words are confirmed by his own experience. In the following prose fragment, which is incorporated into a larger prose poem, "Di Magilas Fun Aushvits (The Scrolls of Auschwitz)," the author himself speaks:

> It was in Poland that I realized that I was haunted. Yes. "A dibbik is in me. A dibbik is in me." It is the condition of our lives for forty years now. Hijikata confirms it for us, that poetry is the speech of ghosts. The shamans in your books confirm it. In *my* books I meant to say. And didn't. (*K*, 28)

Evidently, Rothenberg's extended preoccupation with shamanism has a strong impact on his Holocaust poetry. By merging shamanistic concepts with motifs from Yiddish folklore, he creates potent and evocative symbols. The dibbiks in *Khurbn* are utterly shocking because they are "living beings reduced to symbols / of what it had been to be alive" (13).

In his poem "Nokh Aushvits (After Auschwitz)" and an accompanying essay of the same title, Rothenberg grapples with Adorno's proposition that it is barbaric to write poetry after Auschwitz ("nach Auschwitz ein Gedicht zu schreiben, ist barbarisch")."[53] This famed dictum initiated a stormy debate among poets, critics, and Holocaust scholars, which raged for decades, but which seems to have died down.[54] Lamping traces the way in which Adorno gradually revises his position in response to the Holocaust poetry of Celan and Sachs.[55] Retrospectively, this controversy seems to have been productive. For it raised many fundamental questions about the role of poetry after Auschwitz. Moreover, in his later writings, Adorno himself proposes some criteria for Holocaust poetry; his key principles are shock, shame, terror, silence, and radicalism. In fact, the philosopher and critic finally advocates a type of Holocaust poetry that alienates and shocks us deeply.[56]

Rothenberg likewise takes account of Adorno's changing positions in his own interpretation of the latter's writings:

> "After Auschwitz," wrote Adorno, "writing poetry is barbaric"; but that poetry he singled out as *lyrik*. Another kind of poetry came to be our central way of speaking: our most human act. It was a poetry that Adorno also recognized, when writing of it some

years later: "Perennial suffering has as much right to expression as a tortured man has to scream; hence it may have been wrong to say that after Auschwitz you could no longer write poems." (*NA*, 140)

From this the poet concludes that after Auschwitz we must endorse a different poetics—a poetics touched by the shoah. First, Rothenberg implies that such a new poetics challenges the contemporary significance of "the lyric." After the mechanized and anonymous death in Auschwitz obliterated the notion of individual suffering, the role of the individual voice in poetry, which may be associated with lyric poetry, can indeed be questioned.[57] In response, Rothenberg quotes a poem by Robert Creeley, an "American poet who, more than anyone else . . . , has saved (that is, transformed) the 'lyric voice' for us."[58] Because of the shoah and in spite of it, Rothenberg insists that poetry after the Holocaust must be human. It is in this sense that even lyric poetry still has legitimacy if it goes through a process of transformation: "As such it is not necessarily a poetry about the Holocaust, but a poetry that characterizes what it means to be human, to be a maker of poems (even lyric poems!) after Auschwitz."[59]

Second, Rothenberg posits that poetry after the Holocaust is to be a poetry of ugliness and screaming. In order to illustrate his point, Rothenberg invokes Antonin Artaud's excremental vision:

> I have seen falling from a great many coffins I know not what black matter, I know not what immortal urine from these forms mute of life which, morsel by morsel, drop by drop, destroyed themselves. . . . The breath of the bones has a center and this center is the abyss of Kah-Kah, Kah the corporeal breath of shit, which is the opium of eternal survival. . . . The odor of the eternal ass of death is the oppressed energy of a soul whom the world refused to let live. (Artaud, cited by Rothenberg, *NA*, 144)

Predominated by the subject of suffering, Artaud's work provides a "phenomenology of suffering."[60] In exploring his own mental and physical suffering, Artaud mapped the consciousness of suffering. This is why Rothenberg draws on the French author, who wrote "locked in the mental hospital at Rodez, while the Holocaust was going on—& in the pit of his own body" (*NA*, 144).

Yet, despite the uncanny effect of Artaud's nightmarish visions as representations of the Holocaust, one may wonder whether Rothenberg's appropriation of the French writer is legitimate. Can individual suffering really represent the suffering of millions of Holocaust victims? Does Rothenberg perhaps "instrumentalize" the shoah in order to support his own aesthetics/poetics?

These questions are justified. However, almost every writer and critic may be accused of utilizing the debate about the problems of poetry/literature after Auschwitz to underscore his or her own poetics and beliefs about literature. Moreover, Rothenberg admits that embracing an aesthetic of the ugly and writing "Nokh Aushvits (After Auschwitz)," "a poem addressed to ugliness," (18) does not come to him easily:

> he must fight
> his rage for beauty must make a poem
> so ugly it can drive out the other voices
> like artaud's squawk the poem addressed
> to ugliness   must resist
>
> (*K*, 18)

This is not an uncommon experience among writers and readers of Holocaust literature. Lawrence L. Langer notes that many people are unwilling to accept the destruction of beauty and of the individual as they occurred at Auschwitz. Rothenberg provides an example for aesthetic resistance to ugliness in a story about his friend Duncan, who reacted with disgust to a poem by Clayton Eshleman:[61]

> In the light of that, I remember sitting with Robert Duncan some years ago, while another friend at a symposium I had brought together read a poem filled with fantastical Artaudian images of the grotesque & warped—so much so that it caused Duncan to withhold applause & to whisper (too loudly I thought) that the poem was nothing but pure ugliness . . . or words to that effect. The comment stuck with me, bothered me a great deal in fact, & came rushing back at me, when I felt myself dibbik-stricken on my first journey to Poland & the death camps at Auschwitz & elsewhere. (*NA*, 145)

In his own poem Rothenberg transforms this experience in the following way:

> the poem is ugly & they make it uglier
> wherein the power resides

that duncan did—or didn't understand
when listening that evening to the other poet read
he said "that was pure ugliness" & oh it was
it was & it made my heart skip a beat
because the poem wouldn't allow it no
not a moment's grace nor beauty to obstruct
whatever the age demanded or the poem
shit poured on wall & floor
sex shredded genitals torn loose by dog claws
& the ugliness that you were to suffer
later that they had suffered
not as dante dreamt it but in the funnel
they ran through & that the others called
the road to heaven . . .
. . . .
prayershawl scraps & scraps of bodies bones
his child's he said leaping
into the mud the pool of bones
& slime the frail limbs separating
each time he pulls at one the mystery of body
not a mystery bodies naked then bodies
bonded & rotten

(*K*, 18)

This passage proclaims a terrifying "revelation"—"the mystery of the body / not a mystery." The shoah violated body and soul to such an extent that "idealized versions of the inviolable self"[62] were destroyed. Langer insists that such a fragmentation of the self results in a literature of fragmentation and decomposition.

Seeking a poetics that would recognize this human crisis, Rothenberg reviews the various strands of modernism and stays with those tendencies that seem prophetic in retrospect. "Artaud's definition of his theater of cruelty, designed to shake human sensibility out of the torpor into which most prior dramatic art had encouraged it to lapse, reads like a manifesto explaining the aesthetic intentions"[63] of Rothenberg's Holocaust poetry. Many poems in *Khurbn* therefore contain revolting, scatological imagery; they describe death by excrement:

THOSE WHO ARE BEAUTIFUL & THOSE WHO ARE NOT
change places to relive
a death by excrement
victims thrown into the pit & drowning
in their ordure
suffocating in the body's dross

this is extremity
these images of shit, too raw
for feeling,
that drips onto their faces

(*K*, 20)

These appalling scenes do not simply arise from the poet's imagination, but they are based on his reading of memoirs and testimonies of eyewitnesses as well as his viewing of photographs and other documentary material.[64] Personal experience also comes into it. Rothenberg recalls that when he crossed the border from Germany to Poland, he had to wait next to

> trucks filled with cattle on their way to slaughter. . . . The air stunk of excrement, became itself animal. I walked into a latrine to relieve myself, to piss, & was overwhelmed by the accumulated human smells. And I remember the books of witness I had read before, the visions of a death by excrement so often written there I felt myself (this man, this animal) in a condition of unrest as never before & in a condition of poetry. (*NA*, 143)

The graphic detail of his poems distinguishes them from earlier American-Jewish Holocaust poetry, which frequently employs synecdoche and, at the most, evokes the images of chimneys, smoke, and ashes. Holocaust poetry before 1974, when Brian Murdoch surveyed the field, contained no further details about people dying.[65]

That this is not true for Rothenberg's poems, makes them all the more upsetting and terrifying. We are not even spared the "vision" of the gas chambers, "where the flesh turned yellow from the gas" (30): "Let the screams take you to a room with small white tiles / Let the tiles vanish beneath the press of bodies let vomit & shit be everywhere let semen & menstrual blood run down his arms" (34). The poet does not shun death scenes because for him poetry after the Holocaust is "poetry in extremis—a poetry at the extremities of language . . . the extremities therefore of thought & feeling" (*NA*, 144):

this is extremity   this place

is where desire ends
where the warm flux inside the corpse
changes to stone

(*K*, 20)

Life ends in the pit. In the Psalms the pit serves as a metaphor for a threatening situation. It symbolizes the speaker's anxiety and emotional turmoil. But in Auschwitz the pits were real places, into which living people and corpses were thrown and burned ruthlessly, though according to the Jewish ritual law, corpses must be buried. Another poem, "The Domain of the Total Closes around Them," pictures this dreadful scene:

> "turning the corpses in the pits so densely packed it seemed
> that death had welded them together"
> the faces of the uncovered dead twist in the flames that touch
> them
> seem to come back to life   exuding lymph & fat
> that oozes from them   eyes exploding   like the belly
> of the pregnant woman   bursting open   now expels
> its fetus   that goes up in flames
>
> (*K*, 21)

The outrageous, but realistic imagery of this passage aims to reach the reader. It tries to overcome what Langer calls "reader reluctance," that is, people's unwillingness to think or read about the Holocaust because it is too horrible. Therefore, one of the goals of the literature of atrocity (Langer's term) is "the conquest of this very inability of the mind to contend with the recollections, the emotions, the apprehensions that *l'univers concentrationnaire* evokes."[66] Moreover, in using shock as a literary device, Rothenberg applies Artaud's principles of the theater of cruelty. The power of this strategy for Holocaust poetry was recognized early on by Adorno in his remark that nowadays there is only one way of reaching people—shock.[67] Consequently, Lamping argues that the creation of shock effects is the chief criterion for "successful" Holocaust poetry. What specific methods a poet employs to achieve this goal is of secondary importance.[68]

Rothenberg has many ways of stirring the reader's emotions. In the following passage, for example, he imagines his family members in the pit. Like the speakers in the Psalms, they cry out to God for help. Yet the experience of salvation seems to be denied to the victims of the shoah. This desolate situation addresses the problem of theodicy, that is, the question of how a benevolent, omniscient, and omnipresent God can allow such suffering. The non-intervention of God during the Holocaust throws into doubt the traditional Jewish belief in a God of history:

5
the grandfather who would have carried god with him
into the pit would he have cursed as I will for him?

or for that uncle who died, surely, with a malediction on his tongue
screamed it until the tongue dissolved the bullet achieved its mark
bit deeper

into a world of fact (alas) the mind that cries cried out
"the god is real he whom the dead bear with them

"who bear witness to the death of metaphor & cry:
"do not forget us! help us! think of us!"

(*K*, 25)

This is the only place in this sequence where the poet employs the word "god." It is spelled in small letters to represent a God who is out of control. Rothenberg characterizes this helpless God as the Suffering Servant Jesus, whose Yiddish name is Yoshke: "he is a man called yoshka is a name we share that grandfather & I / name that the jews called jesus that they screamed out of the slime" (25). Even though there are certain traditions in Judaism that view Israel as the Suffering Servant of Isaiah 53, Rothenberg's explicit mentioning of Jesus is risky, since it can be misunderstood.[69] It implies a comparison between Israel and Jesus, which may come over as insensitive and offensive. For hundreds of centuries Jews were persecuted in the name of precisely this Christian savior. However, Rothenberg deliberately invokes this history in order to adduce the argument that the God of history is in fact a God of cruelty and ugliness, a demiurge who deserves no respect: "the world is god's then & its ugliness follows from his" (25).

This assertion ties to Artaud's work, which has been described as gnostic. Growing out of tremendous personal suffering, it aims to transcend the physical and material world, which is regarded with disgust.[70] However, after the shoah, such disgust with life and the rejection of beauty has a much broader resonance. Negativity and negation are, therefore, another distinguishing mark of much Holocaust poetry.[71] For Rothenberg, such negativity results in the denial of meaning.

He insists that one must not try to attribute any kind of meaning to the shoah: "no meaning after auschwitz / there is only poetry" (14). Thus, the poet eventually reverses Adorno's dictum. He affirms the need for poetry exactly because of Auschwitz and because no help or healing can be expected from anywhere else. The demiurge does not answer prayers. God's silence, or better, the "darkness" implied in his absence is viewed as detrimental to life and to poetry. Thus, the poem ends enigmatically with the following stanza: "o god of caves (the stricken fathers cry) if you are light / then there can be no metaphor" (26).

Actually, this is a quotation from a poem about Shiva, the Indian God of light and darkness.[72] One reading of this paradoxical verse proposes that if one continues to believe in the absolute goodness of a God (symbolized by the light imagery) who did not intervene in the Holocaust, rather than a God who is "light" and "dark" at the same time, or whose "dark side" has been split off into a demiurge, the notion of a moral universe becomes absurd. No longer can there be a distinction between light and dark, good and evil, the metaphorical and the literal. In other words: there can be no metaphor. In his commentary on this text in *Technicians of the Sacred*, Rothenberg reads this passage in terms of a "denial of metaphor" (*TS*, 582). And indeed, the above poem states that the victims in the pit witness the "death of metaphor" (25).

Touching on the controversial issue of metaphoric language in Holocaust poetry, the poet reveals his awareness of the particular problems of this kind of literature. The use or rejection of metaphor in Holocaust poetry has prompted vehement debates among scholars, critics, and poets. It is a truism that much poetry relies on the use of metaphor, which involves some kind of comparison. However, in the "concentrationary universe"[73] metaphors became literal and the literal became figurative.[74] How then can one—after Auschwitz—continue to use metaphors to describe that which really took place, but goes beyond the imagination? And what is the role of the imagination in dealing with the Holocaust? Should it submit to facts and documents?

In his book *A Double Dying*, Rosenfeld exposes the pitfalls of metaphoric language in descriptions of the shoah. Postulating the uniqueness of the Holocaust, he concludes that this event is incomparable. Hence, "there are no metaphors for

Auschwitz, just as Auschwitz is not metaphor for anything else."[75] However, James E. Young objects to this stricture:

> Indeed, to leave Auschwitz outside of metaphor would be to leave it outside of language altogether: it was known, understood, and responded to metaphorically at the time by its victims; it has been organized, expressed, and interpreted metaphorically by its writers. . . . If carried to its literal end, an injunction against Auschwitz metaphors would place events outside of language and meaning altogether, thereby mystifying the Holocaust and accomplishing after the fact precisely what the Nazis had hoped to accomplish through their own—often metaphorical—mystification of events.[76]

Yet what Young calls "mystification" others take as a negative revelation.[77] Alternatively, they focus on the radical break in our conception of God, history, and humanity. Rothenberg shares both perspectives. On the one hand, he is cognizant of the problems of metaphor in poetry about the Holocaust. On the other, he does not entirely eschew metaphor or the use of the imagination. Like other authors of the literature of atrocity, Rothenberg allows for surrealist and nightmarish images to emerge (dibbiks, etc.). In addition, the prose poem is particularly well-suited to fusing documentary material and nightmares.[78] The poet deploys this device in the following poem:

> THE OTHER SECRET IN THE TRAIL OF MONEY
> & all true all true the poet's vision
> proven in the scraps. Bank notes & zlotys strewn
> over the field. Papers buried. Testaments
> to death & to the acquisitive nature of the guards
> its passage from hand to hand, to make a picnic
> in the Jewish State. Imagine.

> That he is again in the field leading to the showers & that the field is strewn with money. Those who are dead have left it, & the living bend to pick it up. The rhythms of Gold's orchestra drift past him, as in the woods sometimes the squeals of children & women or the deeper bellows of the men. He bends to lift a coin or to remove a bag of chocolates & raisins from a dead girl's coat. Butter. Cheese. White rolls. Roast chicken. Cognac. Cream. Sardines. "More sugar & tea than in the whole Warsaw ghetto." The Jewish workers & their guards feast in the woods. A child is with them—turns her mouth to you—that by gematria becomes a hole.
>
> (*K*, 15)

We do not know the identity of the man in the field strewn with money: Is he the poet imagining the past while crossing a field near a concentration camp? Is he a witness to the Holocaust, or perhaps even a perpetrator? Shifts of identity, time and place within the poem contribute to a sense of irreality. Factuality, on the other hand, is suggested by the references to the buried testaments of Holocaust victims and to Gold's orchestra, a band of camp prisoners who were forced to play music in the midst of Nazi murdering.

The conflation of facts and fantasy/nightmares, which can be observed in the above poem, can be called "irrealism."[79] Langer contends that this phenomenon characterizes much Holocaust literature. The function of irrealism is "[t]o establish an order or reality in which the unimaginable becomes imaginatively acceptable." But since this "exceeds the capacities of an art devoted entirely to verisimilitude . . . some quality of the fantastic, whether stylistic or descriptive, becomes an essential ingredient of the *l'univers concentrationnaire*."[80] On these grounds, Rothenberg's use of nightmares and the fantastic dibbik motif can be understood.

While attempting to evoke the concentrationary irreality, the poem about Auschwitz must eschew dramatization. Though it may be shocking, it needs to be distinguishable from the scenes of a horror movie. For Auschwitz is not fiction, and the function of the literature of atrocity is not to stimulate the reader with terror, but to overcome the reader's reluctance to confront a historical reality. Hence, Rosenfeld demands that Holocaust literature be wary of "theatrical hyperbole."[81] The Nazis themselves had a perverted sense of drama and performance. Rothenberg accentuates this frequently by alluding to Gold's orchestra: "the measure struck by gold's orchestra a sound so sweet that even the masters swayed to it / so did the jews bring tears to eyes already dark with smoke so would the jews bring tears again" (22).

Yet what kind of theater did the Nazis have in mind? The poet dwells on this question and relates it to the concept of "total theater." As we saw earlier, the notion of "total performance" or "total theater" appeals to Rothenberg and the avant-garde because it promises a unification of body and mind, art and life. Yet as he notes, Wagner in nineteenth-century Germany also endorsed the idea of a *Gesamtkunstwerk*. It is this utopian dream of a total art that the Nazis corrupted utterly:

THE DOMAIN OF THE TOTAL CLOSES AROUND
THEM for there is even
totality here a parody of telos of completion
in the monstrous mind of the masters those who give
themselves authority
over the rest of life who dole out life & death proportioned
to their own appetites as artists they forge a world a shadow
image of our own
& are the artists of the new hell the angels of the possible the
vision
passed from them down to the present of what art can do
what constructs of the mind
are thinkable when power assists their hands in the delusion
of the absolute

(*K*, 21)

This poem then deals with the theatricality and "aesthetics" of totalitarianism. What makes this a troubling subject for Rothenberg is that it represents the underside of his own concept of totality and total art. For the dream of unity and completion (*telos*) is wholly perverted by the Nazis, and the poet recognizes and examines this perversion. *Khurbn* prefaced with an obscure motto by Eshleman: "Since the hidden is bottomless, totality is more invisible than visible." Rothenberg explores that totality in the poem "The Domain of the Total Closes around Them."

According to his analysis, it is power that turns the utopian concept of totality into a parody of itself. "[W]hen power assists their hands," art becomes an instrument of death, while the artists, "in the delusion of the absolute," "dole out life & death." Surely, this is hubris. Rothenberg sees this corrupting principle at work in totalitarian states, but also in other situations of total power, such as "the total apparatus of canon-formation both as a religious & secular phenomenon."[82] Such negative totality, manifest in the total state, also creates its own God, "the terror of an angry & devouring god—the total god envisioned in the total state—made real by the imagination" (*NA*, 144).

In the second and fourth section, the poet examines what happens if humans play God. The example he examines is one of sadistic perversion. Here the link with Marquis de Sade's writings is illuminating: "debasement breeds this that de sade forefold that the young mind of isidore ducasse /

tracked to his own destruction so sweet it is so sickening" (24). Just like Pier Paolo Pasolini, who employs de Sade's novel, *The Hundred and Twenty Days of Sodom*, to present his view of Italian fascism in a film, Rothenberg emphasizes the pornographic side of the Nazi cruelty, "the bright pornography of death" (24).[83] He describes a scene in which a Nazi official, Max Bielas, rapes Jewish boys, but cloaks his crimes in kitsch:

> ill-fated Max Bielas handsome man who had a harem
> of little jewish boys . . .
> sent them to tend the flock of geese a row of pretty boys
> dressed up like princes & had a fabled dream house
> built for them. . . .
> they slept they sang they waited in the afternoons
> for uncle Max to come to them sweet
> german daddy bringing little cakes & *schlag* or letters
> from the folks out east they were his dwarfs & he
> their gentle snow white swooning when they pressed around him
> when he touched a tiny hand or let his thumb slide down
> the young back . . .
>
> (*K*, 24)

Not only does this passage illustrate the "eroticization of power" in Nazism[84]—a subject too broad to be discussed here—but it also exposes an important aspect of the Nazi aesthetics. This "aesthetic" serves as a negative foil to the kind of poetics Rothenberg is striving for. In unmasking it, he exposes what Holocaust poetry must shun by all means:

> the perpetrators themselves so often held to a cult of mindless beauty, while commiting [*sic*] the ugliest (because most systematically conceived) of crimes & degradations—as the final issue, so to speak, of a false & lying art. (*NA*, 145)

The notion of "a false & lying art" has often been associated with kitsch.[85] Without debating the benefits and downsides of this concept and its definitions, I would like to draw on Saul Friedländer's hypothesis regarding the instrumentalization of kitsch by the Nazis. Friedländer claims that "Nazism's attraction lay less in any explicit ideology than in the power of the emotions, images, and phantasms."[86] The above passage illustrates one of these phantasms: the rapist and murderer poses as "snow white." This kitschy image of false harmony (kitsch may be defined in these terms) is reminiscent of many well-known portraits of Hitler with children or animals. Friedländer notes that these depictions also frequently incorporate death imagery—blood-red sunsets, destructive fires, and young heroes destined to die in heroic warfare.[87] But exactly this kind of juxtaposition of kitsch and death is characteristic of the Nazi aesthetic. It functions to neutralize the "extreme situation" of death, and—one may add—to conceal violence and perversion.[88] For what really drives the "sugar daddy," Max Bielas, is desire:

> it is desire that compels him
> directs the flow the force engulfing him & them
> all in the name of love that has delivered many to this place
> as hate has the goods of the intellect reduced
> & bounded by the craving self protected from the world
> where the mind & the body go astray theirs is no simple wish
> for death or order but toward that greater ugliness
>
> (*K*, 24)

The Nazi aesthetic parodies Rothenberg's own poetics and the role of the poet who writes after Auschwitz, who must address ugliness, not because he or she wishes to do so ("we pull away from it although it holds us" [24]), but because this is what a truthful poem—the opposite of "false & lying art"—requires. In the present context "truth" can be associated with the principle of conflating art and life. This is where Artaud's notion of the total theater comes back into the argument. For him, cruelty in the theater works like a knife that performs an operation; it cuts straight through into the audience's consciousness.[89] This way theater may unify art and life.

Rothenberg takes this principle and applies it to the Nazis. He suggests that in the concentrationary universe a kind of "total theater" was performed, in which the Nazis tried to unite art and life, yet in an utterly perverse way. Once more, there is the juxtaposition of kitsch/lying art and death: "& sing bravely the song of work & death that the masters had enjoined that gold had written for them / ecstatic jews in wood . . . / yours is the world of art writ large art joined to life until the boundaries split apart" (22). The grammatical antecedent of the pronoun "yours" is ambiguous. Does it allude to the wooden "sculpted images of jews" (22), or rather to the perpetrators? Just one thing is certain: the unification of art and life does not succeed. When "the boundaries split apart," it becomes apparent that what the Nazis pursue is neither art nor life, but death disguised in "doleful music where bad art / to bad art's joined the heart grows murky weeps at its own losses but drones on" (22).

By contrast, Rothenberg's *Khurbn* does not fall into this trap. Rather, the poet demonstrates his astute awareness of the problems and limitations of Holocaust poetry. Being conscious of various pitfalls, he nevertheless succeeds in composing a poetic sequence that gives expression to his own feelings of terror and despair in confronting the shoah and which at the same time seriously addresses many of the questions arising from this experience. It therefore deserves to be included in every major anthology of Holocaust poetry and to be studied in greater detail than the framework of this book permits.

"14 Stations"

In comparison to *Khurbn*, "14 Stations" seems rather impersonal and controlled.[90] The poet's voice is more withdrawn and the meaning less discursive. This sequence presupposes some background knowledge about the shoah. Like much Holocaust poetry, it evokes rather than describes the events, presuming that the historical facts are known.[91] Except for the names of the concentration camps, which appear in the individual titles, there is no definite reference to the shoah. However, the poems induce the reader to understand them on the basis of her historical knowledge.

Moreover, the title of the sequence refers to a historical reality: "Thirteen of the stations are death camps built on or near railroad lines; the fourteenth is Babi Yar, a ravine outside Kiev where tens of thousands of Ukrainian Jews were murdered."[92] The names of the concentration camps and the aerial photographs of them convey this catastrophe of Jewish history "objectively." However, the ambiguous title also suggests a Christian motif—the Stations of the Cross. In Catholicism, a series of fourteen stations serves as an object of contemplation on the Passion of Christ. Through an act of inversion, the title "14 Stations" suggests a series of "meditations" on the Holocaust. Projecting the shoah onto the foil of subjective religious reflection, "14 Stations" proposes an identification of Jewish suffering with Christ, but it also negates it utterly, for Rothenberg here emphasizes the meaninglessness of the Holocaust.

It is interesting that the origin of "14 Stations" is linked to *Khurbn*. The painter Arie Galles originally intended to use quotations from Rothenberg's Holocaust cycle to accompany a series of large

> drawings in charcoal and white conté crayon with wrought-iron frames. The images are based on aerial photographs of concentration camps taken by Luftwaffe and Allied reconnaissance during World War II. Within each drawing is embedded one-fourteenth of the Kaddish. The Aramaic and Hebrew phrases are invisible, interwoven into the pattern and texture of each drawing.[93]

But Rothenberg was not too enthusiastic about the idea of taking verses out of the context of a personal poetic sequence.[94] For that reason he decided to write a new series of poems based on a method that would give them the appearance of objectivity—an "objectivity" that would correspond to the technique Galles employed in his photo-realistic paintings. Thus he chose, once more, gematria as a procedural device:

> As Galles worked from documentary photographs to establish some pretense at distance (=objectivity), I decided to objectify by turning again to gematria (traditional Hebrew numerology) as a way to determine the words and phrases that would come into the poems. The counts were made off the Hebrew and/or Yiddish spellings of the camp names, then keyed to the numerical values of words and word combinations in the first five books of the Hebrew Bible. It is my hope that this small degree of objective chance will not so much mask feelings or meaning as allow them to emerge. (*S*, 100)

At first sight this description seems clear and straightforward. But at second sight it reveals various ambiguities that result from Rothenberg's compositional method and are also inscribed in the poems. Here, the use of gematria involves many paradoxes.

Let me begin with an obvious one: Although "14 Stations" is based on an "objective" method, it nevertheless manages to bring out powerful emotions. The poet achieves this effect by means of juxtaposition. Surrealist juxtaposition, for instance, attempts to reach down into the depth of the psyche and to stimulate intuition.[95] By employing Hebrew numerology, Rothenberg derives a highly emotive and hermetic collage of biblical quotations, which achieves precisely this kind of psychological effect. The fragments from the Torah are arranged in a disjointed, associative way:

torn in pieces
a terror, a god,
go down deeper
("The First Station: Auschwitz-Birkenau," *S,* 101)

If we read this passage as a statement about the poetics of this sequence, the "pieces" may stand for the fragments of the Hebrew Bible, which are assembled by aleatory means into a hermetic, nondiscursive text. Since this kind of poetry cannot be deciphered rationally, it forces the reader to resort to more intuitive, immediate ways of understanding the text—to "go down deeper." In this sense, the reader's personal feelings are allowed to surface, or, if one buys into the surrealist perspective, the hidden meanings of the unconscious are allowed to emerge.

Yet this "subjectivity" is balanced by the seeming "objectivity" of the compositional process. According to traditional Judaism, the objective rules of gematria are revealed by God.[96] Hence, a text derived by gematria overflows with divine meaning. Rothenberg asserts that he employs gematria in order to establish "some pretense at objectivity." Like Galles, who *draws* photographs in order to foreground factuality and objectivity, the poet chooses a method that produces the *appearance* of objectivity. In fact, in both projects "objectivity" and "subjectivity" are intertwined. Galles introduces a personal and spiritual element into his depictions of the Nazi death machinery by weaving Hebrew and Aramaic words into the picture. Similarly, Rothenberg undermines the "objectivity" of his method by resorting to arbitrary constraints, which enable him to manipulate the material.

For example, the poet employs the Hebrew *and/or* Yiddish spelling of names of the concentrations camps. (Galles, a fluent native Yiddish speaker, helped the poet to write down these names.)[97] This implies that the number value can vary depending on which language was chosen. In the process of determining the "basic number" of a poem, Rothenberg would then have some choice.

Furthermore, the instruction to "key" the camp names "to the numerical values of words and word combinations in the first five books of the Hebrew Bible" leaves much room for selectivity. We are not told exactly how the words in the poems are linked/"keyed" to the title—whether they all have the same number value as the title or whether they are added up to obtain a sum that equals the number value of the title, whether the stanza or the verse serves as a numerical unit, etc. Actually, Rothenberg admits that he did not follow his procedural rules strictly. Starting off with the number value of the title of the poem, he expanded on it in various ways looking for words that would "fit."[98]

As with Rothenberg's other gematrias, the forming hand of the poet can be seen in many ways. Stanzas, rhymes, and various patterns of repetition lend the poems an orderly quality. On the one hand, these devices counteract the confusion and disorientation generated by the fragmented syntax of these poems. On the other, phonetic and syntactic repetition increase the emotional intensity of a passage. The poem becomes a cry of pain and terror: "how naked they come / my fathers / my fathers" (101). Repetition also expresses sorrow and lament. Furthermore, it accentuates the horror of the atrocity by forcing the reader to look it straight in the face:

> a carcass
> a carcass
>
> & a dancing
> carcass
> ("The Fifth Station: Bergen-Belsen," *S*, 105)

What is even more disturbing to the reader is that this grotesque imagery is accompanied by a musical texture:

> *For Rachel, twice:*
> She turned aside,
> I thought,
> the wood, the thorns
> wounding my thighs
> ("The Thirteenth Station: Ravensbruck," *S*, 115)

Even though assonance, alliteration, and half-rhyme exist in Hebrew poetry, they are unlikely to underlie the *lists* of Hebrew words that Rothenberg uses as a basis for these poems. Rather, these English sound patterns suggest a carefully prepared collage of words and phrases. Being aware of the role of such devices in Hebrew poetry and oral literature, Rothenberg composes his English poems with an ear for the power of repeated sounds. The musicality of this and other poems evokes a sense of beauty. This takes us back to the controversial question, which has been debated at length in regard to Celan's "Death Fugue": Is it appropriate to write beautiful poems about the Holocaust?[99] Rothenberg's own position on this issue is that such a poem must be "touched" by Auschwitz. This does not necessarily mean that it must eschew musicality. Rather it may utilize the latter in order to expose the conflict between terror and beauty.

Rothenberg diagnoses a similar tension in surrealist poetry. He asserts that surrealism espouses a sense of beauty, but is "infused, infected, with fierce desires for 'transgression' (G. Bataille)."[100] Similarly, his own quasisurrealist Holocaust poems embrace beauty on one level, but are "infected" by the historical events. This creates an unsettling tension. Just like in Celan's "Death Fugue," beauty is called forth and discredited by the terror of history.[101]

Further tensions arise from the evocation of biblical traditions. Rothenberg appropriates the emotive vocabulary of the Hebrew Bible and the tone of prophetic speech.[102] Hence the poems resonate with the biblical tradition, which interprets history in terms of certain schemes and historical archetypes. Moreover, the poet imitates various types of parallelism, which occur especially in the Psalms and in Lamentations. Rothenberg summons these ancient Jewish traditions—"sanctioned vehicles for expressing one's rage both against God and against the gentiles"[103]—only to subvert them. For if they are displaced into the historical context of the shoah, these traditions take on different meanings, and it becomes questionable to what extent these traditions constitute an appropriate and satisfying response to the shoah. This kind of "inversion of liturgical language to repudiate traditional literature's implicit premises of order and explicit philosophic and social affirmation"[104] is indicative of American-Jewish Holocaust literature.

Displacement, for instance, is a perfect strategy for undermining and questioning the traditional Jewish way of interpreting history in terms of sin and retribution.[105] It allows Rothenberg to raise, once more, the subject of theodicy. Indeed, "14 Stations" raises many themes that are stated more explicitly in *Khurbn*. The two cycles complement each other by posing the same questions, but in different ways. The later work, "14 Stations," addresses the problem of theodicy by displacing and estranging biblical speech in such a way that the poems resonate with biblical theology, yet at the same time undermine it. In traditional Jewish thought the Torah constitutes the covenant between God and the Jewish people. By utilizing words from this sacred text Rothenberg implicates the covenant, but also doubts its continuation.[106] Thus, the poem proposes that in the Holocaust, blessings ("be fruitful and multiply" [Gen. 1:28]) are turned into destruction, which renders the covenant absurd:

as he had spoken
from the wilderness
be fruitful

(& they were fruitful)

so he could blind them
with a fist
& cut them—
("The Twelfth Station: Sobibor," *S*, 114)

The biblical idiom enforces the bitter irony of the poem. It portrays a sadistic God, who merely creates in order to destroy. Even if the biblical God is not directly mentioned, "he" is implied by the method of gematria, by the language and the imagery of these poems. Rothenberg employs these devices to draw the picture of a cruel, omnipotent, and temperamental divinity. Along these lines, the poet ruminates over the fact that the word "terror" and the word "God" have the same number value in Hebrew:

> I found that the letters in the Hebrew god-name, *eloha*, aleph-lamed-vav-hey add up numerically [=42] to the Hebrew word *behalah*, bet-hey-lamed-heh, "terror [panic, alarm]." That they also add up to *kvodi*, "my glory," only intensifies the problematic. . . . So, take it any way you choose. *Where God breaks into what I write or think, it is the terror that admits him.*[107]

This startling equivalence (God = terror) sums up a major theme in Rothenberg's Holocaust poetry.[108] He expands on the notion of the gnostic God in the next poem. Particularly disturbing is the idea that the demiurge cannot be distinguished from the perpetrators of the shoah. We are unable to determine whether the speaker of the phrase "I will kill" is God or man:

& I will kill
the fat
& the fat ones

the wicked
the he-goats
your mistress

conceived
like a coat
& torn off

like the twenty
those you ran over
& numbered

& like those
I will kill
("The Fifth Station: Bergen-Belsen," *S*, 105)

The subtle net of repetitions in this passage creates a superficial sense of order and structure. There are four stanzas of equal length; some verses even contain an equal number of words. Typographically the stanzas look like rectangular building blocks and give the impression of stability. Moreover, the first and the last verse frame this section to convey a sense of closure, which represents the irreversible consequence of killing. The mentioning of "he-goats" and "fat" alludes to the sacrificial system of the Torah. Even though Rothenberg rejects the slightest intimation that the shoah could be interpreted in terms of sacrifice, he includes sacrificial imagery into the poems in order to portray a bloodthirsty godhead.

In the above poem, therefore, the loaded sacrificial imagery is blended with allusions to sexual violence ("your mistress / conceived / . . . / & torn off"). But the identities of the mistress, the speaker, and the addressee are uncertain. In one reading, for example, somebody (God or the perpetrator) declares that they will kill "the fat ones," "the wicked," "the he-goats," "your mistress," and "those you ran over." Yet how is this possible? How can one kill again those who have been run over?

Alternatively, we could try the following reading: "I will kill the fat ones etc., who were conceived by your mistress; I will kill like the twenty you have killed." But who are "the twenty"? Who is "you"? The person (or persons) addressed with "you" seems to have a mistress, but is that person identical with the one mentioned in the eleventh verse ("those you ran over")? Many more questions could be asked and many more readings attempted without coming to a conclusion, for identity in this poem is unstable. As Langer notes, it indicates that, as a result of the events of the Holocaust, "identity as a conception of character is obliterated."[109]

Moreover, the shoah challenges our ability to construct meaning. The textual strategies of the poem therefore convey the difficulties of making sense of the shoah in religious or metaphysical terms. In various ways "14 Stations" underscores instability.

Overdetermination is a prominent strategy. The identity-shifts in the above poem, for instance, are the result of an overdetermined syntax. Each phrase/line can be related to a number of other phrases/lines. Such syntactic ambivalence contributes to the endless deferral of meaning.

Roles and identities are invoked only to be deconstructed immediately. Some poems exhibit the features of a role poem. "The Eighth Station: Chelmo" (108–9), for instance, comprises a chorus of children and survivors. Usually, such poems allow the portrayal of the events of the Holocaust from various perspectives (victims, liberator, survivor, perpetrator).[110] But Rothenberg subverts the simplicity of this scheme by conflating perspectives. When identities and roles are shifting, the voice of the speaker becomes arbitrary, which leaves us wondering: Who is speaking? Who is the victim? Who is the perpetrator?

According to Langer, these literary strategies have enormous philosophical implications. They illustrate the radical difference of the concentrationary universe, in which standard notions of tragedy, hero, and culprit are dissolved.[111] Rothenberg makes this point indirectly, but very effectively. Anyone, therefore, who tries to "make sense" of this poetic sequence will necessarily reach a point of frustration because the denial of meaning is inscribed in the text. Yet this perspective is motivated by a historical event and not by linguistic or philosophical speculations (as in deconstructionism).

Furthermore, the use of gematria as a procedural device enhances the hermetic quality of the poems, for gematria provides the poet with a list of disparate words and phrases, which he combines into a cryptic text. Defamiliarization—another strategy typical of Holocaust poetry—increases the opaqueness of "14 Stations."[112] Because the vocabulary of this sequence is limited to the language of the Torah, the poet is compelled to use biblical words to refer to the shoah. For example, the phrase "lords of fat" (103) comes to represent the perpetrators, while the adjective "streaked" (102) alludes to the concentration camp prisoners who wore striped prison suits. Furthermore, the reference to numbers suggests the tattoos with which the Nazis marked their victims. Disconcerting, however, is that the concept of numbers also alludes to Rothenberg's own compositional method—gematria:

> & when they came
> & carried her away
> he gave them numbers
> by the sword
>
> a bell
> for those with numbers
> ("The Thirteenth Station: Ravensbruck," *S*, 115)

Defamiliarization increases the reader's sense of being confronted with something unknown and abnormal. In other words, our sense of reality and our interpretation of it is challenged by the irreality of the Holocaust. The poem does not allow for a comforting and comfortable meaning:

> like the wheat
> on our altars,
> all will be eaten,
> will not be
> a sacrifice
> there with the nations,
> but a curse
> in her womb
> ("The Eighth Station: Chelmno," *S*, 108–9)

By stripping sacrifice of its power to redeem and heal, "14 Stations" resists the projection of any meaning onto the Holocaust. In a way, this sequence illustrates what *Khurbn* states discursively:

> no holocaust because no sacrifice
> no sacrifice to give the lie
> of meaning   & no meaning   after auschwitz
> there is only poetry   no hope

no other language left to heal
no language

("Dibbukim (Dibbiks)," *K*, 14)

Rothenberg exposes "the lie of meaning" after Auschwitz by employing gematria. In "14 Stations," gematria is used as a procedural device to undermine any sense of meaning and stability. This happens in a complex process. The surface of the text invites the reader to look for stable identities, a narrative, and meaning. But this is a trap that subverts our need for meaning. By utterly frustrating every attempt at a determinate reading, Rothenberg stresses the absurdity of finding meaning in the shoah. Hence, the poetry cycle concludes without consolation. Meaning dissolves as

in the blood
they burn

they turn them
into smoke

("The Fourteenth Station: Stutthof," *S*, 116)

Conclusion

Rothenberg's Holocaust poetry represents his most recent and profound Jewish work. It gains special force and relevance because it moderates any absolute claims of his holistic poetics.

This book reveals the poet's persistent "search for wholeness of spirit and clarity of meaning."[113] Yet his strife for totality (in the sense of wholeness) receives a serious blow through the confrontation with the Holocaust and its implications. Auschwitz introduces a new element of negativity into Rothenberg's poetry and poetics—negativity without redress. Whereas the poet usually associates destruction with the renewal that necessarily follows from it, here all emphasis lies on the denial of meaning and affirmation. His poetry is "touched" by the Holocaust to such an extent that Rothenberg's holistic poetics is put at abeyance. This takes a variety of forms.

In "14 Stations" Rothenberg's general drive toward coherence is contrasted by fragmentation. The poet also insists that after Auschwitz the passion for beauty must be controlled; the poet must strive to write a poem addressed to ugliness. In doing so, Rothenberg seeks legitimization from historical sources. The ugly irreality of the shoah is therefore not merely a product of his imagination, but a historical fact. To emphasize this, the poet refers to historical sources, photographs, museum objects, memoirs, and testaments about the Holocaust. These documents give veracity to his poems. In *Khurbn*, appropriation works as a legitimization strategy. For once, trickery is suspended. The same could be said about the use of comic or humorous elements, which otherwise are characteristic of Rothenberg's texts. In writing about the shoah, the poet abstains from laughter. At the most, it is replaced by bitter irony, parody, and sarcasm.

Furthermore, the poet avoids instrumentalizing the perspective of the victims for his own concerns. Instead, the inclusion of Yiddish words and phrases symbolizes respect for victims of the Holocaust and the world that was lost with them. While the poet usually endorses the view that poetry has the power to create meaning and heal, this belief is challenged by his Holocaust poems. In fact, these poems indicate that there is no restitution for the loss of six million Jews and that any attempt at retrospectively giving meaning to the events must be opposed as cruel and inappropriate. In the same vein, Rothenberg rejects the concept of a God who allowed the shoah to take place. But this does not cause the poet to rebuke humanism. Despite the atrocities committed in the Holocaust, Rothenberg insists on the need to write poetry, "but a poetry that characterizes what it means to be human . . . after Auschwitz" (*NA*, 143).

Conclusion: A Jewish Ethnopoetics and Experimental Jewish Poetry

THE READER MAY BE WARNED THAT THIS BRIEF CHAPTER IS NOT A summary of the complex issues explored in this book. Trying to make any conclusive remarks about Rothenberg's work is problematic, as his explorations of Jewish tradition have not ended and every further publication by him changes the shape of his entire work.

Instead, I will open up yet another perspective on various themes and subjects that feature in this study. My present focus is on the poet's dialogue with Otherness. Ethnopoetics may be described in terms of Otherness, that is, it strives to recognize "the 'world of others' both within and without the self."[1] In constructing Jewish identity this means to be open toward the Other wherever it is found. A Jewish ethnopoetics involves precisely this attitude.

But who or what is the Other? For Rothenberg, the Other may take many forms. Obviously, the Other can be found in another culture (non-Western, non-Jewish, tribal) and the poet's involvement with these kinds of Otherness are well known. However, there is also a *Jewish* Other—the repressed, dark, and subterranean side of Jewish tradition. This book concentrates on Rothenberg's reappropriation of this strand of Judaism.

The poet discovers the Jewish Other in different historical periods (ancient, medieval, and Eastern European Jewish culture), in suppressed Jewish voices (the Hebrew Goddess, the Jewish shaman, the kabbalistic magician, "a world of Jewish mystics, thieves & madmen"), or in silent Jewish voices (the victims of the Holocaust). Such Jewish Otherness also resides in repressed Jewish traditions, especially in ecstatic, magic, and transgressive practices (Abulafianism, Shabbateanism, Frankism, etc.). Rothenberg's dialogue with the Jewish Other then involves the recovery of all this material. His reappropriation of Jewish tradition employs appropriative strategies to overcome historical and cultural distance.

Rothenberg's appropriative strategies show intriguing similarities with medieval forms of rewriting. Therefore, Marcus's hypothesis regarding the neomedieval character of postmodernism may be extended to the poet's use of appropriation. In fact, Rothenberg's palimpsestous, imitative, and apocryphal writing, as well as his use of commentary and the habit of misquotation, are postmodern *and* neomedieval. Similarly, the poet's approach to history—his proclivity toward ahistoricism and his love of myth—parallels the medieval mind-set.

But on the other hand, his perspective also differs from a medieval position. For it involves a different kind of self-awareness. In selecting, transforming, and transvaluing Jewish tradition, Rothenberg makes conscious choices. Time and again he demonstrates that he recognizes his own place in history and vis-à-vis other cultures. Even though he tends to emphasize similarity, there is also an acute sense of difference and unbridgeable distance. This feeling of loss propels Rothenberg's reappropriation of tradition.

This reappropriation of Jewish tradition contributes to the construction of a poetics of the sacred. Appropriated materials and forms are used in order to produce a sacred effect so that ultimately poetry takes the place of religion: "after auschwitz / there is only poetry." In this sense, poetry becomes what Roskies calls a "surrogate for faith."[2]

Rothenberg's poetics of the sacred has multiple functions. Above all, it aims to reempower poetry by reappropriating certain traditions. Poetry and the poet may regain a more central role in society if the communal role of poetry is emphasized and explored. And community can be generated by storytelling, performance, entertainment, and ritual, all of which characterize Rothenberg's poetry. At the same time, the poet explores the way in which poetry can satisfy our need for meaning and can be utilized to create new meaning, for instance, by means of displacement (contextualization, decontextualization), or the use of gematria. His interest in Jewish magic also implies the desire to reempower poetry by going back to its roots in naming. Furthermore, it implicates the dream of a language that would overcome the split between word and thing, or between signifier and signified. However, it should be noted that in recent years many aspects of this "holistic" poetics are put at abeyance as a result of the poet's deep confrontation with the Holocaust.

Because of Rothenberg's insistence on continuous change, and his postlogical stance, it is impossible to make any conclusive statements about his writing. Nevertheless, I will turn our attention once again to various innovative aspects of his poetry. They concern the recovery to poetry of various repressed or forgotten forms of writing—the return of number (gematria, numerology), the return of story (storytelling and the incorporation of myths), and the return of comedy (parody, travesty, and the burlesque). According to Perloff, all these tendencies characterize postmodern poetry.

Moreover, Rothenberg's rewriting of Jewish tradition exhibits other postmodern trends. His appropriative strategies imply the destruction and subversion of hierarchies (e.g., between original and translation, or between poetry and commentary) and the dissolution of boundaries (e.g., between poetry and prose); they perform transgressive acts and pursue impurity (thematically and formally). Antinomianism features strongly in Rothenberg's Jewish poetry. Not only does he frequently refer to heretic movements, but his own approach to tradition also resembles that of the trickster who permanently deceives and breaks taboos.

On the one hand, this tricksterish aspect of reappropriation marks a postmodern stance (keyword: "the poet as a trickster"). On the other, Rothenberg's rewriting of Jewish tradition also intimates the need to go beyond contemporary trends. This desire is manifest in his search for meaning, origin, and presence and the implicit denial of deconstructionist presuppositions.[3] Rothenberg's experimental Jewish poetry, which includes new "Jewish genres," such as the Jewish event poem or the gematria poem, invigorates and enriches the American and the American-Jewish poetry scene. It differs from most academic Jewish poetry as well as from the New American Poetry and Language Poetry:

> Rothenberg has managed to mark out a possible poetic practice that extends beyond either the New American Poetry or Language Poetry, although it has elements of both. . . . Not because he achieves some bridging synthesis however, but because he shows that it might be possible to imagine a poetic practice that is performative but does not need the authority of a first person to speak and so can imagine a poem that is not a history of its negotiations

> with the subjectivity of authorship, and yet can go outside any supposedly constraining condition of a language known in the terms of philosophy, linguistics and literary theory.[4]

Moreover, Rothenberg's Jewish poetry participates in the contemporary American-Jewish discourse by constructing a Jewish identity that seeks a dialogue with Otherness. His motivations and methods of selecting, transforming, and transvaluing Jewish tradition parallel certain approaches among the Jewish counterculture and Jewish renewal groups. Acknowledging the significance of Rothenberg's Jewish work, the Orthodox poet Rose Drachler writes in a letter to the poet: "You are an especially strong poet. This is known in places you are not even aware of. Truly. . . . It will outlast us all."[5]

Notes

A Note on Transliteration

1. See "Transliteration Rules," *Encyclopaedia Judaica*, vol. 1, 90–92.

Introduction: "All Poets Are Jews"

1. Jerome Rothenberg, "Prologomena to a Poetics," in *Seedings & Other Poems* (New York: New Directions, 1996), 69.
2. Jerome Rothenberg, *A Big Jewish Book: Poems and other Visions of the Jews from Tribal Times to the Present*, ed. Jerome Rothenberg, Harris Lenowitz, and Charles Doria (Garden City, N.Y.: Anchor Press, 1978), xxxiii.
3. Jack Wertheimer, "Religious Movements in Collision: A Jewish Culture War?" In *Jews in America: A Contemporary Reader*, ed. Roberta Rosenberg Farber and Chaim I. Waxman (Hanover, Mass.: Brandeis University Press, 1999), 381.
4. Kevin Power, "*Poland/1931*: Pack up Your Troubles in Your Old Kit Bag & Smile, Smile, Smile, from Diaspora to Galut," *Boundary 2: A Journal of Postmodern Literature* 3 (spring 1975): 689.
5. Sherman Paul, *In Search of the Primitive: Rereading David Antin, Jerome Rothenberg, and Gary Snyder* (London: Louisiana State University Press, 1986), 136.
6. Charles S. Liebman, "The Reappropriation of Jewish Tradition in the Modern Era," in *The Uses of Tradition: Jewish Continuity in the Modern Era*, ed. Jack Wertheimer (New York: Jewish Theological Seminary, 1993), 473.
7. Michael Meyer, "Tradition and Modernity Reconsidered," in *Uses of Tradition*, ed. Jack Wertheimer, 465.
8. Ibid., 466.
9. Harry Polkinhorn, *Jerome Rothenberg: A Descriptive Bibliography*, American Bibliography Series 3 (Jefferson, N.C.: McFarland, 1988).
10. Meyer, "Tradition and Modernity Reconsidered," in *Uses of Tradition*, 468.
11. Hana Wirth-Nesher, "Defining the Indefinable: What Is Jewish Literature?" In *What is Jewish Literature?* ed. and introd. Hana Wirth-Nesher (Philadelphia: The Jewish Publication Society, 1994), 11.
12. Jerome Rothenberg, *Poland/1931* (New York: New Directions, 1974).
13. Marcus L. Hansen, "The Third Generation in America," *Commentary* 14 (1952): 492–500.
14. This definition is taken from Charles Russell's book. Equating the term "avant-garde" with "experimentalism" is not uncommon in Anglo-

American literary criticism. Much of it draws on Renato Poggioli's *Theory of the Avant-Garde* rather than Peter Bürger's conceptualizations. The latter's theories are historically more specific than Poggioli's and imply the use the historicizing attributes, such as the "literary avant-garde" or the "historical avant-garde." Rothenberg himself conceives of the avant-garde as a subversive underflow of literature emerging from the avant-garde movements at the beginning of the twentieth century. There are many controversies surrounding the definition and periodization of avant-garde literature. However, in the present context, terminological and ideological debates should submit to the main interest of this book, that is, the deployment and function of experimental devices in contemporary avant-garde poetry. See Charles Russell, ed., *The Avant-Garde Today: An International Anthology* (Urbana: University of Illinois Press, 1981); Renato Poggioli, *The Theory of the Avant-Garde*, trans. Gerald Fitzgerald (Cambridge: Harvard University Press, 1968); Peter Bürger, *Theory of the Avant-Garde*, trans. Michael Shaw, foreword Jochen Schulte-Sasse (Minneapolis: University of Minnesota Press, 1984).

15. Jerome Rothenberg, "The Search for a Primal Poetics," in *Conversant Essays: Contemporary Poets on Poetry*, ed. James McCorkle (Detroit: Wayne State University Press, 1990), 417.

16. Jerome Rothenberg, *Symposium of the Whole: A Range of Discourse toward an Ethnopoetics*, ed. Jerome Rothenberg and Diane Rothenberg (Berkeley: University of California Press, 1983), x n. 1.

17. Jerome Rothenberg, ed. with commentaries, *Technicians of the Sacred: A Range of Poetries from Africa, America, Asia, Europe & Oceania*, rev. and expanded 2nd ed. (Berkeley: University of California Press, 1985); Jerome Rothenberg, ed., *Shaking the Pumpkin: Traditional Poetry of the Indian North Americas* (New York: Doubleday, 1972); Jerome Rothenberg and George Quasha, eds., *America: A Prophecy: A New Reading of American Poetry From Pre-Columbian Times to the Present* (New York: Vintage, 1974); Jerome Rothenberg, ed., *Revolution of the Word: A New Gathering of American Avant-Garde Poetry, 1914–1945* (New York: Continuum Book, 1974); Jerome Rothenberg and Pierre Joris, eds., *Poems for the Millennium: The University of California Book of Modern & Postmodern Poetry*, 2 vols. (Berkeley: University of California Press, 1995–1998).

18. Meyer, "Tradition and Modernity Reconsidered," in *Uses of Tradition*, 467.

19. Liebman, "Reappropriation," in *Uses of Tradition*, 473.

20. Ibid., 476.

21. Gavin Selerie and Eric Mottram, eds. *The Riverside Interviews: 4: Jerome Rothenberg* (London: Binnacle Press, 1984), 60.

22. Jerome Rothenberg, "Deep Image & Mode: An Exchange with Robert Creeley," in *Pre-Faces & Other Writings* (New York: New Directions, 1981), 63.

23. Eric Mottram, "Where the Real Song Begins: The Poetry of Jerome Rothenberg," *Vort* 7 (1975): 175.

24. Jerome Rothenberg, "Jerome Rothenberg: A Dialogue on Oral Poetry with William Spanos," *Boundary 2* 3.3 (spring 1975): 525.

25. "Translation by J. R. [Jerome Rothenberg] & H. L. [Harris Lenowitz] from Babylonian Talmud: Berakhot 28b, 29b" in Rothenberg, *A Big Jewish Book*, 579.

26. Jack Wertheimer, "When Modern Jews Appropriate from Tradition: A Symposium," in *Uses of Tradition*, 463.

27. Roberta Rosenberg Farber and Chaim I. Waxman, "Postmodernity and the Jews: Identity, Identification, and Community," *Jews in America*, 403.

28. Both quotes are from Liebman, "Reappropriation," in *Uses of Tradition*, 475.

29. Ibid.

30. Liebman, "Reappropriation," in *Uses of Tradition*, 476.

31. Jerome Rothenberg, *Gematria* (Los Angeles: Sun & Moon Press, 1994).

32. Jerome Rothenberg and Steven Clay, eds., *A Book of the Book: Some Works & Projections About the Book & Writing* (New York: Granary, 2000).

33. "Jerome Rothenberg," *Electronic Poetry Center*, SUNY Buffalo http://wings.buffalo.edu/epc/authors/rothenberg/.

34. Jerome Rothenberg, *Das Hörspiel des Bibers* (Cologne: Westdeutscher Rundfunk, 1984); Jerome Rothenberg, *Das Dadahörspiel* (Cologne: Westdeutscher Rundfunk, 1985).

35. Michael Rodriguez, "An Effort Somehow in Common: An Interview with Jerome Rothenberg," *Samizdat* 7 (winter 2001): 7. In this recent interview Rothenberg enlarges upon his various collaborations. The reader may be referred to this interview for a more comprehensive list of collaborators.

36. Robert Goldenberg, "Talmud," in *Back to the Sources: Reading The Classic Jewish Texts*, ed. Barry W. Holtz (New York: Summit, 1984), 161.

37. For instance, the poem "Abulafia's Circles" was first published in the form of a small booklet as one of the final issues of Meltzer's journal *Tree*.

38. Jerome Rothenberg, *The Notebooks* (Milwaukee, Wis.: Membrane Press, 1976).

39. Jerome Rothenberg, *Vienna Blood & Other Poems* (New York: New Directions, 1980); and Jerome Rothenberg and Harris Lenowitz, eds., *Exiled in the Word: Poems & Other Visions of the Jews from Tribal Times to Present*, with commentaries by Jerome Rothenberg (Washington: Copper Canyon Press, 1989).

40. Rothenberg, "Pre-Face (1967)," *Technicians of the Sacred*, xxix.

41. Charles Olson, "Projective Verse," in *Collected Prose*, ed. Donald Allen and Benjamin Friedlander, introd. Robert Creeley (Berkeley: University of California Press, 1997), 240.

42. "W. B. (Marriage of Heaven & Hell, 1790)," cited by Rothenberg, in *Poems for the Millennium* vol. 1, 24.

43. The following dissertations deal with Rothenberg's approach to Native American culture: Michael Castro, in *Interpreting the Indian: Twentieth-Century Poets and the Native American* (Albuquerque: University of New Mexico Press, 1983); Molly Weigel, *Interactive Poetics: Native-American/European-American Encounter as a Model for Poetic Practice*, PhD diss., Princeton University, 1996; Natalie Irene White, *The Darmouth Seminar and its Study Group on Myth and "Translation": A Retrospective Analysis*, PhD diss., University of New Mexico, 1988. For a study of performance poetry, see Ellen Marcia Zweig, *Performance Poetry: Critical Approaches to Contemporary Intermedia*, PhD diss., University of Michigan, 1980. For discussions of Rothenberg's Holocaust poetry, see Harriet Abbey Leibowitz Parmet, *The Terror of Our Days: Sylvia Plath, William Heyen, Gerald Stern, and Jerome Rothenberg Poetically Respond to the Holocaust*, PhD diss., Lehigh University, 1998; and Devon Miller-Duggan, *After Auschwitz: Rigor,*

Risk and Witness in American Holocaust Poetry, PhD diss., University of Delaware, 1996.

44. For example, most importantly: Rothenberg, "Jerome Rothenberg: A Dialogue," *Boundary 2* 3.3 (spring 1975): 509–48; Selerie and Mottram, *Riverside Interviews*; Barry Alpert, "Jerome Rothenberg—An Interview: Conducted by Barry Alpert with Charles Morrow sitting in, New York City, January 2, 1974," *Vort* 7 (1975): 93–117; Manuel Brito, "Jerome Rothenberg," in *A Suite of Poetic Voices: Interviews with Contemporary American Poets* (Santa Brigida, Spain: Kadle, 1992), 111–34.

45. For a direct treatment of Rothenberg's work, see Marjorie Perloff, "The Contemporary of Our Grandchildren: Pound's Influence," in *Ezra Pound among the Poets*, ed. George Bornstein (Chicago: University of Chicago Press, 1985), 195–229. See also Henry M. Sayre, *The Object of Performance: The American Avant-Garde Since 1970* (Chicago: University of Chicago Press, 1989). See also Paul, "Founding: Jerome Rothenberg," in *In Search of the Primitive*, 73–183.

46. Paul Hoover, ed., *Postmodern Poetry: A Norton Anthology* (New York: W. W. Norton, 1994).

47. Hank Lazer, "Thinking Made in the Mouth: The Cultural Poetics of David Antin and Jerome Rothenberg," *Picturing Cultural Values in Postmodern America*, ed. William G. Doty (Tuscaloosa: University of Alabama Press, 1995), 103.

48. Eliot Weinberger, ed., *American Poetry Since 1950: Innovators and Outsiders* (New York: Marsilio Publishers, 1993); and Douglas Messerli, ed. and introd., *From the Other Side of the Century: A New American Poetry 1960–1990* (Los Angeles: Sun & Moon Press, 1994).

49. Robert Mezey, "A Gathering of Poets,," *Western Humanities Review* 29.2 (1975): 199.

50. Throughout a period of twenty-five years only very few essays discuss Rothenberg's poetry in a Jewish context: Harris Lenowitz, "Rothenberg: The Blood," *Vort* 7 (1975): 179–84; Power, "*Poland/1931*: Pack up," *Boundary 2* 3 (spring 1975): 683–705; R. Barbara Gitenstein, "Coyote Cohen: Or, the Universal Trickster in Jerome Rothenberg's Evolving Collection *Poland/1931*," *Studies in American Jewish Literature* 9.2 (1990 fall): 176–85; Dan Featherston, "Poetic Representation: Reznikoff's *Holocaust* and Rothenberg's *Khurbn*," *Response* 63 (fall 1997, winter 1998): 129–40; Norman Finkelstein, "The Messianic Ethnography of Jerome Rothenberg's *Poland/1931*," *Contemporary Literature* 39.3 (1998 fall): 356–79; Norman Finkelstein, "Between Poland and Sumer: The Ethnopoetics of Jerome Rothenberg and Armand Schwerner," in *Not One of Them in Place: Modern Poetry and Jewish Identity*, SUNY Series in Modern Jewish Literature and Culture (New York: State University of New York Press, 2001), 87–120.

51. Henry M. Sayre, "David Antin and the Oral Poetics Movement," *Contemporary Literature* 23.4 (1982 fall): 428.

52. Richard Kostelanetz, *The Old Poetries and the New* (Ann Arbor: University of Michigan Press, 1981), 241.

53. Gary Pacernick, *Memory and Fire: Ten American Jewish Poets*, Twentieth Century American Jewish Writers 1 (New York: Lang, 1989), 225.

54. Harold Bloom, "The Sorrows of American-Jewish Poetry," *Commentary* 53.3 (March 1972): 69.

55. Jerome Rothenberg, "Harold Bloom: The Critic as Exterminating

Angel," *Sulfur* 2 (1981): 4–26; and Jerome Rothenberg, *That Dada Strain* (New York: New Directions, 1983), 21–23.

56. Even though Bloom does mention Reznikoff, he dismisses him as lacking in "strong" poetic achievement along with a very limited list of other American Jewish poets (Emma Lazarus, Samuel Greenberg, Karl Shapiro, Harvey Shapiro, Irving Feldman, John Hollander, and Allen Ginsberg). Recently, Reznikoff's achievement as a Jewish poet has been reevaluated by Stephen Fredman, *A Menorah For Athena: Charles Reznikoff and the Jewish Dilemmas of Objectivist Poetry* (Chicago: University of Chicago Press, 2001).

57. *Jewish American Poetry: Poems, Commentary, And Reflections*, ed. Jonathan N. Barron and Eric Murphy Selinger (Hanover, NH: Brandeis University Press, 2000); and Finkelstein, *Not One of Them in Place*.

58. R. Barbara Gitenstein, *Apocalyptic Messianism and Contemporary Jewish-American Poetry* (Albany: State University of New York, 1986).

59. Pacernick, *Memory and Fire*; and Gary Pacernick, *Sing A New Song: American Jewish Poetry Since the Holocaust*, Gary Pacernick with photographs by Layle Silbert (Cincinnati, Oh.: The American Jewish Archives, 1991).

60. Stephen Wade, *Jewish American Literature: Since 1945: An Introduction* (London: Fitzroy Dearborn, 1999).

61. Richard S. Chess, *Still A Small Voice: Toward an American-Jewish Poetry*, PhD diss., University of Florida, 1989; and Laurence Roth, *Statues of Liberty: Assimilation and Twentieth-Century American Jewish Poets*, PhD diss., University of California, 1995.

62. Steven J. Rubin, ed., *Telling and Remembering: A Century of American Jewish Poetry* (Boston: Beacon Press, 1997); and Jules Chametzky et al., eds., *Jewish American Literature: A Norton Anthology* (New York: Norton, 2001).

63. Wade, *Jewish American Literature*, 16.

64. Dieter Lamping, *Von Kafka bis Celan: Jüdischer Diskurs in der deutschen Literatur des 20. Jahrhunderts* (Göttingen: Vandenhoeck, 1998), 14.

65. Werner Sollors, *Beyond Ethnicity: Consent and Descent in American Culture* (Oxford: Oxford University Press, 1986), 13.

66. Ibid.

67. Jerome Rothenberg, "Beyond Poetics," in *Coherence: A Gathering of Experiments in Writing*. Toward a New Poetics 1, ed. Don Wellman (Cambridge, Mass.: O. ARS, 1981), 153.

68. On the history of American Judaism, see Nathan Glazer, *American Judaism*, The Chicago History of American Civilization, 2nd ed. (Chicago: University of Chicago Press, 1972).

69. Waxman specifies the following three sociological generations: first generation: 1880–1920; second generation: 1920–1945; third generation: 1945–later 1960s. See Chaim I. Waxman, "The Fourth Generation Grows Up: The Contemporary American Jewish Community," *The Annals of the American Academy of Political and Social Science* 454 (March 1981): 71.

70. Jerome Rothenberg, e-mail to the author, May 1999.

71. All quotations in the following two paragraphs are taken from Rothenberg, e-mail to the author, May 1999.

72. Jerome Rothenberg, "Pre-Face III: Revolution of the Word," *Pre-Faces*, 99.

73. Jerome Rothenberg, "Paper delivered at 'American Poetry in the

1950s': University of Maine, Orono June 1996," http:/wings.buffalo.edu/epc/authors/rothenberg/50s.html, accessed 13 Oct. 1999.

74. Jerome Rothenberg, ed. and trans., *New Young German Poets* (San Francisco: City Lights, 1959).

75. Diane Rothenberg, *Friends Like These: An Ethnohistorical Analysis of the Interaction between Allegheny Senecas and Quakers, 1798–1823*, PhD diss., City University of New York, 1976.

76. Robert Kelly, "Notes on the Poetry of Image," *Trobar* 2 (1961): 14–16; Jerome Rothenberg, "Why Deep Image?" *Trobar* 3 (1961): 31–32; Rothenberg, "Deep Image & Mode," *Pre-Faces*, 52–64.

77. Rothenberg, "Deep Image & Mode," *Pre-Faces*, 59.

78. Beth Fleischman, "Jerome Rothenberg," *Dictionary of Literary Biography*, vol. 5: American Poets Since World War II, part 2: L–Z (Detroit, Mich.: Gale, 1980), 214.

79. Rodriguez, "An Effort Somehow in Common," *Samizdat* 7 (winter 2001): 7.

80. Jerome Rothenberg, *White Sun Black Sun* (New York: Hawk's Well Press, 1960).

81. Jerome Rothenberg, *Poems For The Game of Silence 1960–1970* (New York: The Dial Press, 1971).

82. Paul, *In Search of the Primitive*, 124.

83. Jerome Rothenberg, *Poems 1964–1967: Sightings, Further Sightings, A Steinbook & More, Conversations, The Gorky Poems* (Los Angeles: Black Sparrow Press, 1968), 39–61.

84. Fleischman, "Jerome Rothenberg," *Dictionary of Literary Biography* vol. 5, 215.

85. Eugen Gomringer, *The Book of Hours and Constellations Being Poems of Eugen Gomringer Presented by Jerome Rothenberg* (New York: Something Else Press, 1968).

86. Jerome Rothenberg, *Ritual: A Book of Primitive Rites and Events* (New York: A Great Bear Pamphlet, 1966).

87. Frank Mitchell (1881–1967) was a Navajo singer, whose recordings were given to Rothenberg by David McAllester. See Jerome Rothenberg, *The 17 Horse Songs of Frank Mitchell Nos. X–XIII: Total Translations from the Navaho Indian with Images by Ian Tyson* (London: Tetrad Press, 1969).

88. Jerome Rothenberg, "Total Translation: An Experiment in the Presentation of American Indian Poetry (1969)," *Pre-Faces*, 91.

89. In order to clarify that he does not simply reproduce the meaningless Navaho words, Rothenberg speaks of "analogues." Rothenberg, "Total Translation," *Pre-Faces*, 85.

90. Jerome Rothenberg, *A Seneca Journal* (New York: New Directions, 1978).

91. Rothenberg, "Pre-Face" (1984), *Technicians of the Sacred*, xxi.

92. Jerome Rothenberg, *The Pirke & the Pearl* (Berkeley: Tree, 1975).

93. Jerome Rothenberg, *Poland/1931* (Santa Barbara, Ca.: Unicorn Press, 1970); and Jerome Rothenberg, *Esther K. Comes to America, 1931* (Greensboro, N.C.: Unicorn Press, 1974).

94. For a study of the history of Meltzer's magazine, see Christine Meilicke, "The Forgotten History of David Meltzer's Journal Tree," *Studies in American Jewish Literature* 22 (2003): 52–71.

95. Jerome Rothenberg, *Letters & Numbers* (Madison, Wi.: The Salient Seedling Press, 1979).

96. Jerome Rothenberg, *Khurbn & Other Poems* (New York: New Directions, 1989).

97. Kurt Schwitters, *PPPPPP: Poems Performance Pieces Prose Plays Poetics of Kurt Schwitters*, ed. and trans. Jerome Rothenberg and Pierre Joris (Philadelphia: Temple University Press, 1993).

98. Wirth-Nesher, "Defining the Indefinable," *What is Jewish Literature?*, 5.

99. Ibid., 3.

100. Wade, *Jewish-American Literature*, 7.

101. Lamping, *Von Kafka bis Celan*, 34–36. "Discourse" is not used in the sense of "discourse analysis," but rather historically. See Lamping, *Von Kafka bis Celan*, 169 n. 76.

102. Jerome Rothenberg, letter to Howard Schwartz, 10 Apr. 1978, Jerome Rothenberg Papers, MSS 10, Box 18, Folder 9, Mandeville Special Collections Library, UCSD.

103. Rothenberg, *Poems for the Millennium* vol. 2, 107.

104. Rothenberg, "5/76," *The Notebooks*, 43.

105. "New Ethnicity" refers to the recent (modern and postmodern) invention of ethnic identity, which has the function to provide a sense of belonging and "some kind of identity—smaller than the State, larger than the family." Nathan Glazer, cited by Werner Sollors, "Foreword: Theories of American Ethnicity," *The Invention of Ethnicity*, ed. Werner Sollers (Oxford: Oxford University Press, 1989), xvi.

106. John Hollander, "The Question of American Jewish Poetry," *What is Jewish Literature?*, 40.

107. Rothenberg, "Beyond Poetics," *Coherence*, 153.

Chapter 1. Rothenberg's Reappropriation of Jewish Mysticism

1. The exact relationship between "magic" and "religion" is contentious. Modern anthropology holds that religion, magic, and science in primitive societies are strongly intertwined and cannot be separated. Following this perspective, I take magic as a subcategory of religion.

2. Jerome Rothenberg, "A Poetics of the Sacred," *Picturing Cultural Values in Postmodern America*, ed. William G. Doty (Tuscaloosa: University of Alabama Press, 1995), 89–100.

3. Jerome Rothenberg, "Innovation & Disruption as Ritual Modes (Transcript of a Talk in San Diego)," *The Riverside Interviews*, 74.

4. Rothenberg, "Poetics of the Sacred," *Picturing Cultural Values*, 91.

5. Joseph Dan, "Gershom Scholem: Between Mysticism and Scholarship," *The Germanic Review: Literature, Culture, Theory* 72.1 (winter 1997): 15.

6. Ibid., 19.

7. Bill Novak, "The Making of A Jewish Counter Culture," *Contemporary Judaic Fellowship In Theory and Practice*, ed. Jacob Neusner (New York: Ktav, 1972), 142.

8. Arthur O. Waskow, *The Bush is Burning! Radical Judaism Faces the Pharaohs of the Modern Superstate* (New York: Macmillan, 1971), 85.

9. Sara Bershtel and Allen Graubard, *Saving Remnants: Feeling Jewish in America* (New York: Free Press, 1992), 223.

10. The *Jews for Urban Justice* (Washington), formed in 1966, constituted one of the first radical political organizations of the Jewish counterculture. See Jews for Urban Justice, "The Oppression and Liberation of the Jewish People in America," *Jewish Radicalism: A Selected Anthology*, ed. Peter Dreier and Jack Nusan Porter (New York: Grove Press, 1973), 323–46. For a listing of the numerous radical Jewish groups, newspapers and journals, see *Jewish Radicalism*, 378–98.

11. The given time frame for the first flourishing of the *havurot* is based on an analysis of the *Response* magazine, which after the Yom Kippur War (1973) began featuring articles about the "death" of the *havurah* movement. See *"Have You Sold Out? A Response Symposium: Veterans of the Jewish Student Movement,"* spec. issue of *Response* 29 (spring 1976).

12. Elisabeth Hamacher, *Gershom Scholem und die Allgemeine Religionsgeschichte* (Berlin: Walter de Gruyter, 1999), 50–62.

13. David Biale, *Gershom Scholem: Kabbalah and Counter-History* (Cambridge: Harvard University Press, 1979), 194.

14. Martin Buber, *Tales of Angels, Spirits & Demons*, trans. David Antin and Jerome Rothenberg (New York: Hawk's Well Press, 1958).

15. For his Buberian definition of "deep image," see Rothenberg, *Pre-Faces*, 57.

16. Biale, *Gershom Scholem*, 195.

17. Ibid., 201.

18. Jerome Rothenberg Papers, "Duncan, Robert 1958–1973, n.d.," MSS 10, Box 7, Folder 8, Mandeville Special Collections Library, UCSD.

19. Rothenberg, conversation with the author, 10 Aug. 2000.

20. Michael Davidson, *The San Francisco Renaissance: Poetics and Community at Mid-Century* (Cambridge, Mass.: Cambridge University Press, 1989), 130–33.

21. Michael André Bernstein, "Bringing it All Back Home: Derivations and Quotations in Robert Duncan and the Poundian Tradition," *Sagetrieb* 1.2 (fall 1982): 178.

22. Ibid., 184.

23. Jed Rasula, "The Compost Library," *Sagetrieb* 1.2 (fall 1982): 207.

24. Brito, "Jerome Rothenberg," *A Suite of Poetic Voices*, 118.

25. Robert Duncan, "From 'Rites of Participation,'" *Symposium of the Whole*, 328.

26. "The Hebrew Bible is often known among Jews as *TaNaKh*, an acronym derived from the names of its three divisions: *Torah* (Instruction, or Law, also called the Pentateuch), *Nevi'im* (Prophets), and *Ketuvim* (Writings)." See "Biblical Literature and Its Critical Interpretation," *Encyclopaedia Britannica*, CD-ROM, Version 97 (Encyclopaedia Britannica, Inc., 1997).

27. Raphael Patai, *The Hebrew Goddess*, foreword Merline Stone, 3rd enl. ed. (Detroit: Wayne State University Press, 1990); and Raphel Patai, *Man and Temple: In Ancient Jewish Myth and Ritual,* 2nd enl. ed. with a new introd. and postscript (1947; New York: Ktav, 1967).

28. See "Wars of Yahweh, Book of the," *Encyclopaedia Britannica*, CD-ROM, Version 97 (Encyclopaedia Britannica, Inc., 1997).

29. Michael Heller, "Pale Darkened Moons in the Firmament of Reason," *Parnassus: Poetry in Review* 9.1 (spring/summer 1981): 281.

30. Ibid.

31. Jonathan Cott, "In the Beginning Was Aleph," rev. of *A Big Jewish Book*, ed. Jerome Rothenberg, *The New York Times Book Review* (April 23, 1978): 15–16.

32. Paul Mendes-Flohr, "Introductory Essay: The Spiritual Quest of the Philologist," *Gershom Scholem: The Man and His Work*, ed. Paul Mendes-Flohr (New York: State University of New York Press, 1994), 24.

33. Jerome Rothenberg, *New Selected Poems, 1970–1985* (New York: New Directions, 1986), vii.

34. Rothenberg, *Exiled*, 13. This remark is only found in the revised version of the poet's "pre-face" to his Jewish anthology.

35. Rothenberg, "Poetics of the Sacred," *Picturing Cultural Values*, 93.

36. Gitenstein, *Apocalyptic Messianism*, 133.

37. See Richard Cándida Smith on Berman in his chapter "Utopia and the Private Realm: Wallace Berman on Career, Family, and Community," *Utopia and Dissent: Art, Poetry, and Politics in California* (Berkeley: University of California Press, 1995), 212–68.

38. For more detailed discussions of Meltzer's and Hirschman's Abulafianism and pictorial illustrations, see my article "California Kabbalists," *Judaism Today* 14 (winter 1999–2000): 24–30; and Christine Meilicke, "Abulafianism among the Counterculture Kabbalists," *Jewish Studies Quarterly* 9 (2002): 71–101.

39. Moshe Idel, *The Mystical Experience in Abraham Abulafia*, trans. Jonathan Chipman (New York: State University of New York Press, 1988), 5.

40. The *Sefer Yezirah* is an early example of hermetic Jewish letter mysticism. This opaque book and its commentaries influenced Abulafia. See Gershom Scholem, *Kabbalah* (New York: New American Library, 1974), 21–29, 54. *Tree* 2 (summer 1971) focuses on the *Sefer Yezirah* and the writings of Abulafia.

41. Gershom Scholem, *Major Trends in Jewish Mysticism: Based on the Hilda Strook Lectures Delivered at the Jewish Institute of Religion, New York*, rev. ed. (New York: Schocken, 1946), 136–37, 147–55.

42. For a detailed description, see the studies by Gershom Scholem, Aryeh Kaplan, and Moshe Idel, the current world authority on Abulafia. However, the results of Idel's research were not available in English at the time of Abulafianism. For studies in English, see Scholem, *Major Trends* (1946), 119–55; Idel, *Mystical Experience*; Moshe Idel, *Studies in Ecstatic Kabbalah* (New York: State University of New York Press, 1988); Moshe Idel, *Language, Torah, and Hermeneutics in Abraham Abulafia*, trans. Menahem Kallus (New York: State University of New York Press, 1989); Aryeh Kaplan, *Meditation and Kabbalah* (York Beach, Maine: Samuel Weiser, 1982). Short summaries and translations from the sources may be found in David R. Blumenthal, "The Abulafian Transformation," in *Understanding Jewish Mysticism: A Source Reader*, vol. 2: The Philosophic-Mystical Tradition and The Hasidic Tradition (New York: Ktav, 1978), 37–79. For a very recent book, see Elliot R. Wolfson, *Abraham Abulafia—Kabbalist and Prophet: Hermeneutics, Theosophy and Theurgy* (Los Angeles: Cherub Press, 2000).

43. Blumenthal, *Understanding Jewish Mysticism*, vol. 2, 59–64.

44. This bi-annual journal (1970–1978) was edited and published by Meltzer. Each volume was dedicated to a theme of Jewish mysticism. For a detailed history of this magazine, see my essay "The Forgotten History of David

Meltzer's Journal *Tree*," *Studies in American Jewish Literature* 22 (2003): 52–71.

45. David Meltzer, *Six* (Santa Barbara: Black Sparrow Press, 1976), 139.

46. David Meltzer, ed. *The Secret Garden: An Anthology of Texts from the Jewish Mystical Tradition* (New York: Seabury Press, 1975); David Meltzer, ed. *The Path of the Names: Writings by Abraham ben Samuel Abulafia*, trans. and adapt. Bruria Finkel, Jack Hirschman, David Meltzer, and Gershom Scholem, Tree Texts 4 (Berkeley: Tree, 1976).

47. Abraham Abulafia, "From: *The Book of The Letter*," trans. Jack Hirschman, *Tree* 1 (winter 1970): 139–48; and ibid., 152–53.

48. Idel, *Mystical Experience*, 4.

49. Abraham Abulafia, "Abraham Abulafia: *From* LIFE OF THE WORLD TO COME: Circles," *A Big Jewish Book*, 400–406.

50. Bernstein, "Bringing it All Back Home" *Sagetrieb* 1.2 (fall 1982): 179.

51. Rodriguez, "An Effort Somehow in Common" *Samizdat* 7 (winter 2001): 8.

52. Abraham Berger, "The Messianic Self-Consciousness of Abraham Abulafia: A Tentative Evaluation," in *Essays On Jewish Life and Thought: Presented in Honor of Salo Wittmayer Baron*, ed. Joseph L. Blau et al. (New York: Columbia University Press, 1959), 59. Idel has published several papers on Abulafia's notion of messianism. Most recently, see Moshe Idel, "Abraham Abulafia: Ecstatic Kabbalah and Spiritual Messianism," in *Messianic Mystics* (New Haven: Yale University Press, 1998), 58–100.

53. Berger, "Messianic Self-Consciousness," *Essays On Jewish Life and Thought*, 55–61; and Idel, *Mystical Experience*, 140–41.

54. Jack Hirschman, "Eluardian Elohenu for Allen Ginsberg," *Black Alephs, Poems 1960–1968* (London: Trigram Press, 1969), 123.

55. Idel, *Mystical Experience*, 143.

56. David Meltzer, *Isla Vista Notes: Fragmentary Apocalyptic Didactic Contradictions* (Santa Barbara: Christopher, 1970), n. pag.

57. Idel, *Mystical Experience*, 249.

58. In conversation, Dietmar Becker suggested to me that "cracks" and "blasts" are drug-related motifs.

59. David Meltzer, "Abulafia," in *Yesod* (London: Trigram, 1969), 24.

60. Gershom Scholem, "Abulafia, Abraham Ben Samuel," *Encyclopaedia Judaica*, vol. 2 (Jerusalem: Keter, 1972), 185.

61. "Abraham Abulafia: HOW HE WENT AS MESSIAH IN THE NAME OF ANGEL RAZIEL TO CONFRONT THE POPE," *A Big Jewish Book*, 305–6.

62. Rothenberg, "Abraham Abulafia (1978)," *Pre-Faces*, 161.

63. "Abraham Abulafia: *From* LIFE OF THE WORLD TO COME: The Permutations," *A Big Jewish Book*, 390–91.

64. Al-Botini, cited by Blumenthal, *Understanding Jewish Mysticism* vol. 2, 72–73.

65. Jackson Mac Low, "J. Mac Low: Interviewed by Kevin Bezner," *New American Writing* 11 (summer/fall 1993): 109.

66. Ibid., 114.

67. See, for example, "A Word Event for George Brecht," in Jackson Mac Low, *Representative Works: 1938–1985* (New York: Roof, 1986), 134.

68. Scholem, *Major Trends*, 146–55.

69. Ibid., 151.

70. Rothenberg, "Deep Image & Mode" *Pre-Faces*, 58.

71. Jack Hirschman, "On the Hebrew Letters," *Tree* 2 (summer 1971): 38.

72. Hirschman, "The Letters," *Black Alephs*, 34.

73. Hannah Weiner, "Mar 7 SIGNAL," *Clairvoyant Journal, 1974: March–June Retreat* (New York: Angel Hair, 1978), n. pag.

74. Robert Alter, *Necessary Angels: Tradition and Modernity in Kafka, Benjamin, and Scholem* (Cambridge: Harvard University Press, 1991), 37.

75. This is succinctly summarized by Smith: "Interpreters of the kabbalah gave three primary meanings to aleph (א): primal chaos as potentiality of meaning; Adam in his capacity as the bestower of names upon the divine creation; and the ox, the beast of burden that brings order to the wilderness and yet can never be fully tamed of its own streak of inner wilderness." Smith, *Utopia and Dissent*, 496 n. 15.

76. Jacob Frank, *Sayings of Yakov Frank*, trans. Harris Lenowitz, Tree 6: Aleph (Berkeley, CA: Tree; Oakland, CA: Tzaddikim, 1978); and Jerome Rothenberg, *Abulafia's Circles*, Tree 6: Beth: Messiah (Milwaukee, Wis.: Membrane Press, 1979).

77. The properties of the long poem are summarized by Lynn Keller, "The Twentieth-Century Long Poem," *The Columbia History of American Poetry*, ed. Jay Parini et al. (New York: Columbia University Press, 1993), 534–63.

78. Idel, *Mystical Experience*, 17.

79. Mircea Eliade, *Shamanism: Archaic Techniques of Ecstasy*, trans. Willard R. Trask (1964; Princeton: Princeton University Press, 1972).

80. Alter, *Necessary Angels*, 63.

81. Dan, "Gershom Scholem," *Germanic Review* 72.1 (winter 1997): 12.

82. This is pointed out by R. Barbara Gitenstein in her essay "Coyote Cohen," 176–85.

83. The exact relationship between the shaman and the trickster is contested. In the above argument, I follow Mac Linscott Ricketts, "The Shaman and the Trickster," *Mythical Trickster Figures: Contours, Contexts, and Criticism*, ed. William J. Hynes and William G. Doty (Tuscaloosa: University of Alabama Press, 1993), 87–105; and William J. Hynes, "Mapping the Characteristics of Mythic Tricksters: A Heuristic Guide," *Mythical Trickster Figures* 33–45.

84. Lewis Hyde, *Trickster Makes This World: Mischief, Myth, and Art* (New York: North Point Press, 1998), 49.

85. Hynes, "Mapping the Characteristics of Mythic Tricksters" *Mythical Trickster Figures*, 37.

86. Rothenberg, note preceding Alfonso Ortiz, "The Sacred Clown," *Symposium of the Whole*, 270–71.

87. Rothenberg, *Poems for the Millennium* vol. 1, 434.

88. Hyde, *Trickster Makes This World*, 71–72.

89. Scholem, *Kabbalah*, 295. For general information about Frank and Zevi, see relevant chapters in Scholem's *Major Trends* and *Kabbalah*.

90. Lenowitz, "Preface," *Sayings of Jakov Frank*, n. pag.

91. Hyde, *Trickster Makes This World*, 71–72.

92. Ibid., 64.

93. Laura Makarius, "The Myth of the Trickster: The Necessary Breaker of Taboos," *Mythical Trickster Figures*, 73.

94. Gershom Scholem, "Redemption Through Sin," in *The Messianic Idea in Judaism: And Other Essays on Jewish Spirituality* (New York: Schocken,

1971), 78–141; and Gershom Scholem, *Sabbatai Ṣevi: The Mystical Messiah*, trans. R. J. Zwi Werblowsky (1957; Princeton: Princeton University Press, 1973).

95. Robert Alter, "Scholem and Sabbatianism," *Gershom Scholem*, ed. and introd. Harold Bloom (New York: Chelsea, 1987), 24.

96. Finkelstein discusses this subject from a different perspective in his essay "The Messianic Ethnography," *Contemporary Literature* 39.3 (1998 fall): 356–79.

97. See Rothenberg, *A Big Jewish Book*, 162, 311–12, 314–16, 321–28, 535, 536. See also Rothenberg, "Satan in Goray," *Poland/1931*, 7–9. See Isaac Bashevis Singer, "*From* SATAN IN GORAY: The Faithful," in *A Big Jewish Book*, 312–14.

98. Scholem, *The Messianic Idea in Judaism*, 112.

99. David A. Gerber, "Nativism, Anti-Catholicism, and Anti-Semitism," *Encyclopedia of American Social History*, ed. Mary Kupiec Cayton, Elliott J. Gorn and Peter W. Williams, vol. 3 (New York: Scribner's; Toronto: Maxwell Macmillan; New York: Maxwell Macmillan International, 1993), 2111.

CHAPTER 2. ROTHENBERG'S REAPPROPRIATION OF JEWISH RITUAL

1. Following a common practice among many avant-garde artists and performers, I will use the words "ritual," "rite," and "ceremony" interchangeably.

2. Nathaniel Tarn, "Foreword: 'Child as Father to Man in the American Universe,'" in *Nathaniel Tarn: A Descriptive Bibliography*, ed. Lee Bartlett, American Poetry Contemporary Series 2 (Jefferson, N. C.: McFarland, 1987), 16.

3. Paul Christensen, "Some Bearings on Ethnopoetics," *Parnassus: Poetry in Review* 15.1 (1989): 162.

4. Rothenberg, "Poetics of the Sacred," *Picturing Cultural Values*, 98.

5. Jerome Rothenberg and Dennis Tedlock, "Statement of Intention," *Alcheringa* 1: Ethnopoetics (autumn 1970): 1.

6. Christensen, "Some Bearings," *Parnassus* 15.1 (1989): 140.

7. Stanley Diamond, "Plato and the Definition of the Primitive," *Symposium of the Whole*, 85.

8. Gary Snyder, "The Politics of Ethnopoetics," *The Old Ways: Six Essays* (San Francisco: City Lights, 1977), 42.

9. Jerome Rothenberg, "Craft Interview with Jerome Rothenberg," *The Craft of Poetry: Interviews from The New York Quarterly*, ed. William Packard (New York: Doubleday, 1974), 38.

10. Rothenberg, "Beyond Poetics," *Coherence*, 151.

11. Kevin Power, "Conversation with Jerome Rothenberg," *Vort* 7 (1975): 147.

12. Finkelstein, "The Messianic Ethnography," *Contemporary Literature* 39.3 (1998 fall): 366.

13. Ibid., 359.

14. Tarn, "Foreword," *Nathaniel Tarn*, 19–20.

15. Richard Schechner, *The Future of Ritual: Writings on Culture and Performance* (London: Routledge, 1993), 229.

16. Victor Turner, "A Review of 'Ethnopoetics,'" *Symposium of the Whole*, 338; and Spanos cited by Rothenberg, "Jerome Rothenberg: A Dialogue," *Boundary 2* 3.3 (spring 1975): 518.

17. Eliot Weinberger, "Rothenberg: New York / 1968," in *Written Reaction: Poetics Politics Polemics (1979–1995)* (New York: Marsilio, 1996), 130.

18. The *Encyclopedia Britannica* defines ritual as "the performance of ceremonial acts . . . prescribed by tradition or by sacerdotal decree." See "Sacred Rites and Ceremonies: The Concept and Forms of Ritual," *Encyclopaedia Britannica*, CD-ROM, Version 97 (Encyclopaedia Britannica, Inc., 1997). Most anthropologists agree that rituals are characterized by formalization/ patterning and by repetition: "Ritual is an act or actions intentionally conducted by a group of people employing one or more symbols in a repetitive, formal, precise, highly stylized fashion." See Barbara G. Myerhoff, "We Don't Wrap Herring in a Printed Page: Fusion, Fictions and Continuity in Secular Ritual," *Secular Ritual: Form and Meaning*, ed. Barbara G. Myerhoff and Sally Falk Moore (Assen/Amsterdam: Van Gorcum, 1977), 199.

19. Rothenberg, *Symposium of the Whole*, xi.

20. Rothenberg, "Innovation & Disruption," *Riverside Interviews*, 85.

21. Waskow, *The Bush is Burning*, 27.

22. Arthur Waskow, telephone conversation with the author, 13 Apr. 2000.

23. Charles S. Liebman, "Ritual, Ceremony and the Reconstruction of Judaism in the United States," in *Jews in America*, 309.

24. Richard Siegel, Michael Strassfeld, and Sharon Strassfeld, comp. and eds., *The First Jewish Catalogue: A Do-It-Yourself Kit* (Philadelphia: Jewish Publication Society, 1973); Michael Strassfeld and Sharon Strassfeld, comp. and eds., *The Second Jewish Catalog: Sources and Resources* (Philadelphia: Jewish Publication Society, 1976); Michael Strassfeld and Sharon Strassfeld, eds., *The Third Jewish Catalog: Creating Community* (Philadelphia: Jewish Publication Society, 1980); see also *Menorah: Sparks of Jewish Renewal* (1979–1982). For further innovative experiments with ritual, see Michael Lerner, "Renewing the Life Cycle," *Jewish Renewal* (New York: Harper, 1994), 385–93.

25. Victor Turner, *Dramas, Fields, And Metaphors: Symbolic Action in Human Society* (Ithaca: Cornell University Press, 1974), 47.

26. Richard Schechner, *Performance Theory: Revised and Expanded Edition* (London: Routledge, 1988). 141.

27. Richard Schechner, *Environmental Theater* (New York: Hawthorn, 1973), 110.

28. Turner, "A Review of 'Ethnopoetics,'" *Symposium of the Whole*, 341–42.

29. "Normative communitas" refers to "a subculture or group which attempts to foster and maintain relationships or spontaneous communitas on a more or less permanent basis." See Victor Turner, *From Ritual to Theatre: The Human Seriousness of Play* (New York: PAJ Publications, 1982), 49.

30. Stanley Jeyaraja Tambiah, "A Performative Approach to Ritual," in *Culture, Thought, and Social Action: An Anthropological Perspective* (Cambridge, Mass.: Harvard University Press, 1985), 145.

31. Myerhoff, "We Don't Wrap Herring," *Secular Ritual*, 199.

32. Arthur O. Waskow, *Godwrestling Round 2: Ancient Wisdom, Future Paths* (Woodstock, Vt.: Jewish Lights, 1996), 289.

33. Gary Snyder, *Gary Snyder: The Real Work: Interviews & Talks 1964–1979*, ed. and introd. William Scott McLean (New York: New Directions, 1980), 49.

34. Judith Malina and Julian Beck, "Vision I: The Vision of the Death and Resurrection of the American Indian," in *Paradise Now: Collective Creation of The Living Theater* (New York: Random, 1971), 19.

35. Arthur O. Waskow, "Is the Earth a Jewish Issue?" *Tikkun* 7.5 (Sept./Oct. 1992): 35–37.

36. Carol Ascher, "The Return of Jewish Mysticism: Try It, You'll Like It," *Present Tense* 17.3 (spring 1980): 38; see also "ALEPH," *On Common Ground: World Religions in America*, ed. Diana L. Eck, CD-ROM (New York: Columbia University Press, 1997).

37. Myerhoff, "We Don't Wrap Herring," *Secular Ritual*, 218.

38. Turner, *From Ritual to Theater*, 18.

39. Riv-Ellen Prell, *Prayer & Community: The Havurah in American Judaism* (Detroit: Wayne State University Press, 1989), 233.

40. Rothenberg, "Innovation & Disruption," in *Riverside Interviews*, 87.

41. Rothenberg, conversation with the author, 5 Mar. 2000. Allan Kaprow coined the term "happening" to describe one of his artworks, which extended beyond the frame into space and time by incorporating real people. See Allan Kaprow, *Assemblage, Environments & Happenings*, text and design by Allan Kaprow (New York: Harry N. Abrams, 1966). Various definitions of the terms "happening" and "event" are found in the books by Kaprow and Michael Kirby. See Michael Kirby, *Happenings: An Illustrated Anthology*, scripts and productions by Jim Dine, Red Grooms, Allan Kaprow, Claes Oldenburg, Robert Whitman (New York: Dutton, 1966).

42. Rothenberg, *Technicians of the Sacred*, 111–46; and Rothenberg, *Shaking the Pumpkin*, 147–208.

43. For example, he transposed a Seneca Indian ceremony into a contemporary "Gift Event," which then was performed as a happening at the Judson Memorial Church. See Rothenberg, *Technicians of the Sacred*, 378–82. Rothenberg removed the event from the revised edition.

44. The term "event poem" is taken from Castro. See Castro, *Interpreting the Indian*, 134.

45. Rothenberg, "Innovation & Disruption," *The Riverside Interviews*, 74.

46. The following exposition draws on basic Jewish knowledge that may be gathered from any Jewish primer. See *Back to the Sources*. The more complex aspects of the Jewish tradition of commentary cannot be elaborated here as they would require a whole chapter, even though Rothenberg's work certainly could be reread in terms of this tradition. However, I completely reject the polemic approach taken by Jonathan N. Barron in his essay "Commentary in Contemporary Jewish American Poetry," *Jewish American Poetry*, 233–50. Barron claims that the difference between Jewish and non-Jewish (Christian) writing concerns the tradition of commentary. Yet he readily ignores the fact that the Catholic Church has its own tradition of commentary, that is, the tradition of interpreting the canon law. Barron's argument rests on a misrepresentation of Christianity.

47. Gershom Scholem, *On the Kabbalah and Its Symbolism* (New York: Schocken, 1965), 11–12.

48. Marjorie Perloff, *Poetic License: Essays on Modernist and Postmodernist Lyric* (Evanston, Ill.: Northwestern University Press, 1990), 143.

49. Editorial Staff, "Magic: Talmudic Period," *Encyclopaedia Judaica* vol. 11, 706–07.

50. Sayre, "David Antin and," *Contemporary Literature* 23.4 (1982 fall): 439.

51. Ibid., 441.

52. Compare to Scholem, *Kabbalah and Its Symbolism*, 187–88. Scholem suggests that this ritual is related to Abulafia's ecstatic kabbalah. Abulafia regarded the golem-making as a purely mystical process.

53. Scholem, *Kabbalah*, 25.

54. Ibid., 158–204; and Gershom Scholem, "Magische und tellurische Elemente in der Vorstellung des Golem," *Eranos-Jahrbuch* 22 (1952): 235–89.

55. Ibid., 269.

56. Rothenberg, "Beyond Poetics," in *Coherence*, 153.

57. Ibid.

58. Scholem and Joshua Trachtenberg describe the ritual. See Scholem, *Kabbalah and Its Symbolism*, 136–37; and Joshua Trachtenberg, *Jewish Magic and Superstition: A Study in Folk Religion* (New York: Meridian, 1961), 83.

59. Scholem, *Kabbalah and Its Symbolism*, 136–37.

60. Castro, *Interpreting the Indian*, 135.

61. See Heller, "Pale Darkened Moons," *Parnassus* 9.1 (spring/summer 1981): 279.

62. Ibid., 278.

63. Rothenberg, "Beyond Poetics," in *Coherence*, 152.

64. Schechner, *Future of Ritual*, 253.

65. Ibid., 246.

66. Ibid., 253.

67. Rothenberg recalls that Grotowski, who was teaching at the University of Irvine, California, got in touch with him and came to visit San Diego with two dancers from Haiti. They planned to meet up again, but nothing came of it before Grotowski moved away. Rothenberg, conversation with the author, 19 July 2000.

68. This critique of Rothenberg and other ethnopoets is summarized by Castro. See *Interpreting the Indian*, 163–72. See also Schechner, *Future of Ritual*, 254.

69. Rothenberg, "Innovation & Disruption," in Selerie and Mottram, eds., *Riverside Interviews*, 88.

70. Ibid., 78.

71. Ibid., 81.

72. Michail M. Bachtin, "Der Karneval und die Karnevalisierung der Literatur," in *Literatur und Karneval: Zur Romantheorie und Lachkultur* (Frankfurt: Fischer, 1996), 47–60.

73. I am drawing on Bakhtin's distinction between the "authoritative word" and "internally persuasive discourse." The former is "the word of the fathers. Its authority was already *acknowledged* in the past. . . . It is given (it sounds) in lofty spheres, not those of familiar contact. Its language is a special (as it were, hieratic) language. It can be profaned." By contrast, internally persuasive discourse "awakens new and independent words" and is "freely developed, applied to new material, new conditions; it enters into in-

teranimating relationships with new contexts." See Mikhail M. Bakhtin, *The Dialogic Imagination*, ed. Michael Holquist, trans. Caryl Emerson (Austin: University of Texas Press, 1981), 342, 345–46.

74. Rothenberg, "Innovation & Disruption," *Riverside Interviews*, 78.

75. "Etrog," *Encyclopaedia Britannica*, CD-ROM, Version 97 (Encyclopaedia Britannica, Inc., 1997).

76. Patai, *Man and Temple*, 54–104.

77. For a discussion of lists as the roots of poetry, see Hugh Kenner, *Magic and Spells (About Curses, Charms and Riddles)*, originally delivered at Bennington College as Lecture Ten in Ben Belitt Lectureship Series, 29 Oct. 1987 (New York: Bennington College, 1988).

78. For a general overview, see Abraham Milgram, *Jewish Worship* (Philadelphia: Jewish Publication Society, 1971), 39–88.

79. Rothenberg, "Innovation & Disruption," *Riverside Interviews*, 78–79.

80. Ibid., 80.

81. Arthur Waskow, telephone conversation with the author, 13 Apr. 2000.

82. For further examples, see Michael Strassfeld, *The Jewish Holidays: A Guide and Commentary*, illustrated by Betsy Platkin Teutsch (New York: Harper, 1985), 135.

83. See, for instance, Isaac Klein, "Family Purity (*Tohorat Hamishpaḥah*) (I)," in *A Guide to Jewish Religious Practice* (New York: Jewish Theological Seminary of America, 1979), 510–16.

84. Lenowitz, "Rothenberg: The Blood," *Vort* 7 (1975): 180.

85. Ibid., 182.

86. Ibid., 180.

87. Alfred J. Koltach, *The Second Jewish Book of Why* (New York: Jonathan David Publishers, 1985), 149.

88. Lenowitz, "Rothenberg: The Blood," *Vort* 7 (1975): 184.

89. Ibid., 181.

90. Jerome Rothenberg Papers, "Food," Ms. 10, Box 28, Folder 7, Mandeville Special Collections Library, UCSD.

91. Jerome Rothenberg Papers, "Forbidden Foods, Clean Foods," Ms. 10, Box 28, Folder 7, Mandeville Special Collections Library, UCSD.

92. Rothenberg, conversation with the author, 26 June 2000.

93. Alpert, "Jerome Rothenberg—An Interview," *Vort* 7 (1975): 105.

94. Ibid., 99.

95. Ibid., 105.

96. Rothenberg, conversation with the author, 5 Mar. 2000.

97. The poem is adapted from Trachtenberg, *Jewish Magic and Superstition*.

98. Kaprow, cited by Rothenberg, *A Big Jewish Book*, 472.

99. Rothenberg, "New Models, New Visions," *Pre-Faces*, 167.

100. Louis Jacobs, "Bar Mitzvah," *A Concise Companion to the Jewish Religion*, Oxford Paperback Reference (Oxford: Oxford University Press, 1999), 15.

101. Rothenberg, "Innovation & Disruption," in Selerie and Mottram, *Riverside Interviews*, 81.

102. Jerome Rothenberg Papers, "BAR MITZVAH EVENTS: for Matthew Rothenberg," Ms. 10, Box 1, Folder 3, Mandeville Special Collections Library, UCSD.

103. Turner, *Dramas, Fields, and Metaphors*, 273.

104. A "Big Jewish Band was assembled for the occasion and played traditional klezmer tunes based on the Kamen song sheets." Rothenberg, email to the author, 22 July 2000.

105. Jerome Rothenberg Papers, "BAR MITZVAH EVENTS: for Matthew Rothenberg," Ms. 10, Box 1, Folder 3, Mandeville Special Collections Library, UCSD.

106. "S.Z.'s Song" was to be performed by Matthew and Jerome Rothenberg. See Jerome Rothenberg Papers, "'BAR MITSVA [*sic*] EVENT'—events," Ms. 10, Box 1, Folder 3, Mandeville Special Collections Library, UCSD.

107. Scholem, *Kabbalah and Its Symbolism*, 118–57.

108. The readings include poems on the Shekhinah by the kabbalist Isaac Luria, the heretic Shabbatai Zevi, as well as a contemporary poem by Nathaniel Tarn. Further texts from *A Big Jewish Book* are Rothenberg's own translation from the Song of Songs, the permutation text, "Havdala of Rabbi Akiba," and a performance piece by Jackson Mac Low, "Kaddish Gatha." See Jerome Rothenberg Papers, "'BAR MITSVA [*sic*] EVENT'—events," Ms. 10, Box 1, Folder 3, Mandeville Special Collections Library, UCSD.

109. Myerhoff, "We Don't Wrap Herring," in *Secular Ritual*, 201.

110. Meyer, "Tradition and Modernity Reconsidered," in *Uses of Tradition*, 468.

Chapter 3. A Jewish Poetry of Names, Numbers, and Letters

1. Craig Williamson, Introduction to *A Feast of Creatures: Anglo-Saxon Riddle Songs*, ed. and trans. Craig Williamson (Philadelphia: University of Philadelphia Press, 1982), 36. The observations about riddles and charms in this chapter are condensed from Williamson's introduction as well as the following texts: Northrop Frye, "Charms and Riddles," in *Spiritus Mundi: Essays on Literature, Myth, and Society* (Bloomington: Indiana University Press, 1976), 123–47; Andrew Welsh, *Roots of Lyric: Primitive Poetry and Modern Poetics* (Princeton, New Jersey: Princeton University Press, 1978); Mark Bryant, *Riddles: Ancient & Modern* (London: Hutchinson, 1983); Kenner, *Magic and Spells*.

2. Rothenberg, "Poetics of the Sacred," in *Picturing Cultural Values*, 97.

3. Theodor H. Gaster, "Amulets and Talismans," in *Encyclopedia of Religion*, ed. in chief Mircea Eliade, vol. 1 (New York: Macmillan, 1987), 243.

4. Trachtenberg, *Jewish Magic and Superstition*, 83.

5. See Theodore Schrire, *Hebrew Magic Amulets: Their Decipherment and Interpretation* (New York: Behrman, 1966), 3; Joseph Dan, "Magic: In Medieval Hebrew Literature," in *Encyclopaedia Judaica* vol. 11, 714; Lawrence H. Schiffmann and Michael D. Swartz, eds., *Hebrew and Aramaic Incantation Texts from the Cairo Genizah: Selected Texts from Taylor-Schechter Box K1.*, Semitic Texts and Studies 1 (Sheffield: JSOT P, 1992), 33.

6. Schrire, *Hebrew Magic Amulets*, 14.

7. Rothenberg, *A Big Jewish Book*, 393–94, 395, 423, 442, 508, 531, 535.

Besides, the anthology also includes many magic incantations, which cannot be listed here.

8. Rothenberg, "Total Translation," *Pre-Faces*, 83–84.
9. Rothenberg, *Poland/1931*, 55, 59, 63, 71, 75, 81, 123.
10. This text is taken from Schrire, *Hebrew Magic Amulets*, 171.
11. Power, "*Poland/1931*: Pack up," *Boundary 2* 3 (spring 1975): 696.
12. Rothenberg, *Shaking the Pumpkin*, 456.
13. Armand Schwerner, *The Tablets* (Orono, Maine: National Poetry Foundation, 1999), 140.
14. Gaster, "Amulets and Talismans," *Encyclopedia of Religion*, 243.
15. Rothenberg, *Shaking the Pumpkin*, 456–57.
16. Kenner, *Magic and Spells*, 24.
17. Patai, "Lilith," *The Hebrew Goddess*, 221–54. For a short summary, see Scholem, *Kabbalah*, 356–61.
18. "No she-demon has ever achieved as fantastic a career as Lilith, who started out from the lowliest of origins, was a failure as Adam's intended wife, became the paramour of lascivious spirits, rose to be the bride of Samael the Demon King, ruled as Queen of Zemargad and Sheba, and ended up as the consort of God himself." Patai, *Hebrew Goddess*, 221.
19. Trachtenberg, *Jewish Magic and Superstition*, 260–64.
20. Paul Schmidt and Charlotte Douglas, cited by Marjorie Perloff, "Soundings: *Zaum*, Seriality and the Discovery of the 'Sacred,'" *American Poetry Review* (February 1986): 37.
21. Rothenberg, "Total Translation," *Pre-Faces*, 88–89.
22. Bronislaw Malinowski, "The Meaning of Meaningless Words and the Coefficient of Weirdness," *Symposium of the Whole*, 112.
23. Ibid., 108.
24. The Hebrew version of the amulet can be found in Schrire, *Hebrew Magic Amulets*, 113.
25. Brito, "Jerome Rothenberg," *A Suite of Poetic Voices*, 121.
26. Frye, *Spiritus Mundi*, 136.
27. Ibid., 126.
28. Ibid., 142.
29. Rothenberg, *A Big Jewish Book*, 388.
30. Schrire, *Hebrew Magic Amulets*, 115–16.
31. Rothenberg appropriated this amulet from a book by Scholem. See Gershom Scholem, *Jewish Gnosticism, Merkabah Mysticism, and Talmudic Tradition* (New York: Jewish Theological Seminary, 1960), 73. This text is also cited by Rothenberg in the appendix of *A Big Jewish Book*, 628.
32. "these terms possessed significance because they were "names" and not because they "meant something." Trachtenberg, *Jewish Magic and Superstition*, 99.
33. Rothenberg, "Poetics of the Sacred," *Picturing Cultural Values*, 97.
34. Ibid.
35. Sayre, "David Antin and," *Contemporary Literature* 23.4 (1982 fall): 438.
36. Rothenberg, "Poetics of the Sacred," *Picturing Cultural Values*, 98.
37. Rothenberg, "The Poetics of Sound," *Pre-Faces*, 144.
38. Peter Middleton, "Seven Words for Jerome Rothenberg," *Samizdat* 7 (winter 2001): 5.
39. Perloff, *Poetic License*, 95.

40. For a general background on number symbolism, see Christopher Butler, *Number Symbolism* (New York: Barnes & Noble, 1970).

41. Rothenberg, *Poland/1931*, 75–78; and Rothenberg, *Vienna Blood*, 57–68.

42. George Ifrah, *The Universal History of Numbers from Prehistory to the Invention of the Computer*, trans. David Bellos et al. (London: Harvill Press, 1998), 589.

43. "Cipher," *Encyclopaedia Britannica*, CD-ROM, Version 97 (Encyclopaedia Britannica, Inc., 1997).

44. "The form of *gematria* which consists of changing the letters of the alphabet according to *atbash*, i.e., the last letter ת is substituted for the first א, the penultimate ש for the second ב etc., already occurs in Scripture: Sheshach (Jer. 25:26, 51:41) corresponding to Bavel ('Babylon')." Scholem, *Kabbalah*, 338.

45. Brito, "Jerome Rothenberg," *A Suite of Poetic Voices*, 119.

46. Ibid., 120.

47. Scholem, *Kabbalah*, 337.

48. This is the title of Perloff's essay, which deals with this subject. See Marjorie Perloff, *Radical Artifice: Writing Poetry in the Age of Media* (Chicago: University of Chicago Press, 1991), 134–70.

49. Traditional riddle, cited by Bryant, *Riddles: Ancient & Modern*, 27.

50. Riddles involve vision and cognition because they "can work from either of two basic elements, the metaphorical presentation of an image or 'picture' or the presentation of an intellectual paradox in which the sense of picture is slight or non-existent." Welsh, *Roots of Lyric*, 30.

51. Gutman G. Locks, "The Torah by Gematria," *The Spice of Torah*, introd. Rabbi J. Immanuel Schochet (New York: Judaica Press, 1985), ii.

52. Moshe Idel, "Gematria," in *The Encyclopedia of Language and Linguistics*, ed. in chief R. E. Asher, coordinating editor J. M. Y. Simpson, vol. 3. (Oxford: Pergamon Press, 1994), 1347.

53. Rabbi J. Immanuel Schochet, "Gematria: the Principle of Numerical Interpretation," in *The Spice of Torah—Gematria*, viii.

54. Ibid., v–ix.

55. Perloff, *Radical Artifice*, 139.

56. Schochet, "Gematria," *Spice of Torah*, xxv, xxvi–xxvii.

57. Idel, "Gematria," *The Encyclopedia of Language and Linguistics*, 1347.

58. Karl Young, email to the author, 3 Feb. 2001.

59. Brito, "Jerome Rothenberg," *A Suite of Poetic Voices*, 120.

60. Eugen Gomringer, ed. *konkrete poesie: deutschsprachige autoren* (1972; Stuttgart: Philipp Reclam Jun., 1991), 158–59.

61. Rothenberg, "Rothenberg's Pre-Face" [From a letter to Eugen Gomringer 9 Nov. 1967], *The Book of Hours and Constellations*, n. pag.

62. However, Young admits that "some of the correspondences were semi-intentional. That is, as I was setting the work up to be printed on two large master sheets, I noticed some possible correlations, and did a bit of rearranging and 'massaging' to enhance them." Young, email to the author, 3 February 2001.

63. Samuel Johnson, cited by Welsh, *Roots of Lyric*, 40.

64. Pierre Reverdy, cited by Rothenberg, *Technicians of the Sacred*, 456.

65. Williamson, Introduction to *A Feast of Creatures*, 32.

66. An astute analysis of *Sightings* and *Further Sightings* is provided by Antin. See David Antin, "Why 1964–1967?" *Vort* 7 (1975): 128–31.

67. However, he also continues to publish minimalist gematrias. His collaboration with the artist Ian Tyson has resulted in a number of beautiful artists' books. See Jerome Rothenberg, *Surimo: To Celebrate 25 Years of Collaboration between Jerome Rothenberg and Ian Tyson* (London: Tetrad Press, 1992); Jerome Rothenberg and Ian Tyson, *Gematria 643* (London: I. Tyson, 1997); Jerome Rothenberg and Ian Tyson, *Six Gematria* (London: Tetrad Press, 1992); Jerome Rothenberg and Ian Tyson, *Twin Gematria* (London: I. Tyson, 1997); Jerome Rothenberg and Ian Tyson, *Delight/Délices and Other Gematria* (Nîmes: Editions Ottezec, 1997).

68. For this terminology, I am indebted to Avram Sachs. See Avram Sachs, "Jerome Rothenberg's *Gematria*," unpublished essay, n.d., 7.

69. Sachs, "Jerome Rothenberg's *Gematria*," 13.

70. Rothenberg, email to the author, 9 Feb. 2001.

71. Perloff reminds us that Cage coined the term "chance operation," but later on preferred to speak of "nonintentionality," which has to be distinguished from randomness. See Perloff, *Radical Artifice*, 150.

72. Mac Low speaks of "'nonegoic' methods in which the artist's tastes, passions, and predilections intervene much less than when artwork is made in other, more traditional, ways." See Jackson Mac Low, "Buddhism, Art, Practice, Polity," in *Beneath A Single Moon: Buddhism in Contemporary American Poetry*, ed. Kent Johnson and Craig Paulenich, introd. Gary Snyder (Boston: Shambhala, 1991), 177.

73. Fred Muratori, "Remixing Lorca, Recounting the Word," review of *The Lorca Variations* and *Gematria*, by Jerome Rothenberg, *American Book Review* (Dec. 94–Feb. 95): 31.

74. The same poem also occurs in one of the gematria sequences. See Rothenberg, "Tenth Gematria: 'Nations,'" *Gematria*, 84.

75. Charles Reznikoff, *Testimony: the United States, 1885–1890* (New York: New Directions, 1965); and Charles Reznikoff, *Holocaust* (Los Angeles: Black Sparrow Press, 1975).

76. Scholem, *Kabbalah*, 341.

77. Schochet, "Gematria," *Spice of Torah*, xv.

78. Carl Gustav Jung, trans. R. F. C. Hull, *Synchronicity: An Acausal Connecting Principle*, The Collected Works of C. G. Jung, vol. 8., Bollingen Ser. 20 (Princeton: Princeton University Press, 1973), 109.

79. David F. Peat, *Synchronicity: The Bridge Between Matter and Mind* (Toronto: Bantam, 1987), 24.

80. Muratori, "Remixing Lorca," *American Book Review* (Dec. 94–Feb. 95): 31.

81. Rothenberg, *Gematria*, 148, 149, 151, 152, 162.

82. Muratori, "Remixing Lorca," *American Book Review* (Dec. 94–Feb. 95): 31.

83. The second part of this poem (not printed here) actually corresponds to a passage from *Khurbn*. Compare to Rothenberg, "Khurbn," *Khurbn*, 39.

Chapter 4. Imagining History

1. Alpert, "Jerome Rothenberg—An Interview," *Vort* 7 (1975): 114.
2. In his book, *Beyond Ethnicity*, Sollors explores the basic tension in

American culture between consent (the choice of a set of American values and beliefs) and descent (blood relations). See in particular Sollor's introduction and chapter 1.

3. Sollors mentions the book by Nathan Glazer and Daniel Patrick Moynihan, *Beyond the Melting Pot: The Negroes, Puerto Ricans, Jews, Italians, and Irish of New York City* (Cambridge: MIT Press, 1963). As regards the revival of theories of descent, he refers to the writings of Andrew Greeley, Michael Novak, and Pierre van Berghe. See Sollors, *Beyond Ethnicity*, 20–21.

4. Alpert, "Jerome Rothenberg—An Interview," *Vort* 7 (1975): 114.

5. Ibid. The mentioned poem is entitled "Seeing Leni Riefenstahl's Triumph of the Will, San Francisco, 1959," *White Sun Black Sun*, 17.

6. Jerome Rothenberg, "Satan in Goray," *some/thing* 1.2 (Winter 1965): 46–48; Rothenberg, *Poems 1964–1967*, 43–45; Rothenberg, *Poland/1931*, 7–9.

7. Gertrude Stein, "Dates," *The Yale Gertrude Stein: Selections*, introd. Richard Kostelanetz (New Haven: Yale University Press, 1980), 199.

8. Alpert, "Jerome Rothenberg—An Interview," *Vort* 7 (1975): 114.

9. Sayre, *The Object of Performance*, 189.

10. For a comprehensive summary of the factors that affected Jewish identity, see Waxman, "The Fourth Generation Grows Up," *Annals of the American Academy of Political and Social Science*, 71–72.

11. David Glanz, "An Interpretation of the Jewish Counterculture," *Jewish Social Studies* 24.1–2 (winter–spring, 1977): 126.

12. For this observation, I am indebted to Alan Bern.

13. *Israel: After the War and Before the Peace*, spec. issue of *Response* 20 (winter 1973–74). In the fall of the following year, the editorial stance of the journal changed. Issue 23 of *Response* clearly shifts its emphasis toward the diaspora; it criticizes the nation state and puts forward diaspora Jewishness. Indicative of this new stance is also the fact that the journal prints two poems by Rothenberg. See, for example, Everett Gendler, "To Be a Jew in the Diaspora—An Affirmation," *Response* 23 (fall 1974): 105–16. See Jerome Rothenberg, "Ancestral Scenes," *Response* 23 (fall 1974): 30; and Jerome Rothenberg, "A Polish Anecdote," *Response* 23 (fall 1974): 117.

14. Melton J. Gordon, Jerome Clark, and Aidan A. Kelly, "Kabbalism and Hassidism," *New Age Almanac*, ed. Melton J. Gordon (New York: Visible Ink, 1991), 332.

15. David Roskies, email to the author, 25 May 2000.

16. Gordon et al., "Shlomo Carlebach," in *New Age Almanac*, 330.

17. David G. Roskies, "The Story's the Thing," in *What is Jewish Literature?*, 120.

18. Glanz, "An Interpretation of the Jewish Counterculture," *Jewish Social Studies* 24.1–2 (Winter–Spring, 1977): 123.

19. Peter Eli Gordon, "Imagining Hasidism," *Tikkun* 5.3 (May/June 1990): 50–51.

20. Roskies analyzes the discourse of authenticity raised by modern Yiddish literature. His observations can also be applied to the neo-ḥasidic revival of the 1970s. See David G. Roskies, "The People of the Lost Book," in *A Bridge of Longing: The Lost Art of Yiddish Storytelling* (Cambridge: Harvard University Press, 1995), 1–19.

21. On this subject, see Hugh Kenner, *The Pound Era* (Berkeley: University of California Press, 1971), 363–78.

22. Yosef Hayim Yerushalmi, *Zakhor: Jewish History and Jewish Memory* (Seattle: University of Washington Press, 1982), 14.
23. Ibid., 8.
24. Ibid., 97.
25. Ibid., xv.
26. Ibid., 40.
27. Ibid., 93, 101.
28. Roskies, *Bridge of Longing*, 9, 14.
29. Ibid., 17.
30. See Roskies, "The Story's the Thing," in *What is Jewish Literature?*, 124–25.
31. Scholem, *Major Trends*, 350. Here is the German version of the same passage: "Die Verwandlung, die so tief ist, daß vom Mysterium schließlich nur noch die Geschichte übrigbleibt." Gershom Scholem, *Die jüdische Mystik in ihren Hauptströmungen*, 5th ed. (Frankfurt/Main: Suhrkamp, 1993), 384.
32. Scholem, *Major Trends*, 350.
33. Olson, "Human Universe," *Collected Prose*, 163.
34. Under the term "image-making," Rothenberg subsumes the following Jewish traditions: apocalyptic and mystic visions, "the fantastic life of the gods & the individualized visions emerging therefrom." Rothenberg, *A Big Jewish Book*, 21.
35. Rothenberg, "Poetics of the Sacred," *Picturing Cultural Values*, 91.
36. Yerushalmi, *Zakhor*, 74.
37. For the visual poem, see Rothenberg, *Poland/1931*, 120. "A Book of Histories" comprises approximately twenty pages. See Rothenberg, "A Book of Histories," *Poland/1931*, 121–39.
38. ". . . things repeated, as the Steinesque writing of the facing mandala reminds us (is history circular, Viconian?)." Paul, *Search for the Primitive*, 144.
39. The speaker states that he is "being made brothers" with another male character. From this I conclude that the speaker must be male.
40. Paul, *Search for the Primitive*, 144. Rothenberg himself also speaks of "simple collages from fragments of prose material." See Brito, "Jerome Rothenberg," *A Suite of Poetic Voices*, 129–30.
41. Paul, *Search for the Primitive* 144.
42. Jerome Rothenberg Papers, "The Materials," MSS 10, Box 29, Folder 4, Mandeville Special Collections Library, UCSD.
43. Brito, "Jerome Rothenberg," *A Suite of Poetic Voices*, 130.
44. Rothenberg cited by Paul, *Search for the Primitive*, 182.
45. Spanos cited by Rothenberg, "Jerome Rothenberg: A Dialogue," *Boundary 2* 3.3 (spring 1975): 518.
46. Ibid., 535.
47. Frederick Garber, "The Histories and Poetics of Jerome Rothenberg," *Repositionings: Readings of Contemporary Poetry, Photography, and Performance Art* (University Park, Pa.: The Pennsylvania State University Press, 1995), 45–49.
48. Ibid., 48.
49. Yerushalmi, *Zakhor*, 17.
50. See, for instance, Rothenberg, *Revolution of the Word*, 78.
51. Yerushalmi, *Zakhor*, 96.
52. Ibid., 26.

53. Ivan G. Marcus, "Postmodern or Neo-Medieval Times?," *Uses of Tradition*, 479–80.

54. This criticism is raised as part of a larger critique of Rothenberg's nonacademic translation methods. See William M. Clements, "Faking the Pumpkin: On Jerome Rothenberg's Literary Offenses," *Western American Literature* 16 (1981–1982): 195.

55. Marcus, "Postmodern or Neo-Medieval Times?," *Uses of Tradition*, 484.

56. Arthur Green, "After Itzik: Toward a Theology of Jewish Spirituality," in *The New Jews*, ed. Alan Mintz and James Sleeper (New York: Vintage, 1971), 202.

57. Brito, "Jerome Rothenberg," *A Suite of Poetic Voices*, 127.

58. Ibid., 133.

Chapter 5. *Poland/1931*

1. Rothenberg, *Poland/1931* (1970).

2. Rothenberg, *Symposium of the Whole*, xii.

3. Lazer, "Thinking Made in the Mouth," in *Picturing Cultural Values*, 139.

4. Rothenberg, letter to Robert Kelly, 9 May 1977, Jerome Rothenberg Papers, "Kelly, Robert 1958–1980," Ms. 10, Box 11, Folder 30, Mandeville Special Collections Library, UCSD.

5. Lazer, "Thinking Made in the Mouth," in *Picturing Cultural Values*, 139.

6. Jerome Rothenberg, "Nokh Aushvits (After Auschwitz)," in *Jewish American Poetry*, 140.

7. Frederic Jameson, "Postmodernism and Consumer Society," in *Postmodern Culture*, ed. Hal Foster (London: Pluto Press, 1983), 116.

8. Herbert J. Gans, "Symbolic Ethnicity: The Future of Ethnic Groups and Cultures in America," in *On the Making of the Americans: Essays in Honor of David Riesman*, ed. Herbert J. Gans et al. (Philadelphia: University of Pennsylvania Press, 1979), 204.

9. Ibid., 202.

10. Jerome Rothenberg, letter to Sherman Paul, 31 July 1983, *Search of the Primitive*, 181.

11. Finkelstein, "The Messianic Ethnography," *Contemporary Literature* 39.3 (1998 fall): 372.

12. I heard this version on an unpublished tape I received from the poet. For an audio clip of Rothenberg's performance at the first People's Poetry Gathering in New York City in 1999, see "Jerome Rothenberg & The Klezmatics: Galician Nights," <http://www.peoplespoetry.org/pg_clips_audvid.html>, accessed 25 Feb. 2002.

13. "Cuba," *Encyclopaedia Judaica*, CD-ROM, Version 1.0 (Jerusalem: Keter, 1997).

14. Paul, *Search of the Primitive*, 147.

15. Rothenberg, "Beyond Poetics," in *Coherence*, 152–53.

16. The poems Schwartz has in mind are "The Beadle's Testimony," "The Neolithic Dream of Rabbi Nachman," "More Visions from the Neolithic Rabbi," and "A Poem from the Saint's Life." See Howard Schwartz, letter

to Jerome Rothenberg, 11 Dec. 1977, Jerome Rothenberg Papers, "Howard, Schwartz 1974–1980," Ms. 10, Box 18, Folder 9, Mandeville Special Collections Library, UCSD. For the anthology, see *Voices Within the Ark: The Modern Jewish Poets*, ed. Howard Schwartz and Anthony Rudolf (Yonkers, N.Y.: Pushcart Press, 1980).

17. Rothenberg, letter to Howard Schwartz, 10 Apr. 1978, Jerome Rothenberg Papers, "Howard, Schwartz 1974–1980," Ms. 10, Box 18, Folder 9, Mandeville Special Collections Library, UCSD.

18. Here Perloff draws on a definition by David Antin. See Perloff, *Poetic License*, 137.

19. Rothenberg, *Poland/1931* (1970); Jerome Rothenberg, *Polish Anecdotes* (Santa Barbara: Unicorn Press, 1970); Jerome Rothenberg, *A Book of Testimony* (Santa Barbara: Tree, 1971); Rothenberg, *Esther K. Comes to America, 1931* (1974). Rothenberg also planned a separate edition of *Galician Nights* with Black Sparrow Press, but the plan did not materialize.

20. Brito, "Jerome Rothenberg," *A Suite of Poetic Voices*, 130.

21. William S. Seitz, *The Art of Assemblage* (Garden City, N.Y.: Doubleday, 1961), 150 n. 5.

22. Alpert, "Jerome Rothenberg—An Interview," *Vort* 7 (1975): 117.

23. Howard N. Fox, *Eleanor Antin*, with an essay by Lisa E. Bloom (Los Angeles: Los Angeles Country Museum of Art, 1999), 23.

24. Garber, "The Histories," *Repositionings*, 49.

25. Power, "*Poland/1931*: Pack up," *Boundary 2* 3 (spring 1975): 686.

26. André Breton, cited by Max Ernst, *Beyond Painting: And Other Writings by the Artist and his Friends* (New York: Wittenborn, 1948), 21.

27. Marjorie Perloff, *The Dance of the Intellect: Studies in the Poetry of the Pound Tradition* (Evanston, Ill.: Northwestern University Press, 1985), 63.

28. "[For] Luminous Details are the transcendentals in an array of facts: not merely "significant" not "symptomatic" in the manner of most acts, but capable of giving one 'a sudden insight into circumjacent conditions, into their causes, their effects, into sequence, and law." Pound, cited by Kenner, *Pound Era*, 152–53.

29. Rothenberg, letter to Robert Kelly, 9 May 1977, Jerome Rothenberg Papers, "Kelly, Robert 1958–1980," Ms. 10, Box 11, Folder 30, Mandeville Special Collections Library, UCSD.

30. According to a family tradition, the reason for his grandfather's return to Poland was that "he felt alienated as a foreigner and a religious Jew." Rothenberg, email to the author, 2 Nov. 2001.

31. Rothenberg, telephone conversation with the author, 19 Sept. 2000.

32. Power, "*Poland/1931*: Pack up," *Boundary 2* 3 (spring 1975): 695.

33. Pacernick, *Memory and Fire*, 38.

34. Paul, *Search of the Primitive*, 131.

35. Alpert, "Jerome Rothenberg—An Interview," *Vort* 7 (1975): 117.

36. Alfred Hornung defines this term in the following way: "By this term I want to characterize those contemporary texts which explore some aspects of the writer's self in a factual or fictional way and use narration as a form of recollection and presentation of earlier stages in life." See Alfred Hornung, "The Autobiographical Mode in Contemporary American Fiction," *Prose Studies* 8.3 (December 1985): 72.

37. Rothenberg, "Craft Interview with Jerome Rothenberg," *The Craft of Poetry*, 39.

38. Ibid.

39. The map actually comes from the Ostrow memorial book. Rothenberg, email to the author, 27 Jan. 2002.

40. Translation of the Yiddish: the city hall, the synagogue, the old synagogue, the new synagogue, the yeshiva, and high school.

41. Rothenberg, letter to Alan Brilliant, 24 Aug. 1969, Jerome Rothenberg Papers, "Esther K. Comes to America—Business Correspondence 1967–1969," Ms. 10, Box 27, Folder 10, Mandeville Special Collections Library, UCSD.

42. Rothenberg, letter to Alan Brilliant, 24 Aug. 1969, Jerome Rothenberg Papers, "Esther K. Comes to America—Business Correspondence 1967–1969," Ms. 10, Box 27, Folder 10, Mandeville Special Collections Library, UCSD.

43. Rothenberg writes: "the book I have is in Yiddish and Hebrew, called *Yizkor Bukh Fun der Yidisher Kehilah in Ostrov-Mazovietsk* and published I would guess around 1960. Two of my uncles have articles in it, and I was once drawn (almost) into translating a part of it but never followed through." Rothenberg, email to the author, 14 Jan. 2002.

44. "Yizkor Book Project: Frequently Asked Questions," http://www.jewishgen.org/yizkor.html, accessed 15 Jan. 2002. There is even a web page for Ostrow-Mazowiecka, the hometown of Rothenberg's family, which contains a necrology of the Jews who were killed there during the Holocaust. See "Memorial Book of the Community of Ostrow-Mazowiecka (Poland)," http://www.jewishgen.org/yizkor/ostrow/Ostrow.html, accessed 20 Feb. 2002.

45. Rothenberg, email to the author, 2 Nov. 2001.

46. Rothenberg, email to the author, 24 Aug. 2000.

47. Rothenberg, email to the author, 14 Jan. 2002.

48. For an overview of Antin's work, see Fox's book, *Eleanor Antin*.

49. Alpert, "Jerome Rothenberg—An Interview," *Vort* 7 (1975): 115.

50. Rothenberg, "Craft Interview with Jerome Rothenberg," in *The Craft of Poetry*, 45.

51. Brad Sabin Hill, email to the author, 2 Nov. 2001.

52. Rothenberg, email to the author, 2 Nov. 2001.

53. See, for instance, the texts in "A Book of the Wars of Yahveh," and section 3 and 4 of "A Book of Writings" in *A Big Jewish Book*.

54. Alpert, "Jerome Rothenberg—An Interview," *Vort* 7 (1975): 115.

55. Jerome Rothenberg Papers, "Poland/1931 Translations: German, Hebrew, Spanish, Polish," Ms. 10, Box 28, Folder 22, Mandeville Special Collections Library, UCSD.

56. Paula Orth, "Rothenberg Reads Poems," *The Wisconsin Jewish Chronicle* 27 Nov. 1975: 6.

57. Rothenberg, conversation with the author, 1 Dec. 2001.

58. For this suggestion, I am indebted to Brad Sabin Hill.

59. Gérard Genette, *Palimpsests: Literature in the Second Degree*, trans. Channa Newman and Claude Doubinsky, foreword by Gerald Prince (Lincoln: University of Nebraska Press, 1997), 85.

60. Ibid., 87.

61. Rothenberg, email to the author, 2 Nov. 2001.

62. Brito, "Jerome Rothenberg," *A Suite of Poetic Voices*, 123.

63. Alpert, "Jerome Rothenberg—An Interview," *Vort* 7 (1975): 116.

64. Jerome Rothenberg Papers, "Notes for Poland/1931: Includes News-

paper Clippings, Unpublished Poems, Part I. ca. 1968–1973," Ms. 10, Box 28, Folder 7, Mandeville Special Collections Library, UCSD.

65. Rothenberg, *Revolution of the Word*, 85.

66. Marjorie Perloff, *The Futurist Moment: Avant-Garde, Avant Guerre, and the Language of Rupture* (Chicago: University of Chicago Press, 1986), 75.

67. Rothenberg, *Revolution of the Word*, xvii.

68. The earliest performances of Rothenberg's Poland poems were accompanied by music by Cyrelle Foreman at The Folklore Center (New York City), 13 March 1968. For more details, see Jerome Rothenberg Papers, "Artwork: Mixed Media of *Poland/1931*: Including Photography of Collage Paste-Ups Advertising Poland/1931 Show at UCSD," Ms. 10, Box 27, Folder 16, Mandeville Special Collections Library, UCSD.

69. Sayre, *The Object of Performance*, 189.

70. Jerome Rothenberg Papers, "'Poland/1931: All-Jewish Dream Fantasy Show': UCSD Art Gallery, 26 May 1971," Ms. 10, Box 28, Folder 13, Mandeville Special Collections Library, UCSD.

71. Alpert, "Jerome Rothenberg—An Interview," *Vort* 7 (1975): 107.

72. For some memorable examples of Antin's storytelling, see David Antin, *talking at the boundaries* (New York: New Directions, 1976).

73. Middleton, "Seven Words," *Samizdat* 7 (Winter 2001): 3.

74. Perloff, *Dance of the Intellect*, 169.

75. Middleton, "Seven Words," *Samizdat* 7 (Winter 2001): 3.

76. This useful phrase is taken from Perloff, *Dance of the Intellect*, 155–71.

77. Like Perloff, I will distinguish between "story" and "narrative" according to a definition by Robert Scholes: "A story is a narrative with a very specific syntactic shape (beginning-middle-end or situation-transformation-situation) . . . When we speak of narrative, we are usually speaking of story, though story is clearly a higher (because more rule-governed) category." Robert Scholes, cited by Perloff, *Dance of the Intellect*, 157.

78. Among critics, the "prose poem" is a strongly contested "genre." In the present context, I postulate the existence of prose poems. Furthermore, I assume that there are different types of prose poems. The French symbolist and the surrealist prose poem need to be distinguished from American prose poems and postmodern prose poems. See, for instance, Renée Riese Hubert, "Characteristics of an Undefinable Genre: The Surrealist Prose Poem," *Symposium* (spring 1968): 25–34; Michael Benedikt, ed. and introd., *The Prose Poem: An International Anthology* (New York: Dell, 1976); Margueritte S. Murphy, *A Tradition of Subversion: The Prose Poem in English from Wilde to Ashbery* (Amherst: University of Massachusetts Press, 1992); Stephen Fredman, *Poet's Prose: The Crisis in American Verse*, 2nd ed. (Cambridge, Mass.: Cambridge University Press, 1990).

79. Murphy, *A Tradition of Subversion*, 65.

80. Ibid., 82.

81. Renée Riese Hubert makes this point regarding the surrealist prose poem. See Hubert, "Characteristics of an Undefinable Genre," *Symposium* (spring 1968): 25–34.

82. On Pound's strategy of layering time, see Kenner, *Pound Era*, 418–19.

83. Rothenberg, cited by Paul, *Search for the Primitive*, 181.

84. Ibid., 182.

85. Rothenberg, "Isaac Luria's 'Hymn to Shekhinah for the Feast of the Sabbath' Newly Set Rosh Hashonah 5733 by Jerome Rothenberg," *Poland/ 1931*, 97–99.

86. Rothenberg, email to the author, 24 Aug. 2001.

87. Northrop Frye, "Literature and Myth," in *Relations of Literary Study: Essays on Interdisciplinary Contributions*, ed. James Thorpe (New York: MLA, 1967), 27.

88. Brito, "Jerome Rothenberg," *A Suite of Poetic Voices*, 126.

89. For a history of the development of the concept of the Shekhinah, see Patai, *Hebrew Goddess*, 137–56, 186–206, 246–69.

90. Eric Murphy Selinger, "Shekhinah in America," in *Jewish American Poetry*, 252.

91. Ibid., 250–56.

92. Scholem, *Kabbalah and Its Symbolism*, 104.

93. Ibid., 88.

94. Selinger, "Shekhinah in America," in *Jewish American Poetry*, 266.

95. Patai, *Hebrew Goddess*, 154.

96. Ibid., 144–45.

97. Selinger, "Shekhinah in America," in *Jewish American Poetry*, 259.

98. Patai, *Hebrew Goddess*, 249; and Scholem, *Kabbalah and Its Symbolism*, 107.

99. Power, "*Poland/1931*: Pack up," *Boundary 2* 3 (spring 1975): 691–94.

100. Scholem, *Kabbalah and Its Symbolism*, 116.

101. Patai claims that the mythical character of the story gets covered up if it only appears in bits and pieces in a great body of different Jewish texts. See Patai, *Hebrew Goddess*, 155–60.

102. Scholem, *Kabbalah and Its Symbolism*, 105.

103. Selinger, "Shekhinah in America," in *Jewish American Poetry*, 260.

104. Rothenberg, *The Notebooks*, 9. The poem is reprinted with slight modifications in *Vienna Blood*.

105. Scholem, *Major Trends*, 63–65.

106. Rothenberg, *A Big Jewish Book*, 22–23.

107. Nathaniel Tarn, *Lyrics for the Bride of God* (New York: New Directions, 1975), 3–24. See also, Tarn, cited by Rothenberg, *A Big Jewish Book*, 39–40, 565–68.

108. An outstanding example is Rothenberg's thematizing of the Austrian depiction of the "*Heilige Kümmernis*." See Rothenberg, "The Ikon (1)," "The Ikon (2)," *Khurbn*, 44–48.

109. Hynes, "Mapping the Characteristics of Mythic Tricksters," in *Mythical Trickster Figures*, 33.

110. Paul, *Search for the Primitive*, 144.

111. Pacernick, *Memory and Fire*, 51.

112. Ibid., 52.

113. Gitenstein, "Coyote Cohen," *Studies in American Jewish Literature* 9.2 (1990 fall): 180.

114. Ibid.

115. This term is adapted from E. E. Evans-Pritchard who analyzes the role of the anthropologist between different cultures. See E[dward] E[van] Evans-Pritchard, *Witchcraft, Oracles, and Magic among the Azande*, introd. Eva Gillies, abr. ed. (Oxford: Clarendon Press, 1976), 243.

116. Brito, "Jerome Rothenberg," *A Suite of Poetic Voices*, 128.

117. Gary Snyder, "The Incredible Survival of Coyote," *The Old Ways*, 71.

118. Ibid., 82–83.

119. In his elaborate commentary on the figure of Coyote, Rothenberg cites C. G. Jung. See Rothenberg, *Shaking the Pumpkin*, 422–23. All the unmarked quotations in the next two paragraphs are from these pages.

120. Perloff, *Dance of the Intellect*, 181.

121. Hynes, "Mapping the Characteristics of Mythic Tricksters," in *Mythical Trickster Figures*, 42.

Chapter 6. Confronting the Holocaust

1. Rolf Hochhuth, *The Deputy: A Drama*, adapt. and trans. Jerome Rothenberg (New York: S. French, 1964).

2. Alvin H. Rosenfeld, *A Double Dying: Reflections on Holocaust Literature* (Bloomington: Indiana University Press, 1980), 140.

3. "He [Shumlin] was unhappy with the language of the earlier translation, but I did use that as a kind of reference point to check my own understanding of the German, given the lack of time." Rothenberg, email to the author, 4 Jan. 2002.

4. Jerome Rothenberg, "The Deputy: The War Behind the Scenes," *Ramparts* 3.4 (Dec. 1964): 35.

5. Ibid., 34.

6. Ibid., 40.

7. Ibid., 35.

8. Ibid., 38.

9. Rothenberg, conversation with the author, 19 July 2000.

10. See Harriet A. L. Parmet's discussion of John Simon's review in *The Nation*. Parmet, *The Terror of Our Days*, 173–74.

11. Rothenberg, "The Deputy," *Ramparts* 3.4 (Dec. 1964): 35.

12. Ibid.

13. Rothenberg, "Seeing Leni Riefenstahl's Triumph of the Will, San Francisco, 1959," *White Sun Black Sun*, 17; Rothenberg, "The Wedding," "King of the Jews," "The Connoisseur of Jews," "The Student's Testimony," *Poland/1931*, 3–4, 4–5, 12, 43–47; Rothenberg, "Vienna Blood," *Vienna Blood*, 18–23.

14. See, for instance, *Blood to Remember: American Poets on the Holocaust*, ed. Charles Fishman (Texas: Texas Tech University Press, 1986); *Ghosts of the Holocaust: An Anthology by the Second Generation*, ed. Steward J. Florsheim, foreword Gerald Stein (Detroit: Wayne State University Press, 1989); *Holocaust Poetry*, comp. and introd. Hilda Schiff (London: Harper, 1995); *Beyond Lament: Poets of the World Bearing Witness to the Holocaust*, ed. Marguerite M. Striar (Evanston, Ill.: Northwestern University Press, 1998).

15. Paul Goetsch, "Der Holocaust in der englischen und amerikanischen Lyrik," in *Jewish Life and Suffering as Mirrored in English and American Literature*, ed. Frank Link (München: Ferdinand Schöningh, 1987), 186.

16. Ibid., 167.

17. Gloria L. Young, "The Moral Function of Remembering: American Holocaust Poetry," *In the Shadow of the Holocaust*, spec. issue of *Studies in American Jewish Literature* 9.1 (spring 1990): 63.

18. Pacernick, *Sing A New Song*, 9.
19. Rosenfeld, *A Double Dying*, 34.
20. Rothenberg, *New Young German Poets*, 16–24.
21. Jack Hirschman, "Jack Hirschman," *Paul Celan*, spec. issue of *Studies in 20th Century Literature* 8.1 (fall 1983): 122.
22. Jerome Rothenberg, "Paul Celan: A Memoir and a Poem," *Paul Celan*, spec. issue of *Studies in 20th Century Literature* 8.1 (fall 1983): 110.
23. Ibid., 111.
24. I am citing "12/75 a letter to Paul Celan in memory" from *Vienna Blood*, 42–44, because this edition is more readily available. However, the poem was first published in *The Notebooks*. See Rothenberg, "12/75 a letter to Paul Celan in memory," *The Notebooks*, 25–27.
25. For a biography, see John Felstiner, *Paul Celan: Poet, Survivor, Jew* (New Haven: Yale University Press, 1995).
26. S. Lillian Kremer, *Witness Through the Imagination: Jewish American Holocaust Literature* (Detroit: Wayne State University Press, 1989), 15.
27. Rothenberg, "Paul Celan," *Studies in 20*th Century Literature 8.1 (fall 1983): 111.
28. Ibid., 111–12.
29. Rothenberg, conversation with the author, 10 Aug. 2000.
30. Rothenberg, "Paul Celan," *Studies in 20th Century Literature* 8.1 (fall 1983): 112.
31. Sidra DeKoven Ezrahi, *By Words Alone: The Holocaust in Literature* (Chicago: University of Chicago Press, 1980), 179–80.
32. Compare to Neugroschel's translation: "there is, / from below, a / light knotted into the air- / mat on which you set the table, for the empty chairs and their / sabbath splendor, for—." See Paul Celan, *Speech-Grille and Selected Poems*, trans. Joachim Neugroschel (New York: Dutton, 1971), 199.
33. Rosenfeld, *A Double Dying*, 107.
34. Celan's poem "Benedicta" ends in the following way: "Ge- / trunken. / Ge- / segnet. / Ge- / *bentscht*." Neugroschel renders it as follows: "Drunk. / Blessed. / *Gebentsht*." Rothenberg assimilates these final verses to his own style by opening up the syntax (he removes the periods and the capitals), by introducing quotation marks and by changing the verb from "blessed" to "blesst." Thus, he incorporates Neugroschel's gloss (see next note). See Celan, *Speech-Grille*, 196–97.
35. Celan, *Speech-Grille*, 254.
36. In this subchapter all subsequent references to page numbers (parentheses) are from the book *Khurbn*.
37. Ezrahi, *By Words Alone*, 108.
38. James E. Young, *Writing and Rewriting The Holocaust: Narrative and the Consequence of Interpretation* (Bloomington: Indiana University Press, 1988), 87.
39. Rosenfeld, *A Double Dying*, 4.
40. Dieter Lamping, ed. *"Dein aschenes Haar Sulamith": Dichtung über den Holocaust* (München: Piper, 1992), 271–92.
41. Devon Miller-Duggan provides such a close reading in *After Auschwitz*, 108–31. Unfortunately, the author completely misreads Rothenberg's work, inasmuch as he has no understanding of the poet's literary strategies.
42. I[oan] M[yrddin] Lewis, *Ecstatic Religion: An Anthropological Study*

of Spirit Possession and Shamanism (Harmondsworth: Penguin, 1971), 28–29.

43. Rosenfeld, *A Double Dying*, 15.

44. Menachem Mendel of Kotsk, per Abraham Heschel, cited by Rothenberg, "Beyond Poetics," in *Coherence*, 154.

45. Rosenfeld, *A Double Dying*, 113.

46. Both spellings and pronunciations of the word are possible depending on one's respective Yiddish dialect.

47. Scholem, *Kabbalah*, 349.

48. Both quotes are from Finkelstein, "Between Poland and Sumer: The Ethnopoetics of Jerome Rothenberg and Armand Schwerner," *Not One of Them in Place*, 109.

49. Eliade, *Shamanism*, 206.

50. Susan Gubar, *Poetry After Auschwitz: Remembering What One Never Knew* (Bloomington: Indiana University Press), 192.

51. Dieter Lamping, "Gedichte nach Auschwitz, über Auschwitz," in *Poesie der Apokalypse*, ed. Gerhard R. Kaiser (Würzburg: Königshausen und Neumann, 1991), 241, 246.

52. Ibid., 242.

53. Theodor W. Adorno, "Kulturkritik und Gesellschaft (1951)," in *Lyrik nach Auschwitz? Adorno und die Dichter*, ed. Petra Kiedaisch (Stuttgart: Reclam jun., 1995), 49.

54. For an anthology with texts from this debate, see *Lyrik nach Auschwitz?*

55. Dieter Lamping, "Sind Gedichte über Auschwitz barbarisch? Über die Humanität der Holocaust-Lyrik," *Moderne Lyrik: Eine Einführung* (Göttingen: Vandenhoeck, 1991), 100–119.

56. Ibid., 106.

57. Lamping, "Gedichte nach Auschwitz," *Poesie der Apokalypse*, 247.

58. Rothenberg cites Creeley's poem "Ever Since Hitler." See Rothenberg, "Nokh Auschwitz," *Jewish American Poetry*, 143.

59. Ibid.

60. Susan Sontag, "Artaud [An Essay by Susan Sontag]," *Antonin Artaud: Selected Writings*, ed. and introd. Susan Sontag, trans. Helen Weaver, notes by Susan Sontag and Don Eric Levine (New York: Farrar, 1976), xx.

61. Rothenberg, conversation with the author, 6 Apr. 2001. Rothenberg dedicates *Khurbn* to Duncan with the words "Now be the angel of my poem." But he also selects a remark by Eshleman as the motto of the book: "Since the hidden is bottomless, totality is more invisible than visible."

62. Lawrence L. Langer, "The Literature of Auschwitz (1991)," in *Admitting the Holocaust: Collected Essays* (Oxford: Oxford University Press, 1995), 105.

63. Lawrence L. Langer, *The Holocaust and the Literary Imagination* (New Haven: Yale University Press, 1975), 183. Langer makes this apt observation with regard to Jerzy Kosinski's book, *The Painted Bird* (1965; New York: Grove Press, 1976).

64. Rothenberg, conversation with the author, 6 Apr. 2001.

65. Brian Murdoch, "Transformations of the Holocaust: Auschwitz in Modern Lyric Poetry," *Comparative Literature Studies* 11.1 (March 1974): 133, 143.

66. Langer, *Holocaust and the Literary Imagination*, 91–92.

67. "Künstlerisch zu erreichen sind die Menschen überhaupt nur noch durch den Schock."Adorno, cited by Lamping, "*Dein aschenes Haar Sulamith*," 279.

68. Lamping, "*Dein aschenes Haar Sulamith*," 280.

69. For a modern Orthodox interpretation of the Holocaust, which views Israel as the Suffering Servant, see Eliezer Berkovits, *Faith after the Holocaust* (New York: Ktav, 1973), 124–27.

70. Sontag, "Artaud," *Antonin Artaud*, xlvi.

71. Lamping, "Gedichte nach Auschwitz," in *Poesie der Apokalypse*, 245.

72. "O lord of Caves, / if you are light, / there can be no metaphor." Allama, cited by Rothenberg, *Technicians of the Sacred*, 318.

73. The term "concentrationary universe" is a translation from the French and was originally coined by David Rousset. For some writers, who survived the concentration camp, the Holocaust turned the entire universe into a "concentrationary universe." The term implies the notion that the shoah brought about a radical change in our perception of reality. Ezrahi, *By Words Alone*, 111.

74. Rosenfeld, *A Double Dying*, 135.

75. Ibid., 27.

76. Young, *Writing and Rewriting the Holocaust*, 91.

77. See, for instance, Irving Greenberg, "Cloud of Smoke, Pillar of Fire: Judaism, Christianity, and Modernity after the Holocaust," in *Auschwitz: Beginning of a New Era? Reflections on the Holocaust*, ed. Eva Fleischner (New York: Ktav, 1974), 7–55. Furthermore, Elie Wiesel, Emil L. Fackenheim, and Richard L. Rubenstein are Jewish thinkers who interpret the Holocaust as a kind of negative revelation.

78. See also the prose poem "Di Magilas fun Aushvits (The Scrolls of Auschwitz)," *Khurbn*, 27–28.

79. Langer, *Holocaust and the Literary Imagination*, 49.

80. Ibid., 43.

81. Rosenfeld, *A Double Dying*, 139.

82. Rothenberg, "Harold Bloom . . . ," *Sulfur* 2 (1981): 25.

83. *Salo, or The 120 Days of Sodom*, dir. Pier Paolo Pasolini (Italy, 1975).

84. Saul Friedländer, *Reflections of Nazism: An Essay on Kitsch and Death*, trans. Thomas Weyr (New York: Harper, 1982), 75. In his brief analysis of this subject, Friedländer draws on the work of Michel Foucault.

85. See, for instance, Ludwig Giesz, *Phänomenologie des Kitsches* (1971; Frankfurt: Fischer, 1994), 88–89.

86. Friedländer, *Reflections of Nazism*, 14.

87. Ibid., 28–36, 39.

88. Ibid., 27.

89. Sontag, "Artaud," *Antonin Artaud*, xxxiv.

90. In this subchapter, all page numbers in parentheses refer to Rothenberg, "14 Stations," *Seedings & Other Poems*, 99–116. The sequence has also been published in a bilingual German-English edition. See Jerome Rothenberg, *14 Stations/14 Stationen*, trans. Stefan Hyner (Berlin: Stadtlichter Presse, 2000). Of great interest is also Rothenberg's recording of "14 Stations" and his reading of passages from *Khurbn*, accompanied with music by Charlie Morrow. See Jerome Rothenberg and Charlie Morrow, *Signature*, compact disc (New York City: Granary, 2001).

91. Goetsch, "Der Holocaust," in *Jewish Life and Suffering*, 167.

92. Arie A. Galles, "Fourteen Stations Suite," *Response* 63 (fall 1997/winter 1998): 118.

93. Ibid.

94. Rothenberg, conversation with the author, 1 Dec. 2001.

95. Karl Riha, "Über den Zufall—in der Literatur der Moderne," in *Zufall als Prinzip: Spielwelt, Methode und System in der Kunst des 20. Jahrhunderts*, ed. Bernhard Holeczek and Lida von Mengden (Heidelberg: Braus, 1992), 78.

96. Locks, *The Spice of Torah*, xiii.

97. Rothenberg, conversation with the author, 1 Dec. 2001.

98. Rothenberg, conversation with the author, 6 Apr. 2001.

99. Dieter Lamping, *Literatur und Theorie: Poetologische Probleme der Moderne* (Göttingen: Vandenhoeck, 1996), 117–18.

100. Rothenberg, *Poems for the Millennium* vol. 1, 466.

101. Lamping, *Literatur und Theorie*, 118.

102. For a striking example of prophetic speech, see Rothenberg, "The Ninth Station: Treblinka," *Seedings & Other Poems*, 110.

103. David G. Roskies, *The Literature of Destruction: Jewish Responses to Catastrophe* (New York: Jewish Publication Society, 1988), 3–4.

104. Kremer, *Witness Through the Imagination*, 10.

105. "The sages of biblical-rabbinic Judaism intimately identified the Covenant with God's justice. When Jews do the good, God blesses them abundantly; when they sin, God punishes them." Eugene B. Borowitz, *Renewing the Covenant: A Theology for the Postmodern Jew* (Philadelphia: The Jewish Publication Society, 1991), 34.

106. Post-Holocaust Jewish theology also struggles with these issues. See Borowitz, *Renewing the Covenant*, 32–52.

107. Rothenberg, "A Poetics of the Sacred," in *Picturing Cultural Values*, 92.

108. Rothenberg includes this gematria into the poem "The First Station: Auschwitz-Birkenau," *Seedings & other Poems*, 101. Yet he also employs it in his earlier gematria book. See Rothenberg, *Gematria*, 21.

109. Langer, *Holocaust and the Literary Imagination*, 161.

110. Goetsch, "Der Holocaust," in *Jewish Life and Suffering*, 172.

111. Langer, *Holocaust and the Literary Imagination*, 164.

112. Lamping, "Gedichte nach Auschwitz," in *Poesie der Apokalypse*, 248.

113. Gavin Selerie, cited by Selerie and Mottram, *Riverside Interviews*, 52.

Conclusion

1. Middleton, "Seven Words," *Samizdat* 7 (winter 2001): 3.

2. Regarding secular Yiddish literature, Roskies notes that stories became a "surrogate for faith." See Roskies, "The Story's the Thing," in *What is Jewish Literature?*, 125.

3. Of course there are exceptions to this—Rothenberg's circular poem (deconstruction of historicism) and "14 Stations" (deconstruction of meaning). However, it seems to me that these two "deconstructive" pieces are not

motivated by poststructuralist thought, but (in the first example) by the poet's attraction to a circular, mythical view of history resembling a medieval mind-set and (in the second example) by the shocking realization of the implications of the Holocaust.

4. Middleton, "Seven Words," *Samizdat* 7 (winter 2001): 5.

5. Drachler, letter to Jerome Rothenberg, 17 Jan. 1978, Jerome Rothenberg Papers, "Drachler, Rose 1974–1982," Ms. 10, Box 7, Folder 6, Mandeville Special Collections Library, UCSD.

Works Cited

Primary Sources

Abulafia, Abraham. "From: *The Book of The Letter*." Trans. Jack Hirschman. *Tree* 1 (winter 1970): 139–48; 152–53.

Antin, David. *talking at the boundaries*. New York: New Directions, 1976.

Benedikt, Michael, ed. and introd. *The Prose Poem: An International Anthology*. New York: Dell, 1976.

Buber, Martin. *Tales of Angels, Spirits & Demons*. Trans. David Antin and Jerome Rothenberg. New York: Hawk's Well Press, 1958.

Celan, Paul. *Speech-Grille and Selected Poems*. Trans. Joachim Neugroschel. New York: Dutton, 1971.

Chametzky, Jules, et al., eds. *Jewish American Literature: A Norton Anthology*. New York: Norton, 2001.

Drachler, Rose. Letter to Jerome Rothenberg. 17 Jan. 1978. Jerome Rothenberg Papers. "Drachler, Rose 1974–1982." Ms. 10, Box 7, Folder 6. Mandeville Special Collections Library, UCSD.

Fishman, Charles, ed. *Blood to Remember: American Poets on the Holocaust*. Texas: Texas Tech University Press, 1986.

Florsheim, Steward J., ed. *Ghosts of the Holocaust: An Anthology by the Second Generation*. Foreword Gerald Stein. Detroit: Wayne State University Press, 1989.

Frank, Jacob. *Sayings of Yakov Frank*. Trans. Harris Lenowitz. Tree 6: Aleph. Berkeley, Ca.: Tree; Oakland, Ca.: Tzaddikim, 1978.

Gomringer, Eugen, ed. *The Book of Hours and Constellations Being Poems of Eugen Gomringer Presented by Jerome Rothenberg*. New York: Something Else Press, 1968.

———. *konkrete poesie: deutschsprachige autoren*. 1972. Stuttgart: Philipp Reclam Jun., 1991.

Hirschman, Jack. *Black Alephs, Poems 1960–1968*. London: Trigram Press, 1969.

Hochhuth, Rolf. *The Deputy: A Drama*. Adapt. and trans. Jerome Rothenberg. New York: S. French, 1964.

Hoover, Paul, ed. *Postmodern Poetry: A Norton Anthology*. New York: W. W. Norton, 1994.

"Jerome Rothenberg & The Klezmatics: Galician Nights," http://www.peoplespoetry.org/pg_clips_audvid.html, accessed 25 Feb. 2002.

Jerome Rothenberg Papers. "Artwork: Mixed Media of *Poland/1931*: Including Photography of Collage Paste-Ups Advertising Poland/1931 Show at

UCSD." Ms. 10, Box 27, Folder 16. Mandeville Special Collections Library, UCSD.

———. "'BAR MITSVA [*sic*] EVENT'—Events." Ms. 10, Box 1, Folder 3. Mandeville Special Collections Library, UCSD.

———. "BAR MITZVAH EVENTS: for Matthew Rothenberg." Ms. 10, Box 1, Folder 3. Mandeville Special Collections Library, UCSD.

———. "Duncan, Robert 1958–1973, n.d." Ms. 10, Box 7, Folder 8. Mandeville Special Collections Library, UCSD.

———. "Food." Ms. 10, Box 28, Folder 7. Mandeville Special Collections Library, UCSD.

———. "Forbidden Foods, Clean Foods." Ms. 10, Box 28, Folder 7. Mandeville Special Collections Library, UCSD.

———. "The Materials." Ms. 10, Box 29, Folder 4. Mandeville Special Collections Library, UCSD.

———. "Notes for Poland/1931: Includes Newspaper Clippings, Unpublished Poems, Part I. ca. 1968–1973." Ms. 10, Box 28, Folder 7. Mandeville Special Collections Library, UCSD.

———. "'Poland/1931: All-Jewish Dream Fantasy Show': UCSD Art Gallery, 26 May 1971." Ms. 10, Box 28, Folder 13. Mandeville Special Collections Library, UCSD.

———. "Poland/1931 Translations: German, Hebrew, Spanish, Polish." Ms. 10, Box 28, Folder 22. Mandeville Special Collections Library, UCSD.

Kosinski, Jerzy. *The Painted Bird*. 1965. New York: Grove Press, 1976.

Lamping, Dieter, ed. *"Dein aschenes Haar Sulamith": Dichtung über den Holocaust*. München: Piper, 1992.

Mac Low, Jackson. *Representative Works: 1938–1985*. New York: Roof, 1986.

Meltzer, David. *Isla Vista Notes: Fragmentary Apocalyptic Didactic Contradictions*. Santa Barbara: Christopher, 1970. n. pag.

———, ed. *The Path of the Names: Writings by Abraham ben Samuel Abulafia*. Trans. and adapt. Bruria Finkel, Jack Hirschman, David Meltzer, and Gershom Scholem. Tree Texts 4. Berkeley: Tree, 1976.

———, ed. *The Secret Garden: An Anthology of Texts from the Jewish Mystical Tradition*. New York: Seabury Press, 1975.

———. *Six*. Santa Barbara: Black Sparrow Press, 1976.

———. *Yesod*. London: Trigram, 1969.

Messerli, Douglas, ed. and introd. *From the Other Side of the Century: A New American Poetry 1960–1990*. Los Angeles: Sun & Moon Press, 1994.

Olson, Charles. *Collected Prose*. Ed. Donald Allen and Benjamin Friedlander. Introd. Robert Creeley. Berkeley: University of California Press, 1997.

Reznikoff, Charles. *Holocaust*. Los Angeles: Black Sparrow Press, 1975.

———. *Testimony: the United States, 1885–1890*. New York: New Directions, 1965.

Rothenberg, Jerome. *Abulafia's Circles*. Tree 6: Beth: Messiah. Milwaukee, Wis.: Membrane Press, 1979.

———. "Ancestral Scenes." *Response* 23 (fall 1974): 30

———. *A Book of Testimony*. Santa Barbara, Ca.: Tree, 1971.

———. *Das Dadahörspiel.* Cologne: Westdeutscher Rundfunk, 1985.

———. *Das Hörspiel des Bibers.* Cologne: Westdeutscher Rundfunk, 1984.

———. *Esther K. Comes to America, 1931.* Greensboro, NC: Unicorn Press, 1974.

———. *14 Stations/14 Stationen.* Trans. Stefan Hyner. Berlin: Stadtlichter Presse, 2000.

———. *Gematria.* Los Angeles: Sun & Moon Press, 1994.

———. *Khurbn & Other Poems.* New York: New Directions, 1989.

———. Letter to Alan Brilliant. 24 Aug. 1969. Jerome Rothenberg Papers. "Esther K. Comes to America—Business Correspondence 1967–1969." Ms. 10, Box 27, Folder 10. Mandeville Special Collections Library, UCSD.

———. Letter to Howard Schwartz. 10 Apr. 1978. Jerome Rothenberg Papers. "Howard, Schwartz 1974–1980." Ms. 10, Box 18, Folder 9. Mandeville Special Collections Library, UCSD.

———. Letter to Robert Kelly. 9 May 1977. Jerome Rothenberg Papers. "Kelly, Robert 1958–1980." Ms. 10, Box 11, Folder 30. Mandeville Special Collections Library, UCSD.

———. *Letters & Numbers.* Madison, Wis.: The Salient Seedling Press, 1979.

———. *New Selected Poems, 1970–1985.* New York: New Directions, 1986.—

——. *The Notebooks.* Milwaukee, Wis.: Membrane Press, 1976.

———. *The Pirke & the Pearl.* Berkeley, Ca.: Tree, 1975.

———. *Poems For The Game of Silence 1960–1970.* New York: The Dial Press, 1971.

———. *Poems 1964–1967: Sightings, Further Sightings, A Steinbook & More, Conversations, The Gorky Poems.* Los Angeles: Black Sparrow Press, 1968.

———. *Poland/1931.* New York: New Directions, 1974.

———. *Poland/1931.* Santa Barbara, Ca.: Unicorn Press, 1970.

———. "A Polish Anecdote." *Response* 23 (fall 1974): 117.

———. *Polish Anecdotes.* Santa Barbara, Ca.: Unicorn Press, 1970.

———. *Ritual: A Book of Primitive Rites and Events.* New York: A Great Bear Pamphlet, 1966.

———. "Satan in Goray." *some/thing* 1.2 (winter 1965): 46–48.

———. *Seedings & Other Poems.* New York: New Directions, 1996.

———. *A Seneca Journal.* New York: New Directions, 1978.

———. *The 17 Horse Songs of Frank Mitchell Nos X–XIII: Total Translations from the Navaho Indian with Images by Ian Tyson.* London: Tetrad Press, 1969.

———. *Surimo: To Celebrate 25 Years of Collaboration between Jerome Rothenberg and Ian Tyson.* London: Tetrad Press, 1992.

———. *That Dada Strain.* New York: New Directions, 1983.

———. *Vienna Blood & Other Poems.* New York: New Directions, 1980.

———. *White Sun Black Sun.* New York: Hawk's Well Press, 1960.

Rothenberg, Jerome, ed. and trans. *New Young German Poets.* San Francisco: City Lights, 1959.

———, ed. *Revolution of the Word: A New Gathering of American Avant-Garde Poetry, 1914–1945.* New York: Continuum Book, 1974.

———, ed. *Shaking the Pumpkin: Traditional Poetry of the Indian North Americas*. New York: Doubleday, 1972.

———, ed. with commentaries. *Technicians of the Sacred: A Range of Poetries from Africa, America, Asia, Europe & Oceania*. Rev. and expanded 2nd ed. Berkeley: University of California Press, 1985.

Rothenberg, Jerome, and Steven Clay, eds. *A Book of the Book: Some Works & Projections About the Book & Writing*. New York: Granary, 2000.

Rothenberg, Jerome, and Pierre Joris, eds. *Poems for the Millennium: The University of California Book of Modern & Postmodern Poetry*. 2 vols. Berkeley: University of California Press, 1995–98.

Rothenberg, Jerome, and Harris Lenowitz, eds. *Exiled in the Word: Poems & Other Visions of the Jews from Tribal Times to the Present*. With commentaries by Jerome Rothenberg. Washington: Copper Canyon Press, 1989.

Rothenberg, Jerome, Harris Lenowitz, and Charles Doria, eds. *A Big Jewish Book: Poems and other Visions of the Jews from Tribal Times to the Present*. Garden City, N.Y.: Anchor Press, 1978.

Rothenberg, Jerome, and Charlie Morrow. *Signature*. Compact Disc. New York City: Granary, 2001.

Rothenberg, Jerome, and George Quasha, eds. *America: A Prophecy: A New Reading of American Poetry From Pre-Columbian Times to the Present*. New York: Vintage, 1974.

Rothenberg, Jerome, and Ian Tyson. *Delight/Délices and Other Gematria*. Nîmes: Editions Ottezec, 1997.

———. *Gematria 643*. London: I. Tyson, 1997.

———. *Six Gematria*. London: Tetrad P, 1992.

———. *Twin Gematria*. London: I. Tyson, 1997.

Rubin, Steven J., ed. *Telling and Remembering: A Century of American Jewish Poetry*. Boston: Beacon Press, 1997.

Russell, Charles, ed. *The Avant-Garde Today: An International Anthology*. Urbana: University of Illinois Press, 1981.

Salo, or The 120 Days of Sodom. Dir. Pier Paolo Pasolini. Italy, 1975.

Schiff, Hilda, comp. and introd. *Holocaust Poetry*. London: Harper, 1995.

Schwartz, Howard. Letter to Jerome Rothenberg. 11 Dec. 1977. Jerome Rothenberg Papers. "Howard, Schwartz 1974–1980." Ms. 10, Box 18, Folder 9. Mandeville Special Collections Library, UCSD.

Schwartz, Howard, and Anthony Rudolf, eds. *Voices Within the Ark: The Modern Jewish Poets*. Yonkers, N.Y.: Pushcart Press, 1980.

Schwerner, Armand. *The Tablets*. Orono, Maine: National Poetry Foundation, 1999.

Schwitters, Kurt. *PPPPPP: Poems Performance Pieces Prose Plays Poetics of Kurt Schwitters*. Ed. and trans. Jerome Rothenberg and Pierre Joris. Philadelphia: Temple University Press, 1993.

Stein, Gertrude. *The Yale Gertrude Stein: Selections*. Introd. Richard Kostelanetz. New Haven: Yale University Press, 1980.

Striar, Marguerite M., ed. *Beyond Lament: Poets of the World Bearing Witness to the Holocaust*. Evanston, Ill.: Northwestern University Press, 1998.

Tarn, Nathaniel. *Lyrics for the Bride of God*. New York: New Directions, 1975.

Weinberger, Eliot, ed. *American Poetry Since 1950: Innovators and Outsiders*. New York: Marsilio Publishers, 1993.

Weiner, Hannah. *Clairvoyant Journal, 1974: March–June Retreat*. New York: Angel Hair, 1978.

Williamson, Craig, ed. and trans. *A Feast of Creatures: Anglo-Saxon Riddle Songs*. Philadelphia: University of Philadelphia Press, 1982.

SECONDARY SOURCES

"ALEPH." *On Common Ground: World Religions in America*. Ed. Diana L. Eck. CD-ROM. New York: Columbia University Press, 1997.

"Biblical Literature and Its Critical Interpretation." *Encyclopaedia Britannica*. CD-ROM. Version 97. Encyclopaedia Britannica, Inc., 1997.

"Cipher." *Encyclopaedia Britannica*. CD-ROM. Version 97. Encyclopaedia Britannica, Inc., 1997.

"Cuba." *Encyclopaedia Judaica*. CD-ROM. Version 1.0. Jerusalem: Keter, 1997.

"Etrog." *Encyclopaedia Britannica*. CD-ROM. Version 97. Encyclopaedia Britannica, Inc., 1997.

"Have You Sold Out? A Response Symposium: Veterans of the Jewish Student Movement." Spec. issue of *Response* 29 (spring 1976).

"Jerome Rothenberg." *Electronic Poetry Center*. SUNY Buffalo. http://wings.buffalo.edu/epc/authors/rothenberg/, accessed 3 Mar. 2002.

"Memorial Book of the Community of Ostrow-Mazowiecka (Poland)." http://www.jewishgen.org/yizkor/ostrow/Ostrow.html, accessed 20 Feb. 2002.

"Sacred Rites and Ceremonies: The Concept and Forms of Ritual." *Encyclopaedia Britannica*. CD-ROM. Version 97. Encyclopaedia Britannica, Inc., 1997.

"Transliteration Rules." *Encyclopaedia Judaica*. 16 vols. Jerusalem: Keter, 1971–72.

"Types of Ritual." *Encyclopaedia Britannica*. CD-ROM. Version 97. Encyclopaedia Britannica, Inc., 1997.

"Wars of Yahweh, Book of the." *Encyclopaedia Britannica*. CD-ROM. Version 97. Encyclopaedia Britannica, Inc., 1997.

"Yizkor Book Project: Frequently Asked Questions." http://www.jewishgen.-org/yizkor.html, accessed 15 Jan. 2002.

Adorno, Theodor W. "Kulturkritik und Gesellschaft (1951)." In *Lyrik nach Auschwitz? Adorno und die Dichter*. Ed. Petra Kiedaisch. Stuttgart: Reclam jun., 1995.

Alpert, Barry. "Jerome Rothenberg—An Interview: Conducted by Barry Alpert with Charles Morrow sitting in, New York City, January 2, 1974." *Vort* 7 (1975): 93–117.

Alter, Robert. *Necessary Angels: Tradition and Modernity in Kafka, Benjamin, and Scholem*. Cambridge: Harvard University Press, 1991.

———. "Scholem and Sabbatianism." In *Gershom Scholem*. Ed. and introd. Harold Bloom. New York: Chelsea, 1987.

Antin, David. "Why 1964–1967?" *Vort* 7 (1975): 128–31.

Ascher, Carol. "The Return of Jewish Mysticism: Try It, You'll Like It." *Present Tense* 17.3 (spring 1980): 36–40.

Bachtin, Michail M. *Literatur und Karneval: Zur Romantheorie und Lachkultur*. Frankfurt: Fischer, 1996.

Bakhtin, Mikhail M. *The Dialogic Imagination*. Ed. Michael Holquist. Trans. Caryl Emerson. Austin: University of Texas Press, 1981.

Barron, Jonathan N. "Commentary in Contemporary Jewish American Poetry." In *Jewish American Poetry: Poems, Commentary, And Reflections*." Ed. Jonathan N. Barron and Eric Murphy Selinger. Hanover, N.H.: Brandeis University Press, 2000.

Barron, Jonathan N., and Eric Murphy Selinger, eds. *Jewish American Poetry: Poems, Commentary, And Reflections*. Hanover, N.H.: Brandeis University Press, 2000.

Berger, Abraham. "The Messianic Self-Consciousness of Abraham Abulafia: A Tentative Evaluation." In *Essays On Jewish Life and Thought: Presented in Honor of Salo Wittmayer Baron*. Ed. Joseph L. Blau et al. New York: Columbia University Press, 1959.

Berkovits, Eliezer. *Faith after the Holocaust*. New York: Ktav, 1973.

Bernstein, Michael André. "Bringing it All Back Home: Derivations and Quotations in Robert Duncan and the Poundian Tradition." *Sagetrieb* 1.2 (fall 1982): 176–89.

Bershtel, Sara, and Allen Graubard. *Saving Remnants: Feeling Jewish in America*. New York: Free Press, 1992.

Biale, David. *Gershom Scholem: Kabbalah and Counter-History*. Cambridge: Harvard University Press, 1979.

Bloom, Harold. "The Sorrows of American-Jewish Poetry." *Commentary* 53.3 (March 1972): 68–74.

Blumenthal, David R. *Understanding Jewish Mysticism: A Source Reader*. Vol. 2: The Philosophic-Mystical Tradition and The Hasidic Tradition. New York: Ktav, 1978. 2 vols.

Borowitz, Eugene B. *Renewing the Covenant: A Theology for the Postmodern Jew*. Philadelphia: Jewish Publication Society, 1991.

Brito, Manuel. "Jerome Rothenberg." *A Suite of Poetic Voices: Interviews with Contemporary American Poets*. Santa Brigida, Spain: Kadle, 1992. 111–34.

Bryant, Mark. *Riddles: Ancient & Modern*. London: Hutchinson, 1983.

Bürger, Peter. *Theory of the Avant-Garde*. Trans. Michael Shaw. Foreword Jochen Schulte-Sasse. Minneapolis: University of Minnesota Press, 1984.

Butler, Christopher. *Number Symbolism*. New York: Barnes & Noble, 1970.

Castro, Michael. *Interpreting the Indian: Twentieth-Century Poets and the Native American*. Albuquerque: University of New Mexico Press, 1983.

Chess, Richard S. *Still A Small Voice: Toward an American-Jewish Poetry.* PhD diss., University of Florida, 1989.

Christensen, Paul. "Some Bearings on Ethnopoetics." *Parnassus: Poetry in Review* 15.1 (1989): 125–62.

Clements, William M. "Faking the Pumpkin: On Jerome Rothenberg's Literary Offenses." *Western American Literature* 16 (1981–82): 193–204.

Cott, Jonathan. "In the Beginning Was Aleph." Review of *A Big Jewish Book*, ed. Jerome Rothenberg. *The New York Times Book Review* (April 23, 1978): 15–16.

Dan, Joseph. "Gershom Scholem: Between Mysticism and Scholarship." *The Germanic Review: Literature, Culture, Theory* 72.1 (winter 1997): 4–23.

———. "Magic: In Medieval Hebrew Literature." *Encyclopaedia Judaica.* 16 vols. Jerusalem: Keter, 1971–72.

Davidson, Michael. *The San Francisco Renaissance: Poetics and Community at Mid-Century.* Cambridge, Mass.: Cambridge University Press, 1989.

Diamond, Stanley. "Plato and the Definition of the Primitive." In *Symposium of the Whole: A Range of Discourse toward an Ethnopoetics.* Ed. Jerome Rothenberg and Diane Rothenberg. Berkeley: University of California Press, 1983.

Dreier, Peter, and Jack Nusan Porter, eds. *Jewish Radicalism: A Selected Anthology.* New York: Grove Press, 1973.

Duncan, Robert. "From 'Rites of Participation.'" In *Symposium of the Whole: A Range of Discourse toward an Ethnopoetics.* Ed. Jerome Rothenberg and Diane Rothenberg. Berkeley: University of California Press, 1983.

Editorial Staff. "Magic: Talmudic Period." *Encyclopaedia Judaica.* 16 vols. Jerusalem: Keter, 1971–72.

Eliade, Mircea. *Shamanism: Archaic Techniques of Ecstasy.* Trans. Willard R. Trask. 1964. Princeton: Princeton University Press, 1972.

Ernst, Max. *Beyond Painting: And Other Writings by the Artist and his Friends.* New York: Wittenborn, 1948.

Evans-Pritchard, E[dward] E[van]. *Witchcraft, Oracles, and Magic among the Azande.* Introd. Eva Gillies. Abr. ed. Oxford: Clarendon Press, 1976.

Ezrahi, Sidra DeKoven. *By Words Alone: The Holocaust in Literature.* Chicago: University of Chicago Press, 1980.

Farber, Roberta Rosenberg, and Chaim I. Waxman. "Postmodernity and the Jews: Identity, Identification, and Community." In *Jews in America: A Contemporary Reader.* Ed. Roberta Rosenberg Farber and Chaim I. Waxman. Hanover, N.H.: Brandeis University Press, 1999.

Featherston, Dan. "Poetic Representation: Reznikoff's *Holocaust* and Rothenberg's *Khurbn.*" *Response* 63 (fall 1997, winter 1998): 129–40.

Felstiner, John. *Paul Celan: Poet, Survivor, Jew.* New Haven: Yale University Press, 1995.

Finkelstein, Norman. "The Messianic Ethnography of Jerome Rothenberg's *Poland/1931.*" *Contemporary Literature* 39.3 (1998 fall): 356–79.

———. *Not One of Them in Place: Modern Poetry and Jewish Identity.* SUNY Series in Modern Jewish Literature and Culture. New York: State University of New York Press, 2001.

Fleischman, Beth. "Jerome Rothenberg." In *Dictionary of Literary Biography*. Vol. 5: American Poets Since World War II, part 2: L–Z. Detroit: Gale, 1980.

Fox, Howard N. *Eleanor Antin*. With an essay by Lisa E. Bloom. Los Angeles: Los Angeles County Museum of Art, 1999.

Fredman, Stephen. *A Menorah For Athena: Charles Reznikoff and the Jewish Dilemmas of Objectivist Poetry*. Chicago: University of Chicago Press, 2001.

———. *Poet's Prose: The Crisis in American Verse*. 2nd ed. Cambridge: Cambridge University Press, 1990.

Friedländer, Saul. *Reflections of Nazism: An Essay on Kitsch and Death*. Trans. Thomas Weyr. New York: Harper, 1982.

Frye, Northrop. *Relations of Literary Study: Essays on Interdisciplinary Contributions*. Ed. James Thorpe. New York: MLA, 1967.

———. *Spiritus Mundi: Essays on Literature, Myth, and Society*. Bloomington: Indiana University Press, 1976.

Galles, Arie A. "Fourteen Stations Suite." *Response* 63 (fall 1997/winter 1998): 118–23.

Gans, Herbert J. "Symbolic Ethnicity: The Future of Ethnic Groups and Cultures in America." In *On the Making of the Americans: Essays in Honor of David Riesman*. Ed. Herbert J. Gans et al. Philadelphia: University of Pennsylvania Press, 1979. 193–220.

Garber, Frederick. "The Histories and Poetics of Jerome Rothenberg." *Repositionings: Readings of Contemporary Poetry, Photography, and Performance Art*. University Park, Pa.: The Pennsylvania State University Press, 1995.

Gaster, Theodor H. "Amulets and Talismans." In *Encyclopedia of Religion*. Ed. in chief Mircea Eliade. 16 vols. New York: Macmillan, 1987.

Gendler, Everett. "To Be a Jew in the Diaspora—An Affirmation." *Response* 23 (fall 1974): 105–16.

Genette, Gérard. *Palimpsests: Literature in the Second Degree*. Trans. Channa Newman and Claude Doubinsky. Foreword Gerald Prince. Lincoln: University of Nebraska Press, 1997.

Gerber, David A. "Nativism, Anti-Catholicism, and Anti-Semitism." *Encyclopedia of American Social History*. Ed. Mary Kupiec Cayton, Elliott J. Gorn and Peter W. Williams. Vol. 3. New York: Scribner's; Toronto: Maxwell Macmillan; New York: Maxwell Macmillan International, 1993. 2101–13. 3 vols.

Giesz, Ludwig. *Phänomenologie des Kitsches*. 1971. Frankfurt: Fischer, 1994.

Gitenstein, R. Barbara. *Apocalyptic Messianism and Contemporary Jewish-American Poetry*. Albany: State University of New York, 1986.

———. "Coyote Cohen: Or, the Universal Trickster in Jerome Rothenberg's Evolving Collection *Poland/1931*." *Studies in American Jewish Literature* 9.2 (1990 fall): 176–85.

Glanz, David. "An Interpretation of the Jewish Counterculture." *Jewish Social Studies* 24.1–2 (winter–spring, 1977): 117–28.

Glazer, Nathan. *American Judaism*. The Chicago History of American Civilization. 2nd ed. Chicago: University of Chicago Press, 1972.

Glazer, Nathan, and Daniel Patrick Moynihan. *Beyond the Melting Pot: The Negroes, Puerto Ricans, Jews, Italians, and Irish of New York City*. Cambridge: MIT Press, 1963.

Goetsch, Paul. "Der Holocaust in der englischen und amerikanischen Lyrik." In *Jewish Life and Suffering as Mirrored in English and American Literature*. Ed. Frank Link. München: Ferdinand Schöningh, 1987.

Goldenberg, Robert. "Talmud." In *Back to the Sources: Reading The Classic Jewish Texts*. Ed. Barry W. Holtz. New York: Summit, 1984.

Gordon, Melton J., Jerome Clark, and Aidan A. Kelly. "Kabbalism and Hassidism." In *New Age Almanac*. Ed. Melton J. Gordon. New York: Visible Ink, 1991.

———. "Shlomo Carlebach." In *New Age Almanac*. Ed. Melton J. Gordon. New York: Visible Ink, 1991.

Gordon, Peter Eli. "Imagining Hasidism." *Tikkun* 5.3 (May/June 1990): 49–51.

Green, Arthur. "After Itzik: Toward a Theology of Jewish Spirituality." In *The New Jews*. Ed. Alan Mintz and James Sleeper. New York: Vintage, 1971.

Greenberg, Irving. "Cloud of Smoke, Pillar of Fire: Judaism, Christianity, and Modernity after the Holocaust." In *Auschwitz: Beginning of a New Era? Reflections on the Holocaust*. Ed. Eva Fleischner. New York: Ktav, 1974.

Gubar, Susan. *Poetry After Auschwitz: Remembering What One Never Knew*. Bloomington: Indiana University Press, 2003.

Hamacher, Elisabeth. *Gershom Scholem und die Allgemeine Religionsgeschichte*. Berlin: Walter de Gruyter, 1999.

Hansen, Marcus L. "The Third Generation in America." *Commentary* 14 (1952): 492–500.

Heller, Michael. "Pale Darkened Moons in the Firmament of Reason." *Parnassus: Poetry in Review* 9.1 (spring/summer 1981): 269–83.

Hirschman, Jack. "Jack Hirschman." *Paul Celan*. Spec. issue of *Studies in 20th* Century Literature 8.1 (fall 1983): 122–26.

———. "On the Hebrew Letters." *Tree* 2 (summer 1971): 34–45.

Hollander, John. "The Question of American Jewish Poetry." In *What is Jewish Literature?* Ed. and introd. Hana Wirth-Nesher. Philadelphia: The Jewish Publication Society, 1994.

Holtz, Barry W., ed. *Back to the Sources: Reading The Classic Jewish Texts*. New York: Summit, 1984.

Hornung, Alfred. "The Autobiographical Mode in Contemporary American Fiction." *Prose Studies* 8.3 (December 1985): 69–83.

Hubert, Renée Riese. "Characteristics of an Undefinable Genre: The Surrealist Prose Poem." *Symposium* (spring 1968): 25–34.

Hyde, Lewis. *Trickster Makes This World: Mischief, Myth, and Art*. New York: North Point Press, 1998.

Hynes, William J. "Mapping the Characteristics of Mythic Tricksters: A Heuristic Guide." In *Mythical Trickster Figures: Contours, Contexts, and Criti-*

cism. Ed. William J. Hynes and William G. Doty. Tuscaloosa: University of Alabama Press, 1993. 33–45.

Idel, Moshe. "Gematria." In *The Encyclopedia of Language and Linguistics*. Ed. in chief R. E. Asher. Coordinating editor J. M. Y. Simpson. Vol. 3. Oxford: Pergamon Press, 1994. 1346–47. 10 vols.

———. *Language, Torah, and Hermeneutics in Abraham Abulafia*. Trans. Menahem Kallus. New York: State University of New York Press, 1989.

———. *Messianic Mystics*. New Haven: Yale University Press, 1998.

———. *The Mystical Experience in Abraham Abulafia*. Trans. Jonathan Chipman. New York: State University of New York Press, 1988.

———. *Studies in Ecstatic Kabbalah*. New York: State University of New York Press, 1988.

Ifrah, George. *The Universal History of Numbers from Prehistory to the Invention of the Computer*. Trans. David Bellos, et al. London: Harvill Press, 1998.

Israel: After the War and Before the Peace. Spec. issue of *Response* 20 (winter 1973–74).

Jacobs, Louis. *A Concise Companion to the Jewish Religion*. Oxford Paperback Reference. Oxford: Oxford University Press, 1999.

Jameson, Frederic. "Postmodernism and Consumer Society." In *Postmodern Culture*. Ed. Hal Foster. London: Pluto Press, 1983.

Jung, Carl Gustav. *Synchronicity: An Acausal Connecting Principle*. Trans. R. F. C. Hull. The Collected Works of C. G. Jung. Vol. 8. Bollingen Ser. 20. Princeton: Princeton University Press, 1973.

Kaplan, Aryeh. *Meditation and Kabbalah*. York Beach, Maine: Samuel Weiser, 1982.

Kaprow, Allan. *Assemblage, Environments & Happenings*. Text and design by Allan Kaprow. New York: Harry N. Abrams, 1966.

Keller, Lynn. "The Twentieth-Century Long Poem." In *The Columbia History of American Poetry*. Ed. Jay Parini et al. New York: Columbia University Press, 1993.

Kelly, Robert. "Notes on the Poetry of Image." *Trobar* 2 (1961): 14–16.

Kenner, Hugh. *Magic and Spells (About Curses, Charms and Riddles)*. Originally Delivered at Bennington College as Lecture Ten in Ben Belitt Lectureship Series. 29 Oct. 1987. New York: Bennington College, 1988.

———. *The Pound Era*. Berkeley: University of California Press, 1971.

Kirby, Michael. *Happenings: An Illustrated Anthology*. Scripts and productions by Jim Dine, Red Grooms, Allan Kaprow, Claes Oldenburg, Robert Whitman. New York: Dutton, 1966.

Klein, Isaac. *A Guide to Jewish Religious Practice*. New York: Jewish Theological Seminary of America, 1979.

Koltach, Alfred J. *The Second Jewish Book of Why*. New York: Jonathan David Publishers, 1985.

Kostelanetz, Richard. *The Old Poetries and the New*. Ann Arbor: University of Michigan Press, 1981.

Kremer, S. Lillian. *Witness Through the Imagination: Jewish American Holocaust Literature*. Detroit: Wayne State University Press, 1989.

Lamping, Dieter. "Gedichte nach Auschwitz, über Auschwitz." In *Poesie der Apokalypse*. Ed. Gerhard R. Kaiser. Würzburg: Königshausen und Neumann, 1991.

———. *Literatur und Theorie: Poetologische Probleme der Moderne*. Göttingen: Vandenhoeck, 1996.

———. *Moderne Lyrik: Eine Einführung*. Göttingen: Vandenhoeck, 1991.

———. *Von Kafka bis Celan: Jüdischer Diskurs in der deutschen Literatur des 20. Jahrhunderts*. Göttingen: Vandenhoeck, 1998.

Langer, Lawrence L. *Admitting the Holocaust: Collected Essays*. Oxford: Oxford University Press, 1995.

———. *The Holocaust and the Literary Imagination*. New Haven: Yale University Press, 1975.

Lazer, Hank. "Thinking Made in the Mouth: The Cultural Poetics of David Antin and Jerome Rothenberg." In *Picturing Cultural Values in Postmodern America*. Ed. William G. Doty. Tuscaloosa: University of Alabama Press, 1995.

Leibowitz Parmet, Harriet Abbey. *The Terror of Our Days: Sylvia Plath, William Heyen, Gerald Stern, and Jerome Rothenberg Poetically Respond to the Holocaust*. PhD diss., Lehigh University, 1998.

Lenowitz, Harris. "Rothenberg: The Blood." *Vort* 7 (1975): 179–84.

Lerner, Michael. *Jewish Renewal*. New York: Harper, 1994.

Lewis, I[oan] M[yrddin]. *Ecstatic Religion: An Anthropological Study of Spirit Possession and Shamanism*. Harmondsworth: Penguin, 1971.

Liebman, Charles S. "The Reappropriation of Jewish Tradition in the Modern Era." In *The Uses of Tradition: Jewish Continuity in the Modern Era*. Ed. Jack Wertheimer. New York: Jewish Theological Seminary, 1993.

———. "Ritual, Ceremony, and the Reconstruction of Judaism in the United States." In *Jews in America: A Contemporary Reader*. Ed. Roberta Rosenberg Farber and Chaim I. Waxman. Hanover, N.H.: Brandeis University Press, 1999.

Locks, Gutman G. "The Torah by Gematria." In *The Spice of Torah—Gematria*. Introd. Rabbi J. Immanuel Schochet. New York: Judaica Press, 1985.

Mac Low, Jackson. "Buddhism, Art, Practice, Polity." In *Beneath A Single Moon: Buddhism in Contemporary American Poetry*. Ed. Kent Johnson and Craig Paulenich. Introd. Gary Snyder. Boston: Shambhala, 1991.

———. "J. Mac Low: Interviewed by Kevin Bezner." *New American Writing* 11 (summer/fall 1993): 109–24.

Makarius, Laura. "The Myth of the Trickster: The Necessary Breaker of Taboos." In *Mythical Trickster Figures: Contours, Contexts, and Criticism*. Ed. William J. Hynes and William G. Doty. Tuscaloosa: University of Alabama Press, 1993.

Malina, Judith, and Julian Beck. *Paradise Now: Collective Creation of The Living Theater*. New York: Random, 1971.

Malinowski, Bronislaw. "The Meaning of Meaningless Words and the Coefficient of Weirdness." In *Symposium of the Whole: A Range of Discourse toward an Ethnopoetics*. Ed. Jerome Rothenberg and Diane Rothenberg. Berkeley: University of California Press, 1983.

Marcus, Ivan G. "Postmodern or Neo-Medieval Times?" In *The Uses of Tradition: Jewish Continuity in the Modern Era*. Ed. Jack Wertheimer. New York: Jewish Theological Seminary, 1993.

Meilicke, Christine. "Abulafianism among the Counterculture Kabbalists." *Jewish Studies Quarterly* 9 (2002): 71–101.

———. "California Kabbalists." *Judaism Today* 14 (winter 1999–2000): 24–30.

———. "The Forgotten History of David Meltzer's Journal *Tree*." *Studies in American Jewish Literature* 22 (2003): 52–71.

Mendes-Flohr, Paul. "Introductory Essay: The Spiritual Quest of the Philologist." In *Gershom Scholem: The Man and His Work*. Ed. Paul Mendes-Flohr. New York: State University of New York Press, 1994.

Menorah: Sparks of Jewish Renewal (1979–1982).

Meyer, Michael. "Tradition and Modernity Reconsidered." In *The Uses of Tradition: Jewish Continuity in the Modern Era*. Ed. Jack Wertheimer. New York: Jewish Theological Seminary, 1993.

Mezey, Robert. "A Gathering of Poets." *Western Humanities Review* 29.2 (1975): 195–203.

Middleton, Peter. "Seven Words for Jerome Rothenberg." *Samizdat* 7 (winter 2001): 3–5.

Milgram, Abraham. *Jewish Worship*. Philadelphia: Jewish Publication Society, 1971.

Miller-Duggan, Devon. *After Auschwitz: Rigor, Risk and Witness in American Holocaust Poetry*. PhD diss., University of Delaware, 1996.

Mintz, Alan, and James Sleeper, eds. *The New Jews* (New York: Vintage, 1971).

Mottram, Eric. "Where the Real Song Begins: The Poetry of Jerome Rothenberg." *Vort* 7 (1975): 163–79.

Muratori, Fred. "Remixing Lorca, Recounting the Word." Review of *The Lorca Variations* and *Gematria*, by Jerome Rothenberg. *American Book Review* (Dec. 94–Feb. 95): 20, 31.

Murdoch, Brian. "Transformations of the Holocaust: Auschwitz in Modern Lyric Poetry." *Comparative Literature Studies* 11.1 (March 1974): 123–50.

Murphy, Margueritte S. *A Tradition of Subversion: The Prose Poem in English from Wilde to Ashbery*. Amherst: University of Massachusetts Press, 1992.

Myerhoff, Barbara G. "We Don't Wrap Herring in a Printed Page: Fusion, Fictions and Continuity in Secular Ritual." In *Secular Ritual: Form and Meaning*. Ed. Barbara G. Myerhoff and Sally Falk Moore. Assen/Amsterdam: Van Gorcum, 1977.

Novak, Bill. "The Making of A Jewish Counter Culture." In *Contemporary Judaic Fellowship In Theory and Practice*. Ed. Jacob Neusner. New York: Ktav, 1972.

Orth, Paula. "Rothenberg Reads Poems." *The Wisconsin Jewish Chronicle* 27 Nov. 1975: 6.

Ortiz, Alfonso. "The Sacred Clown." In *Symposium of the Whole: A Range of Discourse toward an Ethnopoetics*. Ed. Jerome Rothenberg and Diane Rothenberg. Berkeley: University of California Press, 1983.

Pacernick, Gary. *Memory and Fire: Ten American Jewish Poets.* Twentieth Century American Jewish Writers 1. New York: Lang, 1989.

———. *Sing A New Song: American Jewish Poetry Since the Holocaust.* Gary Pacernick with photographs by Layle Silbert. Cincinnati: The American Jewish Archives, 1991.

Patai, Raphael. *The Hebrew Goddess.* Foreword Merline Stone. 3rd enl. ed. Detroit: Wayne State University Press, 1990.

———. *Man and Temple: In Ancient Jewish Myth and Ritual.* 2nd enl. ed. with a new introd. and postscript. 1947. New York: Ktav, 1967.

Paul, Sherman. *In Search of the Primitive: Rereading David Antin, Jerome Rothenberg, and Gary Snyder.* London: Louisiana State University Press, 1986.

Peat, David F. *Synchronicity: The Bridge Between Matter and Mind.* Toronto: Bantam, 1987.

Perloff, Marjorie. "The Contemporary of Our Grandchildren: Pound's Influence." In *Ezra Pound among the Poets.* Ed. George Bornstein. Chicago: University of Chicago Press, 1985.

———. *The Dance of the Intellect: Studies in the Poetry of the Pound Tradition.* Evanston, Ill.: Northwestern University Press, 1985.

———. *The Futurist Moment: Avant-Garde, Avant Guerre, and the Language of Rupture.* Chicago: University of Chicago Press, 1986.

———. *Poetic License: Essays on Modernist and Postmodernist Lyric.* Evanston, Ill.: Northwestern University Press, 1990.

———. *Radical Artifice: Writing Poetry in the Age of Media.* Chicago: University of Chicago Press, 1991.

———. "Soundings: *Zaum,* Seriality and the Discovery of the 'Sacred.'" *American Poetry Review* (February 1986): 37–46.

Poggioli, Renato. *The Theory of the Avant-Garde.* Trans. Gerald Fitzgerald. Cambridge: Harvard University Press, 1968.

Polkinhorn, Harry. *Jerome Rothenberg: A Descriptive Bibliography.* American Bibliography Series 3. Jefferson, N.C.: McFarland, 1988.

Power, Kevin. "Conversation with Jerome Rothenberg." *Vort* 7 (1975): 140–53.

———. "*Poland/1931*: Pack up Your Troubles in Your Old Kit Bag & Smile, Smile, Smile, from Diaspora to Galut." *Boundary 2: A Journal of Postmodern Literature* 3 (spring 1975): 683–705.

Prell, Riv-Ellen. *Prayer & Community: The Havurah in American Judaism.* Detroit: Wayne State University Press, 1989.

Rasula, Jed. "The Compost Library." *Sagetrieb* 1.2 (fall 1982): 190–219.

Ricketts, Mac Linscott. "The Shaman and the Trickster." In *Mythical Trickster Figures: Contours, Contexts, and Criticism.* Ed. William J. Hynes and William G. Doty. Tuscaloosa: University of Alabama Press, 1993.

Riha, Karl. "Über den Zufall—in der Literatur der Moderne." In *Zufall als Prinzip: Spielwelt, Methode und System in der Kunst des 20. Jahrhunderts.* Ed. Bernhard Holeczek and Lida von Mengden. Heidelberg: Braus, 1992.

Rodriguez, Michael. "An Effort Somehow in Common: An Interview with Jerome Rothenberg." *Samizdat* 7 (winter 2001): 7–9.

Rosenfeld, Alvin H. *A Double Dying: Reflections on Holocaust Literature*. Bloomington: Indiana University Press, 1980.

Roskies, David G. *A Bridge of Longing: The Lost Art of Yiddish Storytelling*. Cambridge: Harvard University Press, 1995.

———. *The Literature of Destruction: Jewish Responses to Catastrophe*. New York: Jewish Publication Society, 1988.

———. "The Story's the Thing." In *What is Jewish Literature?* Ed. and introd. Hana Wirth-Nesher. Philadelphia: The Jewish Publication Society, 1994.

Roth, Laurence. *Statues of Liberty: Assimilation and Twentieth-Century American Jewish Poets*. PhD diss., University of California, 1995.

Rothenberg, Diane. *Friends Like These: An Ethnohistorical Analysis of the Interaction between Allegheny Senecas and Quakers, 1798–1823*. PhD diss., City University of New York, 1976.

Rothenberg, Jerome. "Beyond Poetics." In *Coherence: A Gathering of Experiments in Writing*. Towards a New Poetics 1. Ed. Don Wellman. Cambridge, Mass.: O. ARS, 1981.

———. "Craft Interview with Jerome Rothenberg." In *The Craft of Poetry: Interviews from The New York Quarterly*. Ed. William Packard. New York: Doubleday, 1974.

———. "The Deputy: The War Behind the Scenes." *Ramparts* 3.4 (Dec. 1964): 33–40.

———. "Harold Bloom: The Critic as Exterminating Angel." *Sulfur* 2 (1981): 4–26.

———. "Jerome Rothenberg: A Dialogue on Oral Poetry with William Spanos." *Boundary 2* 3.3 (spring 1975): 509–48.

———. "Nokh Auschwitz." In *Jewish American Poetry: Poems, Commentary, And Reflections*." Ed. Jonathan N. Barron and Eric Murphy Selinger. Hanover, NH: Brandeis University Press, 2000.

———. "Paper delivered at 'American Poetry in the 1950s': University of Maine, Orono June 1996." http:/wings.buffalo.edu/epc/authors/rothenberg/50s.html, accessed 13 Oct. 1999.

———. "Paul Celan: A Memoir and a Poem." *Paul Celan*. Spec. issue of *Studies in 20th Century Literature* 8.1 (fall 1983): 110–14.

———. "A Poetics of the Sacred." In *Picturing Cultural Values in Postmodern America*. Ed. William G. Doty. Tuscaloosa: University of Alabama Press, 1995.

———. *Pre-Faces & Other Writings*. New York: New Directions, 1981.

———. "The Search for a Primal Poetics." In *Conversant Essays: Contemporary Poets on Poetry*. Ed. James McCorkle. Detroit: Wayne State University Press, 1990.

———. "Why Deep Image?" *Trobar* 3 (1961): 31–32.

Rothenberg, Jerome, and Diane Rothenberg, eds. *Symposium of the Whole: A Range of Discourse toward an Ethnopoetics*. Berkeley: University of California Press, 1983.

Rothenberg, Jerome, and Dennis Tedlock. "Statement of Intention." *Alcheringa* 1: Ethnopoetics (autumn 1970): 1.

Sachs, Avram. "Jerome Rothenberg's *Gematria*." Unpublished essay, n.d., 1–23.

Sayre, Henry M. "David Antin and the Oral Poetics Movement." *Contemporary Literature* 23.4 (1982 fall): 428–450.

———. *The Object of Performance: The American Avant-Garde Since 1970*. Chicago: University of Chicago Press, 1989.

Schechner, Richard. *Environmental Theater*. New York: Hawthorn, 1973.

———. *The Future of Ritual: Writings on Culture and Performance*. London: Routledge, 1993.

———. *Performance Theory: Revised and Expanded Edition*. London: Routledge, 1988.

Schiffmann, Lawrence H., and Michael D. Swartz, eds. *Hebrew and Aramaic Incantation Texts from the Cairo Genizah: Selected Texts from Taylor-Schechter Box K1*. Semitic Texts and Studies 1. Sheffield: JSOT P, 1992.

Schochet, Rabbi J. Immanuel. "Gematria: the Principle of Numerical Interpretation." In *The Spice of Torah—Gematria*. Introd. Rabbi J. Immanuel Schochet. New York: Judaica Press, 1985.

Scholem, Gershom. "Abulafia, Abraham Ben Samuel." In *Encyclopaedia Judaica*. 16 vols. Jerusalem: Keter, 1971–72.

———. *Die jüdische Mystik in ihren Hauptströmungen*. 5th ed. Frankfurt/Main: Suhrkamp, 1993.

———. *Jewish Gnosticism, Merkabah Mysticism, and Talmudic Tradition*. New York: Jewish Theological Seminary, 1960.

———. *Kabbalah*. New York: New American Library, 1974.

———. *On the Kabbalah and Its Symbolism*. New York: Schocken, 1965.

———. "Magische und tellurische Elemente in der Vorstellung des Golem." *Eranos-Jahrbuch* 22 (1952): 235–89.

———. *Major Trends in Jewish Mysticism: Based on the Hilda Strook Lectures Delivered at the Jewish Institute of Religion, New York*. Rev. ed. New York: Schocken, 1946.

———. *The Messianic Idea in Judaism: And Other Essays on Jewish Spirituality*. New York: Schocken, 1971.

———. *Sabbatai Ṣevi: The Mystical Messiah*. Trans. R. J. Zwi Werblowsky. 1957. Princeton: Princeton University Press, 1973.

Schrire, Theodore. *Hebrew Magic Amulets: Their Decipherment and Interpretation*. New York: Behrman, 1966.

Seitz, William S. *The Art of Assemblage*. Garden City, N.Y.: Doubleday, 1961.

Selerie, Gavin, and Eric Mottram, eds. *The Riverside Interviews: 4: Jerome Rothenberg*. London: Binnacle Press, 1984.

Selinger, Eric Murphy. "Shekhinah in America." In *Jewish American Poetry: Poems, Commentary, And Reflections*." Ed. Jonathan N. Barron and Eric Murphy Selinger. Hanover, N.H.: Brandeis University Press, 2000.

Siegel, Richard, Michael Strassfeld, and Sharon Strassfeld, comp. and eds. *The First Jewish Catalogue: A Do-It-Yourself Kit*. Philadelphia: Jewish Publication Society, 1973.

Smith, Richard Cándida. *Utopia and Dissent: Art, Poetry, and Politics in California*. Berkeley: University of California Press, 1995.

Snyder, Gary. *Gary Snyder: The Real Work: Interviews & Talks 1964–1979*. Ed. and introd. William Scott McLean. New York: New Directions, 1980.

———. *The Old Ways: Six Essays*. San Francisco: City Lights, 1977.

Sollors, Werner. *Beyond Ethnicity: Consent and Descent in American Culture*. Oxford: Oxford University Press, 1986.

———. "Foreword: Theories of American Ethnicity." In *The Invention of Ethnicity*. Ed. Werner Sollors. Oxford: Oxford University Press, 1989.

Sontag, Susan. "Artaud [An Essay by Susan Sontag]." In *Antonin Artaud: Selected Writings*. Ed. and introd. Susan Sontag. Trans. Helen Weaver. Notes by Susan Sontag and Don Eric Levine. New York: Farrar, 1976.

Strassfeld, Michael. *The Jewish Holidays: A Guide and Commentary*. Illustrated by Betsy Platkin Teutsch. New York: Harper, 1985.

Strassfeld, Michael, and Sharon Strassfeld, comp. and eds. *The Second Jewish Catalog: Sources & Resources*. Philadelphia: Jewish Publication Society, 1976.

———, comp. and eds. *The Third Jewish Catalog: Creating Community*. Philadelphia: Jewish Publication Society, 1980.

Tambiah, Stanley Jeyaraja. *Culture, Thought, and Social Action: An Anthropological Perspective*. Cambridge: Harvard University Press, 1985.

Tarn, Nathaniel. "Foreword: 'Child as Father to Man in the American Universe.'" In *Nathaniel Tarn: A Descriptive Bibliography*. Ed. Lee Bartlett. American Poetry Contemporary Series 2. Jefferson, N.C.: McFarland, 1987.

Trachtenberg, Joshua. *Jewish Magic and Superstition: A Study in Folk Religion*. New York: Meridian, 1961.

Turner, Victor. *Dramas, Fields, And Metaphors: Symbolic Action in Human Society*. Ithaca: Cornell University Press, 1974.

———. *From Ritual to Theatre: The Human Seriousness of Play*. New York: PAJ Publications, 1982.

———. "A Review of 'Ethnopoetics.'" In *Symposium of the Whole: A Range of Discourse toward an Ethnopoetics*. Ed. Jerome Rothenberg and Diane Rothenberg. Berkeley: University of California Press, 1983.

Wade, Stephen. *Jewish American Literature: Since 1945: An Introduction*. London: Fitzroy Dearborn, 1999.

Waskow, Arthur O. *The Bush is Burning! Radical Judaism Faces the Pharaohs of the Modern Superstate*. New York: Macmillan, 1971.

———. *Godwrestling Round 2: Ancient Wisdom, Future Paths*. Woodstock, VT: Jewish Lights, 1996.

———. "Is the Earth a Jewish Issue?" *Tikkun* 7.5 (Sept./Oct. 1992): 35–37.

Waxman, Chaim I. "The Fourth Generation Grows Up: The Contemporary American Jewish Community." *The Annals of the American Academy of Political and Social Science* 454 (March 1981): 70–85.

Weigel, Molly. *Interactive Poetics: Native-American/European-American Encounter as a Model for Poetic Practice*. PhD diss. Princeton University, 1996.

Weinberger, Eliot. *Written Reaction: Poetics Politics Polemics (1979–1995)*. New York: Marsilio, 1996.

Welsh, Andrew. *Roots of Lyric: Primitive Poetry and Modern Poetics*. Princeton, New Jersey: Princeton University Press, 1978.

Wertheimer, Jack. "Religious Movements in Collision: A Jewish Culture War?" In *Jews in America: A Contemporary Reader*. Ed. Roberta Rosenberg Farber and Chaim I. Waxman. Hanover, NH: Brandeis University Press, 1999.

———. "When Modern Jews Appropriate from Tradition: A Symposium." In *The Uses of Tradition: Jewish Continuity in the Modern Era*. Ed. Jack Wertheimer. New York: Jewish Theological Seminary, 1993.

White, Natalie Irene. *The Darmouth Seminar and its Study Group on Myth and "Translation": A Retrospective Analysis*. PhD diss. University of New Mexico, 1988.

Wirth-Nesher, Hana. "Defining the Indefinable: What Is Jewish Literature?" In *What is Jewish Literature?* Ed. and introd. Hana Wirth-Nesher. Philadelphia: The Jewish Publication Society, 1994.

Wolfson, Elliot R. *Abraham Abulafia—Kabbalist and Prophet: Hermeneutics, Theosophy and Theurgy*. Los Angeles: Cherub Press, 2000.

Yerushalmi, Yosef Hayim. *Zakhor: Jewish History and Jewish Memory*. Seattle: University of Washington Press, 1982.

Young, Gloria L. "The Moral Function of Remembering: American Holocaust Poetry." *In the Shadow of the Holocaust*. Spec. issue of *Studies in American Jewish Literature* 9.1 (Spring 1990): 61–72.

Young, James E. *Writing and Rewriting The Holocaust: Narrative and the Consequence of Interpretation*. Bloomington: Indiana University Press, 1988.

Zweig, Ellen Marcia. *Performance Poetry: Critical Approaches to Contemporary Intermedia*. PhD diss. University of Michigan, 1980.

Index of Names

Index of Titles

Index of Subjects